THE TRIUMPH OF INTEGRITY

THE MACMILLAN COMPANY
NEW YORK · CHICAGO
DALLAS · ATLANTA · SAN FRANCISCO
LONDON · MANILA

IN CANADA
BRETT-MACMILLAN LTD.
GALT, ONTARIO

THE
TRIUMPH
OF INTEGRITY

A Portrait of
CHARLES DE GAULLE

Duncan Grinnell-Milne

New York
THE MACMILLAN COMPANY
1962

FOR

PAULINE

a small reward

for so much patience

© Duncan Grinnell-Milne 1961, 1962

First Printing

Printed in the United States of America

Library of Congress catalog card number : 62-9294

CONTENTS

LIST OF ILLUSTRATIONS

The Portrait and the Painter

WHEN GENERAL DE GAULLE was told by Geoffroy de Courcel—it was during the State Visit to London in April 1960—that I was writing a book about him, he turned to me to say: 'I hope you are finding the subject agreeable.' The jesting tone, faintly ironical, marked the double meaning so distinctly that, now the work is done, I can only hope that the Subject, in his turn, will find the Portrait agreeable.

That it is a Portrait is stated in the sub-title, but it seems advisable to stress the point here so as to explain the book's intention and account for its limitations. For if it is generally accepted that the business of the Historian is to know what to leave out; as I see it, the business of the Painter is to know what to put in. His purpose must surely be to present in the first place a recognizable likeness, upon which he can then brush in the traits of a comprehensible character. Next, the background, of men even more than of events, is of paramount importance both to balance the composition and to heighten the effect, and the 'characters' selected must be those who had some lasting influence upon the character of the Subject. But once these few essential figures have been placed and accurately drawn, the Portrait Painter, unlike the Historian, must come to a stop; or else, with too large a canvas, he will carry attention away from the central figure and by wearying the eye incur the deadly criticism of being tedious.

Pétain, for instance, exerted great influence upon de Gaulle's early military life and the development of his military thinking, whilst his subsequent doctrine of defeatism was directly responsible for de Gaulle's doctrine of defiance and for the expansion of his character from that of a brilliant strategist to that of a great national leader and statesman. Pétain must therefore be depicted in some detail; so must Weygand, Laval, Darlan, each of whom contributes a shadow to enhance the brightness of the Subject; but not the lesser figures of later years who contribute nothing. The darkening political sky above the Third Republic in the nineteen-thirties must come into the picture, as must the black clouds over Vichy, since both profoundly affected de Gaulle's thoughts and actions; but not the murky political confusion of the Fourth Republic, which in no way altered the character of de Gaulle who had predicted it. The day-to-day politics of the years leading up to the Algiers revolt of 1958 have no place in this Portrait; moreover, they have been thoroughly examined in numerous works, perhaps the best in English being those cited in the Bibliography, by Williams and Harrison, Dorothy Pickles and Alexander Werth.

But, of course, if an Author thus limits his responsibilities as a Historian by claiming to be an Artist he lays himself open to an easier and more commonplace form of criticism. As John Sargent put it, 'a portrait is a painting in which there is always "something wrong with the mouth".' Someone is bound to say, with a knowing shake of the head, that I have not quite caught the Subject's expression, that I have made him too tall, too straight and too silent, or that by stressing his difficulties I have insufficiently portrayed his capacity for being difficult. On the last point, however, one has only to study the *Algiers* chapter in Duff Cooper's *Old Men Forget* to perceive that de Gaulle's 'difficult' attitude was largely due to the British failure to understand the French point of view or, worse still, to admit that there was one. 'Why must we quarrel? Why can't we be friends?' asked Churchill at Marrakesh, apparently incapable of realizing that friendship had been ruled out by, amongst other things, the shady anti-French policy he had sanctioned, or at least connived at, in the Levant.

But whether or not there is 'something wrong with the mouth' can only be a matter of opinion; and the Painter is certainly entitled to his when he has been favoured, as I was, by a large number of sittings, even though neither the Subject nor the Painter was conscious at the time that they were 'sittings'. But why they were granted and how I came to serve under General de Gaulle are questions which require some answer here.

When, at the time of Pétain's surrender at Bordeaux, the remaining 'British Air Forces in France' were withdrawn to England from the neighbourhood of Nantes, their Commander-in-Chief, Air Marshal Barratt, left me behind—not, I may say, without my own keen agreement—to carry out a last mission to the French. To the various Army and Air Force Generals, with whom we had co-operated and who might now be in the dark as to our intentions, I was to deliver personally, together with my own verbal assurances, a number of letters in which the Air Marshal stated unambiguously that Britain was determined to continue fighting to the end and that the end was victory. The slender hope which formed the object of the mission was that these senior French officers might be enlightened and given some last-minute encouragement to fight on, if not in France, then in North Africa. An additional letter, to General Vuillemin, commanding French Air Forces, re-appointed me, subject to his approval, as liaison officer in touch with the Air Ministry —I was provided with a portable wireless transmitter, a call-sign and code. For so long as the French continued to resist, I was to stay with them.

Just how forlorn was our hope became clear as, driving first to Bordeaux, then back to Angoulême, I followed a mazy road through the Limousin and the Dordogne. True, those senior French officers whom I was able to find were surprised to hear that Britain intended to fight on, if necessary alone; but they no longer set much store by the news. '*Vous ne comprenez pas. Sans la France tout est perdu.*' To my expostulations the majority remained indifferent. Pétain and Weygand had done their work too well. I drove on at speed.

In the evening of June 18 I came to a hotel in Agen, last resting-place of GHQ French Air Forces. There, after some slight delay, I was shown into a private *salon* where I found General Vuillemin. I knew him of old, an honest, loyal friend, and a gallant airman if not a brilliant commander; but, though he welcomed me, and my new appointment, warmly enough, I had the immediate impression that he too had lost heart. There was about his drawn face and its unnatural pallor something that betokened an inner and moral exhaustion. He would, he explained at some length, be glad to accept me as liaison officer with the Air Staff in England—for as long as might be possible. He broke off in some confusion to add: 'As you are aware, certain negotiations are in progress—' he dodged saying *with the Germans*, '—and if these are brought to a conclusion, then, with the greatest regret, I shall be forced to ask you to leave. You understand?'

I understood only too clearly. The Pétain Government was breaking with Britain as a first step towards making a separate peace with the Nazis. 'I had hoped,' Vuillemin went on, 'to continue operations from North Africa.' Aircraft had already been flown out, arrangements made for the ground staff to follow by sea. 'But now I have orders to stop all movements. The capitulation is to extend to Algeria. And I can do nothing, you understand—nothing. The orders come from the authorities in power . . .' His voice trailed away miserably. I tried to give him some comfort, to express sympathy with France's terrible predicament and to stress the promise of British support in the War; but it was to no purpose. He stood silent with lowered head, and when he raised his eyes I saw to my embarrassment that they were filled with tears.

In the passage outside the *salon* I ran into the Chief of Staff, General Mendigal; he was deeply distressed—not at the War situation, at the mislaying of his *nécessaire de voyage*, 'with my shaving kit and silver-mounted brushes.' He gave me a smile and a handshake, and wandered unhappily away. But in the entrance hall I found a small knot of old friends, junior officers from the *Deuxième Bureau*, who were waiting to see me and who all spoke at once, though in cautiously lowered voices. What news had I of the armistice negotiations? What did I think of the prospects of getting out of France, to Algiers, to Spain, or even to England? Had I listened to the broadcast just heard from London? *General de Gaulle was appealing for volunteers . . .*

Next morning I drove to Bordeaux to deliver the last of my letters; but it was clear there that the end was fast approaching. French staff officers were obstructive when not openly hostile; when I spoke of returning to Agen, it was hinted coldly that I might be stopped. At the temporary British Embassy, I learned that the Pétain Government, having refused every offer of help from Britain, were 'falling over each other' in their indecent haste to rush into the arms of the enemy; but I also heard that, from Brittany, numerous French airmen were getting out to continue the fight. And in the street outside, among an anxious crowd pressing forward to get visas, I found a couple of French non-commissioned pilots; when I asked them what they wanted, they said: 'To get to England, either by sea or through Spain and Gibraltar.' *General de Gaulle had broadcast from London . . .*

Within a few hours it became plain that my mission had no future. Nothing was to be hoped from the senior staff and the Generals; for the junior officers and men the centre of resistance had shifted to Britain. On the following evening a passage was offered me in the *Arethusa*; I took it.

Two days later, in London, I was offering my services—with Air Ministry sanction—as liaison officer to General de Gaulle. Thus there began what may be called without disrespect a close association, that was to last for four months before other tasks—still, but less openly, connected with France—took me elsewhere; an association in which I saw the General every day, travelled with him frequently and occasionally alone, and eventually accompanied him from the banks of the Thames, via Dakar, Freetown and Lagos, to the banks of the Wouri and the quayside at Duala.

And so it happened that the 'sittings' for the Portrait were granted at what were almost certainly the most testing moments of the Subject's life, when under a strain reaching to the limits of endurance there were revealed the essential and simple components of his character. It seems probable that these were also the last moments in which such a revelation could be made to any individual outside the narrow circle of his family; thereafter, in single-minded devotion to a high purpose, he bound himself to silence and to solitude. I know this from personal experience, but I am not wholly dependent upon memory; in the Second World War, while the Generals wrote their diaries, I took notes. From that experience it appears to me that his character rests, as Conrad's Marlow said, 'on a few very simple ideas . . . notably among others on fidelity.' And it is this aspect, of fidelity to principles of 'honour and honesty' as he was to name them, which I have depicted, not exclusively, but 'notably among others'.

I was very much tempted to paint the Portrait differently, to see the Subject from another angle and to illustrate his life with a greater number of anecdotes. But I do not believe that de Gaulle's character and qualities would be more clearly illuminated by such treatment. The wide sweep of military action and political controversy, the bold strokes of achievement in peace and war, the successive and vital struggles against men mightier than himself but less magnanimous, this is the setting in which I have seen de Gaulle. Some personal touches have been allowed in the Portrait, some asides, some unfamiliar details, but none of the sort of keyhole prying and gossip-writing intimacy best described, in a phrase from Shaw, as 'combinations of Tappertitian romance with the police intelligence.' In my view there is little to be gained from a closer study of the Subject's private life; it was not marriage that shaped his character, but rather his already developed character and the 'simple tastes' he shared with his wife that conditioned his everyday existence. De Gaulle *en robe de chambre* has no reality; devotion to the task is complete, and the task is never completed. Some have said that he has little capacity for enjoyment, but at best this can be no more than a superficial judgment since, to recall another Shavian opinion, 'the true joy in life' is 'the being used for a purpose recognized by yourself as a mighty one; the being thoroughly worn out before you are thrown on the scrap-heap; the being a force of Nature instead of a feverish selfish little clod of ailments and grievances complaining that the world will not devote itself to making you happy.' In that sense de Gaulle has savoured joy to the full. Others have seen him as a 'puritan', which is certainly going too far; and yet, when the time comes, it is a great Puritan writer who will supply him with the most fitting valediction. 'My Sword, I give to him that shall succeed me in my Pilgrimage, and my Courage and Skill, to him that can get it.' No one better than de Gaulle, can echo Mr Valiant-for-truth.

As for the background figures, there too I have been able to draw to some extent upon personal experience. Concerning France, for example, there is scarcely one of the persons described or mentioned with whom at one time or another I have not had some acquaintance however slight, from Foch down to Gamelin, from Clemenceau to Darlan; and I do not think I will be accused of lacking in sympathy for the people of a country in which, before, after and during two Wars, I have lived and served for something more than fifteen years. The same goes, though to a more limited extent, for the other countries and peoples involved, from the United States to the Middle East.

But having thus, in some sort, presented my credentials as an eye-witness, I must hasten to acknowledge my indebtedness to the writers of Memoirs listed opposite.

In the various controversies and 'difficulties' dealt with, it will be seen that each man has been allowed to speak for himself, either from his Memoirs or from the documents he produces. To avoid the tiresome interruption of footnotes, however, I have preferred to list separately in the bibliography the works from which passages are quoted. For those who left no Memoirs—such as Pétain, Darlan, Laval—I have accepted, for their reported words, the evidence given by Robert Aron (in *The Vichy Régime*) whose original sources are unimpeachable. The relevant documents supplied by Churchill (in *The Second World War*) and those, far more numerous, by de Gaulle (in the *Mémoires de Guerre*) are unchallengeable secondary sources upon which also I have relied.

My sincerest thanks are due to those who have so painstakingly read the script and given such helpful advice. And that old friend in France who insists on remaining nameless, but whose criticism was so valuable, will believe this expression of my gratitude. He, at any rate, is unlikely in contemplating the Portrait to find anything seriously 'wrong with the mouth'.

ACKNOWLEDGMENTS

Grateful acknowledgments are made to the authors and publishers of the following works for permission to quote passages and documents:

Aron, Robert, *The Vichy Régime* (The Macmillan Company)
Bryant, Sir A., *The Turn of the Tide* (Doubleday)
Churchill, Sir Winston S., *The Second World War* (Houghton Mifflin Company)
Clark, Gen. Mark, *Calculated Risk* (Harper & Brothers)
De Gaulle, Gen. Charles, *The War Memoirs of Charles de Gaulle* (Simon and Schuster)
De Gaulle, Gen. Charles, *The Edge of the Sword* (Faber & Faber)
Eisenhower, Gen. D., *Crusade in Europe* (Doubleday)
Glubb, Gen. Sir J., *Britain and the Arabs* (Hodder & Stoughton)
Hassett, W. D., *Off the Record with F. D. R., 1942–1945,* copyright 1958 by Warm Springs Foundation. Reprinted by permission of Rutgers University Press.
Hull, Cordell, *Memoirs* (The Macmillan Company)
Leahy, Adm. W., USN, *I Was There* (McGraw-Hill, Brandt & Brandt)
Weygand, Gen. M., *Rappelé au Service* (Flammarion)
Wilmot, Chester, *The Struggle for Europe* (Harper & Brothers)

OTHER WORKS CONSULTED

Aron, Robert, *Histoire de la Liberation* (A. Fayard)
Bonheur, Gaston, *Charles de Gaulle* (Gallimard)
Clark, Brig. Stanley, *The Man who is France* (Harrap)
Cooper, Sir A. Duff, *Old Men Forget* (Hart-Davis)
Führer Conferences on Naval Affairs—in *Brassey's Naval Annual for 1948* (Clowes)
Gellhorn, Martha, *The Face of War* (Hart-Davis)
Goutard, Colonel, *The Battle of France 1940* (Muller)
Hart, B. H. Liddell, *The Other Side of the Hill* (Cassell)
MacIntyre, Captain D., RN, *Fighting Admiral* (Evans)
Pickles, Dorothy, *The Fifth French Republic* (Methuen)
Remy, *Mémoires d'Un Agent Secret* (R. Solar, Paris)
Roskill, Captain S. W., RN, *The War at Sea,* Vol. I (H.M.S.O.)
Stead, P. J., *Second Bureau* (Evans)
Werth, Alexander, *De Gaulle's Revolution* (Hale)
Williams, P. M., and Harrison, Martin, *De Gaulle's Republic* (Longmans)
Woolcombe, R., *The Campaigns of Wavell* (Cassell)

PART ONE

1. The Two Voices

C'était pendant l'horreur d'une profonde nuit.

(Racine: *Athalie*)

As DARKNESS fell on the evening of Tuesday, June 18, 1940, the people of France, stupefied by the suddenness of overwhelming military defeat, pondered with sinking hearts the appalling prospect of national surrender. The official intimation first broadcast on the preceding day and now spread throughout the land still seemed incredible: a nightmare in which fevered minds had dreamed that in five weeks the five million mobilized men of the French Army had been scattered like dust, that Paris had been given up without a fight, and that nothing but prompt submission could halt an irresistible invasion.

An unworthy dream it had seemed at first, one from which men had struggled to awake, to rise above the mounting wave of despair, only to be thrust back into the depths by the lengthening catalogue of catastrophic events, by sights and sounds that could not be denied. By newspaper headlines and official communiqués; by raucous loudspeakers in cafés and restaurants; by the plodding procession of horse-drawn farmcarts piled high with chattels and the pathetic débris of abandoned homes. By the endless road-blocking stream of cars and lorries, the mighty exodus of Paris, swollen by tributary streams from the industrial north, thrusting on towards an ever-receding zone of imagined safety. By the menacing sounds of approaching war, the rumble of military transport retiring in the night, the distant thudding of mysterious explosions, the rhythmical drone of enemy aircraft. At length, and after mid-June in how many ancient provinces, by the crescendo hum of massed motor-cycles heralding the invader.

As the flood-tide swept on—westward through Normandy into Brittany, southward across the upper Seine towards the upper Loire, towards Dijon, towards Besançon and the encirclement of Lorraine—the people of France had watched and listened, impotent, despondent, yet not wholly without hope. A new army, it had been rumoured, was assembling in Africa; fresh divisions were coming from England; Canada was landing troops, America about to intervene. A front was

17

to be established south of the Loire; after the Somme and the Seine, upon this last river a new 'miracle of the Marne' might yet be accomplished. Had not the Premier, Minister of Defence and of War Paul Reynaud, hinted as much?—'If a miracle is needed to save France, then I believe in miracles.' Had not the Commander-in-Chief, General Weygand, bidden everyone stand fast?—this was 'the last quarter of an hour', with the exhausted enemy almost at the end of his tether. Only some startling gesture of inspired leadership was needed to turn the tables.

Towards midnight of June 16 the startling gesture had been made. Wire and wireless had carried the news: Reynaud had resigned; in Bordeaux President Lebrun had called upon Marshal Pétain to form a new government. What did it mean? Had Reynaud, after all, despaired? No matter; in this grave hour the Marshal, many believed, was the man to lead the nation—Pétain the hero of Verdun in 1916, the victorious commander of 1918, the greatest military chief surviving from the other War, a patriot, wise, experienced. So they thought of him, and wondered only why he had not been summoned sooner. At his side stood Weygand, the disciple of Foch, who might yet turn disaster into triumph. Surely, by these two, something would at last be done to stop the rot, a great blow struck for the salvation of France. Of the well-prepared conspiracy to surrender the nation to the enemy, the people of France knew nothing.

Early in the morning of June 17, by all the broadcasting stations in France, relayed by the Germans, the great blow was struck in Bordeaux. An important announcement: the Head of the Government was to speak. '*Voici le Maréchal Pétain.*'

'*Francais!* . . .' All France knew his reputation; few in recent years had heard his voice. How old it sounded! A sorrowful quaver, bleating words that struck the nation dumb. '. . . assured of the confidence of the whole population, I give myself to France in order to mitigate her disasters. . . . It is with a sad heart that I tell you today that we must stop fighting. I have this night approached the enemy and asked him if he is prepared to negotiate with us, as between soldiers and after the battle has been fought in all honour, the means of putting an end to hostilities.

'Let all Frenchmen gather loyally during these hard trials in support of the Government over which I preside, and let them turn a deaf ear to their anguish and listen only to their faith in the destiny of our fatherland.'

* * *

The shock was so terrible that to many it brought a curious numbness akin to relief—a sensation, it may be, like that of a dying man abandoned by his doctor and clutching at consolation from the priest of a religion in which he has not hitherto believed. Reynaud, the doctor, had given up; there would be no miracle of recovery. Pétain, the priest, was speaking now, bidding them forsake all hope save in the enemy's mercy, calling them not to resistance, but to prayer. A Marshal of France would not say such things were they not true; his plea for loyal 'support of the Government' implied that all the Ministers stood firmly behind him. Not for many a weary day of doubt and humiliation would they, the people of France, come to know that he had misled them. There had been no general agreement to surrender; many in the Cabinet—as well as in the Senate and in the Chamber of Deputies—had violently opposed the suggestion. In his haste to accomplish a long-planned purpose, Pétain consulted only his fellow-conspirator Weygand and his pro-fascist adviser the Foreign Secretary Baudouin.

The effect of the announcement was devastating. Save in the Maginot garrison where the relayed broadcast was thought to be an enemy trick, French troops almost everywhere immediately ceased their resistance to the enemy's advance. Whole regiments either laid down their arms or refused to obey their officers' orders. Weygand was alarmed; the plot, because of Pétain's hasty phrasing, was going too far and too fast. An Order of the Day was issued, explaining that since no more than an inquiry for terms had been made the troops must continue to fight. It was useless; the moral paralysis was complete. With a cease-fire now inevitable and close at hand, the scattered remnants of the Army were unwilling to give their lives or, as prisoners, their freedom for a cause Pétain had declared to be lost.

Almost the whole nation, moreover, had now been deprived of its will to fight. There were protests of course, but they were inaudible and unavailing. Paris, more than half empty, lay silent under the enemy. Bordeaux was bewildered, with German aircraft overhead, its hotels and public buildings overcrowded with members of the

Government, of Parliament, of the *corps diplomatique*; its streets were jammed with refugee cars driving on, throughout the 17th and 18th, up the Garonne Valley or towards the Pyrénées, many of them down the long straight road south to Bayonne, Biarritz and the Spanish frontier. Elsewhere, in provincial towns and villages, despair had brought apathy. Of what use now to cry '*aux armes, citoyens,*' when there were no arms and no Army? What good to shout: '*Vive la France!*' when France lay mortally wounded? Somehow or other life had to go on, bread had to be found, the daily tasks performed. Passers-by in the streets exchanged whispered gossip: rumour had it that President Lebrun and half the Government were to leave for North Africa to negotiate more freely. If so, they had better make haste, for it was also being said that the Germans were across the lower Loire, were motoring south through Vendée, along the Atlantic coast, heading for Bordeaux, that other columns were driving towards Limoges and Clermont-Ferrand, that yet another was moving down the Saône towards Lyons. In the night the inhabitants of still unoccupied regions listened for the dreaded approach of the now unopposed enemy.

They listened too, when and where possible, to wireless broadcasts. The vast disturbances of population, part mobilized and now largely captured or scattered, part in flight and dispersed throughout the land, had greatly reduced the numbers of those able, or willing, to listen attentively to news generally unreliable and always bad; but since the War's outbreak many listeners had become accustomed to tuning in, if no more than intermittently, to the news from Britain and especially to the BBC's French-language service which, initiated at the time of 'Munich', had established a reputation for truthful objectivity. It may be that, in the prevalent emotional confusion, only one or two thousand French citizens in all were listening in, on the evening of June 18, to the calm voices from London. Voices that, whilst they boldly reasserted England's determination to continue the struggle and to remain faithful to the alliance, could but confirm the facts of a disastrous military situation in France and of the request for armistice terms by Marshal Pétain. For the immediate future, they hinted, there could be little hope.

And then without preamble a new speaker was introduced: '*Voici le Général de Gaulle.*'

Of those few who listened, fewer still had ever seen him. But almost everyone had heard his name, had read it in the papers in mid-May as that of the hero of two ephemeral victories, at Montcornet and Abbeville; and by many it was also remembered that a fortnight ago he had become Reynaud's Under-Secretary for War. Only a few government officials and senior army officers, however, would know that twice recently he had been sent on missions to the British Government, from the second of which he was understood to have returned. Yet now, astonishingly, he spoke from London.

The voice was not youthful, but young, deep, authoritative. The manner of speaking was unemotional, the enunciation clear; vibrant oratory was excluded and replaced by a level tone with a firm stress upon certain words, and certain syllables, that brought out effectively the simple logic of his argument.

'Those leaders who, for many years, have been at the head of the French forces have formed a government.

'This government, alleging the defeat of our forces, has approached the enemy to obtain a cease-fire.

'Admittedly, we have been, and are, overwhelmed by the enemy's mechanical strength on the ground and in the air... But is this the last word? Must hope vanish? Is the defeat final? No!... The same means that conquered us can one day bring us victory.

'For France is not alone.... She has a vast Empire behind her. She can join forces with the British Empire which has command of the sea and is continuing the fight. She can, like England, make limitless use of the immense industrial power of the United States.

'This war is not confined to the territory of our unhappy country. This war has not been decided by the battle of France. This is a world-war. And all the mistakes, all the delays, all the suffering, do not alter the fact that there are in the world all the means of some day crushing our enemies. Stricken today by mechanized force, we shall be able in the future to conquer by superior mechanized force. Therein lies the destiny of the world.'

Then followed a personal appeal.

'I, General de Gaulle, at present in London, ask all those French officers and soldiers now on British soil, or who should find themselves on it in future, with or without their arms, I ask engineers and specialists in the armaments industry... to get in touch with me.

'Whatever happens, the flame of French resistance must not, and shall not, be extinguished.'

The broadcast ended with the promise that he would speak again on the following day.

*　　*　　*

In France, to those few who had been able to listen, the appeal brought mixed sensations. To some the suggestion that resistance should be continued was disquieting, distasteful even, since it came too late; and yet the thought that Frenchmen might soon be gathering beyond the seas under one who raised their eyes to a reasoned victory however distant was what, at heart, every loyal citizen wanted to believe. But between wanting to believe and ability to act a gulf was now set. Bidden by their own Government to submit, forbidden by the enemy to move, few on either side of the ever-advancing German tide could escape the double domination. Immobilized and inarticulate, they could do little else than wait upon events.

Hardly any in the scattered remnants of the conscript Army heard the call or, if they heard, heeded it; the War was lost and, now that fighting had ceased, all that the great majority wanted was to get back to their homes to care for their women and children. Amongst a minority of younger men, of keen professional officers and junior staff—those who, with access to radio communications, were perhaps best able to listen in—if interest was considerable, opinions were divided. Two voices had spoken. The first, that of a Marshal of France, had to some extent propounded the obvious: military defeat had made resistance futile, *ergo* 'all fighting must cease.' The opinion might be contested, the order—coming from the Head of the Government backed by the Commander-in-Chief—could scarcely be disobeyed. To submit was the way of discipline; it might not be easy, it was easier than to rebel.

The second voice, for all its logical reasoning, offered little of value in the immediate present whatever it argued for the future. Like the whisper of an uneasy conscience it might stir anew the ancient spirit of national pride and patriotic defiance; it could, as yet, have little practical effect. Action required courage less physical than moral, a courage too often sapped by elderly superiors who, from motives not always of the purest, scoffed at the slender hope held out by the voice from London. What could he do, this junior general so recently promoted, this ex-Under-Secretary without power or influence? By what right did a general of brigade dare to challenge the authority of a Marshal of France?

In Bordeaux, if the broadcast was not directly heard, reports of it spread rapidly in military circles; and whilst approval was limited and hushed—it was already unwise to speak against the new authority—protest was loud-voiced and indignant. What, in the first place, was the ex-Under-Secretary for War doing in London? And what was the meaning of this senseless appeal for volunteers when the armistice *pourparlers* were now well under way? Of the two voices speaking to the nation one must be silenced forthwith, before its dangerous doctrine of 'resistance' could gain popular support.

In the morning of July 19 the new Defence Ministry, on Weygand's instructions, cabled to the French Military Attaché in London.

> *'Inform General de Gaulle that he has been returned to duty under the Commander-in-Chief and that he is to come back without delay.'*

That same evening the voice from London was heard again:

> 'By this time all Frenchmen must be aware that the ordinary conditions of authority have vanished. Faced by the bewilderment in the minds of all, by the liquidation of a government fallen under enemy domination, by the impossibility of giving play to our national institutions—I, General de Gaulle, French soldier and military leader, am conscious of speaking in the name of France.'

The first broadcast, explaining that in the causes of defeat lay the hopes of victory, had called only for volunteers on British territory to keep alight the flame of resistance. In the second there was no qualification.

> 'Every Frenchman still bearing arms has an absolute duty to continue the fight. To lay down his arms . . . would be a crime against the nation . . .
> 'At this time it is above all to French North Africa that I am speaking —to a French North Africa still intact. . . . It would be intolerable to allow the Bordeaux panic to spread overseas.'

No longer an appeal to a few this second broadcast, by denouncing the surrender and by opposing to it the duty of all Frenchmen under arms to continue the struggle, openly defied the authority of Pétain and Weygand. It was a declaration of war.

To those, from a fractional audience, able to act freely the call was urgent for time was short. A small fleet of crowded fishing-boats set sail from Brittany; young men of military age slipped across the border to the doubtful hospitality of Franco's Spain; a score of airmen flew their planes over the Channel into Devon and Cornwall, one or two sensing restrictions to come, made their way from North Africa to Gibraltar. In all but a tiny handful they were presently to prove that the ancient fighting spirit of France had not succumbed at Bordeaux.

But the great mass of the people of France remained inert, spell-bound by catastrophe; even had they heard the broadcasts from London they would scarcely have heeded them. Communist workers, who from the outset had stood aside from the 'capitalist war' and listened to the party propaganda urging them to lay down their arms and desert, were waiting for a lead from Moscow. On the political 'right' smaller groups, dazzled by the gleaming machinery of fascism, were waiting to take part in the installation of a new régime. Defeatists and unprincipled place-seekers waited to be called to power. Army leaders, obedient to orders, waited for terms to be negotiated by Pétain and Weygand, who waited for the Germans. The people waited for peace. Everyone waited. No one any longer dreamed of victory.

Nevertheless the fight was on, the war within the War, the struggle for the hearts and minds of the people of France. In the beginning it was centred upon little else than points of military honour and of military common sense. Of the points of honour the shameful sequence had been set in motion at Bordeaux: to cover the Army's 'honour', and to ensure its obedience to the cease-fire order, Weygand required the surrender of the Government; to negotiate with the enemy, the Government must dishonour the indissoluble treaty of alliance signed by France and Britain three months previously; and the signing of the armistice convention would set the seal upon national humiliation. Of all the conquered countries—Poland, Norway, Holland, Belgium, Luxembourg, France—only the government of Marshal Pétain would submit to the enemy. Dire necessity could not justly be pleaded; surrender was not the only way out. The point of common sense had been well put by de Gaulle, that though France had lost a battle she, and her Empire and her Allies could yet win the war. Since surrender was unnecessary, it was morally indefensible.

Thus, inevitably, from the conflict of opinion so plainly stated in the opposing calls to 'cease fire' and to 'fight on', the struggle grew to be one between the assertion of principles accepted as fundamental by enlightened humanity and the negation of those principles as a matter of convenience, either to serve a callous conqueror or to flatter the vanity of men lusting for personal power. Honour *versus* Dishonour, it was soon much more than that: a struggle for the very souls of men across a broad chasm separating integrity from duplicity, honest dealing from sly dissembling, selflessness from self-seeking, uncompromising resistance to evil from a tame and often willing submission to the powers of darkness. Once the first submission had been made, the further degradation could never be resisted. Compelled downward step by step, blindly yet with imagined cunning the aged Marshal herded his silenced and deluded people into the pen of slavery whilst, despite the anathemas of men evil or demented, the voice of reasoned truth, denouncing a course that could lead only to national extinction, proclaimed defiance 'in the name of France'.

From barely audible at first the voice of Resistance grew in strength until its echoes were heard throughout the land; until, across the years and an infinity of human suffering, it wrought a 'miracle' far greater than that of 'the Marne'. Against the reluctance of a whole nation, hopeless, humiliated and embittered, against the immense influence of the legendary hero of Verdun as against the crafty enticement and more open compulsion of the confident enemy, against indifference and comfortable inertia—against these mountains there triumphed the faith and steadfast character of one man. In time all France responded to the call and followed the obscure figure of Charles de Gaulle up the stony and perilous path that led back to national greatness. But, in the black night of June 1940, he walked alone.

2. Search for Survivors

'Si j'eusse été présent quand l'écharpe coula—nos courages, Monsieur,
diffèrent en cela—Je l'aurais ramassée et me la serais mise.'
(*Cyrano de Bergerac;* Act IV, Scene iv)

OF GENERAL DE GAULLE'S situation on his return to London from
Bordeaux on June 17 and his decision to denounce the Pétain Government's surrender, some were to say that it recalled great deeds from
the heroic past—Desaix converting Bonaparte's defeat into the
triumph of Marengo, or Gambetta's balloon-flight from beleaguered
Paris to head resistance in the provinces—whilst others saw it as that
of a castaway from some *Titanic* shipwreck, calling through the darkness for survivors. His own comment showed an almost ironic
appreciation of the immensity of the task ahead.

'I saw myself,' he was to write in his *Mémoires*, 'as one standing,
alone and without resources, upon the shore of an ocean across which
he had announced his intention of swimming.'

But however bold the swimmer it is plain that he could not even
take the first plunge without assistance. Only Churchill's prompt
intervention could save him from being left high and dry, and he was
the first to admit it: 'What would I have been able to do without him?'
was how he put it. On the day of his arrival in England, after an interview with the Prime Minister, he was granted cable and broadcasting
facilities without which his voice would never have been heard at all.

The first use made of these facilities, however, was far from constituting an act of defiance to the new Government, for whose continued resistance overseas there was still some hope. In a cable to
Bordeaux, sent in the late afternoon of June 17, de Gaulle offered his
services, suggesting that he be authorized to resume the work in
London interrupted by his brief return to France on the previous day.

The mission upon which, as Under-Secretary for War, he had been
sent by Reynaud was in itself of considerable importance to both
France and Britain. It concerned three main points:

(i) the diverting to British or North African ports of vessels
carrying war material from the United States to France;
(ii) the provision of British shipping to carry French troops and

equipment, from Atlantic and Mediterranean ports, to continue the War from North Africa;

(iii) the transfer to Britain of 400 German air-crew prisoners shot down during the battle of France.

On the first point he had already achieved much, notably by diverting to Britain the steamship *Pasteur*, carrying arms from America, which would otherwise certainly have fallen into German hands. On the second point he had obtained an official assurance that 500,000 tons of shipping would be available for the evacuation to North Africa.

The third point, given that massive German air assaults across the Channel could now be regarded as certain, was of great importance to Britain and, therefore, to the Allied cause. In France the German air losses in trained bomber-crews and fighter pilots had been heavy; they had been caused in no small degree by the Royal Air Force. Four hundred was an imposing figure, one that might make all the difference to the weight and timing of the forthcoming attack. Foreseeing this, as also the dire possibility of a French collapse, Churchill (at Tours, on June 13) had asked for an assurance that these air-crew prisoners should be handed over to British custody whatever might happen in France. The assurance had been solemnly, and willingly, given by the French Government, a fact of which the authorities in Bordeaux had recently been reminded.

To de Gaulle's cabled offer of service in this and other matters there was no reply. Nor did any action follow the British Government's more urgent representations. The promise was conveniently forgotten by those now more interested in seeking the favour of an 'invincible' enemy than in maintaining friendship with an apparently doomed Ally; the enemy airmen were presently handed back as a propitiatory gift to the *Luftwaffe* which was later to find in them a valuable reinforcement for the Battle of Britain. Consequences tragic for France were to follow this foolish breach of faith, for it inevitably strengthened the suspicion that the Bordeaux Government would be unlikely, under enemy pressure, to keep its word of honour concerning the disposal of the French fleet.

*   *   *

It had been agreed between Churchill and de Gaulle that no broadcast to France should be made until the intentions of Pétain and his associates were certainly known. By the 18th there was no longer any room for doubt and, at six o'clock that evening, the first appeal was made.

Destined to become memorable in French history, the event itself can be seen as the initial test of one man's character, his moral courage and his self-control. To the refugee in a foreign land, broadcasting for the first time and marking the occasion with a declaration as momentous as it was startling, the experience might well have been wholly disconcerting. Oppressive thoughts of disaster, of a shattered Army, of leaders who had lost their heads, added to the natural timidity of an unpractised orator, might have gripped him by the throat; and when in the quiet studio the flick of red light, enjoining silence, paradoxically commanded sound, the sudden impact of his own voice upon the stillness might have inhibited speech. The sound-deadened walls gave back no echo; the unchallenged words went out into the shadows beyond the unresponsive microphone; words that once spoken could not be modified, nor ever be recalled.

He spoke gravely and with admirable clarity, master of himself and of his speech. Even as he spoke he was aware of the dread significance of the step he had taken. At one stride he had broken with the past, with family tradition, with thirty years of service in the Army, with military discipline as with conventional behaviour, to set out, at the age of forty-nine, upon a most uncertain journey. The voice of reason had sounded the call of duty; but in an unpredictable future it was a call that might lead him as easily downward to the depths as upward to the stars. The imagined 'swim' had begun; he must now strike out across the uncharted ocean, or drown.

Disenchantment followed the restrained emotion of the appeal. The broadcast ended as it had begun, in silence. From the unseen audience, of whose very existence he was unsure, there was no swift reply. Had he been so much as heard?—anywhere, by anyone? And who would heed him? 'De Gaulle'—to the masses the name was almost unknown. 'Pétain', 'Weygand', not only were the names of longstanding renown, their bearers were known by sight. De Gaulle was a man without a face.

On the following morning he had the consolation of limited publicity, when the Press of the free world accorded him headlines and printed his call to arms. Sufficiently widespread, the news gave him the opportunity to follow up with a series of cables.

'General de Gaulle to all French communities abroad.
I invite you to appoint a representative who will be directly in touch with me. Wire name and particulars of this representative. . . .'

But the fact that, by broadcast and cable, he had thus signified his intention of hoisting in London the flag that had been hauled down in Bordeaux did not imply that he expected to be the only one to fly it or that others would not raise it elsewhere. Many, he was convinced, must already have made the decision to follow, not him, but the path he had chosen: men of note to speak for France, military commanders ready to denounce the unnecessary cease-fire. Indeed, reports of protests against the surrender were even now coming in from prominent men in overseas dependencies. To those he deemed most likely to assume the leadership of continued resistance, and to be most capable of doing so, he again offered his services.

He began with General Noguès, Commander-in-Chief in French North Africa, couching his message in modest terms.

'Am in London in semi-official and direct contact with British Government. Hold myself at your disposal, either to fight under your orders, or to take any step you may consider useful.'

To this offer, too, there was no reply. The only message to come in that day (19th) from any French personality of mark was the brief telegram from Weygand demanding de Gaulle's immediate return.

News from France, meanwhile, had made it plain that the leaders in Bordeaux, acting with a speed none had displayed in the conduct of the War, were rushing headlong into the vortex of their own contriving. Nothing could now deter them, not even the knowledge imparted by the enemy that North Africa was to be included in the surrender terms and that Italy was demanding her share. Before the shameful tragedy should be consummated someone had to speak, to cry out against the treason of some, the blind stupidity of others, to rouse France from the apathy of despair. That night de Gaulle's second broadcast sounded the new note of authority:

'. . . *j'ai conscience de parler au nom de la France.*'

Circumstances had arisen that compelled him to speak out. In the absence of recognized political leaders, of military commanders better known to the nation, he saw it as an inescapable duty to call upon all French fighting men and, since he alone was free to speak, in no other name than that of France.

Long ago, in his schooldays in Paris, he had laboriously copied out a pregnant paragraph. It came from a book, *Le Réveil de la Race*, written by an uncle and namesake, Charles de Gaulle, but the lines might have been traced by Destiny.

'When, in some camp surprised by night-attack, every man fights on alone against the enemy, one does not inquire of him who first raised the flag and gave the rallying cry "What is his rank?"'

By a tragic twist of fate it had fallen to him to utter the rallying cry on behalf of combatant Frenchmen; but that the assumption of authority was intended to be no more than temporary had already been made plain in the cable to Noguès asking for orders, and it was to be stressed again and again in the next few days. First of all in a letter to Weygand, dated June 20.

In this, acknowledging the order to return to France, de Gaulle affirmed his desire to obey if it were possible—'for my only resolve is to serve by fighting'—provided that the armistice convention was not signed within the next twenty-four hours. In fact the condition was already all but negatived. The armistice, whatever its terms, would be signed, if not within twenty-four, then almost certainly within forty-eight hours. In that case, he declared, 'I shall join any French resistance wherever organized. In London, in particular, there are military elements—others will doubtless come in—which are determined to fight on whatever may happen in metropolitan France.'

The letter's tone was courteous, but the hint it contained was broad. 'I think I ought to tell you very simply that I wish, for France's sake and your own, that you may see your way, and be able, to escape from disaster so as to reach France overseas and continue the war. At present no armistice is compatible with honour.' Even under Weygand—who at the very peak of the battle had, as de Gaulle knew at first hand, advocated surrender—he would still be willing to serve. 'I would add,' the letter ended, 'that my personal contacts with the British Government—particularly with Mr Churchill—might allow me to be useful to you or to any other high French personality who would be willing to put himself at the head of continued French resistance.'

Knowing Weygand he may have thought it improbable in the extreme that so erratic a schemer, believing as he did in the speedy defeat of Britain, would consider for a moment the idea of detaching himself from a government he had just helped to form for the express purpose of surrendering the French nation to the enemy. It was not even desirable that a man of proven instability should assume the leadership of those determined, at whatever cost to themselves, to fight on overseas. The assurance given in the letter was none the less sincere and deserves to be noted: de Gaulle would, at that time, willingly have served under any 'high French personality' coming from France or her dependencies to continue the struggle.

There was no reply to the letter. Months later it was returned with a paper slip attached to it, on which was typed a single sentence: 'If Colonel de Gaulle, retired, wishes to communicate with General Weygand he must do so through the usual channels.'

The events set in motion by Pétain and Weygand followed the now unavoidable course of national degradation. The victor imposed his will through the defeatists of Bordeaux. The earlier movement to North Africa was stopped; aircraft flown out were flown back. The four hundred German air-crew prisoners were released. The senators and deputies who had embarked in the *Massilia* at Le Verdon for Casablanca were prevented from sailing. The fleet remained inactive. On the 21st the French delegates went forward penitently to receive the enemy's orders. On the 22nd, at Rethondes, upon the very spot where Germany's defeat had been acknowledged in 1918, the appalling humiliation was inflicted by Hitler in person.

In London the immediate result was the publication, on the 23rd, of three declarations by the British Government. The first made it plain that the Franco-German armistice convention was 'in contravention of agreements solemnly made between the Allied Governments' and that its terms reduced the Bordeaux Government to 'a state of complete subjection to the enemy', depriving it not only of all freedom of action, but of 'all right to represent free French citizens.'

The statement ended: 'His Majesty's Government therefore now declare that they can no longer regard the Bordeaux Government as a government of an independent country.'

Even though the withdrawal from France of all British diplomatic and consular representation was to sever all direct communication with the unoccupied part of the country, and therefore to drive underground many useful channels of intelligence, in this hour of crisis the British Government's action appears justified and indeed essential. The Bordeaux leaders, confused in their thinking, persistent in their folly, had, whether they realized it or not, sold France into slavery. Britain, condemning defeatism, must resume her freedom of action. But it follows that, since recognition was to be withheld from Bordeaux, it would be only wise to accord it to some other body of Frenchmen, in Britain or overseas, capable of representing the opinion of those determined to honour the Alliance and to fight on.

De Gaulle, in his letter to Weygand, had mentioned the existence in London of French 'military elements' ready to continue in the War, but there were also civilians anxious to offer their services, men of standing like René Pléven and Jean Monnet of the late French Government's Economic Mission. Admittedly Monnet, after a meeting with de Gaulle, wrote to say that he thought 'it would be a great mistake to try to set up in England an organization which might appear in France as an authority created abroad under British protection.' He did state, however, that he fully shared de Gaulle's 'determination to prevent France from abandoning the struggle,' and added a postscript that 'the setting up of a Committee which would be charged with helping any Frenchman wishing to continue the struggle alongside England ... would be extremely useful.'

The idea of a London Committee was the natural sequel to de Gaulle's first broadcast call for volunteers and to his cabled invitation to all French communities abroad to appoint representatives. Put forward by de Gaulle, the formation of the Committee was approved by the Foreign Office and given official support in the second declaration of June 23.

'His Majesty's Government have taken note of the proposal to form a Provisional French National Committee fully representing independent French elements determined on the prosecution of the war in fulfilment of the international obligations of France.

'His Majesty's Government declare that they will recognize such Provisional French National Committee and will deal with them in all matters concerning the prosecution of the war so long as that Committee continues to represent all French elements resolved to fight the common enemy.'

The wording of the final sentence might seem to be oddly at variance with the paragraph's earlier recognition of the Committee, since it laid down a condition that obviously could not be fulfilled immediately. The Committee, only now in course of formation, could not *continue* to represent', since it did not yet claim that it represented *all* French elements of resistance; it could, initially, only endeavour to unite from London those scattered few who were responding to the appeals. The intention, however, was in line with de Gaulle's initial belief that others would soon be coming in overseas to widen the scope of the Committee.

Here and there in the French empire some, momentarily free to speak, were, it seemed, ready to act. The Commander-in-Chief in Syria, General Mittelhauser, had affirmed that his forces would never lower the French flag to the enemy; and somewhat similar announcements were being made by General Catroux, Governor-General of Indo-China, by the Resident-General, Peyrouton, in Tunisia, and by prominent officials in various French African provinces. To them the British Government addressed its third declaration of the day.

'The signature of the armistice by the French Government brings to an end the organized resistance of the French forces at home. In the French Colonial Empire, however, there are encouraging signs that a more robust spirit prevails.'

After naming those who had proclaimed their resolve to fight on, the declaration continued:

'His Majesty's Government are prepared to make the necessary financial arrangements to enable the French Colonial Empire to play its part. As stated by the Prime Minister, the British aim is the complete restoration of the metropolitan and overseas territory of France.'

Again, although this offer appeared to nullify the recognition of the National Committee in London—by making sure that it could not represent *all* Frenchmen, since other bodies were to be recognized in the Colonies—it was entirely in keeping with de Gaulle's repeated attempts to rally any French authority of sufficient influence to take over the leadership. To persuade men in command of considerable forces in strategically important areas to throw in their lot with Britain, only the British Government, given de Gaulle's lack of resources, could make the necessary 'financial arrangements'. Purposely, no mention was made in the declaration of either de Gaulle or the proposed Committee, so that a door might be left open through which colonial governors or military leaders might honourably enter without prior reference to the junior general and his handful of refugees.

With no wish to thrust himself forward, de Gaulle was in full agreement with this procedure, for he was still hoping—though perhaps now against hope—that someone of suitable stature would declare himself. Hard upon the British offer of support, he cabled again to Noguès (24th). From this message, reporting the formation of the Committee with its purpose of 'binding together all French elements of resistance', two sentences stand out to bear witness to his self-effacement.

'We ask you personally to join this Committee. All here consider you as marked out to be the great leader of French resistance.'

But he called in vain. Noguès hesitated, and was presently lost for ever.

To those whose voices had been raised in protest against the surrender other cables were sent out on the same day. To Mittelhauser, to Puaux (French High Commissioner in Syria and the Lebanon), to Catroux in Indo-China.

'Wholly united with you in determination to continue war, we are constituting a French National Committee. . . . We ask you personally to join this Committee. . . . On behalf of the French National Committee—General de Gaulle.'

For a few days it seemed as if the hopes might be justified. There were encouraging signs overseas; opinion appeared to be hardening against Bordeaux. Further cables were dispatched, with the additional suggestion that each recipient should join a 'Defence Council of Overseas France' to unite all resistance 'in the Empire and in England'.

The telegrams ended with a renewed reminder of the fundamental object of armed resistance:

'Faced by the fact that the Bordeaux Government has lost its independence, it is our duty to defend the honour and integrity of the Empire and of France.'

The days passed, and the hopes faded. All too quickly the paternal admonitions of Pétain, the waspish commands of Weygand, silenced the momentary defiance of men irresolute, bewildered, or dominated by voluble defeatists. On June 25 they listened to a broadcast by Pétain. Instead of a stout-hearted call to resistance in the empire, they heard him urge all Frenchmen 'to an intellectual and moral regeneration'. It was not that sort of revival the French needed just then, rather was it a rejuvenation of military thinking among her leaders. But the gilded oak-leaves of the Marshal outweighed the two small stars of the temporary Brigadier-General. Soon, of all the Generals and Governors, only Catroux stood by his decision to refuse surrender.

No top-ranking public figure came out of France. Those who had tried to leave for North Africa—President Lebrun, Herriot, Mandel, the Senators and Deputies in the *Massilia*—all had been stopped. In the confusion sinister influences were at work: Alibert the mentally deranged political theorist who swayed Pétain, Laval the corrupt politician, Darlan the frustrated admiral—by these the disaster was made absolute.

The Allied search for survivors was called off. A few might yet swim to safety, but the lifeboats that should have steered boldly towards the beacon of resistance had been drawn back into the whirlpool of the sinking ship. The proffered lifebelt of financial help remained ungrasped; to the broadcast appeals and the cabled messages there was no response. France was submerged.

On June 28 the British Government, its survey completed, named the only man who, with a small band of followers, inflexibly denounced the surrender and defied the enemy in the name of France.

'His Majesty's Government recognize General de Gaulle as leader of all free Frenchmen, wherever they may be, who rally to him in support of the Allied cause.'

A page of French history had been turned, a new name added to the long list of heroes.

3. The Standard-bearer

'Here is the Constable of France.'
(Churchill: *Second World War, Vol. II.*)

THE COLLAPSE of France in May and June 1940 will always stand as
one of the great disasters of military history. It was unexpected, it was
abrupt, it was total. Its consequences were dire to civilization everywhere; it brought about the minor intervention of Italy and encouraged
the major aggression of Japan; it allowed Hitler to attack Russia; it
permitted the Nazi tyranny, invested with a specious aura of invinci-
bility, to display its power in the cold-blooded murder of defenceless
millions; it immeasurably prolonged the War in the world. It may thus
be seen, not as a transient defeat for one side, to be regarded as a
military triumph for the other, but as a calamity for all men.

The Pétain–Weygand surrender at the end of the battle in France
was a very different matter. It did not affect the ultimate decision of the
War in Europe. It did not contribute so very much more to the
material strength or strategic advantage which the enemy had already
taken since May 10. Of momentarily acute embarrassment to the
British Government, it did not affect that Government's determination
to continue the prosecution of the War until Germany should be
defeated. Nor did it, in the long run, shield the French people from the
horrors and devastations of total war, from Nazi atrocities and whole-
sale massacre. Pusillanimity brought no reward.

What it did achieve was with one stroke to erase the name of France
from the recognized category of Great Nations. Even wholly occupied,
but with her Government resolutely fighting on from North Africa,
with her Empire behind her, Britain her ally, America supporting, she
would have commanded the respect and admiration of the free world;
she would have been a Power, to be considered, consulted. Humbly
begging for terms, surrendering and withdrawing from the struggle
after so brief a campaign, she was immediately negligible, no more than
a painful memory, an object of pity when not of scorn. The harm done
was incalculable and lasting. As time and the War went on and men's
thoughts were drawn to events elsewhere—to the air-bombardment
and threatened invasion of Britain, to the growing menace in the

Atlantic, to the first battles in Egypt's Western Desert, at length to
the Russian, Japanese and American extensions of the conflict—even
the memory became dim; and distant nations with troubles of their
own grew indifferent to the fate of France, caring little on which side
she stood since, worthless as an ally, she was impotent as a foe. Her
soil might some day provide a convenient battlefield upon which
German military power should finally be defeated, but scarcely anyone in the world, least of all in America, expected a Frenchman to be
present at the victory. To the long story of French honour and glory
it seemed that *Finis* had been written.

All this had been brought about by the crime of unnecessary surrender, for which the prime responsibility rested upon Pétain and
Weygand. Their crime was the more heinous for the skill with which,
shielding the military hierarchy, including themselves, whose blind
incompetence in modern warfare had caused the defeat, they placed
the blame squarely upon the French people: Weygand by pretended
fears of popular riots and a Communist uprising to suppress which he
needed the troops engaged in fighting the Germans, Pétain by alleging
that the people were in need of 'moral regeneration', thereby implying,
as the world understood it, that their degeneracy had earned their
defeat. Other and more blatant defeatists were in due course to take
over leadership and to lower still further the credit of France in the
world; they would never have flourished had not the initial surrender
—perhaps the greatest crime ever committed against the staunch
people of France, ignorant of the truth and powerless to resist—been
plotted and perpetrated by Pétain and Weygand.

Against the black curtain that, falling at Rethondes to mark the end
of Act I of the tragedy of France, now obliterated the nation, the
candle-flame of French resistance held aloft by Charles de Gaulle
gleamed with suddenly augmented brightness. As one by one the protests from overseas territories were silenced, his voice alone rang
through the free world to rescue his country's name from obloquy
and oblivion. To his opponents the echoes might sound hollow and
unreal, no more valid than the call of some passing adventurer crying
a lost cause for motives of ambition, vain and scarcely creditable. To
those who, despite the totality of eclipse, believed that the light of
France must shine again the call to arms seemed not only honourable
but vitally necessary, the defiance of the enemy as logical as it was

courageous, the denunciation of surrender a matter less of pride than of military common sense. Failing all others, for whatever reason detained, this man with the symbolic name who dared to speak, in darkness and solitude, 'in the name of France' stood forth as the champion and standard-bearer behind whom the overseas legions of liberation would presently arise.

*   *   *

What the submission of France and her Empire to Pétain's command had involved, in terms of lost strength and influence, could be measured in London. Of the will of a great nation to fight, not for honour, but for her very existence, all that remained was enclosed within the bare walls of a four-roomed office in an old-fashioned building overlooking the Thames Embankment. It was little enough.

On that Sunday, June 23, when the British Government first declared its recognition of a provisional French National Committee, those who had heard the news might have imagined a headquarters bustling with activity; in fact the building was silent and almost deserted. The rare caller found that the lift was not working and, after walking up three flights of echoing stone stairs, came to a door standing ajar which he had perforce to push open since the bell was out of order. Beyond, in a dark alcove, a French soldier in shirt-sleeves busied himself with a telephone switchboard, also out of order; at his direction the visitor crossed the narrow entrance-hall and entered an office-room so small that it hardly contained the furniture of one table and two chairs. Upon the wall above the fireplace was gummed, like the portrait of an absent friend, a small-scale map of France. At the table sat Lieutenant Geoffroy de Courcel, peacetime diplomat and wartime cavalryman.

Courcel, the only Frenchman to accompany General de Gaulle on his journey from Bordeaux to England, was at this time the man of all work: personal assistant, secretary, liaison officer, interviewer. He was also the usher who conducted infrequent visitors down the uncarpeted passage between empty rooms to the General's larger office whose windows, facing across the Thames, opened upon south London's unlovely skyline above which, like silver fish in a blue bowl, floated the tethered balloons.

Of his first meeting with de Gaulle in Downing Street, Churchill was to write: 'Under an impassive, imperturbable demeanour he seemed to me to have a remarkable capacity for feeling pain.' To which he added his impression of a 'very tall, phlegmatic man.' It was not, it could not be on first acquaintance, a complete or very profound estimate; but it was fair, and certainly more penetrating than the many snap judgments subsequently pronounced by various Allied leaders, political or military, who were to label him frigid and arrogant without understanding the causes of his aloofness or the reasons for his austerity. It may be that what they sought, those others, was someone cast in the mould of what they believed a Frenchman ought to be: voluble, witty, gesturing, perhaps tearfully pleading, certainly pliant to their views—for once France had fallen every outsider was ready to state the reasons for the fall and to assert his expert knowledge of the means by which the corpse should be resuscitated. To these experts it was disconcerting to find an unknown French general of junior rank persistently avowing that he knew better. All the more brilliant must Churchill's foresight and understanding of character appear—even if modified subsequently—when so early as June 1940 he could note: 'Here is the Constable of France.'

True, this latter-day Constable never laughed and seldom smiled; concerning France there was little to smile about just then. That he spoke slowly and, it might seem, coldly was due to a natural reserve amounting to shyness with strangers; and in those days all men in England were strangers to him; but he welcomed those who came to call upon him, courteously and with a dignity that was habitual. Standing, he held himself very straight so that all were immediately conscious of his lean height enhanced by the tall cylindrical *képi*. Seated at his desk, studying documents or discussing grave events, from the drawn features of a long face, the eyes dark-lidded and heavy from lack of sleep and excessive reading, it was not stretching imagination very far to deduce that the calm was controlled, that behind the impassive manner were concealed deep emotions and anguished thoughts. His voice was firm; only occasionally did a sharp intake of breath, scarcely a sigh, betray that 'remarkable capacity for feeling pain' which Churchill had observed. Put in other words it was a capacity for taking punishment, of which in the course of self-imposed duty he was to stand in great need in the years to come.

In those early days what he most desired was news from France.

Had his broadcasts been heard? Would combatant Frenchmen respond to the appeal? Were they getting out—to Africa, to Spain? Any encouraging details drew a fleeting smile and a noticeable increase of warmth. Acutely aware of his solitude in London, he was athirst for information from visitors recently arrived from France, for news of those statesmen, generals, well-known personalities who, having played their part in the drama, had now, it seemed, been stricken dumb. However painful the events, he was ready to discuss them provided they shed light upon future action.

Nor was he averse to giving forthright opinions concerning some of those involved in the tragedy. Many at that time were still wondering how it had come about that the French Premier, till then so resolute, had so suddenly, during de Gaulle's brief absence in London on the 16th, despaired and resigned. A shrug of the shoulders accompanied the explanation: 'Reynaud? He was in the hands of his mistress, Madame de Portes. I believe that in the end he was *too tired* to go on.' The allusion to *L'Aiglon* seemed unmistakable; the play had made a deep impression upon him in boyhood and the bitter stress upon the two words in their present context clearly recalled Flambeau's protest. '*Et nous . . . nous ne l'étions pas, peut-être, fatigués?*'

Others had been surprised by the suddenness of Weygand's collapse. Was there not some mystery about it?

The reply was almost toneless; the sorry truth had long been known and digested. 'No, there's nothing mysterious. General Weygand made up his mind to capitulate within a few days of taking over from Gamelin. He talked a great deal about the honour of the Army, but he was thinking more about his own career.'

To the question whether Clemenceau, had he been alive and in power in Reynaud's place, would have handled Weygand differently, the answer was short. 'Clemenceau? He would have had him arrested on the spot—and probably shot the next morning.'

Discussion of the campaign of France was neither vain nor purely academic; it disclosed both de Gaulle's purpose in coming to London and his future intentions already firmly decided. In conversation he made clear his view that once Weygand had realized at the end of May that the gap between the Allied armies in the north and the French armies in the south could not be closed he should not have staked all upon the line of the Somme, for which he lacked both the strength on the spot and the time to bring up reinforcements, but should at once have prepared to fall back to the line Seine–Paris–Marne or even farther, to the Loire, to Britanny, the coast. 'Such is the speed of mechanized warfare,' he said, 'warfare for which we were ill-prepared, that the only remedy was to cede space so as to gain time, if necessary by moving out of metropolitan France. We ought to have taken as much as could be saved of the Army, its equipment, its Air Forces, to North Africa, the Fleet as well. We should have regarded the Mediterranean in 1940 as the Marne of 1914. That's what I told Monsieur Reynaud. And that was what he agreed to do. Only he waited too long, until it was too late.'

In his view the Germans, whom the completeness of their victory had taken by surprise, had no wish to stretch their forces by an occupation of all France—another point that made surrender unnecessary —and wanted still less to embark upon an invasion of North Africa that, whether they went by Spain or by Italy, involved in the end a *seaborne* invasion for which they were wholly unprepared and entirely unequipped. England was now the main German objective; but England, unfaltering in her determination to fight on and still supreme at sea, was also the one sure base and centre of communications from which any French colonial territory anxious to resist would be accessible to re-equipped French combatants. London, moreover, was the headquarters of that loyal friend of France to whom de Gaulle— already officially deputed by Reynaud—most naturally turned for initial support.

But to seek Churchill's aid was not to become his pensioner; of that de Gaulle was prompt to express both his aversion and his awareness of the damage which the very hint of such dependance must cause him personally. He had spoken 'in the name of France', and in that name alone he must plan and strive. There could be no other loyalty. Alliance with Britain, yes, but no subservience. Malicious tongues in Bordeaux—soon to become Vichy—would argue that he and his followers were, as Monnet had put it, 'under the protection of England, inspired by her interests'; at all times and by all means he must assert and prove the contrary. The French volunteers must remain Frenchmen, not become British mercenaries; the Committee now forming would be 'French' and 'National', dedicated to the liberation of the country under that country's flag; and, of this movement of free men towards national resurgence, the independence of action must constantly be affirmed. 'France' must be the slogan, the watchword, the inspiration. However uncompromising the attitude, few knowing him could doubt the purity of his motives. To his selfless if unaccommodating patriotism, Churchill, naming him Constable, gave unqualified approval.

From the outset de Gaulle's military intentions had been made clear. Shortly after his arrival in England he had declared (June 22) in answer to a question: 'As soon as I have assembled such men and material as are available, I intend to take them out of England to some point on French overseas territory; rally other forces in the colonies, and at once start active operations against the enemy.'

There were, at the time of the surrender, some thousands of French troops in Britain, notably a Light Alpine Division (ex Norway), a large number of convalescent wounded (ex Dunkirk) and several thousand French sailors in warships that had taken refuge in British ports in accordance with the initial plan for continuing the fight from overseas bases. It was hoped that a high proportion of these men would volunteer at once, so that they could be transported to Africa while it yet seemed likely that Morocco would continue to play a part in the War. Hence the appeal to Noguès and the suggestion that he assume the leadership.

Of these hopes the disappointment was twofold and swift. Noguès chose obedience to Bordeaux; and in Britain, where the majority of the French naval units now remained inactive, General Bethouart, commanding the Alpine division, requested repatriation for his troops. His attitude was reasonable, for the greater part of the conscripted men were disheartened by recent events, and he was given little encouragement to stay by the British Government. He did, however, permit de Gaulle to visit and address the men, with the result that some 2,000 —including two battalions of the Foreign Legion and a miscellaneous collection of all arms—decided to stay. The remainder of the division was held concentrated and presently shipped back to France.

The intention remained, though the plans had perforce to be modified. The force would be small; it would take longer to assemble and, in the case of the airmen, to re-equip. The destination would of necessity be more distant; time must elapse before it could be ascertained

with certainty which French dependency was most ready to partici-
pate in the resistance movement and which offered the greatest advantages as a base for operations. But whatever the decision, the expedition
would be French.

Never for a moment did de Gaulle contemplate the possibility of
taking service under the British Crown, a hireling soldier of fortune
owing allegiance to a foreign power; the very thought was abhorrent
to him. Not for that had he broken with the past, with tradition and
discipline and issued his call to arms; not for love of fighting, but for
love of France. Nor could he ever accept, though he might have been
powerless to prevent it had others insisted, that the fighting troops of
France in exile should be enrolled in the British services as a 'French
Legion'. Over isolated refugees landing in England, solitary airmen
dropping from the skies or seamen putting into British ports, he had
no jurisdiction; he could only invite and persuade.

In this persuasion, however, he had the warm encouragement of
British authorities who, once individual Frenchmen had been identified as something else than 'fifth columnists', were quick to see the
advantage of uniting all under de Gaulle rather than of accepting them
one by one into British units where, apart from other considerations,
ignorance of the English language would have been a bar to efficiency.
Action, on the other hand, was far from speedy, partly because of the
suspicion with which all foreigners were then regarded, more largely
because of the national preoccupation with a German invasion believed
to be imminent. To accelerate the assembly and recruitment of volunteers, as well as the recuperation of French equipment returned from
Norway or brought over from France, British liaison officers from the
three services were early appointed.

De Gaulle saw these officers daily, either separately and alone or
together, in the presence of his staff, at the evening conferences held
in the largest room of those temporary offices overlooking the Thames
Embankment. More often than not the staff would include Courcel,
Captains Tissier and de Boislambert for the Army, and Admiral
Muselier for the Navy and Air Forces: a total, together with the British
officers, of perhaps a dozen persons crowded about a narrow table.
Reports would be made, and questions put, regarding accommodation
available for newly-arrived volunteers or the transfer of free French
units to suitable training areas; but discussion was always liveliest

when it concerned the discovery of French war material landed in Britain and supposedly seized without right by local authorities.

Muselier was an adept at uncovering, with the help of officers dispatched to northern ports, such acts of alleged piracy. Himself something of a pirate—a swarthy, voluble little meridional who would have been better suited with a colourful bandana about his head than with the goldlaced cap of admiralty—he would press his claims with uncontrolled vehemence, putting the harassed War Office representative at considerable pains to prove that a given incident was due to a simple misunderstanding and that the specified war material, if in fact it turned out to be French which was not always the case, would soon be released. De Gaulle, though he backed his countryman's claim whenever it was reasonable to do so, endeavoured to conciliate so as to obtain practical results. His comments were matter-of-fact, his suggestions logical; he spoke slowly, with a certain authority, yet without raising his voice above conversational level. If sometimes he displayed impatience with unnecessary delay, it was hard to blame him in the circumstances under which he laboured, and no one did. On the whole he remained calm and, as Churchill had noted, imperturbable; so that it was easy to see, as time went by, that behind the constrained manner there lay an honest simplicity of purpose more winning than fiery eloquence, easy charm, or any of the tricks of hearty, joke-cracking bonhomie of which he had none. His purpose was to uphold the honour and independence of France, his sole immediate interest the prosecution of the war.

Even before the formation of the French National Committee had been completed, and before he himself had been officially designated as its rightful head, he had drawn up and submitted (June 26) to the British Government a Memorandum outlining the organization, supply and maintenance of the proposed French forces. Pending final agreement, including financial arrangements, pending also a decision regarding the expedition's destination, he made it clear that he was anxious to contribute, in however small a way, to the defence of Great Britain. For this he had early suggested the sending of suitable French fighter pilots to Royal Air Force units, instead of keeping all concentrated under his own supervision. For the same reason he made frequent inquiries at the evening conferences to discover the whereabouts of half a dozen light tanks (French, ex Norway) believed to be in Newcastle.

'Those six tanks are urgently needed,' he told the War Office representative. 'With the trained crews already with us, they will form the nucleus of a French armoured force. Meanwhile, they can be placed at the disposal of the British military commander. They might be very useful if the invasion takes place.'

Six light tanks to repel Hitler? Why not? With a small improvised force, at Montcornet a few weeks earlier, he had delayed and all but halted the German Army's westward advance. Now, despite the débâcle, the spirit was the same, resolute, indomitable. He might not be able to appreciate—any more than French and German, and even British, military thinkers then appreciated—that command of the sea rightly applied ruled out the possibility of a successful seaborne invasion by an enemy of limited naval means. To him the invasion of the country in which he had chosen to take his stand was a probability to be faced without dismay, for he no more doubted Britain's determination to fight and ability to win than he doubted the ultimate victory of France. The survival of Britain was essential to the restoration of France; faith in the former expressed loyalty to the latter.

Of his position as leader of all Free Frenchmen to which he was named on June 28, he was not slow to perceive the responsibility. In broadcasts to France he might still appeal; to the Free French Forces he must now command. In the name of the National Committee, of which by common consent he was the official head, he must assume a wider authority. For the first time, in his relations with British delegates, he used a significant phrase.

At one of the evening conferences the War Office representative was giving some account of equipment recently sorted out in a British port. Certain items, he declared, were the property of the British Government; other equipment belonged 'to France' and would be moved by the War Office. De Gaulle interrupted.

'That is for me to decide. *Pour l'instant, c'est moi qui suis la France ici.*'

A proud thing to say: 'I am France.' Louis XIV might have said it at Versailles; Pétain, in the near future to assume the powers of an absolute monarch, might vainly assert it in Vichy. Here it was not said proudly; not, at least, with arrogance or presumption. De Gaulle spoke gently, almost diffidently, as one deprecating the unhappy circumstances that caused the assertion to be no more than the truth. No one at the conference table raised so much as an eyebrow. The War Office representative muttered 'Yes, of course'; his French colleagues nodded agreement. The statement was accepted as the logical conclusion to be drawn from recent events.

It did, however, mark an important step forward. No longer did a solitary castaway call in the darkness to scattered survivors. Now from all over the world groups of defiant Frenchmen were raising clamant voices to proclaim their will to fight on; to that will the body of fighting men in Britain gave growing force, the National Committee expression. By their will and common consent a leader was designated. The failure or inability of others to come forward, to risk all in the cause of France at war, was seen as a challenge. Without bombast, but firmly and with notable dignity, de Gaulle took it up. Thenceforward, no one had a better right than he to say: 'I am France.'

4. The Stages of Destiny—I

I had no doubt but that France must undergo trials befitting a giant, nor that the purpose of life lay in rendering her, one day, some signal service, and that I should find occasion to do so.
(General de Gaulle on his boyhood: *Mémoires de Guerre*, Vol. I)

OVER THE months and the years ahead it was not only in German-dominated France, and in Pétain's entourage, that de Gaulle was to find bitter enmity and personal condemnation; considerable hostility to him and to his movement sprang up in political circles elsewhere, in Washington even more than in London. In fact it was to be the paradox of his wartime endeavours that, whilst inside France and within the French colonial Empire he slowly gained popular support, as his aims and those of the resistance movement became better known, in the White House and in the State Department he came, by stages of progressive dislike, to be regarded as one so entirely detrimental to the Allied cause that to condemn him no words were too severe. Roosevelt labelled him a self-seeking egoist. Admiral Leahy, for a time ambassador to Pétain at Vichy and thereafter the President's personal Chief of Staff, spoke of the 'self-appointed leader' of a 'so-called resistance movement' who was 'lusting for power' like Laval, and referred to his supporters in the United States as 'a group of Jews and Communists'—a classification oddly reminiscent of Hitler's intemperate ranting, which the Secretary of State, Cordell Hull, put more succinctly by terming them 'polecats'. Others were quick to follow the official lead and to discern a character inconsequently summed up by Hull as 'desperately temperamental'.

Most of this, admittedly, was said or written much later in the War, after America had entered the struggle. It might well be passed over here, as something done in the heat of the moment under the stress of events, were it not that those who emitted the opinions chose to re-state them in print after the War's ending, when it might have been expected that they would have checked their allegations with the record of General de Gaulle's antecedents and remarkable achievements. Although the books of tainted war Memoirs may no longer be read, they still stand upon dusty shelves waiting to transmit the erroneous impressions of men who, long dead and half forgotten, may yet be regarded by some as reliable authorities; and it is therefore necessary, so as to refute the accusations and efface the impression, to recall some of the salient events of de Gaulle's life prior to 1940.

*   *   *

It must first be recalled that he did not begin in London; he began anew. The events of a long and outstanding military career had already marked him as a person of importance. Indeed, upon at least three occasions, he had been the most important man in France—though few of his compatriots would willingly have admitted the fact. Time had been when, midway between the wars, some of the best-known figures in the Army, Pétain amongst them, had seen in him a future commander-in-chief. That those who had descried the promise then opposed its fulfilment because they were too small to accept its greatness was to lead directly to France's military downfall, to surrender and national discredit, eventually to their own ruin. In the fullness of time and of human misery the wheel would turn full circle to the vindication of de Gaulle and the restoration of France; but the tragedy of war could have been averted—for France, for Europe, for the world—had his clear-sighted logic not been rejected by men obstinate, jealous, and conceited.

It has been said that if a man sow a thought he will reap an action, from the sown action reap a habit, from the habit a destiny. It is not quite so simple as that; to some extent the concatenation must always be affected by Chance, and for too many young men in the twentieth century the links were broken by the chances of war. For de Gaulle, however, wartime misfortune, ensuring survival, enabled the chain to be forged and the destiny to be accomplished.

The first thought of boyhood, after the usual Jules Verne dreams of journeys to the Moon and beyond, was implanted by his father, retired army officer, Professor of Philosophy at Lille, and later Director of Studies at the Jesuits' great Stanislas College in Paris where the young Charles—he was the second of four brothers—received the profound if somewhat one-sided education of the cultured Catholic Frenchman. The thought was of France, of the traditions of her long and turbulent past, of her misfortunes, her dark hours, her glory and recurrent greatness—of all that tumultuous history which seems to have been inspired by a wayward genius and written with the point of a sword. By it, all at once, the boy was enthralled. His grandfather had written a life of St Louis; losing himself in its pages he found himself again in distant centuries, tracing his own forbears back to the gallant Jean de Gaulle who had fought the English in the Hundred Years War or, farther back, to the shadowy ancestor who had originated the name: taken perhaps from the *gaule*, that slender yet sturdy wooden rod still in use today for bringing down the olive-tree harvest, and before the coming of firearms a handy improvised lance—in England might not the name have been 'Longstaff'? Or was it that some nomadic warrior straying within the purlieu of a northern tribe came to be known as the man 'from Gaul', more simply *the* Gaul, the Frenchman? Such speculations linked to the facts of recorded history stirred the imagination. In summer, from a small family estate in the Dordogne, high spirits and long legs might carry him off with his brothers in search of physical adventure; it was to the crowded pages of the book of France that he turned for sheer delight. The seed had fallen upon fertile ground.

The action, reaped in adolescence, was the decision to make the Army his profession. All his reading drew him to it, and not only reading. The Franco–Prussian War was fresh in living memory; his father's tales of the siege of Paris when, a young officer taking part in a famous sortie, he had been wounded at Le Bourget, echoed his mother's childhood remembrance of Bazaine's surrender at Metz. The symbols of past glory, 'the evening majesty of Versailles, sunlight upon the Arc de Triomphe, captured flags fluttering beneath the dome of the Invalides',[1] awakened the desire to serve. The raging of '*l'Affaire*' —in which his father sided with the luckless Dreyfus—did nothing to discourage his youthful ambition; and presently, in the first decade of the new century, the ominous roll of still distant war-drums came to strengthen his determination.

But there was no short cut to an officer's career. Military service was obligatory upon all Frenchmen; before admittance to St Cyr a full year had to be served in the ranks; and because—though now a Parisian as much by upbringing as by domicile—he had been born in Lille, it was to the north-east that he was directed when, a raw recruit

[1] From the *Mémoires de Guerre,* Vol. I.

among the recruited miners and peasants of Artois, he joined the 33rd
Infantry stationed at Arras.

Those who served with him then were to recall an amiable overgrown youth, reserved but not aloof, whose erudition all respected
and whose tales of their country's history—of the many wars that had
swept over this land, of Spanish incursions, of fighting on the Scarpe
and of the siege of Arras—held the rapt attention of men ignorant but
eager enough to draw him out and to learn. A young man whose
height begged the mockery of nicknames—'Big Charles', 'double-
metre', 'asparagus'—and who took them good-naturedly, he seemed
at first an awkward soldier, clumsy at building up the monumental and
all-comprehensive marching pack then carried by French infantrymen;
a possessor of books, too, of too many books that, at inconvenient
moments, would slide from ill-contrived hiding-places to cause confusion and untidiness, to the greater annoyance of an irascible inspect-
ing sergeant. During his year's service he was not selected for promotion.

Despite its moments of comic relief, and its days of instructive field
training, it was a hard life; by modern standards almost brutish. But
Arras can scarcely have been an unhappy garrison, for when at long
last he passed triumphantly out of St Cyr he chose to return there, a
fledgling officer appointed to the 33rd Regiment. And, in the very
hour of his joining, he was brought face to face with one whose ultimate destiny, running counter to his own, was then so distant and so
unimaginable that, even had the future been revealed from on high,
Providence itself would have been laughed to scorn.

The Regiment had changed commanders during de Gaulle's term
at St Cyr. The new Colonel was an oldish man, or so it seemed to his
young officers, for he was well into his fifties and his years of service,
not so very far short of forty, implied that retirement was all to which
he could now look forward. But he was young enough in health and
physical appearance: straight-backed, clear of eye, a commanding
presence. About the care and handling of an infantry regiment, a
lifetime of service had taught him almost all there was to be known;
but his world was narrow; the Army was everything. From his peasant
origin he had derived both the qualities and the faults: a rugged constitution, a capacity for hard work, and a kindly nature conditioned by
a strictly limited intelligence which he endeavoured to supplement

with caution and cunning. Unmarried, he was wedded to the Service and regarded the Regiment as his family. Such was Philippe Pétain, from whom the young de Gaulle learned his first practical lessons in the exercise of command, and by whom his ability and incipient merit were first noted.

*   *   *

Colonel Pétain was no military genius, but he was sufficiently clear-sighted to perceive that in matters of tactical theory the French Army authorities were out of touch with reality. According to the official doctrine, the continual offensive—to be put into operation the instant the opposing armies had made contact—must certainly triumph, since nothing could resist the overwhelming impetus of a French infantry charge. Little account was taken of varying circumstances, of the enemy's dispositions, of the power and range of German weapons. And it was the danger of this fire-power that Pétain vainly urged: faced with massed artillery, rifles and machine-guns, the premature infantry attack would result in terrible losses. The solution, he claimed, lay in concentrating forces behind defensive positions from which the enemy's initial attack would be beaten off; and from out of which, with the enemy weakened and exhausted, the infantry, its concentration completed and heavily supported by artillery, would then advance to complete the victory.

But, however prudent the advice, the Colonel's superiors did not heed it. Swift-moving audacity, involving an immediate attack whatever the circumstances, was thought to be the prime lesson of the Franco–Prussian War. Thus, with a strategic plan whose tactical implementation might well have ensured success in 1870, the gallant French infantry was thrown into 1914—with its red trousers, its blue overcoats and scarlet-topped *képis*, and its long bayonets. Though it gained much glory, its losses were appalling.

De Gaulle was severely wounded in the early fighting across the Belgian border. By the time he had fully recovered and rejoined the Regiment, it was 1915 and the stagnation of trench warfare had set in. From the North Sea to the Swiss frontier both sides stood almost motionless; and in Champagne, where the Regiment was engaged, French attacks large or small invariably ended in costly failure. Presently de Gaulle was wounded again, twice; but not before official note had been taken of his conduct, not only of his courage in the face of the enemy: of his proficiency, his grasp of detail and—most significantly —his devoted care of his men. When, once more, he returned to the front it was as Captain in command of a company. The year was 1916 and the theatre of operations Verdun.

Neither the French nor the German High Command displayed anything that can be classed as brilliance in the ensuing battle whose outcome, in any event incapable of affecting the war's decision, was largely a question of military prestige and national pride. The German Crown Prince and his advisers sought to add to their laurels by the elimination of a fortified salient whose conquest would gain them another important slice of French territory. The French Command, anxious to avoid any further encroachment of their country's soil, were determined at all costs to hold the world-famous, if obsolete, fortress; and General Pétain was the chosen instrument of their will.

His tactical theories vindicated by practice, the almost-retired Colonel of pre-war days had made swift progress: brigadier, divisional commander, now in command of the army defending Verdun. But it was little enough that he could contribute to the war of attrition. His difficulties enhanced by a tenuous line of supply, he might watch from the steps of his headquarters mansion the fresh divisions marching up to the line, see them through tear-filled eyes return a few days later decimated, tattered, borne down with fatigue; to the enemy's massive assault he could oppose no more than the heroism of his men and his own resolute prudence. Too prudent by far, his critics were to say; an early and unnecessary withdrawal from the east bank of the Meuse only prolonged the struggle and made it costlier.

With no great generalship in evidence on either side, the battle was soon little else than a hard slogging-match on the lower plane, the level of battalion commanders, of junior officers, of companies and detachments, of small groups of weary men fighting on amid an incessant deafening din, beneath a smoke-blackened sky in a world of shattered trenches and crumbling brick and flying splinters. One such isolated company, heavily attacked upon its front near the ruined Fort Douaumont, saw through the smoke the enemy creeping about its flanks; heard, moments later, the crack of rifle fire upon its rear. The position was surrounded. At this the company commander rose up defiantly, gathered his surviving men, and led them into hand-to-hand fighting in a furious counter-attack. Almost at once he was knocked unconscious and severely wounded. At nightfall the enemy inched forward, stretcher-bearers following. Captain de Gaulle came to in a German field hospital.

Amid countless deeds of gallantry his own might well, in the confusion of unending battle, have passed unnoticed. But for a long time now his conduct had been outstanding, and the glowing Army citation—published when he was reported missing—did no more than recognize the truth. It began by stating that Captain de Gaulle was 'renowned for his high intellectual and moral worth'; and it went on to describe the events leading up to his wounding and capture, declaring that his decision to counter-attack when outnumbered and surrounded was the only one 'compatible with his sense of military honour'. The concluding sentence summed him up for all time: 'In all respects an officer without equal.' The tribute was signed 'Philippe Pétain'.

Twenty-four years later the same de Gaulle, facing the same enemy, was again to cry out defiantly in the name of military honour; and this time an aged Pétain would sign a sentence of death.

5. The Stages of Destiny—II

Travailler sans souci de gloire ou de fortune.
(*Cyrano de Bergerac:* Act II, Scene viii)

HAD DE GAULLE not been captured it seems almost certain that, recovering from his wounds in France, rejoining a unit at the front, he would not have survived to see the end of the War. But captivity, however detestable, not only spared his life; by its chance circumstances it forced him into a different way of life. He began by trying to escape.

Not all men just recovering from a fourth serious wound would have risked it. But to so keen a young officer—he was twenty-six at the time of his capture—the desire to return to France, to serve again in the great battles, made of an impulse an irresistible yearning. The first camp to which he was sent, Friedberg-in-Hessen, was an unpromising place: two tall modern barrack blocks stood at right-angles about a vast parade-ground open to constant inspection by authorities already alerted by escape-attempts, and beyond the double line of sentries patrolling barbed-wire fences lay a wide area of flat country devoid of cover. Undaunted, the lanky de Gaulle, still limping from his wound, found a way of getting smuggled out in a horse-drawn supply wagon; only to be spotted by a watchful sentry. He tried again; police dogs tracked him to recapture. Transferred to another camp, he made his third attempt with Roland Garros, first of the great French fighter-pilots; their failure was rewarded by separation and removal to the special camps for persistent escapers: Garros to Fort Zorndorf, near Küstrin, de Gaulle to Fort 9 at Ingolstadt.

Escape from Fort 9 had never been easy, but by the time de Gaulle arrived the many efforts of determined prisoners, French and British, had exhausted all practicable means of egress. Cooped up within the narrow stone walls of the fort whose perimeter was limited by a broad water-filled ditch, the best hope for the would-be escaper was to earn, by patient good behaviour, an eventual transfer to a more promising camp. This circumstance was to determine de Gaulle's future.

Hitherto action had sown the seed, now inaction fostered its growth and determined the habit. During the thirty-two months of his captivity the deprivation of physical liberty was made tolerable only by the freedom of thoughts ranging restlessly, at first over the field of events in France in the light of his own experience, then over the wider field now open to him, through German newspapers and periodicals, of events in Germany, of the trend of politics, the mentality of leaders, the character of the people—signs and portents that outlined the stormy future. He took to jotting down his impressions, discussing them with kindred spirits among his fellow-prisoners, amplifying them with the help of such works on military history as were available to him. As weeks lengthened into months the jottings became carefully considered notes, a record reflecting his views, alleviating the tedium of an endless succession of uneventful days. Time formed the habit, the notes became a narrative. By the end of the long seclusion his military thinking was clarified, his prose lucid. A destiny was fore-shadowed.

He tried to escape it at the War's ending. After so long a period of inactivity the keen professional soldier demanded action, if not in France then abroad, if possible at war. A corps of Poles was being formed, with French support, to assist the reborn Polish State in its life-and-death struggle with Bolshevik Russia. French officers were welcome; de Gaulle—after a brief recuperation with his family—volunteered; went to Poland and, in the upshot, stayed for a year and a half. The actual campaigning was of short duration, lasting little more than a month as far as he was concerned; but thereafter his services were required as instructor in infantry tactics at a training establishment on the outskirts of Warsaw, where his wide knowledge and clear thinking presently gained so much favourable notice that the Polish Government offered him permanent employment. In France, however, watchful authorities took note of his evident ability and, recalling him, announced his appointment to St Cyr as lecturer in military history, the appointment to date from October 1, 1921.

Meanwhile another sort of appointment had been made, and kept. On leave in Paris, at the end of 1919, a relative had introduced him to a friend, a quiet young girl, brunette, pretty—Yvonne Vendroux, daughter of a wealthy biscuit manufacturer of Calais. But, although the mutual friend had early foreseen a possible match, it seems that any romantic attachment between the pair—the one reserved and almost awkward in the presence of women, the other withdrawn and shy in the company of men—would have been painfully slow in developing had it not been for the trivial, but later notorious, incident of the tea-cup. At a stiffly formal party he spilled it into her lap; and in the ensuing profuse and embarrassed apologies on one side, and the warm and smiling reassurance on the other, something was started that was to have no end. When he left for Poland there was already an understanding between them; when he came back to France they were formally betrothed. At Calais, in the spring of 1921, they were married.

Employment at St Cyr lasted for a year, after which he was posted to the Senior War School for a two-year staff course; so that for the greater part of the first three years of their life together the de Gaulles were able to live in Paris where presently their son was born.[1] It was, from the start, a quiet well-ordered existence in which he was devoted to his profession and she to her home, and in which neither derived much joy from starchy social functions; a happy, rather humdrum life, in a 'left bank' flat where their circle was restricted to near relatives and a few close friends; the sort of private life that has no public history, but which in due course reaped its projected reward. When he passed brilliantly out of the War School, the way was open to advancement towards the highest posts in the Army.

One very small cloud then came to darken the horizon of his military ambition. In the practical test of small-scale manoeuvres in the field which, for the successful candidate, traditionally marked the ending of the staff course, he tactlessly won the 'battle'—against a crusty senior officer at that—whereas, according to the textbook, he ought to have lost it. Men in high places shook anxious heads. De Gaulle was unorthodox; he had a mind of his own, was 'self-willed', opinionated. Little enough as a black mark, it had a considerable effect. Instead of being appointed to the General Staff, which was the normal practice after success at the Senior War School, he was posted to Mainz, to the staff of the Army of Occupation on the Rhine.

Except for having to move house, he was not sorry to go. The post allowed him to see Germany again, to confirm his wartime views on the philosophy of German military leaders and on the character of the nation. It enabled him to revise and complete the task so painstakingly

[1] There were to be three children: Philippe, Elizabeth and Anne.

hammered out in captivity. The work—his first book, *Le Désordre chez l'Ennemi*—was published in Paris in 1925.[1]

In military circles it brought him immediate, if strictly limited, fame. This man, it was clear, had the makings of a strategist and of something more: if his thinking was sound, his prose was masterly. The book offended no one and it found favour in circles higher than those which had previously criticized him for unorthodoxy: his old Colonel, for instance, now a Marshal of France, who had never lost sight of his one-time subaltern, who had followed his career with interest from Poland to St Cyr and through the War School, and had laughed at the *gaffe* of the tactless 'victory'. Pétain had congratulated him on his marriage and had been touched when the firstborn was named Philippe; and now, as it happened, he had need of just such a man: a clear-thinking staff officer who could write. Towards the end of the year he summoned him to the Boulevard des Invalides, to the office of the Superior War Council of which he was Vice-President.

De Gaulle, needless to say, was greatly encouraged by the Marshal's interest in his affairs. Under him, he felt, much might be accomplished, now that the immediate post-war period was past, to safeguard France against a distant, but in his view, not improbable resurgence of German military might. Pétain in fact had intended that his protégé should undertake the writing of a monumental work, involving lengthy historical research, recording the development of French armed forces throughout the ages. But before de Gaulle could do much more than make a start with it, he was allotted another task of more vital consequence: a re-examination of the whole military position along France's north-eastern frontiers over which had flowed, in past centuries, so many tides of invasion.

Throughout 1926, applying his now profound knowledge of military history and science, he studied to devise a fortified line that should not only protect France, but would also provide, should ever the eastern enemy attack again, suitable bases for a spearhead thrust into Germany. By French military authorities the first part of the plan was readily accepted. A 'line of fortifications'—did it not embody the lessons of recent war? Was it not in accordance with the views Pétain

---

[1] It was not quite his first literary effort. At the age of fifteen he had written a fable in verse, *Une Mauvaise Rencontre*, which his family caused to be printed in the provinces in 1906.

himself had put forward?—that initially a prudent defensive was the answer to the enemy's first onslaught, that behind a fortified line, not improvised this time, the citizen-army would assemble in its millions, beat off the enemy with superior fire-power, and, once that enemy had been exhausted, advance to victory with little loss of life. The line it must be, and nothing but the line. In vain de Gaulle protested subsequently that this was only half the plan, that to the shield must be added a sword; the half-idea was welcomed in political circles which saw in it a saving of money in peacetime and a saving of man-power in war. An able Defence Minister, an ex-soldier who had lost a leg in the War and whose name was Maginot, saw to its realization. The General Staff nodded complacently. A German military threat was, after all, a very long way off.

Pétain was delighted to find that his own perspicacity had enabled him to pick out de Gaulle—a colt from his own stable, now the most promising runner in the stakes of military advancement. Early in 1927, before an august assembly at the War School, to which de Gaulle was to give a lecture, he introduced his young subordinate—lanky, awkward, but with a strangely authoritative manner—in words of startling, if unwitting, foresight.

'Gentlemen, listen to Captain de Gaulle. Listen to him attentively, for the day will come when a grateful France will call to him.'

In the autumn de Gaulle was promoted and given command of a battalion of Light Infantry stationed in the Rhineland. He was only thirty-seven—which was young for a Major in peacetime France and should have been a cause for satisfaction. But already he was uneasy. From beyond the Rhine, scarcely audible as yet, there came to his expectant ears the same distant roll of drums to which he had listened in boyhood.

6. The Stages of Destiny—III

Tout ce qui trop longtemps reste dans l'ombre et dort
S'habitue au Mensonge et consent à la Mort!
(*Chantecler:* Act IV, Scene iv)

THE CLOSE of the nineteen-twenties marked not only a point in time midway between two ruinous wars, but also the bright summit, for the greater part of the civilized world, of hopes for lasting peace and prosperity. Those were the years when the League of Nations, despite the unfortunate abstention of the United States, exercised its benign influence and foreshadowed the coming of European disarmament; when men believed for a while that the Great War had ended all great wars and, placing their faith in the freely negotiated Locarno Treaty between Germany and the Allied Powers, acclaimed with joy the signing of the Briand–Kellog Pact that outlawed war as an instrument of national policy. By many a government the European military horizon was seen to be clear at last. Peace was established; War could not come, nobody wanted it.

The sunshine interval, alas, was brief. Within a decade the whole fabric of peace that had seemed as substantial as the 'Palace of the Nations' in Geneva had been swept away, and the earth trembled once more to the tramp of marching men. So unbelievable was the disintegration that as each stone fell the builders could but reaffirm their faith in the basic strength of the edifice, allaying their fears by mocking those who pointed to its instability even as the last walls crumbled and the arch of European security collapsed; until at length its keystone, the French Army, fell into the dust and was gone. And so horrifying then was the shock of Europe's engulfment, so incredible the military obliteration of France that for long years afterwards men argued the causes of the disaster, blaming it upon the ineptitude, the instability and the corruption of short-lived French Governments, which was only half the story.

It was in the sunshine that tragedy was first outlined for France. As the nineteen-thirties opened, upon no nation did the light fall so brightly. America shrank from the icy blasts of a financial blizzard. Britain, scarcely recovered from grim industrial strife, faced an economic depression that had brought unemployment to record heights.

Italy, black-shirted and over-populated, dreamed in poverty. Germany, frustrated, disarmed, half-ruined by fantastic inflation, trembled between two tyrannies. Russia, under the heel of a new czar, toiled silently in outer darkness. The small nations and the new states of eastern Europe strove to expand their trade, watched their frontiers and huddled for shelter under the League. Alone France appeared prosperous, wealthy, contented and, above all, strong. After the wild post-war fluctuations her currency was stable; the tourist-trade brought in millions, the vast luxury-trade boomed; agriculture was sound; with remarkable speed the devastated areas of the north-east had been brought back to fertility and industrial production. Overseas, her great colonial possessions augmented her commerce and spread her influence throughout the world.

But to the nations of continental Europe it was her armed strength that appealed and drew their admiration. Since the defeat of Germany, the withdrawal of British and American forces and the repulse of the Bolsheviks, the French Army had exercised a mild and undisputed hegemony from the Rhine to the Vistula. Its undoubted heroism during four years of costly warfare, its brilliant victories under Foch in 1918, its stabilizing influence in the initial post-war confusion and its resolute vigilance in support of the peace treaties, all contributed to its immense prestige and surrounded the names of its famous leaders with an effulgent glory. The instability of successive French governments —even of successive French Presidents—was then of little account; the Army had vindicated the Third Republic and guaranteed its permanence. To it France's allies—the Belgians, the Poles, the Yugoslavs and the Czechs—looked for advice and, in the event of trouble, for prompt and decisive assistance. Never since the great days of the First Empire had its reputation stood higher.

That this eulogy, not wholly unmerited, should induce among military authorities—not only in France—a state of complacency bordering on mental lethargy was natural, if regrettable. To a virtually disarmed Germany, the only likely enemy, France opposed her five million mobilizable men, her new eastern fortifications, her hundreds of tanks, her air forces numerically superior to all others in Europe, her sufficient fleet ranking fourth in the world, and the not inconsiderable strength of her European allies. In 1931 the position and power of France and her Army were unassailable. That was the year in which the first distant warning of things to come was given by Japan's invasion of China, an aggression the League of Nations was impotent to arrest; the year in which Britain went off the gold standard, in which part of her fleet 'mutinied' at Invergordon; in which, in Spain, revolution ousted the monarchy and paved the way to civil war. But in France that year, at Vincennes, a resplendent Colonial Exhibition displayed the wealth and world-wide resources that backed a great nation's might.

In 1932 the position was little altered; true, Hitler had come to power, but it would take more than one man's malice to shake the French Army. In right-wing military circles, moreover, the advent of Nazi-fascism was not altogether unwelcome; it was certainly preferable to Communism. Even in 1933, when Germany stamped out of the League, no shadow of anxiety clouded the smiling assurance of France's military advisers. They were still smiling many months later when, over Germany, the danger signals were flying mast-high.

It was not that they slept, those military chiefs, at least not then. Dazzled by too much sunshine, they might blink myopically at progress, but they were wide awake to the supposed requirements of their beloved Army. Against it Germany could do nothing. Everything was ready. Fifteen years after the War they had absorbed all its lessons, so that now they were well-prepared to achieve victory in the pattern of 1914, as in 1914 they had been ready to achieve it in the pattern of 1870. No one could teach them anything new; adulation had made them dangerously over-confident. Looking proudly to their defences, they forgot to look to the future.

*   *   *

The obvious is what most men see too late and men of genius see too soon. De Gaulle belonged to the second category. He was not the first to perceive the immense changes in methods of warfare brought about by the internal combustion engine, any more than he was the first to appreciate the growing importance of the tank. But he was among the first—others included, for France, General d'Estienne and, for Britain, General Fuller and Captain Liddell Hart—to grasp the idea of using a large force of tanks (and other arms) independently of the infantry which hitherto they had been employed only to support; a force of armour to be regarded not so much as cavalry, but rather as it might be a squadron of warships with auxiliaries, compact, self-supporting, under its own commander. He was certainly the first in France to develop the idea in detail, to lay down the composition of the unit, the 'armoured division', to prescribe its organization, and then to examine its purpose and vast strategic possibilities in modern war. In this examination, and in the logical conclusions he drew from it, he led the world.

From prolonged study he deduced, for France, a basic figure of six Armoured Divisions requiring for their service 100,000 men. Since each unit would include, as well as motor-cycle reconnaissance groups, tracked vehicles for infantry, motorized artillery and some five hundred tanks, it was evident that the men must be fully trained specialists, just as were the crews of warships or of aircraft, and that therefore the force as a whole was to be regarded as a small standing army ready for instant action on the outbreak of war. Since, moreover, the estimated fire-power of these six Armoured Divisions, supported of course by aircraft, would be superior to that of the entire French Army mobilized in 1914, a very large proportion of the mobilizable five millions would not be required as combatants; there would be a considerable saving in man-power and money, and the economy of the country in wartime would remain largely undisturbed. The provision of such a force, de Gaulle believed, might well deter the enemy from attacking at all; but in the event of war the conflict would be shorter and less costly, since he calculated that the spearhead thrust of the six Divisions would speedily be decisive.

From these calculations the conclusions were inescapable, and diametrically opposed. If war came, the Armoured force assisted by air power would smash through the enemy defences with the first hard blows, and would then proceed to an exploitation of the 'breakthrough' far more devastating than anything contemplated in the previous War. Moving at 20–25 miles an hour, it would dislocate the enemy command, disrupt communications, paralyse troop formations; driving ever deeper into enemy country, it would occupy strategic points, isolate military centres and industrial areas; demoralization would follow swiftly and total collapse might well ensue. But the converse was also true: supposing that *not France, but the enemy* possessed this new weapon, the independent highly-specialized Armoured force, then at some time, at some point, under its assault supported by all arms even the strongest fortifications must be penetrated and the enemy Armour pour through to a similar and equally disastrous exploitation. The slow-moving masses of the French Army would be powerless to stop the drive—unless they could oppose it with an equally fast-moving force. The only answer to Armour, therefore, was Armour. The buckler of the north-eastern defences would be beaten down unless it held a spear.

In effect the design for the standing army of six Armoured Divisions, and the purpose for which they were intended, was an invention as revolutionary as the tank itself. But the inventor is seldom recognized in his own land, and the prophet is notoriously without honour. De Gaulle, after long reflection, began serious work on his project towards the end of 1932. By that time he was back in the office on the Boulevard des Invalides, to which he had returned after serving two years in command of the battalion on the Rhine and a further year on the staff of the commander-in-chief in Syria. In the interval he had also completed and published another book, *Le Fil de l'Epée*,[1] in which he analysed the necessary characteristics of an ideal military commander. A profoundly penetrating work, it found favour in literary, but not in military circles where the author was now seen to be, worse than unorthodox, something of a disturbing influence, a nuisance who might be dangerous. He was given no encouragement in his new task.

The first news of the projected Armoured force was published in the authoritative 'Political and Parliamentary Review' in May 1933. It was warmly welcomed in political circles. A scheme that substituted 100,000 men for five millions, that gave increased security at diminished cost, that would satisfy the League's insistent advocacy of disarmament—and thereby rob Hitler of his principal argument in favour of rearming—such a scheme was exactly what was needed; it was brilliant common sense. At once the military hierarchy took fright. Reducing the mobilizable millions to a few hundred thousand would mean a reduction almost to zero of the cadres of officers; promotion would cease overnight; senior officers would be retired by the hundred. At all costs and without further consideration the scheme must be condemned. Rebuking de Gaulle, who was now looked upon as a

---

[1] The English translation by Gerard Hopkins, *The Edge of the Sword*, published by Faber & Faber, had not yet appeared when these pages were written.

trouble-maker with ideas above his station, the General Staff let it be known that under no circumstances would it tolerate any reorganization of the Army, that nothing need and nothing should interfere with the present super-excellent state of affairs. And the military chiefs, having turned de Gaulle down, turned themselves over and went to sleep.

When, momentarily, they awoke it was 1934 and they were beset with anxieties of a very different sort. The February riots, provoked by political scandals connected with the Stavisky affair and sparked off by right-wing demonstrations against the Chamber of Deputies, ended in considerable disorders and excesses apparently attributable to the Communists, but quite possibly inspired by fascist *agents-provocateurs*. With brickbats flying, armed hooligans dashing about on bicycles breaking windows, and sinister figures loitering at night in the residential quarters of Paris, it was only natural that the attention of respectable, quiet-living, well-to-do citizens—a category that naturally included top-ranking Army officers—should be diverted from the growing external to the lesser internal danger. When a new and more respectable government was formed, an eminently respectable soldier with strong right-wing sympathies was chosen to be War Minister: the ageing, easily flattered Marshal of France, Pétain.

Under him the hierarchy could be sure that there would be no drastic changes in the Army, nothing of the sort suggested by de Gaulle. Whispered prejudice had caught the Marshal's ear. And not only whispered; Weygand, now Chief of the General Staff, had reacted violently and publicly to the projected Armoured force. Moreover, this was no time to relax control over the five millions; in the event of nation-wide Communist trouble the workers could be mobilized, following the successful precedent long ago established by Briand. Pétain no longer listened to de Gaulle. The Nazis were grinning through the windows, the Marshal was not afraid of them; the windows were barred.

The tumultuous events of 1934—the death of King Albert of the Belgians, and the subsequent renunciation by Belgium of the alliance with France; the murder by Hitler of his opponents in Germany, the murder by his supporters of Chancellor Dollfuss in Vienna; the death of Hindenburg and the assumption of supreme power by the *Führer*—amid these sensational happenings one thing of greater consequence to the fate of Europe than all the rest passed almost unnoticed. Failing to impress the General Staff, de Gaulle tried to compel action by interesting the nation as a whole. His book, *Vers l'Armée de Métier*, was published in May. It was logical, convincing, concise. It cost about three shillings. It sold seven hundred and fifty copies; which is as good as saying that no one read it, outside of a few hostile critics and a handful of professional soldiers. The military attaché at the German Embassy bought some copies and sent them back across the Rhine; one of them was passed to an energetic Colonel of Dutch extraction, by name Guderian, whose theories of armoured warfare had been developing along much the same lines. With approval from on high, he got down to practical work. By 1935 the first *Panzer* Division was equipped and ready. It was, in every detail, a replica of de Gaulle's *Division Blindée*—alas, still on paper. Hitler's staff had marked well what Pétain had refused to read.

* * *

It was not the French military authorities, but a French politician who woke up first. Paul Reynaud had read the book and met the author; sending for de Gaulle, recently promoted Lieutenant-Colonel, he had himself briefed upon the project. In the Chamber of Deputies he proposed a Bill authorizing the creation of six Armoured Divisions. The proposal was rejected by the Government on Pétain's advice.

Shelved for a year, the Bill was brought forward again in 1936 by the Socialists under Léon Blum; only to be thrown out, partly on the advice of the new Chief of Staff, General Gamelin, whose thinking, then as later, was well behind the clock, and partly because a 'standing army' had an ugly sound in the ears of anxious parliamentarians. Nothing more could be done. True, Daladier, determined to recognize de Gaulle's merit in spite of Gamelin's disapproval, caused him to be promoted to full Colonel; but the project itself was stone dead. And, barring miracles, France was lost.

Lost because, that same year when Hitler occupied the Rhineland, her Government had made it abundantly clear that it had neither the will nor the strength to act. Lost because Hitler already had three *Panzer* divisions and France had none and because her military leaders had openly declared that she did not intend to have any in the future; lost because without swift-moving Armour she could strike no blow if Hitler, when he was ready, attacked her allies in the East; and because, if those allies were engulfed and Hitler then turned West with vastly increased strength, to the penetrating thrust of Armour she could offer no riposte. All of this was foreseen by de Gaulle, not just intuitively—though he set great store by intuition when it resulted from prolonged study of a given problem—but by careful calculations based on technical knowledge reinforced by soundly reasoned arguments. None of it had been even remotely contemplated by the stubborn or drowsy military minds in the famed *Conseil Supérieur de la Guerre*, or by any of the senior Army chiefs among whom stood, first and foremost, Pétain, Weygand and now Gamelin. Obstinately blind, jealous of the 'conceited' subordinate—'that journalist', Weygand called him—who had dared to read them a lecture, they clung steadfastly to their outdated ideas through all the dire events of successive years, ignoring the countless warnings in peacetime and in war; until, suddenly enlightened by disaster, they sent for de Gaulle on a May morning in 1940 and asked him to save France with a single Armoured 'Division' that did not exist save on paper.

Through those years of military inaction and political decline, de Gaulle's actions and expressed thoughts trace the pattern of his integrity. Frustrated by the rejection of his project, convinced of the accuracy of his forecast, and deeply concerned therefore for the safety of his country, he might well have become embittered, have talked vehemently in public or used violent language in press polemics in which, knowing what he did, he could have accused his superiors of complacency amounting to incompetence. Cold-shouldered by Pétain, scorned by Weygand, disliked by Gamelin, it would have seemed natural had he despaired of the future, his own and that of France, and made the gesture of ultimate discouragement, retired from the Army to seek solace perhaps in some remote academy as professor of military history. Maybe he was tempted, certainly he suffered deeply; outwardly he remained calm and unruffled. In *Le Fil de l'Epée* he had propounded the value of silence; anxiety now increased his natural reserve, but he stayed faithful to his chosen profession.

After a customary course of instruction for senior officers he had been given command of a tank regiment stationed at Metz, where (1937–38) he threw himself into the task of making it at once the most efficient unit of its kind in France and the means wherewith he could put his theories to the test. Under his leadership the regiment's keenness became enthusiasm as the new methods were unfolded and practised. Hitherto trained only to co-operate with slow-moving infantry, soon the men were training for the war of manoeuvre. Rumbling in formation over the rolling hills of Lorraine, they moved as might a battle-squadron following the flagship; and the flagship was the leading tank above which fluttered their Colonel's personal pennant. Appropriately, he had chosen as his emblem the ancient badge of the country, the two-armed cross of Lorraine, red upon a white ground. If France, through the blindness of military chiefs whom he could no longer hope to influence, were to fall, she would at least fall fighting.

In a little while the regiment was brought to the peak of efficiency. The Military Governor of Metz, a certain General Giraud, came to inspect—and was astonished by what he saw. Something new had been created. Moreover, it had been tested and proved. Early in the year of 'Munich' de Gaulle was writing: 'After some detailed experiments I am more convinced than ever of the soundness of the ideas which I have tried to spread, but which, alas! have so far been much more readily accepted by the Germans than by my compatriots.'

But, though his efficiency was applauded, folly triumphed in the end. On the outbreak of war the tank regiment was broken up, the fractions were dispersed, and the tanks returned to their task of supporting the infantry. De Gaulle was appointed to the headquarters staff of the Vth Army in Alsace: 'in command of tanks'. But the tanks failed to arrive. The Army that had no spear stayed motionless behind its shield. Poland was overrun. And the end was near.

7. The Battle

Dauphin—   In cases of defence 'tis best to weigh
              The enemy more mighty than he seems:

French King—'Tis certain he hath past the River Somme.

The Constable of France—
              And if he be not fought withal, my lord,
              Let us not live in France; let us quit all.
                    (Shakespeare: *Henry the Fifth*)

IT SEEMED for a time as if the whole linked chain of de Gaulle's existence was to lead, not to that 'signal service' to France of which he had dreamed in boyhood, but only to a miserable culmination whence, an impotent spectator, he must witness the defeat of his country by the very methods he had devised for her salvation and victory. The thought had been to serve France, the action a military career in peace and war, the habit military thinking and writing; and yet the resulting destiny that had once beckoned so brightly with its quickening hope not merely of winning but of averting war altogether, that had been followed so consistently and so honestly, seemed now to lead to no more than the bleak vindication of a prophet of woe whose efforts must soon be interred under the epitaph 'Too late'. When in due course the lightning struck at France and he learned, from the first news of disaster, that his prophecies were being fulfilled, 'there was nothing', he wrote later, 'that I would not have given to have been wrong.'

That France had not lifted a finger to help her eastern ally by breaking through the lightly manned Rhineland defences whilst Germany was fully occupied in over-running Poland, though it dismayed many a keen French officer, had scarcely surprised him. It was the inevitable continuation of the policy first expressed in March 1936 when Hitler's troops invaded the Rhineland and so clearly reaffirmed in September 1938 at Munich: France, on the recommendation of the Vice-President of the Supreme War Council and Commander-in-Chief of the Armed Forces—now unhappily united in the person of Gamelin—would remain strictly on the defensive. It might seem a damning commentary on the military policy and planning of the past decade that in the hour of crisis, with five million men under arms, the French Army should be compelled to stand inactive behind its eastern fortifications; what caused de Gaulle the gravest anxiety was the fact that, with the brief Polish campaign at an end and all the details known, nothing should be done by the High Command to apply the obvious lessons. They were not even understood. To any inquiry the unvarying reply was returned that between Poland and France conditions were not comparable, that against the fortified line and continuous front no *Panzer* Divisions could prevail, and that since any attack would be repelled with losses that not even the foolish Hitler could endure there was no need for reorganization.

Moreover, the High Command was able to claim that the Army now in fact possessed two Armoured Divisions. At the end of 1938, Léon Blum, momentarily back in office, had sent for de Gaulle much as Reynaud had sent for him three years earlier and had listened again and attentively to his theories and suggestions. The result, however belated, had seemed encouraging. At the request of an enlightened officer, General Billotte, and by order of the Defence Ministry, two Armoured Divisions were created; by the winter of 1939 they were ready. But they were very far from constituting the force de Gaulle had envisaged, that instrument Guderian had copied and with which Poland had been conquered. Instead of 500 tanks per division there were only 120, and the tanks themselves were of a type designed fifteen years previously and now inferior in speed and fire-power to those employed by the Germans.[1] Instead of seven battalions of infantry carried in tracked vehicles, there was one battalion carried in lorries; there were no motor-cycle reconnaissance groups; there was insufficient artillery. Nor were these Armoured Divisions to be used as an independent striking force in a war of manoeuvre; each was embodied in an Army Corps and their tanks were to fulfil their ancient role, traditional since 1918, of supporting the infantry. A third such Division was added early in 1940; a fourth was planned on paper. It was still on paper at May 10.[2]

---

[1] There was no shortage of tanks in France, but they were held in storage, far in rear, as reserves for the support of infantry divisions.

[2] Three 'Light Mechanized Divisions' had also been created, but without Armour they were no match for German divisions. Sent forward into Holland and Belgium in May, they were promptly forced back and were then broken up and used to stop gaps in the Allied line.

In his pre-war writings de Gaulle had taken into full account the importance in the modern battle of air power. It was not, at the outbreak of war, his immediate concern, but he could hardly fail to note the total inadequacy of the French Army's Air Forces as against the strength of the *Luftwaffe*. In the whole of metropolitan France there were less than 500 serviceable fighter aircraft, a considerable proportion of which was held back from the 'front' for the defence of Paris and other centres; there were practically no stored reserves and production could do little more than keep pace with normal wastage. Meanwhile, striking power had been reduced almost to zero; for the War was not many days old when the entire heavy bomber force— about 1,100 strong and consisting principally of the old twin-engined Bloch–110—had been ruled obsolete and placed in reserve. A number of bomber prototypes was being developed and tested, but only one modern 'heavy' (by the standards of the day) was being produced in limited quantity.[1] On May 10, 1940, there were on France's north-eastern front only 31 day bombers and 64 obsolete night bombers.[2] Even taking into account the Royal Air Force contingent—of some 300 aircraft, including a high proportion of obsolescent Fairey *Battle* single-engined bombers—the grand total of Allied air strength available at the front on the day the Germans attacked would scarcely reach 700 aircraft: all, with the notable exception of the British *Hurricanes*, of inferior performance, type for type, to those of Germany.[3] Against this, though it was known to relatively few in France, the *Luftwaffe* could bring to bear some 3,500 aircraft of all types, including transports, with not far short of 100 per cent stored reserves and a production rate reaching up from 500 towards 1,000 aircraft a month.

But it was not alone these considerations of machine-strength on land or in the air that made the situation so frightening. The unshakeable complacency with which it was regarded by the High Command, and through it by both the French and British Governments,

---

[1] Production of French military aircraft of all types had never recovered from the halt caused by over-hasty nationalization of the industry under Blum's 'Popular Front' Government in 1936.

[2] Figures supplied by General Georges and quoted by Weygand in *Rappelé au Service*, Appendix III.

[3] Of French military aircraft in metropolitan France the grand total serviceable on May 10 was approximately 700. But this figure included the large number of fighters held back for air defence far from the battle front and a number of new aircraft not yet fully equipped for operations.

was even more alarming. Though practically nothing was done throughout the winter to even the disparity by intensive training, reorganization or seriously increased production, the confident view was still firmly held that the fire-power of defensive fortifications must triumph over any attack, however heavy. From this proposition it was inferred that a well-informed German General Staff would never countenance the loss of a million men for nothing gained; and that Hitler, baulked from success in the West, would in all probability turn to the East. Should he none the less try to drive through Belgium, an intention indicated by captured documents, he would find the full strength of several French and British armies advancing to meet him. That King Albert's successor had carried Belgium into neutrality and that in consequence the northern end of the Maginot Line had never been completed, that of alternative lines cf defence on Belgian soil no information whatever had been vouchsafed by the Belgian Staff, and that therefore the Allied forces, far from fighting from behind well-established fortifications, would be caught in the open by an enemy vastly superior on land and in the air, and moving at perhaps three times their speed, did nothing to disturb the equanimity of the French, and British, high military authorities. Some went so far as to profess that they would welcome a German attack.

De Gaulle was not the only French officer to be deeply perturbed by this unwarrantable optimism which appeared to have its roots in a blind ignorance of the conditions of modern warfare. But he was the only one whose anxiety was of long date, whose views had clearly and consistently been expressed for all to read; whose contacts in military and political circles gave him access to the highest in the land; and whose name was etched with acid upon the memory of the most obdurate of his opponents. In January 1940 he made a last effort to enlighten the authorities and so to avert catastrophe. From the Vth Army headquarters at Wangenbourg he sent out to the eight most influential personalities in the Army and in political life a Memorandum in which, once more, he summarized from known facts the logical conclusions.

The typed sheets were headed: *The Advent of Mechanized Force.* The argument was simple: the events of the past five years were shown as leading inexorably to the tragedy of Poland, the lesson of whose destruction were studied and applied to the existing peril for France. The language was forceful and telling: 'In modern warfare action can no longer be undertaken save by means of and in relation to mechanized force. . . . If the enemy has not yet been able to build up a mechanized force sufficient to break our lines of defence, everything compels the belief that he is working to that end. . . . A defender who should hold to static resistance with outdated forces would be pledging himself to disaster. Mechanized force is the only effective weapon with which to smash mechanized force. . . . In the present conflict, as in those which have preceded it, to remain inert is to be defeated. . . . Make no mistake, the struggle that has begun might well be the most wide-spread, the most complex, the most violent of all those which have ravaged the world . . . and, in the end, each nation will be judged by the achievements of its armed forces.'

The warning was clear, but perhaps because the argument was unanswerable there was no reply to it. Or scarcely any. The Inspector-General of Tanks took the opportunity to reiterate that the purpose of tanks was to accompany the infantry. The Premier, Daladier, found no time to read the Memorandum. Gamelin, it is said, glanced through it, shrugged his shoulders and made no comment. There would be no change of plan, still possible even at this late hour, concerning the employment of the Armoured Divisions. In April Gamelin was able to tell de Gaulle with chilling serenity: 'I do not share your anxieties.'

*   *   *

In March (1940) a Government crisis brought Daladier down and Reynaud up as Premier. Reynaud, who had read de Gaulle's Memor-andum as well as everything else he had written, wished to bring the expert in mechanized warfare into the Ministry of National Defence of which Daladier was to be the Minister. There were immediate objections on political grounds and the idea was promptly abandoned, but not before de Gaulle, summoned to Paris, had encountered the leading personalities in and about the Government and had seen re-vealed something even more shocking than the over-confidence of the High Command. In certain political circles a passive defeatism at the prospect of a long war had always existed; but now a more active influence was at work preparing what could only be regarded as treason. Worst of all, the plotters were plausible.

Appeasement had borne its bitter fruit. Poland—so ran the argu-ment—to save which had been the object of the War's declaration, was lost as irretrievably as Czechoslovakia. Nothing could be gained by crying over the spilt milk of history; the verdict could not be reversed. The long period of stagnation, as ridiculous in the eyes of the world as it was economically ruinous for France, had proved that neither of the principal opponents intended to give any blood for a cause already decided. The present stalemate in which the troops glared at each other across the Rhine—or, as on New Year's Day, exchanged friendly greetings—must be brought to an end. Peace could be had at any time, so it was learned through contacts in Italy and Spain, and on terms very favourable to France; for Bolshevism was the real peril and all Hitler wanted was a free hand in Eastern Europe. In recent weeks had not the Allies found themselves very nearly on the same side as Germany in the matter of Russia's aggression against Finland? In France, with Communist soldiers deserting and Communist workers 'going slow' or going underground, disorders might break out at any moment, with serious riots if ever the battle started.

Peace, then, the defeatists argued was essential. Peace—and with it a change, not just of Government, but of régime, of constitution, to something more in keeping with modern trends, a 'new order' that would safeguard the interests of all decent people and make quite sure that the industrial working-classes were no longer suborned by Muscovite propaganda. A firm hand was needed, velvet-clad maybe, but strong, the hand of unquestioned authority. And for this the necessary leader was available, ready-made, one whom all France respected and trusted, a man of no political party, yet certainly of the 'right', a great soldier, a national hero: Pétain.

The aged Marshal, hale and hearty at eighty-three, was basking in glory as Ambassador in Madrid. There he was slowly being poisoned; not, unluckily for him and for France, with a lethal dose that might have ended his career before he had outlived his fame, but with the sweet and more insidious toxin of an adulation continual and often obsequious. He had always been susceptible to flattery; now vanity clouded a limited intelligence already dimmed by the shadow of advancing years. In the capital of a land so recently ravaged by civil war, where a junior army officer who had won the victory was accorded the dignity of a king, the Marshal-Ambassador of France was treated with the respect due to a visiting sovereign before whom all men bowed, to whom all deferred. In the ordered calm, the traditional formality and the quiet splendour of Franco's court he was encouraged to appreciate what Falangists had restored, what Communists had attempted to destroy. Few failed to remind him of his great past, his famous victory, his achievements in the councils of his country; many hinted, and more than hinted, at the great future that must surely lie ahead. A leader was what France was going to need in the dangerous times to come, a leader stern but paternal, and who better than her senior and most celebrated Soldier-Statesman, with a constitution patterned perhaps on the Spanish model. The War was a futility, a great mistake; Communism was the danger, for France the growing danger; before it was too late Civil War must be averted and the Marshal appear as the saviour of his country. General Franco was at his service.

To be Head of State, to have Power, to be revered as Royalty—what a culmination to a long life! And what a triumph: to take France out of the War successfully and without loss would be a victory greater than that of 1918, and he, Philippe Pétain, would be the supreme authority. Heady wine for an old peasant; he was soon intoxicated. He did not say much, he seldom did; he was not one to originate ideas and he was no good at intrigue; but it became known that he was amenable to the suggestions put to him, that he would not be averse, if a serious crisis arose, to taking over political power and assuming the leadership of France. In Paris those who proposed to make use of him for their secret ends were emboldened, and presently began to prepare the public.

Enemy propaganda, most of it crude, had not made any serious impression upon the people of France.[1] They had far more avidly listened to the comfortable words of their own spokesmen in the Press or on the radio, assuring them that the Allied leeway in armaments had been made up during the six months' respite, that sea power was playing its twofold part by bringing in supplies from America on the one hand and by strangling Germany on the other, that the north-eastern fortifications were impregnable, that for Hitler it was 'too late'.

[1] One of the few points to stick originated in France itself and concerned the casualties in the First World War. Even by Frenchmen sympathetic to Britain it was honestly believed that the French dead outnumbered the British dead by more than three to one, and that this holding back of British lives had been a matter of policy. Exact figures are impossible to arrive at, but from several sources a reasonably accurate estimate indicates that the totals were almost equivalent. On land, at sea and in the air, on all fronts, France and the French Empire lost 1,350,000 dead; Britain and the British Empire lost 1,250,000 dead.

Doubters in Paris were reassured visually by a flaming poster, prominently displayed, showing the Allied World—France, Britain, Dominions, Colonies—in uniform fire-engine red, with a tiny black dot for Nazi-Germany in the centre, and the boldly printed slogan: *Nous vaincrons parce que nous sommes les plus forts*. A similar flood of fatuity poured in from across the Channel, culminating in Chamberlain's classic statement that 'Hitler has missed the bus.' Thus it did not seem very incongruous that a pamphlet should presently appear and be widely circulated bearing, beneath the oak-leaved *képi*, the handsome features of Marshal Pétain. Below the portrait, on three sides of a folder, the captions read: '*Yesterday the Soldier*', '*Today the Diplomat*', and '*Tomorrow——?*' The inference drawn was natural enough; to many it began to appear that Pétain was the best man to lead France out of the impasse of static war, or to save her if trouble started.

Filled with the gravest misgivings at what he had seen and heard, de Gaulle went back to his post at Wangenbourg. In Paris he had spoken his mind emphatically; and now, according to the rapidly accumulating Intelligence reports, the battle was fast approaching. Of its favourable outcome he had the most serious doubts.

*   *   *

His name, and what it stood for, could no longer be entirely overlooked by the authorities. In April, with the battle raging in Norway, he was summoned to High Command Headquarters.

At Vincennes all was quiet. In the courtyard of the château, before the doorway leading to the Commander-in-Chief's offices, a resplendant *spahi* stood motionless, the white *burnous* thrown back to disclose the scarlet jacket, the drawn sword held up in rigid, gleaming salute. Within the thick stone walls the rooms seemed dingy and cheerless. There was no activity; voices were muted. News came in occasionally, by telephone, for there was no wireless communication with the outside world. Calm, secluded, the atmosphere was that of a monastery of some contemplative order.

Gamelin was in his office. His desk was tidy. A wall map faced him. He spoke little and his manner, though never lacking in courtesy, was noticeably cold. A small man, pink and white, he looked so clean as to give the impression that he had just stepped out of a bath, but that the process of scrubbing had both chilled and stiffened him. Neatly dressed, he wore khaki riding-breeches with canvas leggings and—startling contrast—black elastic-sided ankle boots. He had been a staff officer to Joffre in 1914, a fact from which he retained considerable prestige; unfortunately his military thinking had not progressed very much since then.

Even many years later his backwardness must appear extraordinary. He was loyal, well-intentioned, bent on achieving victory and convinced that he was capable of the achievement. He was cultured, far from unintelligent; he had access to all sources of information. He was not new to the job; for some five years, as well as being Commander-in-Chief of the armed forces, he had held the posts of Vice-President of the Supreme War Council and chief of the General Staff of National Defence. His vast authority—stimulated, it might have been supposed, by even greater responsibilities—demanded close and continual study of international developments, of technical progress at home and abroad, of the trends of military thought. He had before him the copious and on the whole remarkably accurate reports of the French Intelligence, the *Deuxième Bureau*. He had, readily available if he chose to read, the writings of de Gaulle, of Guderian, of General Fuller and Liddell Hart. He had been shown the distant-warning lights of German rearmament; had noted the accelerating tempo of events— the Rhineland, the *Anschluss*, the *Sudetenland*, 'Munich' and the betrayal of Czechoslovakia. He had been supplied with detailed accounts of the Polish campaign and with analyses of its implications. And yet, throughout the winter, he had done what no general can ever do and hope to win: he had done nothing, save plan the advance into Belgium. Now, with all the signals set at danger, he was to drive steadily forward over the brink of catastrophe.

For a man who was no genius, he had too much power, and he failed to delegate enough of it to General Georges who had been expected to assume full command of the North-eastern Armies. At the conferences at which 'Plan D'—the advance into Belgium—had been worked out, there was none to gainsay him. His own staff acquiesced to his suggestions and his British colleague, the Chief of the Imperial General Staff, Ironside, gave him unquestioning support, nodding tacit agreement through a cloud of reassuring pipe-smoke. The role of the British forces was described in detail, as also was that of the French Light Mechanized Divisions and of the French Armies on either flank; there was little, if any, argument. Seldom was any mention made of Armour or Air Power; never were *Panzer* Divisions or *Luftwaffe* discussed. When on one occasion the British Chief of the Air Staff, Newall, had endeavoured to issue a warning to the effect that if the Allied armies were not given sufficient tactical support from the air the battle might go against them and all Belgium be lost, he had been treated with mild ridicule. Newall having suggested that such a defeat might be 'decisive', Gamelin, unruffled, had allowed a slow smile to wrinkle the corners of his eyes before answering that it depended upon what was meant by decisive. 'Does the Air Marshal suggest that, if we lose Belgium, England will ask for an armistice?' The very idea had seemed so preposterous that those about the conference table had tittered with delight; Gamelin, they felt, might as well have postulated the surrender of France; and further discussion of air power had been killed stone dead.

The Generalissimo was still unruffled in April when he received de Gaulle. The '4th Armoured Division', he explained quietly, was now being created; as soon as it was ready the Colonel would assume command with the rank of Brigadier-General. Though the belated creation of one new armoured unit could do little to allay his fears de Gaulle, after so much frustration, would not have been human had he not expressed his pleasure at a promotion which, at forty-nine, would make him the youngest General in the French Army. And it was then that Gamelin, the Supreme Commander responsible for the safety of France, had used that memorable phrase: 'I understand your satisfaction, but *I do not share your anxieties.*'

Five weeks later he was to share them to the limit of what the mind can endure: the front was broken on the Meuse, one of his Armies had vanished altogether and of the others the infantry, falling back at three miles an hour, had been overtaken and passed by enemy Armour advancing at thirty. Four years previously he had heard Pétain formally and officially express the opinion that no fear of attack upon the sector Sedan-Mézières need be entertained, since the Belgian Ardennes lying in front of it were 'impassable' to large enemy forces. That such ignorance of local topography should have been displayed by the Marshal was excusable on the grounds that he was probably thinking back to conditions pertaining to 1914 and earlier; what is astounding and wholly inexcusable is that his views should still have been accepted by the French, and British, High Command in 1939 and during the undisturbed months of preparation for battle. It suggests the incredible: that no Allied staff officer had ever crossed the Belgian frontier in time of peace either to explore the hilly, but far from mountainous, region whose forest areas are patchy and seldom dense or to drive along its several wide and well-laid roads. Certain it is that Gamelin, and Georges with him, was utterly taken aback by the appearance of German Armour upon the French Meuse on May 13. Even so all might have been well, for a time, had the fortifications been strong, the troops first class. But as Georges had to admit, in notes subsequently prepared for Weygand,[1] the divisions of Colonial Infantry on this sector of the front were then undergoing 'a thorough reorganization which, in the case of six of them, consisted in replacing two completely war-trained white regiments by two black regiments a part of which had only recently been raised.'

'On May 10,' Georges continued, 'three Colonial Infantry divisions on the North-eastern Front were still in process of amalgamation. Two of them, *as was to be expected*,[2] were to give cause for grave disappointment.' Since the 'disappointment' was expected, military historians will always wonder why, at a time when an attack of some sort was known to be on the way, unreliable troops were placed in the front line. For this state of affairs General Georges and the local Army commander must bear a large part of the blame, but the supreme responsibility is that of the Supreme Commander. Had Gamelin's honesty and patriotism not been above suspicion, had his errors not been those of a complacent self-assurance, it might have been hard to believe that he had not committed so obvious a blunder deliberately.

*　　*　　*

The manner in which the French Armoured Divisions were handled in the battle justified de Gaulle's worst fears. In the space of four days, from May 13 to the evening of May 16, the three existing Divisions were eliminated. One, sent forward into Belgium, was hastily put into line facing the Meuse, only to be overwhelmed by the enemy's onslaught west of Namur. A second, thrown in piecemeal to support an infantry counter-attack in France, was frittered away in isolated com-

[1] See Appendix III, *Rappelé au Service.*
[2] Author's italics.

bats; whilst the third met with a more humiliating end. Moved up by rail from the Aisne towards Hirson, its troops and supplies were still wandering forward in trains through the French zone whilst the head of the convoy, containing the tanks, was de-training in German-held territory where it was cut off and destroyed. All that remained in the way of Armour to bar the road to Paris, along which the *Panzers* were hurrying, was the 4th Armoured Division whose inadequate forces were not even assembled.

On the 11th de Gaulle had been informed officially that he was now to take command of the promised Division. On the 15th he was summoned to Army Headquarters[1] and told to concentrate its widely scattered elements at Laon. The situation was desperate, a few days earlier it would have been described as unimaginable. Ten German Armoured Divisions—supported by six others, motorized—had erupted into France through the rapidly widening breach caused initially by the failure of the Colonial Infantry. Three of them were containing the Allied northern armies; seven were driving westward from the Meuse towards the St Quentin area, and already their advanced groups were reaching down to Montcornet, junction of main roads to Rheims, to Laon, to Paris. A French Army was moving forward to take position on the Aisne; until it could come up and deploy, de Gaulle must endeavour, for a few vital hours, to hold up the enemy tide. 'Go ahead, de Gaulle,' the harassed Georges told him: 'You who have so long foreseen what the enemy would do—now is your chance to act!'

To act?—to attack from the south against the flank of a westward moving enemy, to cut across his line of advance and thus dislocate his entire plan? With a force of Armour such as he had advocated it could have been done, and the result might have been decisive for the whole campaign, for the War even. Instead of six divisions he had one, most of it 'on paper'. In the evening of the 15th he set up a command-post on the outskirts of Laon; on the 16th he was out on reconnaissance and, taking with him a few hundred men from a local cavalry division armed only with carbines, made contact with the enemy. During the night the

[1] To add to the confusion and delay there were three Headquarters: Gamelin's at Vincennes, Georges's at La Ferté-sous-Jouarre and his Chief of Staff Doumenc's at Montry. Many miles apart these vast organizations were linked by an extremely inefficient telephone service and motor-cyclists; there was no wireless.

promised tanks began to arrive; before daybreak he had assembled four score of them in front of the town. At dawn on the 17th he attacked.

The enemy's reconnaissance troops were close at hand; he was in strength between Laon and Montcornet which he held firmly, and his reinforcements were coming up by lorry. De Gaulle had no supporting infantry and no artillery; but he saw his opportunity. With less than thirty heavy and sixty light tanks, whose engines had not yet been 'run in', whose drivers had no more than a few hours' experience and whose crews were only half trained, he drove forward unhesitatingly.

Once again, as nearly a quarter of a century earlier, he was in the forefront of the battle, striking at the invader. Once again, as during peacetime practice so now under fire, his helmet could be seen emerging from the turret of the leading tank from the slender mast of which fluttered the pennant bearing the two-armed cross of Lorraine. Overrunning hastily contrived enemy defences, silencing machine-guns, setting vehicles on fire, the little force swept forward twelve miles; reached Montcornet, fought in and around it; reached the River Serre and would have crossed it but for the lack of artillery support. In rear an enemy group, by-passed and lying concealed, rose to counterattack; it was dealt with by a newly-arrived battalion of Light Infantry, ordered up by de Gaulle to join the 'Division'. Montcornet was held; the roads to the south and west temporarily denied to the invader. A French communiqué mentioned the success, and that night the rumour spread through France that the enemy advance had been halted.

Had France, had de Gaulle now possessed but three of those six Armoured Divisions of his devising to back the controlled fury of his assault, the calm execution of long-planned methods, there would have been a very different story to tell. Even so, his swift success at Montcornet had an immediate effect upon the enemy; Hitler was alarmed. On the 18th the German Army's Chief of Staff, General Halder, noted in his diary: '*Führer* keeps worrying about south flank. He rages and screams that we are on the way to ruin the whole campaign.' If the French High Command had only listened to common sense and acted upon de Gaulle's Memorandum of January that year, Hitler would indeed have had something to scream about. But north of the Serre was one who had listened five years earlier, and now acted: de Gaulle's disciple, Guderian. The enemy flank-guard was strengthened and heavy artillery brought forward during the night of the

Colonel de Gaulle,
Commanding Tank Regiment, 1938–9

(Monde et Caméra)

Lieutenant de Gaulle,
33rd Infantry Regiment, 1915

(S.C.A.)

June 7, 1940. Paul Reynaud presents new Ministers at the Elysée.
De Gaulle becomes Under-Secretary of State for War

A Few of the First. Breton fishing-boat with French airmen,
sailing for England, June 19, 1940

17th; in daylight dive-bombers were called up, and continued to attack throughout the 18th. The main enemy forces meanwhile, finding the road blocked at Montcornet, thrust downstream to Marle-sur-Serre, aiming to cross the river and head for La Fère.

To oppose them de Gaulle extended his own weak forces to the west, attacking again, this time from north of Laon. He had received some reinforcements, in the shape of a reconnaissance regiment and two batteries of artillery; and more tanks were slowly reaching him, bringing the grand total up to one hundred and forty. Of these, however, only thirty were 'heavy', the remainder being of various lighter types armed with small cannon of too short a range. Against increasingly severe pressure, and under a continued air assault unchecked by French fighters, he could do no more than delay the enemy and make him pay for his advance. Presently, with the enemy forcing the Serre and infiltrating from the east, he was compelled to withdraw from Montcornet, from Marle, eventually from Laon; by the evening of the 19th, skilfully retiring, he had assembled his force, tanks, transport and infantry, to the south-east of the town. On the 20th, with the enemy circling about both flanks, he received orders from General Georges to break off the fight; it was almost too late, only by stubborn fighting did he succeed in cutting his way out. On the 21st he was back on the Aisne where the Army front had now been established.

He had been asked to hold for a few hours; he had held for three days. With half an improvised Division he had faced and delayed the advance to the west of Guderian's *Panzer* Corps. He had inflicted more casualties than he had suffered; he had brought back 150 prisoners. Still a Colonel, he had proved himself a leader upon the field of battle. More important, he had raised the morale of the troops; and, by expert manoeuvring and calm courage, he had carried to safety the last Armoured unit in France.

At once the Division was ordered to the north-west where a counter-attack had been planned by Gamelin to close the fatal gap between the Allied northern and southern army groups. Even without additional Armour something might have been achieved had the Allied attack been made swiftly and with all available strength, for the *Panzers* in their headlong rush to the coast had outdistanced their own supporting divisions; there was a weakness between Arras and the Somme that offered the Allies a chance of victory. But confusion in the High Command, Weygand's failure to follow Gamelin's plan, and thereafter to transmit clear and positive orders to the Northern group, only added to the uncertainty in the minds of bewildered Army Commanders and lengthened avoidable delays; soon it was too late. The German Command, expecting the counter-attack, had observed troop movements north and south of the gap; air reconnaissance had brought news of a force of Armour coming up from the south. In his distant headquarters Hitler was screaming once more, overjoyed at success, terrified of failure; his nervousness, communicated to his generals, may well have contributed to the timid halting of the *Panzers* before Dunkirk until the south-western flank could be secured by bridgeheads upon the Somme at Amiens and Abbeville.

The 4th Armoured Division moved up by road, covering sixty miles a day for five days; shedding worn-out tanks, receiving new ones, collecting bits and pieces of reinforcement; learning that its commander was now, at last, a General. At first directed towards Amiens it was sent forward—after the local Army Commander had robbed it of thirty of its best tanks—to Abbeville, reaching a point some fifteen miles south-west of the town on the evening of the 26th when urgent orders were received to attempt to reduce the newly-established German bridgehead.

The enemy position, forming an arc some twenty miles long with its wings resting upon the Somme, had at its centre the massive hill of Mont Caubert dominating Abbeville and the surrounding country and lying a dozen miles inside the German line of outposts. The rising ground dotted with orchards, the many small villages and farmhouses, gave excellent opportunities for defence of which the enemy had taken full advantage, during several days of undisturbed possession, by occupying strong-points, bringing up anti-tank guns and digging in. An entire German division had been given the task of holding the bridgehead and, established on three lines, it was now ready, with artillery on the steep slopes of Mont Caubert, heavy artillery upon the far bank of the Somme, and as much air support as it needed. The enemy troops were rested, elated by recent events, confident.

De Gaulle now had something approximating to an Armoured Division, but it was still largely an improvised force few of whose components had fought or trained together and whose tank crews, with the exception of those few who had been in action at Laon, had gained most of their experience during the long drive from the south. Moreover, the majority of the men were tired by the journeys involved in their hasty concentration, and, in a confused situation, such news as had reached them was disheartening. The total strength comprised some 140 tanks, most of them light, six battalions of infantry including reconnaissance troops and a Colonial regiment, and approximately a brigade of artillery as well as some anti-tank and anti-aircraft guns. The force was heavily outnumbered by the enemy within the bridgehead.

It was evening (26th) when the Division came within striking distance; nevertheless de Gaulle decided to attack at once, both to avail himself of the slight element of surprise caused by his sudden arrival and to avoid, during the dark hours, the interference of enemy aircraft. At six o'clock the assault was begun; and the men, delighted to be advancing instead of joining in the helpless retreat, threw themselves forward with a will. The enemy's first line was penetrated before nightfall; the first objectives reached and held early in the night. At dawn the attack was resumed and continued throughout the 27th with a three-pronged advance: along the escarpment of Mont Caubert parallel to the Somme, towards the centre with maximum artillery support, on the left with the main force of tanks on a wide sweep up the slope of the hill.

During the night of the 27th–28th the enemy threw in fresh troops, and brought further reinforcements to put up a grim and determined stand on the 28th. De Gaulle had received no reinforcements; his losses had been heavy, many of his tanks had been knocked out; he had requested air support, none was forthcoming. Directing the battle from the ground, his pennant upon its staff planted amid the trees of an orchard,[1] he ordered the attack to be resumed and sent forward his remaining tanks. Furious fighting ensued for a while, and then the spirit of the French infantry, the boldness of the French tank crews, backed by the skill and resolution of the newly-promoted General, triumphed over a tough and numerically stronger enemy. The defence began to waver, then gave way all along the line; the retreat became a rout in which, according to a German eyewitness,[2] the enemy troops,

[1] Members of his staff reported later that the General, smoking incessantly, could always be located by the trail of stubbed out cigarette ends.
[2] Major Gehring, whose published account, *Abbeville*, is quoted by de Gaulle in *Mémoires de Guerre*, Vol. 1.

seized with terror at the rapid advance of the tanks, fled back towards Abbeville and were only rallied by the divisional commander, General Blümm, himself. By evening the French forces, everywhere victorious, were reaching towards the last bastion of defence stretched along the crescent hilltop.

Reinforced again during the night of the 28th, the enemy made desperate efforts to dislodge the French in day-time on the 29th. The attempts failed and the 4th Armoured Division, attacking once more despite the losses and exhaustion of three days' battle, forced the enemy, once again stubbornly fighting, up the steep slopes until little more than the narrow crest of Mont Caubert remained in his hands. Thence, though the enemy might still fire his remaining guns, he was deprived of all freedom of movement upon the west bank of the Somme. The bridgehead had been effectually reduced.

Small, ephemeral, isolated, the operation ended in an indisputable local victory for the French, almost the only offensive victory of the entire campaign. In the course of the three days of hard and nearly continuous fighting a weak Armoured Division had defeated a strong and continually reinforced German division, had driven it from prepared positions and forced it back ten miles on a front of fifteen. Losses had been heavy, those of the Germans heavier; thousands had been killed or wounded; a considerable quantity of arms and equipment had been captured; more than 500 prisoners were brought back to the French lines.

The achievement once again threw into tragic relief the High Command's blindness to long obvious facts, the obstinate deafness of senior military authorities to the loudly audible warnings from across the Rhine, to the facts supplied by their own Intelligence, to the logical arguments of de Gaulle. Their criminal negligence—for their disdainful self-satisfaction amounted to that—cost them the battle of France and France her reputation. Their outmoded thinking and obsession with the past decided the issue, not German strength or German genius; not, above all, a superior German valour based on pretended racial characteristics. Had de Gaulle's proposed six Armoured Divisions, properly handled, been present for only ten days, between May 14 and 24, disaster would have been turned into victory for France and for all the civilized world. As it was the *Panzers* had come and gone before the High Command awoke from its pipe-dream of ancient glory.

*   *   *

On May 30 the much-tried 4th Armoured Division was relieved in front of Abbeville by the 51st Highland Division. Taken out of the line of battle it was sent back to Beauvais to rest and refit. Two days later its General learned of the well-deserved tribute paid him by the Commander-in-Chief in an Army Order of the Day.

More than twenty-four years earlier, at Verdun, Pétain had described him in a similar citation as 'in all respects an officer without equal'. Now he had become this 'admirable leader, bold and energetic', and the Order was signed: Weygand.

Something of a different and more sombre significance was to be found within the citation. Ever since May 10 the High Command, confused by the speed of events, muddled by feeble telephone communications and defective or non-existent wireless liaison, had been getting more and more behind time and out of touch with the realities of the moment. All news was delayed; every move was made too late; the Staff scarcely knew the time of day. When it came to the fighting at Abbeville they were three days out. De Gaulle's attack (26th–29th), they stated, had been made on 'the 30th and 31st of May.'

It had been obvious to any competent observer that the German Command, once it had finished with Dunkirk, would attack upon the Somme and the Aisne. The French High Command, priding itself upon its prescience, believed that the attack might be opened as early as June 6. The Germans attacked on the 5th. And almost immediately the front, for which there had been insufficient time to bring up adequate covering forces, began to crumble.

De Gaulle took no part in the fighting. A few days earlier he had again been summoned to Headquarters where the Commander-in-Chief had consulted him about the use to be made of the 1,200 tanks still remaining to France, but scattered about in distant 'parks'. On the 6th he was summoned to Paris by Paul Reynaud. Now that it was too late all men sought his opinion.

8. The Betrayal

. . . Henri quatre
N'eût jamais consenti, le nombre l'accablant,
A se diminuer de son panache blanc.
(*Cyrano de Bergerac:* Act IV, Scene iv)

IN MID-MAY, with news of disaster pouring in, with Gamelin announcing that the road to Paris was open and that he had nothing with which to block it, Reynaud's courage had all but failed him. 'Capitulate'—the dread word was no longer whispered, it was openly advocated and he had listened. But only momentarily; nobler sentiments had prevailed linked to remembrance of other dark days in France's history, of recollections of Clemenceau, stimulating a renewed determination to fight on 'before Paris, behind Paris, if necessary in Paris'—to fight on with no thought of surrender, in France or overseas, to a victorious end however distant. With this resolve in mind, he invited de Gaulle to join his Government.

Unfortunately, thinking to strengthen his hand, he had already appointed to positions of power and influence two men, each of whom was determined, though for different reasons, that the fight should be short, the end near, and the result the very opposite of what the Government intended. Pétain, recently returned from Madrid, he brought into his cabinet as Vice-Premier, thinking thereby to make use of his prestige and at the same time to wean him from his profascist wet-nurses. Weygand, recently returned from organizing an army in Syria, he made Generalissimo in Gamelin's place, thinking that his very name would rouse the nation and be 'like a banner' to raise the drooping morale of the troops. Aware though he was of the more obvious drawbacks, he was unaware of the intentions already fixed in the minds of both these elderly men; and the double blunder of their respective appointments was so grave that in little more than ten days it was fatal not only to his own position, but also to that of the entire French nation.

Still physically fit, but ageing rapidly in the mind, Pétain's thoughts on the prosecution of the War were now wholly defeatist and almost entirely unconstructive, save that he saw the Vice-Premiership as the necessary stepping-stone to personal power. The War, he dimly perceived, must be ended at once and he was the man to end it; a pity it had not been done sooner. The Germans were willing to negotiate, he knew that for certain; their terms would not be harsh, no worse than after the Franco-Prussian War: a few concessions, measures of disarmament, a period of partial occupation ended by the payment of an indemnity, and then France would live again—not this time, as in the 1870's under Marshal MacMahon and a régime whose hesitations had led only to parliamentary republicanism, but under Marshal Pétain and the New Order. He saw himself as the wise and benevolent peacemaker. The wider implications—the deadly struggle against Nazi oppression, the defiance of the downtrodden nations of Europe, the world-fight developing against Hitler's dream of world-conquest—meant nothing to him; he neither understood nor believed in their existence. As his faithful orderly officer, Captain Bonhomme, was to admit a little later: 'He is very, very old. His thought is no longer geared to action'—which of course made him an ideal tool for his supporters.

In most respects Weygand's case was different, but there were certain similarities in thinking that led him to the same dire conclusion and, for a vital period of time, made of him Pétain's keenest ally. A dapper little man, brisk, intelligent, quick at repartee, he too seemed younger than his age: retired at seventy, he was now in his seventy-fourth year. He too, like Gamelin, had gained much credit from First War association with a great commander; to have been chief of staff to Marshal Foch in the glorious days of 1918 was something that distinguished him from other men, so much so that his qualifications for the highest posts had always been taken for granted. In those far-off times Foch, the warm-hearted soldier and supreme artist in his profession, had been wont to depict, at many an inter-Allied conference, his bold strategy (of concentric and synchronized hammer-blows that was to bring Germany to her knees) by wide-sweeping, arrow-headed strokes upon the map, explaining his intentions with convincing simplicity; but when it came to details, to exact numbers of divisions available, to things pertaining to 'logistics', he would turn to Weygand; and the little man would bustle forward with all the facts and figures at his fingers' ends. From this had stemmed the popular belief that he had been indispensable, that Foch had recognized in him not merely an efficient and hard-working subordinate, but a military leader of genius. It was generally believed that, in Poland in 1921, he alone had devised the plan whereby the Bolshevik Army had been defeated; a story later hotly denied by the Poles. At the time of Foch's death in 1927, it was reported—and it may well have been true—that the dying Marshal, dreaming back to the crisis of wartime stress, had repeatedly mentioned his name. This, as the years passed, grew into the legend that Foch, almost with his last breath, had said: 'If ever France is in danger, send for Weygand.' In 1940 the legend was given wide currency. On the strength of it, and upon little else, Reynaud appointed him Supreme Commander-in-Chief.

It is not enough to say that the appointment should never have been made. He should never have accepted it. Nothing in his military career entitled him to suppose that he was competent to take over, at the height of a most desperate battle, the personal direction and command of the forces, still to be numbered in millions, of the French, British and Belgian Armies; for never in his life had he commanded anything, neither a regiment nor a brigade, much less a division or an army. It seems improbable that he had even been under fire, certainly not under heavy shell-fire, and his only experience of air attack seems to have been gained after he had assumed his first active command when, from a hasty flight to the north, he chose to return by sea.

A moment's self-examination should have told him that he possessed none of the qualifications of a great leader. He was, first and foremost, a staff officer, efficient, even brilliant; an orthodox soldier who went by the textbook, who placed his faith in the dogma, derived from the 1914–18 War, of the continuous line based on defensive positions: if the line was broken, you fell back to a second; if that was pierced you retired to a third; if that went, then all was lost. He had nothing else to offer. Throughout the years of his authority as head of the General Staff he had violently resisted the changes that would have given France the mechanized force with which she was now being conquered. Ageing, long past the compulsory retiring limit, he was set in his ways and unable to adjust his thoughts to swift-moving military events. The true interests of France in the world eluded him; with the interests of France's allies in the War he felt little concern. What did seem to concern him to the exclusion of all else was his personal reputation, his 'career'. For a few days he may honestly have believed that he could win a great battle; but it was the glittering prize of Supreme Command that tempted him. Without compunction he accepted it, even while scorning the high authority to which he owed both the appointment and his allegiance. Of this authority he was later to write, that it was merely 'one of those ephemeral Governments of which the Third Republic had already, in its seventy years' existence, seen more than one hundred.'

It was on June 1 that he had summoned de Gaulle to his Head-quarters at Montry to ask his advice on the use to be made of the remaining 1,200 tanks. That he should send for the undoubted expert at this time must appear wise; that he should have been compelled to do so reveals the straits into which his ignorance of mechanized war-fare had driven him. For years in peacetime he had fought de Gaulle tooth and nail, had written vituperative articles, had used the weight of his prestige in military circles, had spoken bitterly and with spite— and he had an ugly temper when his views were opposed—all to the effect that a specialized force of Armour was useless and wholly un-necessary, that whatever happened, as he told a group of officers, 'it will not be done in my time.' And now his time had come. The rebelli-ous trouble-maker, twenty-five years his junior, had to be conciliated and consulted.

De Gaulle's advice, based now upon experience in the field as upon long-established principles, had been simple. The tanks should be grouped at once in two Divisions of 600 each, allotted infantry and artillery and placed north of Paris and south of Rheims respectively, so as to be ready to strike at the flanks of any *Panzer* Divisions pene-trating the French front. Time, however, was short, troop movements slow and artillery scarce; the advice was acknowledged, but it had seemed clear that at this late hour nothing would be done. For Weygand, turning to the map, had described the situation in terms so black that de Gaulle, hearing him, had not missed the implication spoken almost nonchalantly. If the forthcoming battle on the Somme went as he, Weygand, expected it to go, then defeat all along the line was certain; after which the Commander-in-Chief saw no alternative other than capitulation.

Barely four days previously he had raged at the tidings that the small remnants of the Belgian Army, ill-equipped, demoralized and all but surrounded, had asked for terms: 'I shall never forget,' he wrote in his memoirs, 'that the Belgian Command's decision to withdraw from the struggle stirred up within me a violent feeling of condemnation.' That he now foresaw a rapidly approaching climax in which he too would be asking for terms from the enemy failed to stir him to any equivalent self-condemnation. With such despairing thoughts in mind, he should at once have offered his resignation to that Government, however 'ephemeral', which in making the appointment had implicitly trusted him to fight, not to argue surrender. Instead, he chose to cling to the power and title of Generalissimo. Soon, impelled by defeat upon the Somme, the thoughts developed that led to evil action. An armistice there must be; no greatness of mind or of heart inspired any other course. But, so that neither his own reputation nor that of the military hierarchy should be besmirched by accusations of cowardice or incompetence; so that none, moreover, should be able to question an order to cease fire; he decided that the surrender must be national; by the State; political not military.

To that end he worked as the Allied armies, fighting valiantly, fell back from the Somme to the Seine, from the Aisne to the Marne. Reynaud he could safely betray, for within the despised Government of France he possessed, in the person of Marshal Pétain, a powerful friend and fellow-defeatist.[1]

*   *   *

For ten fateful days, from June 7 to 17, 1940, four men held the stage and played out the tragedy of France.

Reynaud, the Premier—lively, perceptive, clear-cut in speech. A man physically small but wiry and energetic, whose slanting heavy-

---

[1] To some small extent Weygand's birth and parentage may have affected his curious behaviour. That he was not born a Frenchman matters little—a Corsican had once commanded the Armies of France with some success—but, in his determination to thrust humiliation upon his adopted country whilst sparing himself, there was something un-French, illogical, eccentric and perhaps even vindictive. In an early French military record of his name he is listed as: *Maximilien de Niemand, dit Weygand*. His father then was *Niemand*: Nobody. On the other side, it appears to be established beyond doubt—certainly it has never been denied—that his mother was that unhappy Empress Charlotte, widow of the murdered Emperor Maximilian of Mexico, whose demented appeals for help for her dead husband became pathetically notorious all over Europe. Napoleon III abandoned Maximilian to his fate in 1865. *De Niemand, dit Weygand* was born in 1867, the year in which Maximilian was shot at Queretaro. Conceivably, in the moment of crisis these antecedents exerted some recondite influence upon Weygand's character.

lidded eyes belied a bright intelligence; a man of spirit clinging to the ideal of a fiery, unconquerable Clemenceau, but too easily influenced by voluble political associates; a man who, in the crisis of confusion, listened instead of leading, procrastinated instead of commanding. To his daily worries, moreover, he greatly added by the power and proximity he allowed his mistress, Hélène de Portes. Ever present in the ministerial ante-rooms at Paris, later at Tours and Bordeaux, acting the part of a governess severely watchful of her small charge, poking her head in at the door to see that he was not playing too hard at his nasty game of war for which she had no stomach, denying access to those political playmates who were anxious to continue the struggle, her influence was entirely detrimental. No wild passion or profound love inspired her, only the sordid desires of power and pleasure. To the Premier's eventual exhaustion and despair she greatly contributed.[1]

Pétain—straight of back, dull of mind; speaking only of the past or of himself, his wide-open eyes so intensely blue they seemed vacuous, like those of a sleep-walker dreaming of a paradise of personal power even as his ponderous footsteps carried him each moment nearer the rim of disaster. White-haired, white-moustached, his face almost expressionless, he uttered no thought that did not presage peace in defeat.

Weygand—by turn vivacious, calm, panicky, bitterly ironical; always ready to recite, with an almost gloating wealth of detail, the steadily worsening situation of his vanishing command. Never had he seemed more clearly the subordinate staff officer, well-equipped with facts and figures, attentive to details, but incapable of formulating a grand strategic plan—save only that plan which led to surrender. Openly contemptuous of the Government, opposition stung him to sarcastic retorts and, on occasion, to outbursts of bitter laughter not far from hysterical. About his pointed features there had always been something fox-like, now the yellowing skin stretched over unusually high and prominent cheek-bones gave him a notably Mongolian appearance that was unpleasantly enhanced in moments of scornful anger. He talked a great deal about 'honour', never about winning the War. So it had been in the years after Agincourt.

And *de Gaulle*. Every link forged in the chain of destiny was now

[1] Shortly after the Armistice, for which her nefarious activities had been in part responsible, she was killed in a car accident on the road from Bordeaux to Clermont-Ferrand and Vichy.

tested under strain. Others, the majority, had vowed in youth to render France some 'signal service'; others, tragically diminished in numbers, had survived the rendering of those services in the First War to serve again in the Second. To few had it been vouchsafed, after wide experience gained in the years of peace, to serve once more in the forefront of battle; to none had it been given to achieve such distinction, such high if belated recognition as he had earned during those two short weeks in May. These acknowledged services had led him towards the centre of the stage in the political drama whose first act was so soon to end in catastrophe. But what in this hour of crisis proved of even greater worth than the facts of military skill and gallantry, listed in the citations of Pétain and Weygand, was the golden thread of thought that ran throughout the chain: the pure metal first evolved in the tedium of captivity, painfully hammered into the first book, developed and drawn through the years, glowing upon every printed page, bright, enduring.

The thread was fidelity to France, yet analysis of its composition reveals a broader value. For although, initially, the thoughts were evoked by love of French history, and subsequently by a study of technical progress and the search for security, the thinking expressed in his prose was not merely military. Unfolding in his staff lectures as in each of his books, and in his most recent Memorandum, had been the wider considerations of international politics, of world struggle, of the conduct of human affairs and of the quality of leadership. He had not only foreseen the possibility, under given circumstances, of immense disaster, he had gone further; he had foretold the nature and character of the man who must then arise to restore the situation and resume the fight. High military authority might mark and disapprove his audacity; he was not to be deterred. Nor were the gleaming yet sober thoughts expressed solely that others might read and profit; from being his own they came in time to be his own self.

In his first published work—*La Discorde chez l'Ennemi*—he had noted concerning Germany in 1918 what was to be true of France in 1940: 'The sudden collapse of a strong and valiant people bears witness to the revenge of flouted principles.' To this the opening sentence of the lecture given in 1927 at the War School to which Pétain had introduced him seemed complementary: 'The prosecution of war is essentially conditioned by contingency.' Given this element of chance, of the accidental, doctrine and military dogma were all very well, but: 'Those who achieved some great action had often to go beyond the letter of a misunderstood discipline.' As an example he might have quoted Nelson directly, at St Vincent or Copenhagen; instead he quoted a comment attributed to Fisher on Jellicoe: 'He had all the qualities of Nelson, save one—he did not know how to disobey.' However, he went on, such outstanding men are by nature 'usually harsh, unaccommodating, even aggressive.' And thus: 'The choice of those who decide careers is more often drawn to that which pleases than to that which deserves.' The great commander, he had early seen, must possess in addition to more pedestrian qualities the marked abilities 'of concentrating all efforts into a single effort, of constantly raising the stakes and of taking those risks which are the very essence of strategy.' But the great national leader in wartime, he wrote—in *Le Fil de l'Epée*—must rely even more upon his own strength of character, so that in the hour of need 'far from sheltering beneath high authority, from hiding under the textbooks, from seeking cover in official reports, he will take his own stand, rise up and face events. At the crisis, he is the man whom people will follow, the man who will take up the burden with his own arms though they should crack and place it upon his own shoulders though they should break under the strain.'

For the contingencies of uncertain war he was as well-prepared as for the approaching crisis of leadership that would make necessary the act of indiscipline. Of all those who at this time would willingly have given all and life itself to raise their country from the depths, he alone was equipped—by virtue of an appointment gained, never by 'pleasing', solely by 'deserving'—to stand up against the wave of despair sweeping through both Government and High Command. In the end, of the four men upon the central stage, he alone had the strength of character to raise the stakes in the hour of defeat, to bid for victory and to take upon his shoulders the burden of the greatness of France.

*   *   *

At his first official meeting with Reynaud—held in the small hours of the 7th; Reynaud in his dressing-gown, de Gaulle in the black leather jacket of a tank officer, in which he had driven posthaste from the front—he at once expounded, at the Premier's invitation, his logical and far-seeing view that the Mediterranean must henceforth be regarded as the barrier between the future power of France and the actual power of Germany. The fleet must be directed to North Africa, the aircraft be flown over, arms and equipment shipped out; certain classes of young recruits at present under training could also be sent by sea and, eventually, such of the combatant troops as could be detached from the battle and evacuated in time; in all perhaps half a million men to be added to the forces already in North Africa. With the resources of the French Empire, with the support of Britain and aid from America, a modern army could be built up in safety and, in due course of time, brought back to the liberation of France and the defeat of Germany.

It was a bold but commonsense conception and Reynaud, in fighting mood, approved his request to initiate the necessary measures forthwith. At the same time he asked him to go at once to London, in the first place to reassure the British authorities, and Churchill in particular, of the French Government's determination to fight on, legitimate doubts having arisen in their minds after the disasters of mid-May. In the second place he was to ask for increased air support and to inquire when the bulk of the British forces evacuated from Dunkirk might be expected to return, the magnitude of the disaster in which all equipment had been lost not having been appreciated in France.

Before leaving for London, however, de Gaulle wisely decided to discover Weygand's views more exactly, given that in his new capacity of Under-Secretary at the National Defence Ministry he was entitled to be informed. It was as well that he did so, for after no more than a few minutes' conversation at the Montry Headquarters he came to understand beyond all doubt that the Commander-in-Chief was 'resigned to defeat and determined upon an armistice'. It was June 8.

Part of the conversation, reported by de Gaulle in his Memoirs, deserves to be quoted again for the light it sheds upon the attitude which Weygand was to maintain with increasing rancour until the end.

That morning he was calm and collected. After reminding de Gaulle that he had predicted the German attack upon the line of the Somme, he went on to say that the enemy was still attacking, that he had crossed the river and that he could no longer be stopped.

(De Gaulle): ' "Right. He's across the river. What then?"

(Weygand): "Then? It's the Seine and the Marne."

"Yes. And after that?"

"After that? But it's the end."

"How so? The end? What of the world? And the Empire?" General Weygand burst into despairing laughter.

"The Empire? Childish nonsense! As for the world, once I've been beaten here England won't wait a week before coming to terms with the *Reich*." And the Commander-in-Chief, looking me straight in the eyes, added: "Ah, if I could only be sure that the Germans would leave me enough troops to maintain order . . .!" '

Having informed Weygand that this point of view was diametrically opposed to that of the Government which intended to fight on whatever happened, de Gaulle returned to Paris. Reporting to Reynaud, he begged the Premier instantly to dismiss a Commander-in-Chief who had patently abandoned all intention of fighting and all hope of victory. In principle Reynaud agreed wholeheartedly, but although he asked for the names of those who might be capable of replacing Weygand he said that he felt bound, for political considerations, to delay the decision. On the following morning (9th) de Gaulle, accompanied by Courcel, left for London by air.

He was away only for the space of the daylight hours, returning to Paris in the evening and conferring with Reynaud again during the night. But already it was too late. The enemy had reached the lower Seine; Weygand was still in command and had stolen a march on the road to surrender: Paris was to be declared an open city. De Gaulle, with Reynaud's full approval, had previously made all necessary arrangements for the defence of the capital; but in his absence the powerful influence of the Commander-in-Chief within the Government had made itself felt; a Cabinet meeting presently bore down Reynaud's opposition and approved Weygand's decision to abandon Paris to the enemy without a fight.

On the 10th Reynaud was given an opportunity to make good the delay and to repair the initial error of Weygand's appointment. He and de Gaulle were at work together in the War Ministry in the rue St Dominique, when they were interrupted by the sudden appearance of the Commander-in-Chief who claimed that he had been summoned to a meeting. Both men having stoutly denied this, Weygand went on unabashed: 'Then it's a misunderstanding. But a useful one, because I have an important statement to make.' He then made a rapid survey of the situation as he saw it, leading to the predetermined conclusion of a defeat total and inevitable.

As to Foch in the golden past, so now to Reynaud in the sombre present he proffered a sheet of paper upon which facts and figures were meticulously set down. From this the opinion was drawn: no victory, no further resistance, only capitulation. At one point de Gaulle interjected that there were other possibilities in view. But opposition only provoked the little man's spite.

'Have *you* got something to suggest?' he asked mockingly.

De Gaulle had been a junior Minister for only four days, but well aware of his responsibilities he was not to be intimidated by Army rank. His retort was a model of dignified authority. 'The Government has no suggestions to make, but orders to give. I am confident that it will give them.'

Reynaud backed him up loyally, hotly contesting Weygand's defeatist views, but he failed to act as he should have done. Weygand, though reproved for his attitude, was allowed to leave, still Commander-in-Chief, to drive down to his new Headquarters at Briare, there to work a greater mischief.

That night, with the Government withdrawing to Tours, de Gaulle and Reynaud left Paris in the same car. In the small hours of the 11th they reached Orleans and made their way to the Prefecture, linked by telephone with Briare. Shortly after dawn a call came through for Reynaud. Picking up the receiver he heard, to his amazement, Weygand's voice telling him that he had invited Churchill to a meeting at Headquarters that day. The Commander-in-Chief had decided that 'Mr Churchill must be informed personally of the real situation at the front.'

De Gaulle exploded: was the Generalissimo to be allowed to summon the Prime Minister of Great Britain without consulting the Premier of France—was it not evident that Weygand, instead of attending to military operations, was pursuing a political plan of his own—how much longer was this to go on? Reynaud needed no pressing; he was angry and, for the time being, resolute. Weygand must go; the only immediately suitable personality, General Huntziger, must be consulted this day; they would go to see him at once.

(Photos—*Keystone*)

ABOVE. THE CAPITULATORS

LEFT. Pétain, RIGHT. Weygand

THE COLLABORATORS

LEFT. Laval

BELOW. Darlan, greeting Hitler at Berchtesgaden

(Moreau)

Dakar—airview, 1940

Launch leaving for Dakar, September 23, 1940—with
Captains d' Argenlieu, Perrin and Bécourt-Foch

(Associated Press)

At the last minute he changed his mind; he must go first to Briare to make ready for the conference, since conference there was to be, and to receive Churchill. De Gaulle would interview Huntziger alone.

It was still early when de Gaulle drove off and made his way back to Arcis-sur-Aube. There he found General Huntziger, to whom he explained briefly the circumstances of the lost battle of France and the necessity for withdrawing to North Africa, and from whom he obtained the comforting assurance that he would be willing to take over the Supreme Command. Then, held up on roads almost blocked by dense masses of refugees and retreating troops, his car thrust its way back to Briare. It was about noon when he got there; and already, once again, it was too late. Reynaud had weakened; he no longer wanted to hear about Huntziger. Weygand still held the stage as Generalissimo. And now Pétain was coming forward from the wings to speak his shameful lines. 'Monsieur Reynaud,' Churchill noted at the conference that day, 'told me that Marshal Pétain had informed him that it would be necessary for France to seek an armistice.'[1]

Of practical results the conference was entirely unproductive, a waste of valuable time. Weygand began with the usual recital of facts concerning the state of things at the front, of which everyone present was aware, and brought in Generals Georges and Besson to confirm his account which no one challenged. It was the same staff-officer report that de Gaulle had heard on two previous occasions, an able assessment of all the worst factors of an ugly situation, but made now in a critical and at times almost angry tone as if the speaker were determined to show that responsibility for all France's disasters lay upon other shoulders; whereas, having been Chief of the General Staff during the decisive years 1930–35, at which time he had decisively opposed de Gaulle's conception of Armoured warfare subsequently copied by the Germans, he was, even more than Pétain and Gamelin, largely to blame. At the end of his indignant recital he offered no plan of action, made no constructive suggestion for future operations, but came abruptly to the same dire conclusion as the Marshal. 'At one point,' Churchill recorded, 'General Weygand mentioned that the French might have to ask for an armistice. . . . Reynaud at once snapped at him: "That is a political affair".'[2]

---

[1] Churchill: *The Second World War*, Vol. II.
[2] *Ibid.*

Politics, however, was the game at which Weygand was now playing, a double game at that: he aimed to spread the responsibility still
wider by involving Britain as well as France in the capitulation. Given
his repeated insistence upon the need to surrender—on the 8th, the
10th, and now the 11th—how else account for his demand for the
dispatch to France of additional British forces when, in his expressed
view, the battle was already lost beyond retrieve? Churchill reported
that Weygand 'requested that every reinforcement should be sent—
above all, that every British fighter squadron should immediately be
thrown into the battle. "Here," he said, "is the decisive point. . . . It is
therefore wrong to keep *any* squadrons back in England." '[1]

Just how sincere was Weygand in making this request? He was well
aware that from the start Britain had put a large number of aircraft—
relative to the total strength of the Royal Air Force—into the battle;
that these aircraft had fought well and had suffered considerable losses;
that the *Blenheims* and *Battles* and *Hurricanes* were still fighting upon
the Seine and in Champagne; that other fighters were operating out of
England upon the lower Seine by day, whilst heavy bombers were
hammering the Ruhr and German rail communications by night. On
the other hand, he well knew, from his recital of the situation along
the broken front, that not all the fighters in the world at that time would
suffice to hold up the German Armoured thrust to the west and south
of evacuated Paris; and that neither *Hurricanes* nor *Spitfires* could stop
tanks in low level attack for which they were not designed, nor their
pilots trained. He knew, moreover—it had been repeatedly explained
by the British air staff—that fighter squadrons could not be moved
across the Channel with the speed and ease of rooks upon an empty
chessboard. Suitable landing-grounds were few and had to be selected
with care; special fuel had to be brought up, expert ground staff ferried
over together with essential equipment, spares, cannon ammunition.
Days must elapse before any of the remaining twenty-five fighter
squadrons demanded by Weygand could be effective in France; during
those days nothing could stop the German advance; by the time the
fighters were operating from the airfields, the airfields would be in
enemy hands and the fighters with them. Why then did he seek to
draw into a situation from which he saw no issue other than surrender
the last of the British reserves?

[1] Churchill: *The Second World War*, Vol. II.

In part the answer is to be found in Weygand's own confessions.[1] He was, he wrote later, 'aware of the reduced resources then available to England' and therefore 'could not believe that the enemy had not, with the care customary to each of his enterprises, gathered together all the probabilities of success and assembled all the means indispensable to an invasion of England.' Under such 'a massive German attack' or the threat of it England without France, he had assured de Gaulle, would not 'wait a week before coming to terms with the *Reich*.' In his view, then, *both* nations would shortly be compelled to surrender. By drawing the remaining British forces into France within a few days of the end, he sought to make those surrenders concurrent. It was his way of saving his 'honour', for how could France be blamed if Britain, too, capitulated to the Nazis?

It is also noteworthy that, whereas he demanded the transference to France of the whole of the British fighter force, he made no mention of any further support to be given by the French air forces. These had amounted, according to his own figures, to some 700 aircraft of all types serviceable on May 10. Considerable losses had been suffered in the initial frontier battles, but thereafter the forces had been carefully husbanded; the few reserves had been brought forward and factory output stepped up; so that at the end the strength was as great as at the beginning. Afterwards, when de Gaulle's plan of air evacuation to North Africa had been put into operation, Weygand could write: 'The number of aircraft that crossed (the Mediterranean) can be put at seven hundred.' And at Rethondes General Huntziger—not, alas, the new leader of a fighting Army, but the unhappy head of the armistice team—was to inform Hitler's General Keitel: 'Our Fleet is intact, our Air Force is intact.' In the battle for France, in which according to Weygand the need for air support was paramount, why had this force not been used? Of Huntziger's statement to Keitel he was to write that it was a 'proud declaration'. It is a matter of some difficulty to understand how the man who, with Pétain's connivance, had forced his country into surrender could feel 'proud' of having kept his Air Forces intact at a time when, pleading exhaustion of all French resources, he had attempted to extort the last of Britain's fighter squadrons.

Nor was it only the Royal Air Force that he planned to ensnare; the small, re-established British Expeditionary Force was also to be caught

[1] *Rappelé au Service*, pages 325–6 of the French edition.

in the net. Mixed with the débris of the French Xth Army retreating westward, it was to be held until, too late to disentangle, too late to reach the coast, its surrender became inevitable. The time-table of Weygand's actions proves the plot. On the 11th no mention was made of the plan of retreat to North Africa, but the lesser alternative of the 'Brittany redoubt'—approved in principle by both Churchill and de Gaulle—was derisively condemned by the Commander-in-Chief. On the 12th he made his way to Cangey, President Lebrun's temporary residence, and before a full Council of Ministers declared that the enemy must be asked immediately to grant an armistice—a declaration to which Pétain gave unquestioning support. On the 13th he attended the conference at Tours when Churchill, hastily summoned from London, was asked by Reynaud whether Britain would agree to a request for armistice terms being made by France; and heard Churchill reply with deep emotion that, whatever France might feel compelled to do, Britain would never give in under any circumstances. In the course of the conference, 'Mr Churchill,' according to Weygand, 'brought up once more the question of a bridgehead on the Atlantic, a variation of the theme of a Breton redoubt. I explained why I did not think it reasonable to base any hopes on devices of that sort.' Reynaud then told Churchill that in any event it was 'too late' for the Brittany redoubt to be organized, and the matter was closed. In spite of this, on the morning of the 14th at Briare, Weygand sent for General Alan Brooke—who, as commander of the B.E.F., was under his orders—and informed him that 'at the Inter-Allied Council' (i.e. at Tours on the 13th) 'it had been decided to hold a position covering Brittany in front of Rennes.'[1]

Weygand then carried Brooke off in his car to General Georges's headquarters where he was to receive written orders for the operation. On the way the Generalissimo, in a moment of revealing truth, incautiously allowed his real preoccupation to be known. 'This is a terrible predicament I am in,' he told Brooke. 'Yes, I had finished my military career which had been a most successful one.' At hearing him speak with deep concern of his own career—at a time when, with the fate of all France in the balance, thousands were dying without regard for theirs—General Brooke was horrified; but scarcely

---

[1] From Lord Alanbrooke's Diary quoted in *The Turn of the Tide*. The incident is fully dealt with on pages 165–77.

more so than by what Weygand presently told him in front of the map in Georges's office. He was ordered to hold the neck of the Brittany peninsula. Measuring the distance upon the map he found it to be nearly 100 miles; to hold such a line would require at least fifteen divisions at full strength and well equipped; he had less than four, weak, with few anti-tank guns and hardly any tanks. Weygand agreed that the idea was 'fantastic' and that little support could be expected from the French Army, since it 'had ceased to be able to offer organized resistance and was disintegrating into disconnected groups'. Nevertheless, he repeated, the plan was the result of an Inter-Allied agreement and the instructions must be obeyed. He thereupon wrote out the orders, signed them and obtained Brooke's signature in acknowledgment.

Back at his own headquarters at Le Mans, Brooke decided that, given the rapidly worsening situation, he must refer what he termed this 'wild project' to London. At four o'clock that afternoon (14th) he telephoned Dill, now Chief of the Imperial General Staff, to explain Weygand's orders and the peril in which they placed him. In reply Dill said that he must consult the Prime Minister as he himself 'had not heard of the Brittany scheme'. Intermittent phone calls—between Brooke and Dill, and Churchill and Brooke—passed to and fro throughout the night of the 14th and into the 15th. The final result was that Churchill stated categorically that no agreement to hold Brittany had been reached by the Allied Governments, that Brooke was to withdraw to the coast and commence re-embarkation, and that instructions had been sent to Weygand whereby Brooke and the B.E.F. were removed from his command.

The French Government, meanwhile, had retired to Bordeaux. Thence, Pétain, his limpid blue eyes now fixed upon the sombre dawn of personal power, wrongfully and without authority sent for the Generalissimo. Together they concerted their plans for the ultimate ignominy. Even as, on the 16th, these plans began to bear fruit, Weygand was in communication with London, protesting to Dill that Brooke was failing to carry out his instructions, and demanding that the signed order to hold on in Brittany be complied with. Almost simultaneously: 'At about twenty-two hours,' as Weygand later wrote, 'we learned that M. Reynaud had resigned. . . . The Marshal accepted without hesitation the powers which the President of the

Republic asked him to assume. He asked me to take the post of Minister of Defence which I did. . . . I decided to retain the post of Commander-in-Chief. . . . The immediate duty of the government of *the Marshal, who had not ceased since the 12th of June . . . to attempt to obtain a cessation of hostilities*,[1] was to take a decision already too long delayed. . . . A note was at once drafted by the Minister of Foreign Affairs'— the italophile Baudouin—'for the Spanish Government which France had asked to act as intermediary in Berlin. . . . In the early hours of the 17th, Marshal Pétain decided to let the French people know of the formation of his government and of the request made to our enemies.'

Neither the Marshal nor his Minister of Defence and Commander-in-Chief thought fit to inform General Brooke of 'the request made to our enemies'. In Weygand's view the British Expeditionary Force was still under his command; it would find out in course of time about the armistice negotiations since it too would be involved in the cease-fire. Meanwhile it must continue to fight. After all, in his view, Britain herself would shortly capitulate; did it much matter whether her troops surrendered in France or in England? Matters of far greater moment to him had to be considered. Several times during the past ten days he had hinted at the danger of 'anarchy', had stressed the need to bargain with the enemy for a remnant of French force 'to maintain order'. At Tours, on the strength of a wild rumour subsequently proved to be false, he had used the panicky pretext of a 'Communist rising' to accentuate his insistence upon surrender. Now, no longer willing to fight the enemy, he was ready to fight his own people.

From all this dark record one of two conclusions must surely emerge. Either Weygand, after the first few days of his Supreme Command, was paralysed by the disastrous results of a form of warfare he had always contemptuously dismissed as unthinkable and, suddenly realizing his total ineptitude for the post in which he never rose above the level of subordinate staff officer, was driven to save that personal reputation, the 'very successful career' of which he was so inordinately proud, by forcing a national, as distinct from a military, surrender that should absolve him from blame; or, stricken in the mind by the nightmare magnitude of unbelievable disaster, he was the victim of dementia, perhaps hereditary. Perhaps it was a combination of the two, for it is certainly hard to explain his conduct solely upon the basis of either

[1] Author's italics.

one. His outrageous pretence to General Brooke that the Allied
Governments had ordered him to hold on in Brittany when he himself
had officially turned down the proposal must seem as deliberate a
betrayal of trust as does his conspiracy with Pétain to oust Reynaud.
But his persistent efforts to force the French Government to surrender
the moment he had been beaten upon the hopelessly weak position of
the Somme and his scornful refusal to consider any other possibility
whatsoever savour more of lunacy. Always a devout Catholic, after
the armistice he displayed a marked increase of piety, attending Mass
twice a day and, in the intervals, spending long hours with his father-
confessor. Perhaps he had something on his conscience.

However that may be, by the end of the 1940 campaign he had been
found wanting in every essential quality of a Commander-in-Chief.
He was neither a born nor a trained leader. He had no unshakeable will
to win. His strategic outlook was narrow, his technical knowledge out
of date; with no faith in victory, nor any plan, he betrayed the trust
reposed in him by a Government he despised. At the crisis he intervened in politics when his attention to purely military matters should
have been undivided. All this must be taken into account when considering what was seriously proposed some two years later by Roosevelt who would have wished to see him made Commander-in-Chief
again, to lead French forces to the liberation of the country he had
done so much to abase in the eyes of the world.

*   *   *

The last days of the battle in France were passed by de Gaulle in
great agony of spirit. With the Army shattered, the whole edifice of
the French State seemed to be crumbling from within and he who had,
in large measure, foreseen the catastrophe could do nothing to prevent it. Lebrun, President of the Republic, might voice patriotic sentiments, he had neither the character nor the constitutional right to
command. Jeanneney and Herriot, presidents of the Senate and
Chamber of Deputies, might express their passionate determination to
fight on, they could not compel. Loyal and enlightened ministers, such
as the stout-hearted Mandel, Minister of the Interior, might press for
the continuation of the War from North Africa, for a speedy departure
to Algiers; they had to fight the growing influence within the Government of right-wing extremists, men like Baudouin and Prouvost, and

found it daily more difficult to counter the convinced, and convincing, defeatism of the Hero of Verdun and the successor to Foch. Everything depended upon the Premier of France, Paul Reynaud—who had vowed to fight on, come what might, who had taken Clemenceau as his pattern, who believed that France would be saved by a 'miracle' and who favoured Algiers. He still held the power, he yet had the time. All at once and with sinking heart de Gaulle realized that he too was weakening.

On the 12th, at work all day upon plans for the withdrawal to North Africa, de Gaulle was left in ignorance of the Cabinet meeting at Cangey, at which Weygand made his official request for the opening of armistice negotiations. No reason was given for the omission, and when he saw Reynaud that evening, and again on the morning of the 13th, he had the impression that the Premier was stoutly holding his ground against those who were agitating for surrender. That afternoon, however, a telephone call warned him that Reynaud was meeting Churchill at Tours and that he, de Gaulle, was being deliberately excluded from the meeting. Driving over at once, he was in time to hear the astonishing question put to Churchill by Reynaud: Despite the treaty of Alliance signed in March, would Britain allow France to inquire of the enemy on what terms he was prepared to grant an armistice?

To de Gaulle it seemed incredible. The moment the conference was over he marched straight up to Reynaud. 'Is it possible,' he demanded forcefully, 'that you should conceive the idea of France requesting an armistice?'

'Certainly not!' Reynaud answered. And then added a fantastic explanation: 'But we must impress the English so as to obtain greater assistance from them.'

It was a prevarication that, failing to deceive, opened de Gaulle's eyes to the unhappy truth. Reynaud, his immediate superior and close associate who had brought him into the Government for the sole purpose of prosecuting the War without thought of defeat or despair, Reynaud was holding him at arm's length, fobbing him off with lame excuses. Churchill, commiserating with France's plight—instead, as de Gaulle would have wished, of condemning her leaders' pusillanimity—had declared his sympathetic understanding and, whilst insisting that Britain would never withdraw from the struggle, had demanded only, as a possible condition for releasing France from her pledge, certain guarantees concerning the Fleet and the German air-crew prisoners. The alacrity with which the Government had agreed to the second of these terms showed how strongly the tide was flowing and how little resistance Reynaud was now offering to it. The telegram he presently sent to Roosevelt, hinting that without immediate American intervention all was lost for France, proved that he was a drowning man, clutching only at the straw of an unrealizable hope.

That night de Gaulle took stock of his position. The movement towards submission to the enemy, under the pressure of Pétain, Weygand, Baudouin and the surrender-group, was gaining momentum. Once France had been absolved by Britain from the treaty clause forbidding her to make a separate peace, the movement would be irresistible. The very fact that Reynaud had mentioned the word 'armistice' brought the eventuality of surrender measurably nearer. That step, the abandoning of France's honour and independence, de Gaulle refused to contemplate; under no circumstances would he be a party to it. There was but one course open to him: he wrote a letter of resignation from the Government.

Even as he was about to dispatch it, Georges Mandel, warned by a secretary of his intention, asked to see him. As determined to continue the fight from Africa as he was anxious to counter the defeatists and to uphold the honour of his country, he urged de Gaulle to reconsider the decision. Outside the Government he would have no greater influence upon the outcome than any other loyal officer dismayed by events; inside it he might yet sway the weaklings with his own strength of purpose, the more so since, unattached to political party, uninfluenced by parliamentary intrigue, he was a man apart, almost the only one in the present Government whose integrity no one doubted. To serve France must be the only consideration; he could serve best by retaining his post. De Gaulle listened and was persuaded; the letter of resignation was withheld.

On the 14th the Government moved to Bordeaux. De Gaulle had advised Quimper, whence troops and material could be evacuated with easily summoned help from Britain and from which the Government would, sooner or later, be compelled to leave for French territory overseas. Baudouin had insisted upon Bordeaux; and Reynaud, faltering under the burden of events, deeply distressed at ever-worsening

reports—the Germans in Paris, their armies pouring over the Seine—
had given way. The outcome was inevitable: Bordeaux meant delay,
indecision, and the triumph of defeatist intrigue.

The moment he reached the new temporary capital—in the evening,
after an interminable drive along refugee-packed roads—de Gaulle
went to see the Premier. Warning him that were the Government to
slide tamely into capitulation he would refuse to obey the order,
de Gaulle asked him pointblank whether or not he still intended to
withdraw the remnants of the Army to North Africa. Reynaud, with
apparent firmness, asserted that the withdrawal was to commence
forthwith; and agreed further that de Gaulle should go at once to
London to make final arrangements for the necessary half-million tons
of shipping. To de Gaulle's question where they should meet again, he
replied boldly: 'You will find me at Algiers.'

Driving back northward through the night, de Gaulle was in
Brittany on the morning of the 15th; made a hurried inspection of the
principal commands, at Rennes and Brest, to ascertain their embarka-
tion requirements; and sailed, in the afternoon, in a French destroyer
for Plymouth. Thence he reached London at dawn on the 16th.

Hardly had he arrived, at the Hyde Park Hotel, than the French
Ambassador, Corbin, and Jean Monnet of the Economic Mission were
announced. Having handed to him the list of official engagements for
the day, they then produced the remarkable, and indeed startling, plan
elaborated largely by Robert Vansittart with the agreement of the
Foreign Minister, Lord Halifax, whereby France and Britain were to
be indissolubly united by the fusion of all their interests, of all their
resources throughout the world, even of their Parliaments. De
Gaulle saw at once that, although there was much in the plan that
appeared fantastic and incapable of being put immediately into
practice, it was undeniably the most magnanimous offer ever made by
any nation to a friend in distress; if agreed, it would give Reynaud a
weapon with which to beat down the defeatists and to persuade his
reluctant Cabinet to continue the War overseas. As a member of the
French Government he undertook to present the plan to Churchill.
They met for lunch at the Carlton Club.

De Gaulle had first encountered the Prime Minister during his
mission to London on June 9. If the mission, whose main purpose was

to request speedy British reinforcements, had then seemed vain it had not been altogether fruitless, for it had enabled him to gain a clear impression of the outstanding qualities and vast experience of the man upon whose strength and energy, inspiring words and inspired leadership the salvation of half the world must now depend. At Briare he had appreciated both his quick grasp of a desperate military situation and his inflexible determination to fight on. At Tours, though he deplored the gentleness with which the defeatists had been handled, he had discerned, beyond the quicksands of doubt and despair into which so many Frenchmen were being drawn, the basic Churchillian rock of resolve. Upon that rock the future of France in the War might be solidly built.

Churchill had been told of the new plan by Halifax; aware of its complex immensity, he knew that it was a big mouthful to be swallowed at one gulp, that time must elapse and many obstacles be surmounted before it could be digested and take effect. But its very vastness appealed to him; an imaginative gesture, it would surely impress the doubting French with the firmness of Britain's decision and prove that, with their resources pooled, the two nations must triumph in the end. After lunch he took the draft plan back to Downing Street and placed it before the hurriedly assembled Cabinet. De Gaulle waited in the ante-room.

'In these days,' Churchill wrote later, 'the War Cabinet were in a state of unusual emotion. . . . Grief for our ally in her agony, and desire to do anything in human power to aid her, was the prevailing mood.' In under two hours the plan was approved. Well before five o'clock, the hour to which a decisive meeting of the French Cabinet in Bordeaux had been postponed, de Gaulle was on the telephone giving an outline of the great scheme to an excited Reynaud. It was the very thing, the French Premier said in effect, with which to swing the tottering Government back to a decision in favour of continuing the War from North Africa; he had complete confidence in the result. Churchill then took over the receiver, spoke encouraging words, and agreed to meet Reynaud at Concarneau on the following day to make further arrangements for the withdrawal of French forces by sea. Forthwith an aircraft was placed at de Gaulle's disposal for the return journey to Bordeaux and any other journeys that might become necessary on the morrow; and, his business completed, he left at once, accompanied by the faithful Courcel, a draft of the plan in his pocket together with the shipping agreement.

It was nearly half past nine and darkness had fallen when the aircraft, a Lockheed *Hudson*, touched down at the airfield near Bordeaux and taxied over to the sheds. Two members of his official staff came forward to meet him. They bore grave tidings: Reynaud had resigned. Pétain held the stage and this was the end of the act.

Outwardly de Gaulle remained unmoved. The news in no way affected the decision announced two days ago to Reynaud, that in no case would he accept surrender by whatever authority it might be ordered. A stab of pain he must have felt at the sudden announcement of the Premier's abdication, but the tragic possibility had been contemplated for so many weary days that now the blow seemed no more than the booming of a distant gun whose warning flash had long been perceived; it failed to shake him. He had no need to ponder the problem afresh; he had long ago questioned the past for guidance in the present. The years of preparation, of thought and of action, the linked stages of destiny, led him to the new resolve. He had no doubt where his duty lay: now as ever to contribute to the greatness of France by rendering 'some signal service', by taking the burden upon his own shoulders 'though his back should break'.

He hesitated no longer. That night he saw Reynaud who approved his intentions; and in the morning, by the same plane that had brought them, he and Courcel left for London.

9. The Banner of Resistance

Votre Excellence veut, n'est-ce pas? qu'effaçant
Cette tache de ciel, cette tache de sang,
Et n'ayant plus aux mains qu'un linge sans mémoire,
J'offre a la Liberté ce linceul dérisoire?

(*L'Aiglon:* Act III, Scene iii)

FROM THE beginning, the new beginning in London that was to see the rebirth of fighting France, nothing was easy for de Gaulle. In exile, even daily life seemed disconcerting. After the ceaseless toil and constant anxiety of recent weeks, the confusion, the chaotic shifts from Paris, to Tours, to Bordeaux, the almost hourly association with Reynaud, the voluble pessimism of Weygand and the glum expectancy of Pétain, after the babel of angry voices raised in despair and all the tragic hurly-burly of defeat, the tranquillity of England seemed unreal and not altogether reassuring. In the capital traffic circulated normally, people went unhurried about their business, theatres and restaurants were open, taxis plied for hire; it was like Paris before May 10, almost dangerously nonchalant.

In the summer sunshine there were few signs of any war-quickened activity. True, there were some coils of barbed wire in the parks and in the sidestreets near Whitehall; and on the lawns men in denims went through the motions of rifle drill with makeshift weapons; and the silver balloons floated protectively overhead—in Paris they had stayed on the ground because there were no winches. But on some days there were also to be seen the sandwich-board processions of Peace-movement cranks, meandering along main thoroughfares and deflected from whatever goal had been intended by unmoved, and unarmed, policemen. The ubiquitous gasmasks—in Paris too they had been dutifully carried—showed that most of the inhabitants were aware that a war was in progress somewhere, yet the most martial figures in the metropolis were still the heavily bemedalled commissionaires in the clubs and outside the great hotels. That across the narrow seas, at Rotterdam and Dunkirk, at Calais, Boulogne and Cherbourg and round the coast to St Nazaire, the docks, the oil tanks and the stranded shipping still lay smouldering beneath a drifting pall of smoke that marked the end of a tragedy and presaged the wrath to come, appeared to be beyond the ken of the soft-spoken, stolid-seeming English. Fretting at inaction, de Gaulle's uneasiness was excusable in a land 'where it seemed always afternoon' and time for tea.

The one event bringing him peace of mind at this time and a measure of consolation in exile was the arrival of his wife and children. Earlier, when the Government's move to Quimper had seemed likely, he had sent them into Brittany whence, on his advice, they had sailed for Cornwall, taking passage in the last small steamer to escape. His mother, however, had been forced to remain, gravely ill, at St Brieuc; there, a little later, she died. Before the end she had news of her son. In her lifetime two Marshals had brought dishonour to France: Bazaine at Metz, Pétain at Bordeaux. Now, as she lay dying, she learned of her son's call to honour and duty; and to her fading consciousness the nobility of his action brought a last stirring of love and of pride.

By those with whom he came in contact in London, de Gaulle was welcomed with sympathy and respect for the cause he championed; from all sides offers of service were pressed upon him, offers of accommodation, of entertainment, of comforts for the troops, even gifts of money, some pathetically small from anonymous well-wishers. But, however heart-warming and encouraging, such tokens of regard for France could do little to bring in recruits and nothing to supply them with arms. Nor, he soon discovered, could material assistance from the Service ministries be either prompt or extensive; with the Navy silently preoccupied with the grave problems arising from an enemy occupation of the Channel and Atlantic coasts, with the War Office at its wits' ends to re-equip an army sufficient to resist the expected invasion, with the Air Staff devoting all their energies to the strengthening of that fighter defence upon which the brunt of the enemy attack must certainly fall, it was not to be expected that much could be spared for a miscellaneous collection of Frenchmen who, however gallantly volunteering for service, could contribute little of decisive importance to the approaching crisis. Churchill might issue instructions for all possible aid to be given, the obstacles were innumerable and not to be effaced by a stroke of the pen. De Gaulle commanded admiration, it must be some time before he could command an army; such a view, though courteously expressed and rationally explained, was not calculated to allay frustration. His impatience was as natural as the delays were inevitable.

But these anxieties were as nothing compared to the sudden consternation caused to all free Frenchmen by the shattering news given to the world on July 4. In the evening of the previous day a British naval squadron in the Mediterranean had—after a lengthy parley in which alternative proposals offered to a French squadron under Admiral Gensoul had been rejected—opened fire upon the ships at anchor at Mers-el-Kebir (Oran), destroying a number of vessels, seriously damaging others and causing great loss of life. The facts were given banner headlines in the London newspapers.

Authoritative opinion, not only British, has since almost unanimously held that in the wartime circumstances then prevailing the action, both of the British admiral, Somerville, and of the Government which sent him his instructions, was justified. The proposals offered to Gensoul were honourable: he could take his squadron to a British port and either resume the fight against Germany or allow the ships to be interned; or he could be escorted across the Atlantic to the French base at Martinique where he could, if he wished, be placed under American protection; or he could disarm and immobilize his ships at Oran. The proposals were also reasonable; for not only did the German and Italian armistice terms permit a latitude of intervention in French North Africa of which the enemy was certain to take advantage sooner or later; but, far more dangerous, the terms laid down that all French warships were to return to the ports of metropolitan France forthwith. True, the German terms specifically allowed the French under Pétain to retain their fleet, *except* however, for 'vessels required for coastal defence and minesweeping.' In the long and hard run of naval warfare it was more than probable that for 'coastal defence' French heavy cruisers and destroyers would be found necessary.

Reynaud's Government had given verbal assurances that the French fleet would not be handed over to the enemy, and the assurances had been repeated in Bordeaux by members of Pétain's clique; but even more solemn assurances had been given concerning the custody of the four hundred German air-crew prisoners, yet these enemies had now been liberated and returned to the *Luftwaffe*. There was little reason to believe that the Pétain régime, under pressure from its German masters, would be more punctilious in regard to the fleet, the less so given the character of Admiral Darlan whom few were so simple as to trust, whose authority over the French Navy was undisputed and whose conduct was governed by an obsessive hatred of all things British, dating, it seemed, from Trafalgar where his grandfather had been killed.

The necessity for the proposals offered to Gensoul was acute. The sudden turning of the tables caused by the overrunning of Norway, the fall of France, the menace of the Italian fleet in the Mediterranean, had made Britain's position at sea precarious. The Royal Navy was fully extended; the timing of the enemy's next attack was unknown, even the strength available to the German Navy was uncertain; in the Mediterranean the least accretion of force to Axis naval power might tip the scales disastrously. To avert the peril, action—Operation *Catapult*—had to be swift and, to be effective, simultaneous upon each of several divisions of the French Navy. In English ports, despite a few instances of physical resistance, French warships were taken over without difficulty. In Alexandria the squadron under Admiral Godfroy submitted with good grace to immobilization and honourable surveillance. At Mers-el-Kebir the British officer sent in to parley, Captain Holland, was particularly well chosen; he knew France and the French language and had long collaborated with French naval authorities, having been Naval Attaché at the British Embassy until the surrender; but, although he carried out his mission with courtesy and consideration, it was to no purpose. The proposals he brought were curtly rejected, and his further anxious endeavours to persuade were repulsed without serious discussion. He was still trying to reach a compromise when the time-limit set by the British Government expired.

For what followed Gensoul must take his share of responsibility. To the likely, if not obvious, advantages of getting his squadron away from an area dominated by the Axis armistice-commission—a move for which he could easily have pleaded a desire to spare the lives of his men—he appears to have given no thought whatever; and by transmitting a summary and incomplete version of the British proposals, sent via Toulon to Vichy, he ensured their rejection. Nevertheless, it is upon Darlan that the full weight of blame must fall. His authority over the French Navy was sole and undisputed; it could be challenged immediately only by the head of the Government, Pétain, and the Minister of National Defence, Weygand; he avoided the challenge by concealing the facts. Not until the end of the War did Weygand learn the whole truth, and he was then constrained to admit it in his Memoirs so as to clear himself of any suspicion of complicity in the deception.

Darlan, at the hurriedly convened meeting of Ministers in Vichy to discuss the British proposals, had placed the Pétain Government before a *fait accompli* by claiming that the Royal Navy had already opened fire. This claim was false, and, at the hour at which he made the claim, he must have known it to be false. Further, in explaining the British proposals, he omitted altogether the offer of safe-conduct for the French squadron across the Atlantic to the French island of Martinique where, the offer stated, it could remain unmolested until the end of the War. Had this offer been made known, Weygand wrote, an agreement might well have been reached with the British and the tragedy averted. From this it is clear that Darlan intended to provoke the incident and that he took the very steps necessary to make certain that it should be provoked. Dominated by his chronic and unreasoning anglophobia, he may have thought to please his German masters by forcing Britain to take a cruel action that would stimulate, among his fellow-countrymen, a hatred similar to his own. But whatever the cause, by ordering Gensoul to reject the British proposals he sent, without a flicker of compassion, fourteen hundred French sailors to untimely death.

In Europe the action which, between Britain and France, will always stand as one of the most melancholy events of the War, had an unintended, though perhaps not unexpected, effect. It proved to all men, to the doubting Weygand as much as to the hesitant Hitler, that Britain was not open to a negotiated peace, that she would fight on to the end, whatever the end might be, and that she would stick at nothing to safeguard her vital interests. It was this aspect that, at a time when there was little to report and when to the waiting world any event must appear sensational, evoked the staring headlines in the British Press. Unfortunately, in some cases the facts of the bombardment were allowed to appear without even a formal expression of regret for its necessity, so that the impression given was that the Royal Navy—whose responsible officers had protested at their orders and had carried them out with the greatest reluctance—had scored a splendid triumph over its 'enemies'. Among the Free French, to the shock of dismay and grief, the impression added resentment at an unmerited humiliation.

To the leader and initiator of French resistance, who had so recently fought the inner and personal battle of conflicting loyalties, who had sought in the name of France the friendship and support of a trusted ally and who now saw the massacre of French sailors acclaimed almost as a British victory, the callous attitude of the Press was so much of a blow to the heart that Churchill's opinion of his conduct— 'General de Gaulle, whom I did not consult beforehand, was magnificent in his demeanour'—must seem an understatement. Wasting no time upon vain recriminations, he stifled emotion and viewed the incident with notable objectivity. Aware from the outset that, in the course of the struggle against surrender, he and his followers must travel a hard road, he may well have perceived that this was but the first of many bitter trials to be endured before the liberty and greatness of France could be restored. To those British officers most closely associated with him at this time he was as calmly courteous as ever, seeming indeed by some faint and undefinable sympathy to express, in the name of France, his understanding of their embarrassment at what their country had been compelled to do.

'I do not blame the British Government,' he told one of them on the day after the publication of the news, 'for their action at Oran. In their view the shelling of French warships to prevent them from falling into enemy hands must have appeared as an urgent and terrible necessity. Nor do I blame Mr Churchill for not having consulted me—it would evidently have been quite impossible for me to discuss the matter. But I do take exception to what has appeared in one or two of the English newspapers. To treat the affair as a British naval victory is wrong and will have a bad effect upon opinion in France.'

And a bad effect it assuredly had. The propaganda point was too obvious to be missed by the enemies both of de Gaulle and of Britain; in the French Navy in particular, where the truth of the matter was wholly unknown, a spark of resentful hostility was kindled and, kept alight by Darlan, smouldered on for years. Among the French people, however, both inside and out of France, it was surprising how quickly the first flames of anger abated. In part this may have been due to an appreciation of Britain's continued stand in the war, in part to the factual news disseminated by the BBC; but there can be little doubt that in great measure the amelioration was brought about by de Gaulle's own broadcast of July 8 .

Freedom to speak his mind had very wisely been accorded him by Duff Cooper, then Minister of Information, and he made his opinion clear without reckless condemnation, but also without ambiguity. After declaring that not a single Frenchman would have learned of the shelling at Oran without feelings of deepest pain and justifiable anger, and after rebuking the British Press for its tactless approach, he went on to explain the events in detail and to place the responsibility squarely upon the men of Bordeaux, whose surrender had put French warships at the mercy of the enemy. He would rather, he said in effect, see a French warship battered and stranded than manned by the enemy and in action against Britain. The wrath of Frenchmen was being turned against the English by those who, at Bordeaux, had already betrayed their Allies, but no Frenchman worthy of the name would fail to recognize that England's defeat must seal the enslavement of France for ever; the two great nations must either succumb or triumph together. As for the Free French, they had taken once and for all the decision to fight on.

The response, however limited, was almost immediate. Volunteers, who had held back after the news of Oran, began to come forward again; clandestine letters in increasing numbers came out of enemy-held territory, with, just occasionally, news of some incident favourable to de Gaulle's resistance. And presently news of greater significance came in from the Empire: the central African province of Chad, under its enlightened Governor, the West Indian Félix Eboué, cabled London its adherence to de Gaulle.

Further encouraging information came in during the month from French Equatorial Africa, where officials and leading citizens were rejecting the surrender of Bordeaux and refusing submission to the Pétain Government's representatives. From Duala in the mandated Cameroons territory the British Consul sent word that the majority of the people wished to come over to de Gaulle, but that they were being held down by the local governor on the instructions of a French admiral flown out from Vichy. Even in the Pacific the flame of resistance was taking hold. From the New Hebrides in the Coral Sea came a message of loyalty to the movement from the Commissioner, Henri Sautot.

To speed the adherence of the Cameroons, de Gaulle took prompt steps that resulted, towards the end of August, in a romantic and bloodless success. Major Leclerc (de Hautecloque) and Captain de Boislambert were selected for the mission, with orders to proceed first to Accra, then to Lagos to collect a number of Free French volunteers, after which they would move on the Cameroons with British help and take Duala by force. Time being the limiting factor, they were to go by air; but at that period of the War the only British aircraft in service for African (and Eastern) liaison were the two transatlantic 'Empire' flying-boats, *Clare* and *Clyde*; and, although the range of these four-engined boats was considerable, they were compelled to make a number of refuelling stops, of which the first was at neutral Lisbon. The two French officers were thus forced to travel as civilians with false identities, British passports being issued in the names of 'Mr Clark' and 'Mr Lambert'.

On arrival at Lagos—Accra being unsuitable for flying-boats—they met with inevitable delays, some of the red-tape variety, but for the most part due to the need for secrecy and to difficulties of communication. Eventually, with time pressing, the party consisting of but twenty Frenchmen in all made its way by sea to the British Cameroons and set out from Victoria in three native canoes. Paddling by night up the reedy channels of the Cameroon River, the party reached Duala without opposition, made contact with the local resistance leaders and, before dawn, had taken command of the stately government palace. The Governor was ousted and Mr Clark, now temporary Colonel and High Commissioner Leclerc, reigned in his stead in the name of de Gaulle. On the same day, August 28, word came that Colonel de Larminat had crossed the Congo from Léopoldville and had taken over control from the pro-Pétain administration in Brazzaville, capital of French Equatorial Africa.

Together with the Chad province, a vast and valuable area of Central Africa had thus rallied to the cause of freedom. Only Libreville and a stretch of the Gaboon coast still hesitated; a greater show of force would be needed to convince the doubting authorities.

*   *   *

In England, meanwhile, the organization and re-equipping of Free French forces continued as steadily as the times permitted. 'Olympia' and the 'White City', where volunteers assembled and convalescents (ex Dunkirk) were canvassed, Aldershot where the units went into training, and even remote St Athan, in Glamorgan, where the airmen were grouped, entered into French history and took on a French pronunciation. Numerically the strength of the forces was still infinitesimal relative to the immense task that lay ahead; by August the grand total in all services was some 7,000 men, of whom less than half were effective combatant troops. Much later de Gaulle was to refer, not without pride, to the gallant few who stood for France in those early days as *'une poussière d'hommes'*—a little dust of men.

Of that dust the airmen were no more than a sprinkling; but they had their importance, as de Gaulle was quick to realize. They alone of all the impatient band could hope to get into the battle now impending over Britain; they alone might perhaps express in actual fighting the resolve of all to fight on and thus give, in the name of France, a token of the continuing alliance. News of their action would raise the morale of all and echoes of their combats would not leave France unmoved. De Gaulle urged their speedy employment.

But of these, the French 'few', not all were employable. Of under four hundred officers and men, one hundred and twenty were cadets from a training establishment in north-western France, who—led by their officers, Lieutenants Pinaud and Berthier—had made a dramatic escape to England tightly packed in two Brittany fishing-boats. Of the others, less than fifty were either trained or partly-trained fighter pilots; about a hundred could be classified as bomber pilots or navigators, air gunners or radio operators; there were perhaps seventy fitters and riggers; and the balance consisted of some thirty reserve officers and older pilots suitable for staff and administrative duties. Lack of aircraft, equipment and ground staff put out of the question the immediate formation of a French squadron capable of rendering any warlike service; of the score or so of French machines flown out of France, for which there were neither spares nor ammunition, not more than three or four were of the same type. Far away from the rising din of battle, at St Athan, the keen young cadets might continue their training; but for a time the remainder could only kick their heels in idleness; unable, because of security regulations, so much as to engage in practice flying in their own aircraft.

To obtain the admission into Royal Air Force squadrons of French pilots and air-crew was far from easy. Few had more than a smattering of English and not one was trained either in the handling of British aircraft or in British operational methods. Youthful fighter pilots, anxious to get back into the War, might—and frequently did—exaggerate their qualifications with an effrontery as barefaced as it was courageous; so that fifty hours' flying at a training establishment in France was magnified unblushingly into one hundred and fifty hours in a squadron at the front; whilst half-forgotten crumbs of school-fed English became overnight—at least on the paper of a questionnaire—the expert knowledge of a first-class interpreter. In the Royal Air Force training units to which they were sent on probation the deficiencies of these young men quickly became apparent, and they were promptly returned to St Athan. A few did, however, miraculously survive their gallant deception, and lived on to pit their skill and courage with notable success against the *Luftwaffe*.

De Gaulle's suggested introduction of French air-crews into Bomber Command Squadrons was even more difficult to achieve. Language was again the main obstacle; it being easy to imagine how hazardous the inclusion among the crews of the larger aircraft of men using French–English phrase-books would have made inter-communication. In spite of this serious objection the Air Ministry were persuaded to give limited support to the idea, and one or two crews, made up from the most experienced French airmen, were sent in British-piloted bombers on night operations over the Continent. Thus, before the middle of July, Bomber Command was able—at de Gaulle's special request—to issue a communiqué stating that in attacks on targets in Germany 'units of the Free French Air Force' had taken part. It made a brave sound on the radio to France.

But such occasions for active employment were rare, and the majority of those at St Athan soon came to realize that, with a career in the Royal Air Force out of immediate reach, they must stay together and make the best of it. This suited de Gaulle well enough, for if he had shown himself ready to contribute individuals and token forces to the defence of Britain he was naturally far more anxious to provide his few battalions with an all-French air component. Somehow a

Squadron must be formed and, since there were no facilities for such a unit at St Athan, an airfield found, nearer London, where the airmen could train for future operations overseas. This was a commonsense decision, but when it came to finding an airfield with suitable accommodation he ran into further difficulties. In all England just then there was scarcely an air base of any sort that was not either overcrowded or urgently needed for some new requirement; nor was it generally possible to persuade the harassed commanders of stations where space did appear to be available that to receive a handful of refugee French airmen without arms or aircraft was to advance the cause of the Allies in the War.

At length, an impasse having been reached, an appeal was made to the Chief of the Air Staff (Newall) and with his help the necessary accommodation, including hangars and workshops, was discovered at Odiham in Hampshire. Thereafter there was little delay. The main body of airmen was transferred from St Athan; equipment was collected from all points of the compass and a string of recently found French lorries brought down from a dockside in Liverpool; the aircraft were flown over from various fields without incident, despite their unfamiliar appearance in the well-watched English sky whence a descent of 'fifth columnists', quite possibly disguised as Frenchmen, was almost hourly expected. Before the end of the month (July) the first Free French Air Squadron had been formed.

De Gaulle drove down from London to inspect and inaugurate. It was a notable occasion with, as so often then, a deep undercurrent of pathos and romance. In cold fact the unit was small; the sparse line of aircraft numbered only half a dozen serviceable machines— Dewoitine fighters, Caudron *Simouns*, a twin-engined Potez. An 'all-purpose' unit might be its fittest description, though for some time to come its purpose could be no more than training. Yet the wider purpose could be discerned, or perhaps only guessed, in the ranks of those whom their General presently reviewed. Drawn up on the tarmac, before a flagstaff standing in a plot of grass near a camouflaged hangar, stood the three hundred officers and airmen each one of whom must, by virtue of his presence, have come to terms with himself before coming to England. Each had outfaced despair and, taking for all baggage little else than faith, had left his homeland to savour the bitterness of exile for the sake of France's future. Banded together they proclaimed, by a willing discipline visible in the smartness of their appearance and the perfection of their alignment, their certainty of victory in the hour of defeat. And the very smallness of their numbers illuminated the immense courage of their defiance.

Of the cost of this silent victory de Gaulle was as well aware as of the agony of spirit afflicting those lost leaders who yet remained in France. His compassion for their secret sufferings had been revealed during an earlier visit to the airmen, at St Athan shortly after the Oran tragedy. In the aircraft carrying him back to London he had turned to one of his companions.

'You know, for those who are still over there,' he had said abruptly, and with deeper feeling than he normally permitted himself, 'for the younger men as for the senior officers, the military leaders, men like——' he named half a dozen—'it's a dreadful thing to decide. Whether to obey orders, remain under Pétain and the armistice—or to risk everything, defy the authorities, leave France, leave all, in order perhaps to lose all. A terrible choice!'

Unresolved, it could be Hamlet's dilemma. And it may be that some such thought occurred to him, for almost at once he added with more than usual warmth: 'Mark you, it is not the same for me. Not any longer. My choice is made, my decision taken. I have no hesitation, no doubts left—all that is finished.'

For the men of the Squadron, too, it was finished; no trace of conflict remained, no outward emotion marred the simple military formality of the morning at Odiham. Of the depth of their feelings, however, as of the source of the inspiration that guided them, a visible sign was presently given.

The inspection completed, de Gaulle took station at the head of his men, facing the flagstaff. A wholly French occasion, there were no British present.[1] A French trumpeter sounded the call. At the foot of the staff an airman tugged at halyards, the drooped bunting rose slowly. A light south-westerly breeze was rising, a warm wind that on its way up-Channel must have brushed the cheek of France; its sudden gust unfurled the flag crisply, to reveal for the first time the banner under which Free Frenchmen would march for many a long mile through many a hard year. Upon the tricolour's central white ground was displayed the two-armed Cross of Lorraine.

[1] Save for one assistant whose presence de Gaulle had requested.

A moving scene, one whose significance was missed by none of those standing motionless at the salute while the trumpet-call still sounded. But even a new flag must suffer birth-pains; and even in exile military discipline must be asserted, the proper forms observed. When the ceremony was over de Gaulle sent for the responsible officer. Who had authorized him to place the Cross of Lorraine upon the French flag? '*Il n'y a qu'UN drapeau français,*' he declared with chilling logic.

Undeniably he was right, and right to state the case. Individuals, however good their intentions, could not be allowed to go around setting up flags of their own choice and design; it was not in that sense that the 'Free French' were free. Theirs was no breakaway organization, no new small nation seeking independence from the homeland; it was a part of France, the fighting part, claiming that by its morally justifiable defiance of a dishonourable act of surrender it was more truly representative of the French Republic and Empire than the men of Bordeaux and Vichy. Their duty was to keep the French flag flying, undefaced, a symbol of that unity which lay at the very root of de Gaulle's call to arms 'in the name of France'.

To the use of the two-armed Cross, moreover, he perceived a further objection in the fact, widely known in France, that as a tank-commander he had used the emblem upon his personal pennant. In the hands of hostile propagandists the news that he had now placed it upon the national flag would at once be distorted; it would be said that de Gaulle was fighting, not for France, but for personal power as an ambitious adventurer, that he was seeking like one of Alexander's generals to carve up the Empire and to create, not a free army for France, but a free state for himself.

To these logical arguments an equally logical reply was presently voiced by Thierry d'Argenlieu, who in time of peace followed the vocation of priest in the secluded Carmelite order and who, recalled to wartime service as a naval commander, had made his way out of Cherbourg to become one of de Gaulle's most faithful supporters. In his view the emblem was ideal as the badge of resistance, recalling that earlier liberation inspired by Saint Joan, symbolizing nobility of sacrifice in the cause of national freedom; recalling, too, the newly stolen province of Lorraine. De Gaulle need have no misgivings; the accusation that he had filched the emblem for his personal aggrandizement would never stick; that he had used it in battle to lead Frenchmen against the enemy could only heighten its popularity. With its centuries of tradition, all would approve it who remembered the triumph of Orleans, the martyrdom of Rouen. As a symbol of the continuing fight against the pagan swastika it would have, moreover, the advantages of being easily marked and easily recognized; and no true Frenchman, whatever his political colouring, would have it in his heart to despise a sign in which France might find the unity essential to resurgence.

De Gaulle, approving these opinions, gave his consent. The tricolour must remain the national flag; all must continue to serve and respect it. But, for use in the resistance movement, the symbolic badge was approved; and henceforth, in fighting units, the ensigns would carry the Cross of Lorraine until the invader had been thrown out of France.

It did not come into general use, however, until the first overseas expedition had left England.

10. Dakar—Plans and Preparations

The story of the Dakar episode deserves close study, because it illustrates in a high degree . . . the unforeseeable accidents of war. . . .

(Churchill: *The Second World War*, Vol. II)

OF THE failure of the Anglo–French expedition to Dakar in September (1940) the official explanation given shortly after the event was to the effect that, aside from a number of unpredictable accidents on the spot, some confusion among the authorities at Gibraltar had led to a blunder at the Admiralty, excusable because of air-raid precautions in force at the time. It was not long, however, before it began to be put about that the real culprits were to be found among de Gaulle's staff who, it was said, had been guilty of careless talk and had even, in a crowded restaurant, raised their glasses to '*Dakar!*' a few days before the expedition's sailing. In political circles inimical to de Gaulle the tale was accepted apparently without question and, retailed across the world, was presently told in Washington where it took such root that, two years later, Admiral Leahy found it possible to say without further evidence that de Gaulle's whole organization was 'impregnated with German spies'. In less exalted circles in Britain the legend that the expedition had failed because of a leakage from Free French sources persisted through the years with much the same tenacity as that of the arrival of the Russians, 'with snow on their boots', in 1914. Nearly twenty years later a minor personality employed by the BBC was permitted to broadcast, concerning Dakar, that 'the French staff gave the whole plan away'. It is therefore of some importance to the story of the venture and of de Gaulle's part in it to examine closely the known facts.

To deal first with the question of a 'leakage' of information to the enemy: there was none. The three Vichy-French cruisers and three destroyers whose appearance in the Atlantic was to contribute in part, and only in part, to the failure of the expedition's primary purpose, were not sent to Dakar to prevent 'Dakar' (Operation *Menace*). They put in there to refuel on their way to Libreville where they were to oppose the extension of the Free French movement that had so recently, and so easily, assumed control at Brazzaville and Duala. Their arrival at Dakar naturally raised the morale of the local authorities, but neither those authorities nor the Vichy naval staff had any idea of the powerful British forces then assembling off the coast of West Africa, of whose presence they became aware only after mid-September. Nor has any record been discovered in either Vichy-French or German naval archives showing any foreknowledge whatever of the Anglo–Free French plan of operations. It was to be alleged that Vichy's Intelligence knew so much from the 'leak' it was even aware beforehand of the date of de Gaulle's intended arrival at Dakar; but this date, no more than tentative at the beginning of August and continually postponed throughout the month, was only made final at Freetown on September 20, less than three days before zero-hour. It is clear, moreover, from Admiral Räder's lengthy discussion with Hitler on September 6, that the German Naval Staff had no knowledge of an expedition which, by then, had been at sea for a week.[1]

Some months after the event an almost comical attempt to pin the blame for the supposed 'leakage' upon Admiral Muselier was made by the British Intelligence authorities. The charges, based on documents which should have been suspect from the start, were far too readily accepted by the Government; Muselier was arrested and lodged in Pentonville Prison. But for all his indiscretions, and occasional black intrigues against de Gaulle, the voluble little Admiral was no pro-Vichy traitor; an investigation quickly showed that the charges were false, the documents forgeries; and the Government, releasing the prisoner, was compelled to offer him a full and rather shamefaced apology.

The plans, then, were not 'leaked'; they were not 'given away'; there were no 'German spies' in de Gaulle's organization. The arrival of the Vichy cruisers at Dakar on September 14 was entirely fortuitous as far as Operation *Menace* was concerned. Equally fortuitous, in relation to Vichy's intentions, was the presence of British naval forces at Freetown effectually denying access to Libreville, since these British forces had not been sent there for that purpose. West Africa had obviously become a theatre of war, but neither side knew what

[1] See sections 5 and 6 of Räder's report in *Führer Conferences on Naval Affairs*, Brassey's Naval Annual for 1948, pages 134 and 135.

the other intended to do about it. It was not knowledge of *Menace*, but ignorance coupled to anxiety about Equatorial Africa that induced Vichy, with German permission, to despatch its cruisers at this time.

Much of this could not, of course, be appreciated in 1940; but after the War, when the evidence—or the lack of it—was certainly available to Churchill, if to no one else, it may seem regrettable that the accusation against the Free French of having caused a leakage which had not in fact occurred should have been allowed to stand in the pages of a work accepted round the world as an accurate relation of fact. Many of those gallant Frenchmen against whom the accusation, however sugar-coated, was then levelled were to give their lives before the War's end; their protests were never heard; nor were the voices of survivors loud enough to refute a charge so firmly established and so widely disseminated.

* * *

For the rest the principal events concerning the Dakar expedition must be related in chronological sequence. In the first place: Who suggested the direct approach to Dakar? It was certainly not de Gaulle. He had the place in mind, but only as a distant objective to be reached after an initial landing elsewhere.

By mid-July, with his small forces gradually taking efficient shape, he was giving serious consideration to the problem of where best to take them. In his office at the new Headquarters in Carlton Gardens, to which the various sections of the Free French organization had recently moved, he explained his intentions to individual members of his staff before a large-scale map showing the great bulging coastline of West Africa. 'I do not know Africa at all,' he reminded one of them. 'But we have men with us here who do. And from what they tell me it would seem that this will be the best place to land: at Konakry.'

There were sound reasons for the choice. Konakry (in French Guinea) was little more than a hundred miles from the British base at Freetown; it had a small but efficiently organized port, an airfield, a line of railway leading inland some three hundred miles to the upper waters of the Niger. Opinion in Guinea appeared to be favourable to the Free French; it should be an easy matter to land and assemble the troops, put light tanks and transport ashore, erect aircraft. As soon as possible the move inland to the Niger would be made, thence down-stream to Bamako (French Sudan) from which the advance would be continued westward along the line of railway to Kayès close to the Senegal border. By this indirect approach Dakar would be threatened from the rear, and taken probably less by force than by persuasion. From a safe entry to the African continent the plan promised to yield, after a cautious opening, large dividends from a very small expenditure of armed force.

One important qualification had to be taken into account. To pro-tect Konakry during the landing and to block any subsequent inter-vention by sea from Dakar, a strong naval force would be required. This force must, inevitably, be provided by the Royal Navy.

The British view was more ambitious. The general idea of the pro-posed expedition had first been mentioned by de Gaulle to Churchill early in July, but with the Free French forces still embryonic, and the attitude of French Africa far from certain, discussion was premature. Later it was raised again by the Prime Minister's advisers on French affairs, by which time the situation, if it had not improved, was at least clearer. The North African problem was for the time being insoluble; the military leaders were now firm in their support of Pétain; the people, both white and African, were passively content to wait and see; the naval authorities, since Oran, were more actively hostile to Britain than to Germany. No forces sufficient to carry out an opposed landing could then be spared from Britain, nor, had they gained a footing, could they have maintained their positions against an un-friendly garrison spurred to open hostility by Vichy and its German masters. On the other hand, in the East African sphere, Djibouti and Madagascar were not of immediate importance in the War, and to the objection of distance was added the dissuasive argument that both dependencies were likely soon to break with Vichy of their own accord —as the Chad province had already done, as Equatorial Africa was then about to do. Thus, by a process of elimination, the logical choice became the West Coast port with its docks, its big-gun forts, its well-equipped airfield and its dominant position at the 'narrows' between North and South Atlantic. 'My mind,' Churchill wrote, 'naturally turned to Dakar.' Not unnaturally the mind of the enemy also turned that way.

As usual, the Prime Minister moved fast. A proposal for a Free

French landing in Africa was put before him at the beginning of August; on the 3rd he approved it; on the 4th the Chiefs of Staff Committee considered the plan in detail; on the 5th the War Cabinet approved their suggestions; on the 6th he asked de Gaulle to come to Downing Street to discuss the result; on the 7th he presided over a meeting of the Chiefs of Staff Committee, at which it was decided that the Free French should be landed *at Dakar*. Well might Churchill write subsequently: 'I thus undertook in an exceptional degree the initiation and advocacy of the Dakar expedition.'

This sudden decision to make the direct approach had not gone unquestioned. De Gaulle had expressed serious doubts of its wisdom on first hearing it proposed by Churchill on the 6th and had only agreed to it, at a second meeting, after considerable hesitation. Nor had the Chiefs of Staff favoured it in their first report; in fact they had tacitly excluded it by stipulating that, except for the naval escort and some of the shipping, the force must be entirely Free French—of a strength, therefore, of no more than some 3,000 men—and that it should be landed, after inter-French negotiations, only at some West African port where there would be no effective opposition. At Dakar some opposition seemed certain: not only was the new Governor (Boisson) strongly pro-Vichy, the naval authorities, mindful of Oran, had recently been incensed by the torpedo-attack on the battleship *Richelieu* (July 8, part of Operation *Catapult*), which, if it had caused serious underwater damage, had not impaired the firing of her 15-inch guns; and there were other warships in the port, notably submarines.

What overcame de Gaulle's reluctance was not the Prime Minister's eloquent enthusiasm for the project, but two rather more solid arguments. In the first place it was now clear that the British, at Churchill's behest, were bent on obtaining possession of Dakar and would devote to its capture relatively large naval and land forces; and it would therefore be highly desirable that, to assert French sovereignty and if possible to avoid bloodshed, the Free French should go in ahead and attempt a peaceful negotiation. In the second place it was plain that the British naval forces allotted to the expedition would not be able to remain in West African waters for more than a very limited period, since at this crucial time the majority of the vessels would be urgently needed for service elsewhere. If, then, de Gaulle were to insist upon the Konakry landing and the indirect approach he might well find, once the British naval escort had left and his own forces had marched inland, his unprotected rear open to attack by warships from Dakar. On the other hand, whatever the outcome of the direct approach it would probably involve, by negotiation or by sterner action, the elimination of pro-Vichy naval forces in the vicinity, thus leaving the way open to subsequent landings at Konakry or elsewhere in West Africa. But it was nevertheless somewhat against his better judgment that de Gaulle gave his approval to Operation *Menace*.[1]

Once he had agreed, however, he threw himself unreservedly into the task of planning and preparation. Raising few objections to British proposals, he pressed only for speed and still greater speed in the execution of the design, knowing full well that with every day that passed Vichy's authority at Dakar must be the more firmly established, Vichy's defensive measures the more certainly taken. Delays even when unnecessary were unavoidable, but they were also cumulative, leading to changes of detail and thence to further discussion and additional delay (whilst, for instance, ships of appropriate tonnage and requisite speed were sought, moved and loaded) until it became evident that the expected date of arrival off Dakar—August 28—would in fact be no better than the probable date of departure from Liverpool.

In one direction, the re-equipment of the small Free French Air Force, the delay was an advantage. For the approach to the African coast and the landing operation British carrier-borne aircraft would be available, but once de Gaulle had been put ashore he would be dependent, for any action on French territory, entirely upon his own resources. Aircraft were an essential component, but since lack of spares ruled out the mixed and not very suitable collection at Odiham an appeal had to be made to the Air Ministry authorities who were able to supply six *Blenheims* and a dozen *Lysanders*, together with guns, ammunition and supplies for three months' operations. Given the pressing needs of the time, given also the very small number of Free French airmen, the supply might be considered generous; but it is not in the nature of keen young airmen to be satisfied and presently

---

[1] At the start it had been named Operation *Scipio*. Some person in authority had then remarked that Scipio reminded him of Scipio Africanus and therefore of Africa, which was as good as telling everyone where the expedition was going. In consequence the more mysterious code-word '*Menace*' was bestowed. It was appropriate.

the fighter pilots were asking for more, passing their claims upward through staff channels until a note in de Gaulle's handwriting reached the Air Ministry: '*Le Général de Gaulle demande—trois avions "Hurricane."*'

It seemed so little to ask that not until a senior air-staff officer had been brought into the conference room at Carlton Gardens could de Gaulle be convinced that there simply were not any *Hurricanes* to be had. By way of encouragement the staff officer added, heartily but incautiously: 'Wait till October. Give you plenty then, if all goes well—be able to throw them into the sea.' To which de Gaulle very properly retorted: 'But I don't want to throw them into the sea. I want them to fly. Only three!' The fact remained that, with the battle over Britain rising to its climax and seaborne invasion pending, neither *Hurricanes* nor *Spitfires* could be spared for operations anywhere else in the world.[1] It was just as well, for already the training problems were next to insoluble.

It was, of course, unthinkable that the first the French airmen might see of their *Blenheims* and *Lysanders* should be when the crates were unloaded at an African port; yet, given the limitations of time and of language, it was not possible to send the air-crews to a British training unit or the ground-staff to a technical training establishment. By way of compromise Royal Air Force instructors were sent to Odiham with two of each type of aircraft, one of each for flying training, the other two for practice dismantling and reassembly by those who would have to erect and service them in Africa. No more than a fortnight could be allowed for this intensive training, all too short a period and only enough to add a measure of confidence to the French airmen's undoubted courage. Meanwhile, with time running out, another knotty problem was set to de Gaulle's small air-staff.

Initially it had been suggested by Churchill's advisers that, as an *hors d'œuvres* to negotiations at Dakar, pamphlets should be dropped over the town from carrier-borne aircraft; very late in the day it was further suggested that Free French representatives should be landed at the nearby airfield and that, for this purpose, the aircraft should be

[1] Curiously enough, both de Gaulle in Vol. I of his *Mémoires de Guerre* and Churchill in *The Second World War*, Vol. II, mention *Hurricanes* as having been allotted to the Free French for Operation *Menace*. In fact no fighters of any type were taken on this expedition.

French with French markings. The problem was to discover suitable aircraft. They had of necessity to be two-seaters at the least, yet small enough to fit into the hangar of the British cruiser that was to hurry them out to Freetown where they would be transferred to the *Ark Royal*, into whose lifts they must fit and from whose deck they must be able to take off. None of the machines at Odiham was usable; some were single-seat, others had too great a span and their wings could not be folded. De Gaulle's staff, searching through Air Ministry files, in the end discovered that a maintenance depot in Wales had in its keeping two crates containing French aircraft of uncertain type. Rushed by road to Odiham the crates revealed a pair of Caudron *Lucioles*—small biplane two-seaters with folding wings, originally intended for liaison work in Norway. Hurriedly assembled, they were flown to Scotland where they were taken on board HMS *Fiji*, into whose hangar they fitted snugly.

That shortly after putting to sea the *Fiji* was torpedoed and, seriously damaged, forced to put back to port where the *Lucioles* were transferred to another cruiser, *Australia*, added but one more delay to those now causing de Gaulle the most acute anxiety. The expedition sailed on the last day of August, some three weeks later than planned. In all probability it would reach its destination too late for an unopposed entry. News of success at Duala and Brazzaville had come in three days previously; and to this news Vichy would certainly react.

11. Dakar—Doubts and Delays

Experience shows me that, in an affair depending upon vigour and dispatch, the Generals should settle their plan of operations, so that no time may be lost in idle debate and consultations when the sword should be drawn. . . .

(General Wolfe, in a letter on combined operations, dated November 1757)

ON SEPTEMBER 13 the convoy containing the Free French and British forces was steaming south over a calm sea, heading for Freetown. By afternoon its position was approximately two hundred and fifty miles west of Dakar.

It was not a large convoy, half a dozen ships in two lines. *Westernland*, carrying de Gaulle, his staff and some 1,200 men of the Foreign Legion; *Pennland*, with about the same number of French troops, including the airmen; astern a supply ship. To starboard in line astern: three liners—*Sobieski, Kenya, Karanja*—conveyed the British supporting force consisting in the main of a brigade of Royal Marines, and equipment that included some light landing-craft. On either bow of the leading pair of ships was stationed a Free French escort vessel: *Commandant Dominé* and *Commandant Duboc*, each of 630 tons. Ahead steamed the 8-inch gun cruiser *Devonshire* wearing the flag of Vice-Admiral J. H. D. Cunningham, joint commander of the British forces with Major-General N. M. S. Irwin who sailed with him. The main naval force and the remainder of the store ships were to join the expedition at Freetown.

During the two weeks that had elapsed since the departure from Liverpool neither de Gaulle's staff nor his British liaison officers had been idle. Official handbooks on West Africa had been studied as well as the latest available Intelligence reports on Dakar, and almost daily staff meetings had been held to discuss in detail both de Gaulle's plan for the landing and that of the British supporting force should it be required. A meteorological analysis of weather likely to be encountered at this season was given careful attention.

In the end the plan agreed to by de Gaulle was substantially the same as that outlined by Churchill on August 6. The combined force would approach Dakar during the hours of darkness, de Gaulle's ships in the van. At dawn, while pamphlets were being dropped over the town, four Free French airmen would be flown off the *Ark Royal* to land at Wakkam, the Dakar airfield; they would parley with the local authorities and, if all went well, commandeer transport to take them through the town to the quayside where they would meet de Gaulle's emissaries. These emissaries, protected by the French tricolour and a white flag, would enter the harbour in a launch from the *Westernland*; they would be the bearers of a letter from de Gaulle to the Governor, Boisson, to whom they would be driven in the cars commandeered by the airmen. With de Gaulle broadcasting to the population on the Dakar wave-length and with the entire Franco-British naval force now coming over the horizon to display its strength, it was hoped that Boisson and his colleagues would come to a peaceable, if not wholly friendly understanding. If, on the other hand, they showed fight de Gaulle would land the Free French force at the small port of Rufisque, a few miles to the south, and march on the town. If serious resistance were encountered the British supporting force would be landed to the north, to march on Wakkam and take Dakar in rear, whilst the powerful naval squadron would close in menacingly, but not firing unless fired upon. Under this combined pressure it was regarded as certain that the place would be in de Gaulle's hands before nightfall.

To these sanguine hopes the British Intelligence reports, even more than those of the French, gave much encouragement. Up to the fall of France relations with Dakar had been close and cordial; since then they had, to some extent, been maintained through Bathurst scarcely a hundred miles to the south; and all the most recent information coming in during August had tended to show that as a whole the people of Dakar, including the garrison and many of the administrative officials, were anti-Vichy and only awaiting the arrival of Free French representatives to demonstrate their sympathy for de Gaulle. It may be that insufficient stress was laid upon the uncompromising rigidity of Boisson's pro-Vichy sentiments, but in any event it was not believed that he would be able long to resist the pressure of popular sentiment. Since the airmen at Wakkam were thought to be friendly, the only likely trouble-makers appeared to be in the naval units, more especially among the officers of the damaged battleship *Richelieu*. With the majority of the Free French, however, the conviction was now strong that, once the radio and pamphlet appeals had been made and the Franco-British naval force perceived, Dakar's welcome would be tumultuous.

De Gaulle, though he studied the reports and to a limited extent shared their optimism, was far from reassured at the expedition's leisurely rate of progress. Freetown, the essential assembly-point, would not be reached for another three days; two days would be spent there in coaling and in re-distributing troops and equipment; allowing three days for the return journey, Dakar would not be reached before the 21st at the earliest. What had seemed favourable in August might well be unfavourable towards the end of September; aircraft might have been flown down from Casablanca, pro-Vichy men brought in to stiffen resistance and provoke that armed strife he was so anxious to avoid. Left to itself Dakar would in all probability have offered no serious opposition, but he was well aware of Vichy's determination to stick to its shameful course. Of the lengths to which the military hierarchy would go to uphold its authority he knew from his own experience.

At the end of June he had received, through the French Embassy in London, an order from the Military Tribunal at Toulouse commanding him to appear before that court to answer 'for the crime of refusal to obey orders in the presence of the enemy', and informing him that a warrant had been issued for his arrest. This curious document, issued at Weygand's instigation, de Gaulle had returned through the French *chargé d'affaires* with the laconic reply that in his eyes it contained 'no sort of interest whatever'. In July the Tribunal, tacitly condoning the real 'crime in the presence of the enemy' which was that of the surrender contrived by Pétain and Weygand, proceeded to try him *in absentia* and to render without delay a verdict made inevitable once proceedings had been started. On August 2 the news had been made public: de Gaulle was condemned to death.

A minor blunder, compared to those errors of ever-increasing gravity into which Pétain was inexorably compelled by the first folly of desired submission, it served but to enhance the respect with which de Gaulle and his *poussière d'hommes* were regarded by their many sympathizers throughout the free world, French and English-speaking, whose opinion of Vichy could now hardly have been lower. De Gaulle himself received the news of the death sentence with his usual reasoned calm; he neither laughed it to scorn nor did he make it an occasion for violent protestations or eloquent appeals. At luncheon on the day of the announcement he confided to a friend that he did not think it was the Germans who had insisted upon the sentence: 'The men of Vichy were forced to pronounce it in any case, so as to bolster their policy and cover up their own evil actions.'

By way of reply, although the timing was no doubt unintentional, there had been published in London on August 7 the formal agreement between the British Government and General de Gaulle, initially suggested by him in his Memorandum of June 26. By this agreement de Gaulle was recognized, not in any sense as the head of a provisional government—he had never requested it—but as an independent Allied leader in 'supreme command' of a distinctively French force of volunteers subject to French discipline and only temporarily, and of necessity, supplied and financed by Britain. On August 24 an inspection by King George VI symbolically inaugurated the new Army of France.

The agreement had marked an important step forward, one that gave him and his associates a greatly increased authority and the power to deal with those colonial dependencies now joining or about to join the resistance movement. He was no longer without resources; he had something to offer. But he was under no illusions as to the size of his force, or of its fragility; the least set-back might destroy its morale, smash its unity. As the convoy steamed slowly on into the South Atlantic he was aware, too, of his isolation.

No news relative to West Africa, and Dakar in particular, had come in since the departure from England. Wireless silence had consistently been maintained; only the broadcast news bulletins had been received, and they had told chiefly of the intensified *Luftwaffe* assault on Britain, of the bombing of London, of retaliatory attacks on Berlin. Nothing else of immediate interest to the expedition was heard—until the afternoon of the 13th when the thunderbolt fell.

A BBC communiqué announced that two days previously, 11th, three Vichy cruisers had passed through the Strait of Gibraltar heading west.

Much more than the dismay that was felt by all his colleagues, de

Gaulle's worst sensation at this juncture was of his own impotence. Apart from the bare announcement he knew nothing; at the moment he could do nothing. With wireless silence still in force he could make no inquiry; only by Morse lamp could he communicate with Admiral Cunningham who had no instructions and who could not halt the convoy in daylight for an anxiously needed but probably fruitless conference. He must hide his impatience and wait for nightfall. Meanwhile, the convoy and its attendant flagship steamed steadily on to the south.

It was after midnight before Cunningham, at de Gaulle's urgent request, brought the convoy to a stop and, putting off from the *Devonshire*, came to the *Westernland* for a belated discussion at which de Gaulle expressed his anxiety in no uncertain terms. Hours earlier he had made known his opinion that, failing news from London of the whereabouts of the Vichy cruisers, the convoy should turn back or, if not the convoy, at least the *Devonshire* and any other warships in the vicinity, so as to deny access to Dakar which must be—obviously to the Free French, if not to London—the first port of call for the Vichy squadron. By now, however, Cunningham had broken wireless silence and presently received instructions from the Admiralty that accorded with de Gaulle's emphatic request. The discussion at an end, the boat put off from the *Westernland* and, a little later, de Gaulle staring through the night over an oily sea watched the *Devonshire* get under way, turn half-circle and, her wake gleaming, head away to the north. The Admiral was going to intercept. Twelve hours had passed since reception of the BBC's news bulletin.

Three days had gone by since the sighting of the Vichy warships from Gibraltar. This was the 14th. It would be evening before the *Devonshire* and other hastily summoned cruisers could reach the latitude of Dakar. In all probability the Vichy squadron would get there first. It did. But, although the news caused further dismay to the members of the expedition, the event was not decisive.

On the 17th the convoy reached Freetown and met the assembling supply ships, together with the powerful naval force: the 15-inch gun battleships, *Barham* and *Resolution*, the cruisers *Devonshire*, *Australia* and *Cumberland*, the carrier *Ark Royal*, a flotilla of destroyers. With additional French escort vessels, the armada presented an impressive sight; but, for de Gaulle and the Free French staff, the occasion was far from joyful. The views of the War Cabinet had just been received.

'His Majesty's Government', the cable from London said, had decided that Dakar was now 'impracticable', that the alternative landing at Konakry did not offer 'any chance of success', and that the 'best plan' was for de Gaulle to take his troops to Duala. To this the Free French reaction was immediate, violent, and unanimous. The London authorities, it was said—not without justice—had made a disastrous mess of things by letting the Vichy cruisers pass Gibraltar and now, demanding a meek acceptance of their failure, had nothing better to suggest than that de Gaulle should trot off to a place infinitely less important than Dakar and already in Free French hands. It was a suggestion they refused pointblank to countenance; and de Gaulle, though he said nothing to increase their annoyance, was bound to take their point of view into consideration. He might well believe from personal experience that those in London were more capable of honest stupidity than of Machiavellian cunning, but it was not easy to allay the suspicions of some of his followers that the whole affair had been planned in advance to please Pétain and get rid of de Gaulle—*perfide Albion* once again. Although he did not subscribe to such wild imaginings, it was not without resentment that he protested, by cable to Churchill, against the hasty decision to abandon the attempt to seize Dakar.

His arguments had not only the strength of courage and common sense, they had also the strong support of his colleagues, the joint commanders Cunningham and Irwin, who added their opinion that 'the presence of these three cruisers has not sufficiently increased the risks, which were always accepted, to justify the abandonment of the enterprise.' And it was this audacity, more than any reasoning, that convinced Churchill. The War Cabinet's decision was reversed. On the 18th authority was given for the expedition to go ahead.

On the 19th and 20th a series of events occurred at sea that, although their significance does not appear to have been appreciated in London, justified de Gaulle's view that action at Dakar had become essential whatever the risks, and in British as much as in Free French interests. The three Vichy cruisers—*Georges Leygues, Montcalm, Gloire*—together with a fourth cruiser, *Primauguet*, stationed at Dakar before their arrival, and the supply ship *Poitiers*, all steamed out into the

Atlantic, heading *south*. A suspicion already formed was confirmed: no leakage of information had brought the ships to Dakar, Libreville was their destination. Libreville and the regaining for Vichy of Equatorial Africa. Or so it seemed to de Gaulle, whose view it was that the Vichy squadron should be drawn down towards Freetown where, in the presence of overwhelming Allied power, it could be persuaded either to join the Free French or to accept honourable terms and an escort to Martinique. Doubtless this view would have been agreeable to the Admiralty, but as luck would have it the previously ordered interception took place rather too soon, so that the French ships were headed back to the north. Nevertheless, swift action by British cruisers was in part successful: the *Poitiers* scuttled herself, the *Primauguet* accepted escort to Casablanca, and the *Gloire*, having suffered a machinery breakdown, was similarly escorted back to the Moroccan port. Alone the *Georges Leygues* and *Montcalm*, eluding pursuit at high speed in a rain-squall, returned to port at Dakar.

From this it was appreciated by the leaders of the expedition that, with two cruisers sent back and two allowed in, the *net* gain to Dakar was now only one cruiser and three destroyers. No doubt these vessels would have brought a considerable number of embittered men ready to fight the Allies in the mistaken belief that they were doing their duty to France; but, were Free French persuasion to fail, the naval and land forces gathered at Freetown, of whose existence Dakar still had no certain knowledge, would be ample to overcome resistance. Moreover, the news reaching de Gaulle, principally from Bathurst, was firmly to the effect that the original garrison was lukewarm in its support of the Governor and that resistance would be brief. Thus, in the opinion of all concerned, the attempt must be made as planned.

On the eve of departure, however, Boislambert arrived unexpectedly from Duala, by air from Lagos. What he had to tell de Gaulle was far from reassuring. From his own sources of intelligence he had received detailed information of the trend of opinion in official circles at Dakar, and it was his conviction that, unless the expedition were delayed until a party of Free French agents could be sent to win over the officers of the garrison and some of the more prominent officials, the defence of the place would be stubborn. Postponement for at least a few days was essential in his view if de Gaulle did not wish to have a prolonged and costly fight on his hands.

This candid and forceful opinion confronted de Gaulle with an unenviable choice. If he went ahead at once he might fail, and failure now might do irrevocable damage to the cause of resistance. If he postponed the sailing-date the expedition might never start at all, since it had been laid down from the outset that British naval support could only be made available for the very limited period of a specific operation. In the Atlantic there was a grave shortage of destroyers; at home additional cruisers might be needed at any moment to repel the invasion attempt; in the Mediterranean the aircraft-carrier was required even more urgently than the battleships. No large naval force could be allowed to lie idle in the distant waters of a West African port.

He faced the issue squarely. To relinquish naval support was out of the question; whatever ensued at Dakar, the Vichy warships could not be permitted to remain there, undisturbed, to resume at leisure their interrupted voyage to Libreville. Boislambert and three volunteers he sent ahead; by air to Bathurst, thence by launch to the neighbourhood of Dakar; they would have barely two days in which to pave the way for a peaceful entry.[1] On the 21st the expedition sailed from Freetown.

In the events that followed, it was not the Vichy naval squadron that, as Churchill was to put it, 'sealed the fate' of Operation *Menace*. Another factor intervened; one which none had foreseen and which was, on the basis of information supplied, unpredictable.

---

[1] Hardly had they begun work at Dakar when Boislambert was arrested and thrown into prison. Taken back to France, he was tried by Vichy and given a long term of imprisonment; it was two years before he could contrive to escape to North Africa where he rejoined de Gaulle.

12. Three Days' Skirmish

'To know when to retreat. And to dare to do it.'
(Wellington, on the attributes of a great commander)

AT FOUR in the morning of September 23 the lift warning-bell rang in the *Ark Royal* and, within a few moments, the first of the two *Luciole* aircraft appeared in outline upon the flight deck. It was still dark, a calm morning with a clear sky overhead but the horizon obscured by mist. Close by, the black forms of escorting destroyers showed faintly. The course was northerly, the distance from Dakar some twenty miles.

The air operations, with which the *Menace* plan was now to be opened, were of considerable importance both for what they were intended to achieve and for the early information they would give concerning the sentiments of the French at Dakar. It had been agreed with de Gaulle's staff that a first, British, aircraft would be flown from the *Ark Royal* before dawn to scatter leaflets over the town, that a second would follow immediately to take station over the Wakkam, airfield to observe and report, and that then the two *Luciole* machines each carrying two Free French officers, would leave the *Ark* to land on Wakkam at first light. These four men, unarmed, would at once go into the hangars to see if 'the natives were friendly'; and, all being well, they would come out again without delay to place upon the edge of the runway canvas strips denoting 'Success'. The patrolling aircraft would report back by wireless to the *Ark*, from which a succession of aircraft would next be flown with a total of twenty Free French airmen, also unarmed, to be deposited on Wakkam. While some helped the pro-de Gaulle faction to gain control of the airfield and of the local cable and wireless station, others would commandeer those cars in which they were to drive into Dakar to meet the emissaries coming in from the sea. A great deal therefore depended upon the reception accorded to the first four of the Free French.

At the start all went smoothly. Well before daybreak a *Swordfish*[1] rolled forward, roared down the deck, lifted, and turned into the night with its bundles of leaflets and tricolour streamers. A second *Swordfish* followed; climbed and circled to its observation post over Wakkam. The engine of the first *Luciole* was warmed up; her pilot and

[1] This single-engine biplane, torpedo-carrier and maid-of-all-work, was long and affectionately known as the 'Stringbag'. It could carry, with a squeeze, three passengers.

passenger climbed in; the second was wheeled into position. There were some anxious moments, for neither of the French pilots had flown off a carrier before, neither was trained for night flying, neither had ever handled a *Luciole*, nor had flown at all for many weeks. Anxiety, however, was quickly dispelled as each aircraft in turn took off with ease, turned away, and headed for the land. Over Africa it was just beginning to get light. At sea the mist was thickening.

Some twenty minutes later, with a score of French airmen lining up on the flight-deck, the first signals came in from Wakkam. Both *Lucioles* were approaching the airfield. At zero-hour to the minute they landed. A short interval of uncertainty dragged by; then came the welcome news. The four men had gone into the hangars; had reappeared; had laid out the 'Success' strips. From the *Ark Royal* the first passenger-carrying *Swordfish* had already taken off, others now followed in quick succession; by the time the fourth was rolling down the deck the first was going in to land at Wakkam. Signals made by the patrolling aircraft reported a safe landing and the depositing of the three passengers; the second *Swordfish* was just coming in; all was well.

Within seconds the whole situation was changed. A disturbing report from above the airfield announced that French fighters were taking off. A second report added that, although the 'Success' strips were still in position, fire had been opened from the ground. Moments later a third message announced that the 'Success' strips had been removed and that the passenger-carrying *Swordfish* were heading out to sea, pursued by the French fighters. The *Ark Royal*, reporting to the flagship, *Barham*, made the concluding signal: 'All aircraft recalled. Further departures cancelled.'

These events, reported to de Gaulle in the *Westernland*, marked the total failure of the first operation of the day. There would be no taking over of the airfield or of the cable and wireless station, no transport to meet the Free French representatives at the quayside, and no element of surprise in the subsequent operations. Those in control at Dakar had been alerted and some at least had already shown their firm determination to resist de Gaulle's arrival.

In the meantime another part of the plan for a peaceful occupation had been adversely affected by chance. At six o'clock de Gaulle had broadcast (from the *Westernland*) his proclamation to the people of Dakar and, telling them that he had come to protect the place against German domination, had mentioned that he was supported by very considerable Allied forces. At this the inhabitants, as well as their Governor, were expected to throw open their windows to the morning air and to see, across the bay and stretching to the horizon, the battle-ships, the cruisers and destroyers, the aircraft carrier, liners and trans-ports—and the freighter bearing gifts of food—in all some thirty-five vessels. This had been Churchill's vision. But here, as with the epic sung in ancient Greece, Apollo was on the side of the Trojans. The mist, steadily thickening since dawn, was now a dense sea fog. Not one of the impressive fleet was visible from the shore.

Nor, though the fog was less dense in the harbour, did fortune accompany de Gaulle's emissaries. Their two launches, each bearing a white flag beside the French colours, moved safely by the guns on Goree Island, passed between the breakwaters and, turning to port, brought up alongside the landing quay. Four Free French officers—among them Thierry d'Argenlieu and young Bécourt-Foch[1]—at once went ashore and, to the officer in local command, announced that they were bearers of General de Gaulle's letter to Governor Boisson. With evident reluctance the local officer refused to allow either the letter to be delivered or the party to remain, and presently called out to sum-mon the harbour guard; with the result that the Free French repre-sentatives had no course open to them but hastily to re-embark. As their launches moved out into the harbour, still plainly displaying the flag of truce beside the tricolour of France, machine-gun fire was opened upon them from the quayside and two officers, d'Argenlieu and Captain Perrin, fell seriously wounded. An act of rare stupidity, it disclosed the abasement to which the Vichy régime was now com-mitted, for its servants would never have dared to open fire had the national flag been that of Germany.

Even as this avenue of negotiation was closed, unhappy events were gradually developing at sea. Determined not to be baffled by the fog, Cunningham had led his squadron into the bay in support of the Free French vessels. But the move, designed to let Dakar see both the strength and the peaceable intentions of the Allied fleet, was defeated by the fog; less than two miles from the shore the ships were still invisible to the town. Time passed while the leading ships continued

[1] Grandson of Marshal Foch. Captain and pilot in the French Air Forces. Killed in action over North Africa in 1942.

to steam slowly through the mist that severely restricted any further operations, until, towards ten o'clock, first a destroyer and then the *Barham* were sighted from the fort on Goree, which at once opened fire with its batteries of 9·4-inch guns. The fire was described by eye-witnesses as 'extremely accurate', yet with shells falling in profusion about the ships none was hit and Cunningham was able to maintain his course and station whilst inquiring of Boisson by wireless why he was being shelled. So far, he pointed out, not a shot had been fired by either the British or the Free French, but: 'If you continue to fire on my ships I shall, regretfully, have to reply.' To which Boisson answered: 'Withdraw twenty miles to seaward, or fire will be continued.'

And continue it did. To the persistent banging of guns on Goree there was now added the deeper detonation of heavier weapons as the damaged *Richelieu*, shifted from her berth by tugs, brought two of her 15-inch guns to bear. With the fog lifting momentarily, one of the Goree guns presently scored a hit on the cruiser *Cumberland*, the shell penetrating the engine-room, killing a number of ratings, and forcing her to withdraw from the action; and at about the same time minor damage was inflicted upon two destroyers. To this Cunningham replied with the 15-inch guns of the *Barham* and *Resolution*, but with the fog thickening again and heavy French fire continuing he soon found it necessary to open the range; a wise decision for Vichy submarines had been reported in the vicinity of the British ships. All firing then died away.

Towards noon it was agreed between de Gaulle and the joint commanders that the planned landing should be made by Free French troops at Rufisque, the small port some three miles to the south-east of Dakar harbour. Escort vessels were sent forward and the troop-ships ordered to steam towards the coast, near which they were to await the arrival of two British destroyers before commencing the disembarkation. Apart from these two British vessels in support, the operation was still intended to be entirely Free French; no British troops would be landed there or elsewhere, and de Gaulle would be in command. It was mid-afternoon when the attempt was made.

Concerning the weather two points must be noted. First, the meteorological analysis, so carefully studied during the outward voyage, stated unequivocally that at this season and on this stretch of coast conditions would be stable and fair. Blue skies and calm seas were forecast, with occasional brief rain squalls, a chance of thunder, and

some swell from the south-west causing surf on the exposed beaches—
nothing else. 'Fog' was not so much as mentioned. Secondly, whereas it
had for many years been popularly supposed in Britain that a German invasion when it came—and at this very moment it was expected—would
be attempted under cover of a fog that would hide it from the British
fleet, expert naval opinion had always held that such an operation was
impracticable. Both French and British naval officers were to observe,
that afternoon off Dakar, that the word 'impossible' is sometimes justified.

As the hour for the landing approached the fog thickened until,
looking down from the bridge of the leading troopship, the very
surface of the sea became invisible. The shallow-draught Free French
escort vessels, having lain close inshore earlier in the day, were able,
after some hesitation, to locate the jetty at Rufisque; but the troopships,
less handy and drawing far more water, were chary of closing the
unseen coast with its fringe of shelving sand. Behind them the destroyers waited, standing off, fearful of collision; whilst the main fleet,
after its withdrawal of late morning, lay many miles out, still enshrouded by impenetrable mist and unable to give guidance. Uncertainty grew
and with it confusion. A vessel of the intended landing party asking
for assistance from the fleet in fixing her position was given bearings
that, had they been accurate, would have placed her several miles
inland. Nor, at the critical time, was the *Ark Royal* able to give help;
more than twenty miles to westward of the nearest point of land she
could barely make out the grey shapes of her escorting destroyers; had
her aircraft flown off they could hardly have found their way back
through the murk to a flight-deck indistinguishable from the sea.
Over the high land at Wakkam, however, visibility was just good
enough for the Vichy-French to be able to operate aircraft and, even
as the troopships nosed their way uneasily towards the coast, a Glenn-
Martin bomber was heard, and briefly glimpsed, overhead. At about
the same time a faint breeze swayed the curtain of fog and disclosed to
the anxious watchers in de Gaulle's vessels the unmistakable outlines
of two Vichy warships, thought to be the cruisers *Georges Leygues*
and *Montcalm*. Although these alarming apparitions, by air and by sea,
were almost instantly lost to view the situation of the troopships now
seemed precarious, for the British fleet, as uncertain of its own position
as of that of the Free French, could not be counted upon for

protection. It may have been that the Vichy cruisers were themselves in some doubt of their whereabouts, since they neither challenged nor opened fire; and, once they had vanished, the Free French vessels might well have proceeded on their course had it not been for the blank wall of fog blotting out all sight of the land close to which they were to lower the boats, their own deep draught preventing them in any event from entering the harbour at Rufisque. Waiting, almost stationary, there came to them from the east a clatter of small-arms fire.

Some time after three o'clock the escort vessel *Commandant Duboc* entered the little port and, tying up, put a small party of *Fusiliers Marins* ashore. A surprised and excited crowd began to assemble, some running down to the water's edge, when fire was opened upon the ship from a battery of light artillery. Hit by a shell on her upperworks, the *Duboc* suffered a number of fatal casualties; but as soon as fire was returned the Vichy battery fell silent. A body of Senegalese troops then let off a few rounds of machine-gun fire at the landing party, but they too ceased their fire the moment it was returned. No more than a token defence, it seemed evident that few of the local garrison—as distinct from senior Vichy officers and the Governor in Dakar—had much heart for a fight in which the opponents were their own compatriots. Tending her wounded, the *Duboc* waited in port for the troop reinforcements that, had they arrived, might perhaps have marched straight into Dakar.

In the *Westernland*, meanwhile, de Gaulle had been receiving Cunningham's signals reporting the proximity of the Vichy cruisers—a few shells from which would have sent the entire Free French Force to the bottom—and the fleet's inability to move in support. It was now past four-thirty, the light was beginning to fail; in little more than an hour it would be dark, and night would only add to the dangers and uncertainties. Not Vichy's misguided resistance, but the obliterating fog, had won the day. De Gaulle's decision to withdraw seaward was eminently sound.

*   *   *

Sea fog being so unusual a feature of these regions, it was hoped that there would be no recurrence when at dawn on September 24 the horizon was clear. Spurred by a wireless message of Churchillian pugnacity, an ultimatum had been sent during the night to Boisson; the joint commanders stating that the Navy was going to destroy the forts and that the troops would then land to occupy Dakar. But with the broadening of day the mists rose again and it was in steadily decreasing visibility that the bombardment was begun at a range of about eight miles. Aircraft were able to co-operate for a time and good results were observed, hits being scored upon forts and warships; but none of it brought satisfaction to the *Ark Royal*; she was losing men and machines. From the start her air-crews, in *Swordfish* and in *Skua* fighter-bombers, had obeyed strict orders not to attack French aircraft. The Vichy airmen acted under no such restraint.[1]

During the forenoon the mist thickened steadily until it became evident, given the previous day's experience, that the landing attempts must again be postponed. A slight improvement allowed the bombardment to be resumed in the afternoon, but fire from the forts was still heavy and two-gun salvoes from the *Richelieu* were straddling the *Barham* which presently sustained minor damage from shell splinters. Eventually, with the fog closing in more densely than ever, firing had perforce to cease and the ships stood out to sea.

In the evening the *Westernland* drew near the flagship and de Gaulle came on board to confer with the joint commanders. Although the persistent fog had damped the spirits of all, further plans were keenly examined. To Cunningham, as to General Irwin, it was plain that even were the weather to improve on the morrow the forts would still have to be reduced and the *Richelieu* silenced before the landings could take place, since the only suitable beaches in the immediate vicinity, either at Rufisque (for the Free French) or to the north of the Dakar peninsula (for the British land force), were covered by the guns either of the forts or of the Vichy warships. He therefore proposed to resume the bombardment on the following day and to continue it until the Dakar guns had been silenced when, in all probability, the Governor would come to terms.

To this de Gaulle opposed a reasoned argument. He agreed that, since the disembarkation from open boats—and, in the case of the British force, from a few small landing-craft—precluded the putting ashore of all heavy equipment, artillery and transport, the Dakar forts must first be demolished and the Vichy warships silenced. But to do this, in the light of the determined resistance of Boisson and his naval

---

[1] They were using Curtis fighters that, together with Glenn-Martin bombers, had been convoyed across the Atlantic largely by the Royal Navy. Too late to fight the Germans in 1940, obsolete by the end of 1942, this was their only action.

associates, would require a more protracted and even heavier bombardment than hitherto; and, given the unavoidable inaccuracy of naval gunfire at ranges between ten and twelve miles, it was certain that a high proportion of 15-inch shells aimed at Fort Manuel, on the seaward side of the town, and at the *Richelieu*, close to the waterfront, must fall upon the place itself, killing numerous inhabitants and ruining their homes. It was hardly likely that devastation would encourage Free French supporters or induce a friendlier frame of mind among the followers of Vichy; when at length the troops were landed the crews of disabled warships and survivors from the battered forts might well offer in their despair an embittered and long-drawn resistance. On both sides casualties would be heavy.

It was the very situation which de Gaulle, in the initial stages of planning, had resolved to avoid at all costs. Had it been possible to put the whole of his small force ashore on the first day, then despite the chilling reception of the early morning it seemed highly probable that the Foreign Legion battalions could have marched into Dakar against only light opposition; and with the town in his possession the Vichy warships, unsupported from the land, blockaded from the sea, would have been compelled to accept honourable terms. Fog and the inconclusive but damaging bombardment of the second day had affected the situation adversely; because with Boisson and the naval commanders determined, on repeated instructions from Vichy, to fight on to the end it was certain that the landings would be strongly opposed. There would be a hotly contested battle, at the end of which the British would no doubt be able to make themselves masters of the place, but only at the cost to Dakar of much bloodshed. Neither de Gaulle nor his followers had ever supposed that the road back to France could be travelled without the letting of French blood by French fighting men; but were they, at the first step, to stamp death and partial destruction upon a fair French colonial settlement then the road might be long indeed. The terms 'national unity' and 'liberation' would be given so derisory and cynical a twist that the goal might never be reached at all.

It was, as always with de Gaulle, a logical and commonsense argument; but there was more to it than that. The heart reasoned as well as the mind. To the British—who had suffered numerous casualties at the hands of those from whom they had expected, if not a delighted, at least a pacific reception—it might appear that the defenders of

Dakar were no more than a lot of obstinate pro-Nazis who, at a dangerous moment in the War, must of necessity be eradicated. To de Gaulle they were still Frenchmen. Even now many would wish to join him could they but break away from those so blindly obedient to a servile authority. Compassion joined with reason to bid him suggest that, to spare French lives, the shelling should be stopped. The expedition should withdraw to concert a new plan; the Free French might be put ashore at some safe place—perhaps Bathurst—to deploy their strength, their transport and artillery, their light tanks and aircraft, to march inland and, allowing time for their agents to influence opinion, to strike at Dakar from the landward side a rapier thrust more effective than the bludgeon of bombardment from the sea.

To these views the joint commanders listened with sympathy. But that night, when de Gaulle had gone back to the *Westernland*, they found that they were unable to follow his advice. Sound though it was, their orders were explicit: the expedition had been directed to Dakar and nowhere else; in fact it had been specified that no other point was to be considered. To put de Gaulle ashore elsewhere would require authority from London; they had no power to detain the fleet or the British land force for any alternative operation. On the other hand, the War Cabinet's instructions were formal and Churchill, in a message received at noon on the 23rd, had made them imperative: 'Having begun, we must go on to the end. Stop at nothing.' Thus, *even without de Gaulle*, the British attempt to bring Dakar to terms must continue. Early on the 25th, the first clear day since the operations had begun, the bombardment was resumed.

It was not long before a new and final misfortune befell. At about nine o'clock, in bright sunshine, the battleship *Resolution* was torpedoed by a French submarine coming from Dakar. She did not sink, but the torpedo's explosion seemed to echo round the fleet like a command to cease fire. The *Resolution* heeled over to port; slowed, stopped, and was presently taken in tow by the *Barham*. The Free French transports and supply ships had already moved off; the British troopships followed, with their escort. Cruisers circled watchfully, destroyers screened and searched. Soon all were headed south, their guns silent. In the flagship a wireless message had been received from London suggesting that the enterprise be terminated; with this suggestion the joint commanders had concurred. Operation *Menace* was at an end.

13. Aftermath

. . . celui qui voit son rêve mort
Doit mourir tout de suite ou se dresser plus fort!
(*Chantecler:* Act IV, Scene vii)

Upon the *Westernland*, back at her old moorings in Freetown harbour, the unobscured sun beat down so fiercely that the fogs of Rufisque seemed distant as an unhappy dream, half-forgotten and scarcely imaginable. In the cabins the heat was stifling, on deck it was like a leaden hand laid across the shoulders. The ship herself lay silent, motionless. All those faint yet thrilling sounds of a vessel under way, the distant hum of machinery, the creak of plates and panelling, the wash and send of the sea, the stirring breeze of motion, had died with the death-rattle of the anchor's chain running out through a rusty hawsepipe, like the last links of a life without hope of resurgence. The very sense of vitality had departed; even her planks were lifeless to the tread. Her crew had vanished below deck, maybe they slept; her French passengers mysteriously reduced in numbers, or so it seemed, walked softly and rarely spoke, and then only in lowered tones, as though respecting the dead.

Dotted over the vast sheet of placidly gleaming water the vessels of the defunct expedition, the warships and the transports, lay as widely spaced as if they were now disdainful of each other's company. Along a good half-dozen miles they stretched, from the harbour mouth at the foot of Lion Mountain, with its red earth showing through the bright green scrub, upriver towards the steamy creeks and rank vegetation that marked the limits of the estuary. No smoke came from their stacks, no heartening wisp of steam. All rode passively at anchor like so many tethered nags, pensive, drowsy. From a distance there was no sign of life on board, and even from close to there cannot have been much visible activity for the clusters of dugout canoes—bearing those importunate but amiable sharks from the waterfront to dive without cease into the opaque water for tossed coins—had long since moved on to seek more lively victims in newly-arrived merchant vessels. At length only one remained, in proximity to the *Westernland*, a cheerful soul who dived mostly for the fun of it and who signalled his arrival each morning with the innocently ironical greeting: 'Happy Christmas!' He deserves a place in history, however small, for he alone brought mirth to those downcast by undeserved misfortunes and condemned to loiter in soul-wearying idleness through the torrid days of late September.

By de Gaulle those days were never to be forgotten. They seemed so unending, such a nightmare of black doubt, in which there flickered the baleful lightning of dissension among his advisers, British as well as French, that when at length they did end it seemed as if time itself had been stretched through the aggravation of inner conflict by physical discomfort. For in fact the days at Freetown were only three. The ships had reassembled in the harbour by the morning of the 27th; by the 30th de Gaulle had left by air for Lagos; the convoy was to follow immediately.

But so swift a conclusion, while it seemed to falsify that impression of listlessness throughout the fleet of transports, had not been reached without a silent struggle whose severity was accentuated both by imposed inactivity and the obligation to make haste. Within three days the past must be assessed, the present faced, the future decided; there could be no extension of the time limit. The very existence of the Free French movement was now at stake; the unity and purpose of the fighting force here assembled depended upon the decision of one man; and it was a decision to be made in the face of misfortunes that could only be endured in the mind.

Discussions there were, inevitably, and conferences in the *Westernland* called by Cunningham. But the recent unhappy events off Dakar were not recalled by de Gaulle, whose attitude at this time commanded once again the respect of all fair-minded British observers. He uttered no word of recrimination, initiated no fruitless argument to apportion blame for a reverse which could so largely be attributed to the unpredictable fog. The misplaced zeal with which the Vichy leaders had opposed negotiations might be a source of disillusionment; it was far more a source of enlightenment, a clear warning of the lengths to which the Pétain régime would go to protect interests which were, in fact, not those of France but of Germany. Only as a guide to future operations was the action at Dakar to be considered in detail; and, seen from this angle, it was evident that the failure had not been total. True, the declared objective—the occupation of Dakar by Free French forces—had not been reached; but the undeclared purpose—the neutralizing of the Vichy warships—had largely been accomplished. Tragic though the French naval losses might be, they had to be assessed for the new situation to be appreciated. In the course of the three days at Freetown they were fairly accurately established.

Of the warships at Dakar at mid-September two cruisers, it was recalled, had been intercepted and turned back to Casablanca and a supply vessel had scuttled herself. During the action from the 23rd to the 25th one destroyer and two submarines had been sunk, two destroyers damaged beyond repair, minor damage inflicted upon other vessels. The *Richelieu*, in addition to further underwater damage caused by near misses, had received a direct hit by a 15-inch shell, from which it could be said with certainty that she would stay unserviceable, tied up in Dakar harbour where her repair was out of the question. Two cruisers alone remained, but whatever their state of serviceability it appeared highly improbable that they would venture forth again; they had already been turned back once, a second sally towards the Congo would come as no surprise to the British warships based on Freetown which would certainly intercept any attempted move.

Equatorial Africa, then, was safe for the Free French. Vichy's attempt to intervene by swift naval action, authorized and encouraged by Germany,[1] had failed. Almost by chance a considerable success had been achieved.

The fact, coupled to the knowledge that ammunition at Dakar had been very nearly exhausted by the recent firing, led to the suggestion, courageous in the circumstances, of a second attempt upon the place; this time from either St Louis to the north or from some other small port to the south, perhaps Bathurst, possibly Konakry, or even, again, Rufisque. The suggestion was supported by the anger of the Free French at the manner in which they had been received, at the firing upon the flag of truce in Dakar harbour, upon the *Commandant Duboc* at Rufisque, and at the unprovoked attacks by aircraft from Wakkam. But to all such hopeful plans there was the one insuperable objection: neither the British naval squadron nor the land force would be available. They, the warships especially, could be spared no longer for operations likely to be protracted and involving the close blockade of

---

[1] See *Führer Conferences on Naval Affairs*. Räder's report to Hitler, September 6, 1940, paragraph 6.

Dakar. On the other hand, instructions from London to the Admiral offered escort, by the *Devonshire* and sufficient destroyers, to conduct the Free French to any safe port they might choose within reasonable range of Freetown.

Within reasonable time, too, as Cunningham insisted; his chief desire at this time being, as he expressed it, 'to put the French ashore and get away quickly'. It was a desire that met with the full approval of the Free French staff, since the troops, the Foreign Legionaries in particular, were becoming fretful at long confinement on board ship and the airmen, anxious to get to grips with Vichy, were ready to be put ashore at any point where they could erect and operate their crated aircraft. Some of the British staff suggested that the airmen might either be left at Freetown, to build their own base on the 'air-field' (so-called) upriver near the village of Hastings, or else be dropped off at Takoradi (in the Gold Coast) then being developed for aircraft supply to the Middle East. Both bases, however, were on British territory and at neither could the bulk of the Free French troops be accommodated. De Gaulle intervened with a decisive No; he refused to split his forces. He would take them all to Duala.

It then appeared that, although the British Government had suggested the destination and the Admiral had urged its advantages, no one at Freetown knew anything about the place, its port facilities, its crane installations or even the state of its estuary. The Dutch captain of the *Westernland* having wisely questioned whether there was sufficient water to allow the two big liners—his own ship and the *Pennland*—to pass over the bar at the mouth of the River Wouri, his doubts were passed on to the local naval authorities who were inclined to agree with them. But Cunningham's relief at having obtained agreement upon the destination was now such as to give the impression that the buoyancy of his spirits would alone be sufficient to float the vessels in. Without further ado the Free French convoy made ready to sail on October 1.

*　　*　　*

But, however protracted the conferences, however frustrating the forced renunciation of hopes of a return to Dakar, these were not the preoccupations that weighed most heavily upon de Gaulle. Nor did they reside in vain regrets, bitter though the taste of failure might be; if he could not wholly deny his thoughts, he did not allow them to rankle. There were other things, more deeply wounding than the bare facts of a military reverse for which he was less responsible than anyone, British or French, directly connected with the enterprise; things more cruelly calculated to shake his faith and to test, almost to breaking point, his strength of purpose.

That once the Allied expedition had withdrawn from Dakar the German propaganda machine in France should promote the minor events of a three-day skirmish to the level of a great naval victory was only to be expected. That Vichy should follow the example set by its masters, showering Boisson with countless telegrams of fulsome congratulations, was inevitable in the shameful circumstances of national enslavement. What was quite unexpected were the harsh criticisms of the Free French now suddenly voiced in the English-speaking press. In not a few British and many American newspapers the condemnation was so violent, the opinions expressed so unanimous, the information so detailed—and so false—that it was difficult for de Gaulle not to suspect a common origin: an influential source bitterly hostile to him and to his movement and even inimical to Churchill who was also, though less sharply, taken to task.

According to the published story, de Gaulle, first and foremost, was responsible for the whole disgraceful episode. He it was who had initiated the plan for the direct approach to Dakar; he who had thrust his ideas upon the British Government with an infatuated optimism that had persuaded Churchill against his better judgment; he who had overborne the opinion of the joint commanders and had insisted upon continuing the operation at a time when success was manifestly out of reach; he, above all, who by his own proud folly, and the careless talk of those irresponsible adventurers in his service, had caused the fatal 'leakage' that had brought the Vichy cruisers out. The fable of the public toast '*à Dakar*' was already gaining currency; and by many, wise after the event, the impression was given that 'everyone' had known beforehand of the ill-conceived expedition; only to Admiral North at Gibraltar, upon whom much blame for allowing the French cruisers to pass was later and most unfairly to be placed, had the secret not been 'leaked'. In America and, to some extent, in Britain the conclusion was inescapable: it was to be hoped that the British Government would have nothing more to do with one so reckless, so obstinate, and so unreliable, as General Charles de Gaulle.

Impotent at Freetown to reply or to protest, he might rise above these wild accusations with a clear conscience; they were none the less painful. He saw himself condemned not merely by such determined defeatists as Pétain, Weygand and the like, but by those whom he had come to regard, if not as friends, at least as dependable comrades in arms. Mockery, however personal and cruel, he could treat with a tolerant smile; ridicule was damaging to the cause. Caricaturists, writers in search of similes, might find in his gaunt frame, slender equipment and quixotic behaviour, a resemblance to the doleful knight of La Mancha setting forth upon some illusory quest, attended by a handful of scruffy and untrustworthy Sancho Panzas. Others, seeking analogies in French history, alleged a vaulting ambition worthy of a Bonaparte; not, however, of a Napoleon riding to victory, but of Louis-Napoleon landing at Boulogne. Some, pursuing the allegation of an ambition personal and political, descried a second General Boulanger and, the ages being not too dissimilar—de Gaulle would be fifty in November—recalled the chilling rebuff: '*A votre age, Monsieur, Napoléon était mort!*' Kindlier critics compared him to Cyrano de Bergerac, but to the advantage of neither; Cyrano was for ever throwing things away, his purse, his chance of patronage, his hopes of happiness; despite his romantic idealism he was an egoist: '*Ne pas monter bien haut, peut-être, mais tout seul.*' Such a man, however heroic, must be detrimental as an ally in modern war.

Curiously enough none of the inspired critics on either side of the Atlantic appears to have noted the far closer analogy to be drawn from another of Rostand's works; if they did, then perhaps they found it too favourable to de Gaulle. Thierry d'Argenlieu, re-reading *Chantecler* during the voyage out, had drawn attention to the many similarities—in plot and action, in characterization and speech—between the symbolism of the barnyard play and the drama of France. It was a comparison that, far from detracting, added glory both to the poet and to the patriot; the profundity of a dream was ennobled by the reality. All the personages were there, in life as in the play, the faithful and the fair-weather friends, the vain and the pompous, the mocking enemies and the croaking toads, all grouped about the central figure who proclaimed, in the blackest hour of the night, his simple faith that the sun would rise again. Only one character was lacking on the stage of actuality, the dangerous hen-pheasant of gorgeous plumage, beguiling, seductive. And at Freetown, for a while, even her part was briefly filled; but by male voices speaking, on cable forms, from London.

Far more serious than the outcry in the Press—likely to be no more than transient since it lacked substance—were the unpublished opinions emanating from influential and supposedly well-informed circles in Britain and said to represent the views of men in high places or close to the Government. These reports, unanimously hostile, were forwarded by some panicky busybody, whose identity is unimportant but whose malice seems certain, and brought to de Gaulle's notice. Their gist and purport were that the small Free French forces, having demonstrated their inefficacy at Dakar, should now retire from active operations; that de Gaulle as a Brigadier might continue to command them; but that the leadership of the resistance movement in London, henceforth more closely controlled by the British Government, should devolve on Admiral Muselier and General Catroux, whilst any new volunteers—and after Dakar they were expected to be few in number —would be absorbed into the British services. Lest de Gaulle should be putting his trust in Churchill—and he was—it was hinted that the Prime Minister, himself in a difficult political situation, might not be able to give any further support. The insinuation was obvious: de Gaulle must abandon all plans for independent action and 'go quietly'. The proffered naval escort to Duala was seen to be more in the nature of police escort for an unruly failure, a charlatan exposed, discredited and now discarded.

Even allowing that much of all this might be no more, as de Gaulle suspected, than a backstairs intrigue designed to bring pressure upon him for obscure political motives, the danger was real enough. He had no certain idea of the identity of his principal enemies; some, conceivably, might be found at the centre of his own organization. In London he might have uncovered their machinations, have fought back with the help of Churchill upon whose loyalty he counted and upon whose support he must continue to depend for so long as the resistance movement was based in Britain. From Freetown he could do nothing; while the future of the movement and his own fate as leader of Free France were being debated without him, he was held in inactivity, powerless to make himself heard. In his heart he might still have faith in the outcome of his self-imposed mission, might still believe in the moral and logical rightness of the path he had chosen to follow; but it could be that the burden of leadership was, after all, too heavy; perhaps, already, it had broken his back.

Never had he felt more alone. He had the sense of being trapped. These were British waters; across the harbour mouth lay British warships; in the flagship was a British Admiral, waiting impatiently to lead him away to a place to which he had no desire to go. About him were ranged the French transports, the troops in them silent, inarticulate, as impotent as he himself to make their voices heard by those who might even now be deciding their destiny. Dejected by failure but loyal almost to a man, they had, since Dakar, renewed their decision to stand by 'the General'; yet for all the action they could take to make their decision known they might as well be captives held in British prison-hulks. It looked like the end; as if all his plans and hopes and promises might now be bundled together, torn up, and tossed over the side of the *Westernland* to float down with other rotting detritus on the next ebb tide. Long years of frustration had taught him to an unusual degree to master his sentiments; but here in the blinding light of the unrelenting sun his thoughts were black and as near to despair as may be possible for a man of fixed resolve, immutably loyal to simple ideals of honour and honesty.

A stroke of good fortune released him and brought to a sudden end the seeming infinity of those three days. On the 29th a cable reached him from Nigeria. It informed him that his staunch adherent Colonel de Larminat was on his way from Brazzaville to Lagos where, in the course of a brief visit, he was to have discussions with the British military authorities on matters of common policy; de Gaulle's presence was urgently requested. That he was anxious to obey the summons goes without saying, and there can be little doubt that Cunningham would have been willing enough to help. The trouble was that de Gaulle wanted to reach Lagos on the very next day, the 30th, and that not the fastest destroyer in the fleet could make it in less than three days—the distance was 1,400 miles—and that none of the *Ark Royal*'s aircraft had the necessary range.

Quite unexpectedly, in the course of the 29th, one of the two 'Empire' flying-boats appeared over Freetown and touched down in the harbour. She was outward bound and carried no passengers. And so it was that shortly after dawn on the following morning de Gaulle, accompanied only by Courcel and one assistant, took off on the nine hours' flight to Lagos. He was to rejoin the convoy off Duala.

14. A Breath of Fresh Air

Having measured my task, I had to measure myself . . . and the
part that fell to me was solitude.

(De Gaulle: *Mémoires de Guerre*, Vol. I)

THE FIRST week of October, from the arrival at Lagos to the landing
at Duala, marks an important turning-point in the fortunes of Free
France. It was also to mark the beginning of a change in de Gaulle's
appreciation of the task that lay ahead and in his understanding of the
greater role he must perforce play in the political field, through the
months and the years to come, if his goal—not only the military
victory of France, but her restored standing in the eyes of the world—
were ever to be achieved.

The days at Lagos constituted a breathing-space; not a holiday, but
a period of relative relaxation in congenial surroundings; and physical
conditions had their usual effect upon mental outlook. To be away
from superheated confinement in the *Westernland* was as much of a
relief as to be freed from daily discussions with his staff and storm-
charged encounters with the Admiral, whilst the atmosphere at Lagos
was quick to restore a needful measure of self-confidence weakened by
painful reflections at Freetown. The improvement began from the
moment of his arrival.

The manner in which he was received was a model of tact and
courtesy. When the launch meeting the flying-boat had brought him
to the landing-stage in front of Government House, he found waiting
to greet him between two thin but glittering lines of armed guards the
Governor of Nigeria, Sir Bernard Bourdillon, the Chief Secretary
(Sir C. Woolley), the British military commander (General Giffard)
and his staff, together with de Larminat and other French officers.
Allowing that no national anthems were played—a gun-salute would
in any event have been ruled out in wartime—it was a reception that
might well have been accorded to a Head of State, certainly to a
prominent statesman or to a high-ranking personage of international
importance. He was given rooms in Government House; a formal
dinner and reception were arranged to which all local notabilities were
invited; on successive public occasions he was present at the Gover-

nor's side. Later during the five days of his visit he attended Anglo-French conferences on matters relating to joint colonial defence, at which he was able to co-ordinate Free French plans with those of the British staff and to offer detachments of his own forces to help man the northern borders against possible Vichy incursions.

Rather unexpectedly the forthcoming landing at Duala was also the object of official talks. For a warning message was presently received to the effect that, despite Admiral Cunningham's optimism, there would not, after all, be enough water to float the liners over the bar and up the river. The whole contingent of troops would have to be transferred to shallow-draught vessels at the river's mouth. An awkward problem, it was solved only by the prompt assistance of the Nigerian Government, ordering up half a dozen river steamers to meet the Free French convoy in Amherst Bay.

For a man less wary of self-conceit it would have been natural to see in these repeated expressions of amity a personal tribute, a demonstration of sympathy, of admiration for courage in adversity; and it is not given to all men to resist the flattery of pomp, the corrupting influence of personal acclaim. Certainly the warmth of his reception was not lost upon de Gaulle; he was not ungracious, and he was conscious that in the English country-house atmosphere of the Bourdillons' home the hospitality was genuine, the kindness without pretence. To his way of thinking, however, the tributes of respect were paid not to the man but to the Frenchman, one who was regarded less as a friend than as an ally of consequence; he was grateful for them, but only in the name of France—which is not to say that he stood too rigidly upon his dignity and never unbent. Indications of more buoyant spirits were not lacking; he talked more easily, the shy, fleeting smile came more readily to his lips.

Good news reached him at Lagos. Some of it had begun to come in even before the operations at Dakar; now more became known, together with amplifying details and additional information. First, Tahiti and the islands of French Oceania announced that they had deposed their pro-Vichy governor and joined the Free French movement; and a message from the New Zealand Government showed just how strong French public opinion could be when allowed to express itself freely: a plebiscite gave 5,564 votes for de Gaulle, for Pétain and the armistice 18. A few days later the Governor of the French establishments in India (Louis Bonvin) declared that the colonies—Pondicherry, Karikal, Yanaon, Chandernagore—had come over to de Gaulle. In mid-September the Ex-Soldiers' Association in the islets of St Pierre and Miquelon sent a cabled message, via Newfoundland, expressing their confidence 'in the final victory of General de Gaulle and his army' and ending, perhaps for the first time in history, not only with the traditional '*Vive la France!*' but also with '*Vive de Gaulle!*' Towards the end of the month a cable from the Governor of New Caledonia (Henri Sautot) announced the adherence of the colony to Free France, adding that the capital, Noumea, was beflagged with the tricolour bearing the Cross of Lorraine. Thus, in the Pacific, in India, in Africa, very considerable portions of the French Empire had rallied to the cause. Scarcely three months had passed since the first broadcast appeal.

On October 3 a cabled dispatch from Churchill brought news of a very different sort. The Vichy Ambassadeur in Madrid had approached the British Ambassador (Samuel Hoare) with proposals intended, according to Vichy, to re-establish friendly relations between the two countries, for which it was suggested that Britain should raise the blockade in favour of supplies to unoccupied France. By way of guarantee, Vichy declared that were the supplies to be seized by the enemy the Pétain Government would leave for Morocco and rejoin Britain in the War. To de Gaulle it appeared at once that the move was either a sign of despair at the consequences of the surrender policy or, far more probably, a cunning ruse.

Vichy was plainly alarmed at the secession of so many French dependencies, which it was powerless to prevent even by frittering away the remaining vessels of its fleet. The obtaining of a formal and friendly agreement with Britain would involve British recognition of Vichy and of its authority over the colonies; at one blow de Gaulle and the Free French would be eliminated. Worse still, if supplies on a large scale were permitted to enter France the agreement would bolster Vichy's power in the land and make things easier for the Germans. Much earlier de Gaulle had himself suggested measures of relief for France, now he proposed that these measures, strictly limited and carefully controlled, should be carried out by the Americans. In this sense he cabled his reply to Churchill.

Other reports reached him at Lagos, reports coming out of Vichy-France and North Africa and containing rumours of dissension be-tween the leading personalities in Pétain's entourage. Weygand's forthcoming departure from Vichy was cited as a case in point; by some it was believed that his appointment to the chief command in North Africa made probable his return to active participation in the war against Germany. De Gaulle smiled at this.

'Ah, I know my Weygand,' he said tolerantly. 'He'll not change sides yet; to do so would be to admit the wrong he did three months ago. But he is not so sure now which way the wind is going to blow. If he were quite certain of England winning the War, he might come over to our side—and then try to take charge.'

After a pause he added: 'That is a danger we shall have to expect—that those who are now actively opposed to us will want to change sides when things get better, and then try to take the place of those who never stopped fighting.'

In fact a paradox was now discernible, which was greatly to streng-then his position as sole leader of the Free French. Had his forces succeeded in occupying Dakar they could not have remained station-ary; reinforced from Dakar itself they would have moved up the coast. The move had already been outlined by Churchill:[1] '. . . as soon as de Gaulle has established himself there and in the place a little to the north[2] he should try to get a footing in Morocco, and our ships and troops could be used to repeat the process of "Menace", if it has been found to work, immediately and in a more important theatre. The operation may be called "Threat".' Had *Threat* then been successful—as after a successful *Menace* it was likely to be—Casablanca would have been in Anglo–Free-French hands, and it is more than probable that throughout Morocco there would have followed a general defiance of Vichy. Any intervention by the Germans would have cut through the armistice terms, provoking a still wider and more spontaneous change of heart and bringing over to the Allies a number of political personalities and military leaders. With British support and American supplies an Atlantic–North African front could have been set up two years ahead of time and, with it, a legally recognizable French Pro-visional Government. Of such a Government de Gaulle—although he

[1] In a minute to General Ismay, dated September 1.
[2] Presumably St Louis.

would doubtless have been awarded a high post in it—would not have been the supreme head.

Thus, whilst success at Dakar would in the end have forced him down, failure forced him up. Hostile propaganda, exploiting the failure, deterred the waverers; in North Africa the senior members of the armed forces harkened to Weygand's embittered condemnation of De Gaulle's expedition as a 'deplorable adventure' that had 'failed miserably'; inside France no one moved, no prominent personality either political or military tried to escape. To the Free French, therefore—to the slow-growing forces, to the colonial populations and their governors, to small but increasing numbers of the common people of France herself—there could be but one possible leader in the fight for the honour, the liberty and the greatness of the nation. The Pétain Government had already pointed to him with its sentence of death; now it named him with execration and, in the darkness reigning over a land inescapably involved in the German toils, incautiously turned the spotlight of publicity upon him. Whether they liked it or not Frenchmen everywhere became accustomed to the sound of his name.

The paradox thus disclosed by the reports reaching him at Lagos did not escape de Gaulle and did much to counter the dejection caused by the impressions from London received at Freetown. True, the developments, in so far as they were favourable, could only be long-term in their effect; there could be no sudden swing of opinion towards resistance in North Africa any more than in France. The Pétain régime was firmly established; the majority of its military leaders not in German prison camps regarded de Gaulle, as Weygand put it, as one 'in open rebellion against the legal government of France'. But in the long run two undeniable facts must surely prevail: the fact that the war against Germany was continuing, Britain was fighting back and Free France was her ally; and the fact that, named with scornful anger by the German press and radio, de Gaulle was regarded by the conquerors as an enemy and not, like Pétain, Laval or Darlan, as a useful and submissive tool. He had not sought his lonely pre-eminence; from the start he had shown himself averse to it; but no other pretender to leadership had made himself known, no legendary figure had arisen— no Clemenceau, no Gambetta, no heroine from Domrémy. In the cause of Free France his name alone had echoed round the world. To the widely scattered colonial dependencies as to the slowly-awakening few in France, 'de Gaulle' was no longer just the surname of a defiant military commander. Under the Cross of Lorraine, it was a symbol of distant victory.

* * *

For the journey to Duala, de Gaulle took passage in the *Commandant Duboc*, the little escort-vessel that had made the long voyage out from England and that still showed upon her upper-works the scars of Vichy gunfire at Rufisque. He left Lagos upon a day of storm. From a darkened sky the downpour was incessant, a gusty wind bent the tall trees along the waterfront, and beyond the breakwaters steep, yellowish rollers swept drearily over the Gulf of Guinea. The bright interlude was at an end, and the break in the weather seemed to presage the long struggle ahead.

Holding to the rail, de Gaulle watched the low-lying land drift astern until at length it was blotted out by the mist. Then, turning away to face the future, he went below to the trim cabin the *Duboc*'s captain had ceded to him. In a warship of such small dimensions cabin-space could not be other than limited, and the accommodation offered was much the same as that of a French sleeping-car compartment, which the cabin not too distantly resembled; as well as a bunk and a concealed wash-basin, there were a metal chair and a small folding desk. Upon the narrow flap of this desk he spread his papers and, throughout the greater part of the day while the little ship jumped, shuddered, and drove on into the storm, made the first draft of a document that was to become the charter of Free France in the War, and to mark his transition from combatant soldier to soldier-statesman. Through the porthole, as he worked, could be glimpsed at each roll a short stretch of turbulent water merging into spume and rain that called to mind a phrase of Descartes: 'I see myself as a navigator, enshrouded by a dense rain-squall, who is certain, if he but holds to his course, that the horizon will clear.' Just then the navigator's course was taking him farther away from France; on the meridian of Paris, he was more than two thousand miles distant from the capital—and none could tell how many years away from its liberation. He worked on steadily and, for the most part, alone. He had measured the task and he was not daunted by its immensity.

That he felt his solitude keenly was made plain that night. Wind and rain gradually abated during the latter part of the day, so that in the evening, after supper in the wardroom, he was able to go on deck to straighten up; there was little head-room below for so tall a man. Nor was there much room for any regular pacing of the quarter-deck encumbered with gear and fittings scarcely distinguishable in the darkness; presently, with one of his companions, he found a place to sit beneath the black, rain-stretched awning, where facing aft he could see, over the ship's stern, the faintly luminous wake rolling towards the still murky horizon. The lighter mood of the past few days had evaporated; when he spoke it was of those things which, at all times, lay uppermost in his mind: of France and her problems, present and future. He spoke calmly; yet it was with a measure of suppressed bitterness that he chanced to mention the apathy of those whose reputations had seemed to him a guarantee of uncompromising resistance to the enemy. At the end he paused; his cigarette glowed in the night like the spark of a sudden anger; then, quietly but with anguish, he added: '*Pour moi ce qui est terrible c'est de me sentir seul. Toujours seul.*'

It was the penalty of selfless ambition. The verdict had been given long ago, during the years of peace, when against the self-satisfied complacency of careerists like Weygand he had defied the military hierarchy. The sentence of solitude had been pronounced on the day when he had chosen between two opposing conceptions of loyalty and duty, between meek submission to an authority fallen into error and bold resistance to counsels of despair; between career, reputation, personal security, and the way of an outcast defying the majority in the name of principles logical, altruistic and enduring. Recent developments had confirmed the sentence: were he to stand at all, he must stand alone. Far from bowing under the weight of a criticism now almost universal, he raised his sights to a greater and more distant target: the leadership of a unified nation. For that purpose 'de Gaulle' must be more than a single Frenchman defying surrender-terms and fighting the invader, he must be the embodiment of the cause, of the principle of fidelity for which men would give their lives. Rising above self, he must personify the very spirit of France. And that the price would be loneliness he had long been aware.

The ideal leader in war 'is inevitably aloof, for there can be no

authority without prestige and no prestige unless he keeps his distance',
so he had written in the days of peace. That the burden might yet
'break his back' was a risk he must accept; for it must of necessity be
heavy and the journey seem interminable. No sudden victory could be
his; no stroke of genius could raise up France in the twinkling of an
eye. Years must pass and many fresh trials be withstood before the
cause could triumph; and at the end he would still be alone.

*　　*　　*

The very first of the new trials—albeit no more than a minor incident—occurred upon the following afternoon when, during an interval of brilliant sunshine, his ship steamed slowly into Amherst Bay.
The setting was worthy of romantic adventure; in the moist heat, the
air heavy with the presage of further storm, rocky islets overgrown
with dense vegetation shimmered above a sea like polished steel.
Ahead, the little port of Victoria seemed to float above the water;
beyond it the massive slopes of Mount Cameroon swept up to the
clouds. To the east, patches of swampy jungle broke the sea into
narrow channels and concealed the entrance to the broader river
leading to Duala; to the south, clear of the mainland, the glittering
emerald coast of Fernando Po rose sheer from the water's edge.

As the *Duboc* glided into the bay, de Gaulle, standing at the rail
forward, identified the ships of the convoy. Two British destroyers
guarded the approaches; farther in were the *Westernland* and *Pennland*,
behind them the supply ships and the smaller Nigerian steamers sent
to take the troops upriver. A little apart from the scattered group,
towards which she showed her stern as if contemptuous of her shabby
charges, the slim and graceful *Devonshire* lay at anchor, the Admiral's
flag drooping in the breathless air.

All seemed well, save for one thing: the ships lay idle, motionless
and silent. It was disagreeably reminiscent of Freetown. Not a launch
moved between the ships, no boats plied from the shore; when the
Duboc dropped anchor in the midst of the group nothing happened. No
signal flags fluttered, no Morse lamps winked. De Gaulle was puzzled;
he could see French uniforms on the upper decks of the two liners; why
had the troops not been transferred as arranged? By this time the supply
ships and the Nigerian steamers should have reached Duala.

Belatedly, a launch did put off from the *Westernland*. It bore three

Free French officers who, when presently they came on board the *Duboc*, looked unusually grave. An observer who saw the scene then enacted reported afterwards that it reminded him strongly of *Treasure Island*, with the three officers as a 'deputation' of mutineers come to tip de Gaulle the 'Black Spot'. They were, he related, perfectly respectful and polite, but obviously uneasy at having to admit—in answer to de Gaulle's direct question—their personal responsibility for halting the movement of troops to Duala. However, they found the courage necessary to give their astonishing reasons.

Embarrassment robbed their speech of dignified formality. They just didn't fancy Duala as a place, that was the long and short of it. They had learned from local authorities that it rained there more than anywhere else in the world: it was Mount Cameroon that did it, one of them explained turning to point towards the peak about which dark cloud masses were even then gathering. Rain, he added, would be bad for morale, because there would be nothing for the men to do since the whole colony had already come over to de Gaulle and was entirely peaceful; and what the troops wanted, more especially the Foreign Legion, was a taste of real fighting after the frustration of Rufisque. They would get none of it here, and so they didn't want to land. According to the spokesman for the 'deputation', they wanted to suggest another destination. After all, they had the ships, the escort, the necessary equipment; why not go on round the Cape and up the east coast, perhaps to Madagascar, or to Somaliland and Jibouti?

De Gaulle, his face expressionless, listened patiently until each had said his piece. Then, the moment they fell silent, he made his counterattack. He neither barked nor lectured; he made no gestures. In a voice barely raised above conversational level he pulverized that unhappy 'deputation' with simple facts and clear common sense.

They had the ships, had they? What about coal, and food, and fresh water? All were now short in the liners. Escort? What about the Admiral? He had orders to bring them thus far and no farther. Rainfall? No one was going to stop at Duala indefinitely; most of the troops would be moving on at once. As for fighting, there would soon be plenty of that, and first of all against Vichy forces at Libreville.

The observer reporting this noticed something else. In addition to the verbal assault, de Gaulle made a skilful move physically against the would-be mutineers. Motionless whilst they had been speaking, as soon as he commenced his reply he strode forward; advanced with long, measured strides, walking between and straight through them; so that they had first to stand aside, and then to follow so as to catch what he said. Down the ship's side he led them, so timing his argument that as he reached the final point he also reached the head of the companion ladder. There he turned to face them and, in suave almost friendly tones, gave the clearly audible command that the transfer of troops should start forthwith.

'*Messieurs*,' he ended, polite but frigid, 'I will not detain you any longer.'

The audience being plainly at an end, there was nothing the crestfallen three could do but salute, turn about, and get quickly down the ladder into the launch that had brought them. The simple arguments and tactful exercise of authority had recalled them to their duty in such a way that they found mingled with their respect a measure of affection, faint but enduring. Looking back as the launch sheered off from the *Duboc*'s side, they could see him standing at the rail, a spare, somewhat austere but not forbidding figure, unyielding, solitary. Behind him the slanting sunlight shone through the folds of the tricolour at the stern and over his shoulder could be read upon the ship's upperworks the legend: *Honneur et Patrie*. No one seeing him then could doubt the quality of his leadership. Without him to show the way and to direct their steps it seems unlikely that many of his followers would have got much farther along the road back to France than the swamps of an equatorial African river.

*   *   *

On the following day he reached Duala and stood once more upon French soil.

Leclerc met him at the quayside with a guard of honour, and conducted him through the town to the Governor's palace on the leafy promontory overlooking the river now filled with incoming supply ships. The whole place was gay with flags and, along the winding route, the entire population—African and European, official and unofficial, local troops, traders, planters and humbler folk—was joyfully assembled, pressing forward tumultuously at his passing to see and to applaud; to shout a welcome wildly enthusiastic, whose object could as little be mistaken as the clamour could have been silenced. It was '*Vive la France!*', of course, and long live the Free French forces, and Victory, and Liberation; but also, resounding and insistent, it was '*Vive de Gaulle!*' More than a cry of approval, it was a declaration of faith.

Perhaps surprisingly, it was something for which he was unprepared. Accepting the responsibility of leadership, casting his net wide for all things that might favour the cause of France, giving meticulous consideration to all likely circumstances, it was the one foreseeable detail that had eluded him; so that now to hear, for the first time in his life, the sound of his own name, as it were thrown back at him in an acclaim direct, vociferous and personal, came as something of a shock, disconcerting and even distasteful. He would have wished to exchange quiet greetings with these fellow-citizens, these fellow-fighters for the honour of France; he wanted to shake their hands, he even made the gesture; instead he found himself silenced and as if imprisoned by the overwhelming weight of their single-minded applause, by the startling impact of an unaccustomed chant: '*de Gaulle — de Gaulle — de Gaulle!*' ...

It was his initiation to an experience that was presently to be repeated wherever he went; and in time he came to accept the rapturous shouting of multitudes as the unvarying and unavoidable accompaniment to his appearance anywhere on French territory free or liberated. But he was never to accept it as his personal due, regarding it rather as a tribute, through him, to France herself, an explosion, as it were, of approval for the cause and not for the man. Restrained as he was by an honesty of character in which self-adulation had no place, the perpetual acclaim forced him to an even sharper cleavage between the man and the symbol, between de Gaulle and 'de Gaulle'. And the unending self-watch needed to maintain the separation of a personal and inner identity from the figure of popular legend, by which he was increasingly to be identified with the hopes of the nation, heightened the impression of aloofness and austerity that was part of the price exacted for the honour of leading France back to self-respect. His almost total lack of histrionic ability forbade any romantic interpretation of the part of national hero; his integrity forbade pretence. As the object of deafening praise he was never happy; he was glad that the people were glad, that they approved in unison the cause he advocated. But he would sooner, at the end as at the beginning, have shaken their hands.

PART TWO

15. Thrust and Counterthrust

C'est la nuit qu'il est beau de croire à la lumière.
(*Chantecler:* Act II, Scene iii)

FROM DUALA, after a brief visit to Yaoundé, de Gaulle flew north to Fort Lamy and thence made a tour of inspection of the settlements and outposts of the Chad province. He moved fast and purposefully.

Reviewing sparse garrisons meagrely equipped, he raised the spirits of both native and white troops as much by his imperturbable demeanour as by his bold confidence in the future of France in the War, his quick grasp of local conditions and his refusal to be daunted by obstacles regarded as insuperable by an orthodox staff. At first with an amazement amounting almost to blank consternation, presently with elation growing to enthusiasm the officers of the weak defence forces heard him expound plans for offensive operations, not to the west against their sullenly inactive Vichy kinsmen, but to the north, against the Italians. An expedition was to be organized forthwith; supplies, necessarily scant, would be brought up from the south; Colonel Leclerc would take command; and the slender force would then move out across the desert to advance, with the camel corps leading, through the heart of the Tibesti to the borders of Italian Libya and beyond. Motorized columns with air support would take isolated garrisons by surprise, enemy outposts such as Kufra and Murzuk would be carried by assault, airfields overrun; and the raiding force driving ever northward from oasis to oasis—with, as might be expected, powerful British aid upon its eastern flank—would have as its distant objective no less a prize than Tripoli. Thereafter, it might well be hoped that all French North Africa might be drawn back into the struggle for the honour and independence of France.

It was no mere dream; that same winter, despite vast distance and much hardship, and grave shortages of trained men and of equipment, the first part of the mission was to be splendidly accomplished by the capture of Kufra together with 350 Italian prisoners, a battery of artillery and forty machine-guns. But a dream inspired the operation and its subsequent developments, a dream of action against the enemies of France, to which Vichy could oppose only stagnation and servitude, a vision discernible through the darkness as through the mirage shimmering above the unending desert, the image ever present of 'Notre Dame, of sunlight upon the Arc de Triomphe, of captured flags fluttering beneath the dome of the Invalides.' Upon those few hundred combatant Frenchmen de Gaulle bestowed a lasting faith in victory that was to lead them through the years of trial—to the Mediterranean, at length to France, ultimately and still under Leclerc to the freeing of Paris, to the march into Germany, to the Danube and to Berchtesgaden. Even after making full allowance for Britain's initial defiance of the enemy, without which nothing would have been possible at all, and for her growing strength and continued support, the achievement must surely be regarded as outstanding when seen from the starting-point of 1940. Many armies and great powers in a world at war were to contribute to its fulfilment; de Gaulle, alone of all Frenchmen, conceived it.

At Fort Lamy, on his return from the tour of inspection, the cause for which he stood received a noteworthy accretion of strength. General Catroux, unable to persuade Indo-China to break with Vichy and denounce the armistice, had resigned his post and had made his way by sea and air to London. There, it appears, a feeler had been put out by the British authorities, suggesting that he might care to take over de Gaulle's leadership, official ill-feeling at the failure to seize Dakar then being at its height. The suggestion having proved unwelcome, Churchill had then requested him to journey to the Middle East in the hope that he might be able to open negotiations with the French authorities in Vichy-held Syria. De Gaulle, though he appreciated Churchill's reasons, was not best pleased to learn, after the event, of Catroux's mission and waited with some anxiety for news from his old acquaintance: they had been together as prisoners in Germany during the first War. He was not kept long in doubt. Catroux flew down to Fort Lamy from Cairo, and at an official luncheon given by the Governor, Félix Eboué, formally announced his decision: he, the four-star Army-General and ex-Governor, would serve under the temporary two-star Brigadier. A noble example of self-effacement, it emphasized in striking manner de Gaulle's position as unique head of Free France.

Flying south, de Gaulle reached Brazzaville on October 24. There

—with ceremony by armed forces, with dignity by colonial officials, and rapturously acclaimed by the civilian population—he lost no time in putting into effect plans already outlined at Duala for the 'liberation' of the coastal province from Vichy control. From the landward side operations were begun immediately and the first outpost, at Mitzic, was carried on the 27th; but the principal attack, from seaward, upon Libreville took longer to mount, the aircraft in particular requiring more time than had been expected to assemble and test.

At length, on November 6, an expedition of all arms under Leclerc sailed from Duala. On the 7th a Vichy submarine came out of Libreville and attempted to torpedo Admiral Cunningham's flagship which had been directed to block any Vichy interference from seaward; depth-charged and brought to the surface the submarine's crew were taken off, with the exception of her commander who preferred to go down with his ship. Free French troops under Major Koenig were landed during the night of the 8th and sharp fighting broke out on the 9th for the possession of the Libreville airfield, upon which was stationed a flight of Glenn-Martin bombers and where for a time resistance by the Vichy garrison, including four battalions and auxiliary forces, was determined. Meanwhile Thierry d'Argenlieu, entering the harbour in the sloop *Savorgnan de Brazza*, had been heavily engaged by the gunboat *Bougainville* whose fire he was compelled to return and to silence. At about the same time aircraft from Duala bombed the airfield, whose defenders were then successfully attacked by the Foreign Legion, bringing resistance to an end. Before the close of day the local commander, General Têtu, had surrendered; his troops laid down their arms and were interned until they could make up their minds upon whose side they should fight in future. Three days later, after prolonged negotiation, the last remaining Vichy stronghold, Port Gentil, came over without a shot fired and the whole of Equatorial Africa was safely in Free French hands.

In France the enemy-controlled radio advertised de Gaulle's success with an explosion of anger and wild tales of imagined atrocities.

II

At Brazzaville, meanwhile, de Gaulle had been working at speed. On October 27, less than three days after his arrival in the capital, he published a Manifesto setting forth the aims and claims of Free France and creating a 'Council of Defence of the Empire' which, within those colonial territories acknowledging de Gaulle, was to assume the powers of a provisional government.

A further portion of the same Manifesto was released on November 16; a much lengthier document, its many clauses had required a more careful scrutiny and revision. Termed an 'Organic Declaration, in the name of the French People and Empire', and based upon the constitutional laws of the French Republic, it argued first the legal position of the Defence Council and then, point by point with facts too plain to be called in question, the fundamentally unconstitutional nature of the Vichy government which, abolishing the Republic and ousting its President, had set up with an entirely false semblance of legality a 'French State' ruled autocratically by Pétain, without a parliament but with the tacit consent of the enemy.

Taken as a whole the Manifesto constituted the charter of Free France, dedicated to the simple proposition that the republican form of government was still in force, consequently, that, given Vichy's patent illegality and subservience to the enemy, only those laws in force prior to June 23, 1940 (date of the armistice agreement) were to be regarded as valid, and that no Frenchman was to be bound by the acts of the usurper. To this proposition—that the Third Republic, under which France had declared the War now continued by Free France, had not been and could not be arbitrarily abolished by Vichy —de Gaulle remained steadfastly faithful. So consistent was his attitude that when, upon August 25, 1944, he faced the delirious multitudes of liberated Paris from the balcony of the *Hôtel de Ville* and was asked by one of the Resistance leaders (Georges Bidault) to 'proclaim the Republic' he was able to affirm without a moment's hesitation: 'The Republic has never ceased to exist. . . . Why then should I proclaim it?' If, as his detractors claimed, de Gaulle was an obstinate man, it must surely be conceded that in this matter he was obstinately right.

For it was clear from the start, to any impartial observer with the least knowledge of French constitutional law, that Vichy was wrong. Indeed no special knowledge was needed; even a child, provided with a modicum of common sense, could have appreciated that no Republic in the world would have in its written constitution a clause permitting either its self-destruction or the substitution of what amounted to an absolute monarchy; and in fact there were, in the French Constitution, numerous safeguards against such an act of suicidal immolation.

Any revision of the constitution of 1875 could only be made under certain exactly stated conditions, none of which had been observed during the proceedings at Vichy; but, over and above these limiting conditions, there stood the constitutional law added in 1884 which stated without ambiguity that 'the republican form of government cannot be the object of any suggestion of revision.' It was thus beyond question that whereas the political leaders—who, at Vichy in July, had persuaded the National Assembly to vote against the Republic and for Marshal Pétain—might, by kind permission of the enemy, exercise limited power as a *de facto* authority in the unoccupied portion of France, they were debarred, by virtue of constitutional laws they were not competent to modify, from claiming *de jure* recognition as the legitimate Government of France. Since the Republic could not legally be abolished, Pétain's 'French State' was, *ipso facto*, illegitimate; and the assertion sometimes made that the destruction of the Republic and the advent of the new régime were obtained by 'perfectly legal' means cannot be accepted as valid. Within the limits of long-established constitutional law, it simply was not possible to destroy the Republic; any Government proposal to do so was *ultra vires*. De Gaulle, therefore, far from being a rebel against legitimate government, had become the defender of the indestructible legitimacy of the Third Republic.

III

The story of political and moral degradation unfolded at Vichy during the first ten days of July, and resulting from the Pétain–Weygand surrender, might well be dismissed, were it the product of romantic fiction, as too far-fetched to be credible. There is about it a nightmarish quality of confusion that makes it less easily acceptable as fact than as some cautionary fairy-tale in which little frightened men, drawn irresistibly forward by an evil piper (Laval), are led into a pit they cannot see because their eyes are raised in fatuous adoration to an aged father-figure (Pétain) whose god-like qualities and abilities exist only in their imagination.

Fleeing from Bordeaux ahead of the Germans, the scared flock of Ministers, Senators, Deputies, Secretaries and political hangers-on paused for a day at Clermont-Ferrand, found no resting-place, and hurried on to Vichy where it rushed helter-skelter into the numerous hotels of the little place whose only political significance, whatever its value as a health resort, was that of chief town of a remote rural district. For a Government that had already betrayed the nation by unnecessary surrender deliberately contrived, and was now plotting to betray it again, it was perhaps an apt 'capital': a refuge for the aged, the infirm and the diseased, watched with silent contempt by the German Army, halted a score of miles away to the north. Herded into cramped quarters, overflowing into bars, restaurants and cinemas, the sharply divided parliamentary groups and parties, clamorous in their bewilderment, were ruled and to some extent united by two all-dominating sentiments: despair, to which was linked a very natural fear of the future, and unreflecting faith, emotional, almost religious, in Marshal Pétain. Into the ears of these unhappy men, stunned by disaster, wavering in their loyalty, Laval, the evil piper, dinned his subversive music, a twofold theme with variations to suit every shade of political opinion: the 'old order' must go, a New Order must come in; Pétain must be its head, Laval its chief minister.

Unwise though it is to judge a man by what is visible upon the surface, about the features of Pierre Laval, indeed about his bearing, his voice and manner, even his stained and untidy apparel, there was so much in keeping with his character that observers found it difficult to dissociate appearance from personality. At fifty-seven, between stooping shoulders, short-necked, the face was sullen and deeply scored, the eyes half closed by heavy creases. A straggling black moustache drooped about a thick-lipped mouth whose faint smile was at once supercilious and menacing, whilst the very texture and colour of his skin, rugous and unhealthily dark, appeared sinister and repellent. A mysterious atavism may have formed the features and coarsened the skin; those who had watched his career deemed it more probable that the repulsive exterior had been influenced, if not wholly shaped, by an inner malevolence the more dangerous for the man's considerable mental equipment, power of persuasion and complete self-assurance. In the course of the War, singleminded in his ruthless pursuit of power, he was to become directly responsible for the deportation and death of many thousands of his countrymen.

Born the son of an innkeeper in the harsh region of Auvergne, at first the expression of inhibited talents was merely physical; as a boy he was unruly, sacrilegious, violent to his fellows, cruel to animals. A well-meaning schoolmaster presently discovered his mental powers and induced him to study, even as the boy was discovering for himself abilities in another direction by committing, at fifteen, adultery with the schoolmaster's wife. Persuaded to take up teaching he was quick to perceive in the profession an easy way of turning a dishonest penny and, as a young schoolmaster, perpetrated his first major fraud upon the Government, by obtaining a grant of money from the Minister of Education for a 'Society of Schoolmasters' said to number eight hundred members, in reality eight. Emboldened by success, he readily perceived that, for a career in which honesty had no place, a sound knowledge of the law was essential and political influence invaluable. Prolonged study and hard reading, made possible by the 'education grant', gained him admittance to the Paris bar at the age of twenty-four; prolonged canvassing of a Paris suburb, largely populated by fellow-*Auvergnats*, gained him election as a Socialist Deputy before the 1914 War in which he served his hard-pressed country as a militant pacifist.

By nature an extremist in all things he had begun his political career on the extreme Left, but with personal advantage as his sole guiding principle no cause could hold him for long; oscillating from group to group between the Wars, by the late 'thirties he had reached the extreme Right. By that time long experience of political intrigue and crafty manoeuvre—a game at which his sharp wits and lack of scruples made him an adept—had brought him to ministerial rank and so to that merry-go-round of Premiers and Cabinets, every turn of which brought back the same faces, arranged in slightly different order, to form 'one of those ephemeral governments' derided by Weygand in the hour of crisis. By that time, too, he had become wealthy. Though far from being the only corrupt politician in France, he was certainly one of the most successful; by 1940, through persistent abuse of political influence and ministerial power, the once penniless youth had amassed a fortune estimated at more than a million pounds.[1]

[1] One of his most profitable deals concerned the purchase, for his private account, of a small firm of printers in Clermont-Ferrand. For this firm (i.e. himself) he then obtained the Government contract for printing all the ration-cards in France.

Driven from office by reason of his blatantly pro-Italian policy at the time of the Abyssinian War—a policy briefly supported by the Foreign Office under Samuel Hoare, until condemned by British public opinion—he broke with the Socialists and, independent of all parties, remained in the background during the last years of peace, a prophet of doom openly approving fascist principles. Friendless, but not without political sympathizers, the physical violence of youth was turned to the violence of speech by which he expressed his contempt for parliamentary government and bitter hatred alike for the Radicals and Socialists who had deprived him of power and, perhaps most of all, for anti-fascist Britain. When Hitler commenced hostilities in 1939, Laval was the only Senator to vote against the French Government's war subsidies, implying thereby his support of the enemy.

In the political chaos and perplexity following upon the downfall of France his previous attitude suddenly brought him into prominence again. It was not that he gained popularity overnight—he was disliked as much as he was distrusted—but that his earlier policy was seen to have been unhappily justified by events and that therefore, since he was on friendly terms with Mussolini and with some of the leading Nazis, he was almost the only French statesman likely to find favour in the eyes of the conqueror. With the Socialists as unacceptable to the Nazis as were the Communists; with Léon Blum, leader of the Popular Front, a Jew; with Daladier who had declared war and Reynaud who had tried to wage it both regarded as 'warmongers'; the rise to power of Laval was inevitable and not safely to be opposed. At Bordeaux he accepted Pétain's offer of the post of Minister of State, and was almost immediately promoted to be Vice-President of the Council of Ministers, the position Pétain himself had occupied in Reynaud's administration and from which he had plotted the surrender of France. Forthwith, on the road to Vichy, with the febrile assistance of the half-demented Alibert and the fond connivance of the unprotesting Marshal, Laval began plotting the destruction of the Republic.

During those first ten days of July at Vichy he was at the height of his powers of political double-dealing, of forceful speech, of cunning and mendacity. The malign inspiration with which he countered opposition and brushed aside successive obstacles seemed daemonic; nothing could stop him. A restless Lucifer, with astonishing speed he

First landing on French soil. Duala, October 1940

The Start of a Long March—Review of Troops at Fort Lamy, October 1940

Fighters for Free France: General Catroux at Beirut (Gen. Maitland Wilson on right)

General Leclerc   General Koenig

went up and down from one political group to another, urging haste, denouncing indecision; lying to one group concerning the support promised by a second, hurrying round to the second to cover the lie before it was revealed, then back to the first to follow up the advantage gained and, if need be, to lie again. Alternately cajoling and minatory, warning some of the nearness of the German Army, he threatened others that, if opposed, he would resign and that then they would get Weygand as dictator. Tempting a Deputy with the bribe of a high post in the new order—'You have many admirable qualities, we may well have need of you. I ask you, therefore, to consider the matter'—he browbeat a wealthy Senator with the menace of sequestration: 'Take care! . . . if you persist in your attitude, all your profits will be taken from you.' At times he spoke movingly of his desire to 'strengthen the Republic'; at others, with an insolent frankness that displayed his confidence in himself, he would proclaim the necessity for its total destruction and for the creation of 'something entirely different' that must be aligned 'with the German and Italian constitutions', adding that since 'parliamentary democracy has lost the War' it must 'disappear'.

Such blunt disclosures of his true intentions, whilst bringing many of his hidden supporters into the open, served further to alarm and divide the political groups whom he then entertained, and to some extent reunited, by sounding the high note of anglophobia. Britain was and always had been France's bitterest enemy; in peace Britain had frustrated his, Laval's, efforts at *rapprochement* with the Axis powers; in war Britain had used France for her own ends, so that 'today we are at the bottom of the abyss to which Britain has led us'. Worse still, he knew for a fact that Britain was at this moment secretly negotiating a peace treaty with Hitler so as to get in first and 'conclude it at our expense'.

From this it might almost be thought that it was Britain which had conquered France and imposed the surrender terms; but to frightened politicians wholly ignorant of affairs outside France, resentful moreover of the recent naval tragedy at Oran, there seemed to be more than a grain of truth in Laval's fierce denunciation. They saw France ruined, at Hitler's mercy, friendless, alone. Despair deepened until they hardly knew what to think or which way to turn; in stupefied misery they heard Laval declare that 'parliament must be dissolved', that 'the formation of labour camps must be envisaged', that failure to agree would entail 'the German occupation of the whole of France'; and in this mood of dejection not unmixed with terror, towards which Laval had so skilfully led them, they could see but one hope of salvation and it was Laval who supplied it. 'We demand,' he told the Deputies, 'that Marshal Pétain be invested with complete constitutional power.' Upon that point all were soon forced to agree.

Among the politicians at Vichy, as indeed among the greater number of the people of France, faith in Pétain was now nearly absolute; it would have been touching had it not been unwarranted. Quite suddenly he came to be regarded as a saintly and predestined figure who, alone now that the five-million Army had vanished, would miraculously bar the way to Hitler. Upon each and every possible occasion for speechmaking individual Ministers, ex-Premiers, Senators or Deputies would intone a *magnificat* in the old man's honour: he was 'revered', he was 'venerated', he 'represented perfectly the traditional French virtues', with great 'nobility of spirit' he had 'made the gift of his person to the nation' and about that Person 'the nation was gathered in its distress'. He was looked upon, one French writer was to put it,[1] as 'a sort of tricolour Father Christmas', benevolent and omniscient, who would bestow upon his children the unlikely gifts of political harmony, safety of the state and the prompt achievement of an 'honourable peace'. To him they clung with the desperation of drowning men; and in his near-sacred name Laval conquered.

On July 10 the Government's Bill, presented to the National Assembly by Laval (in the name of the Marshal) on the previous day, was voted. Eighty staunch members found the courage to vote against it, seventeen abstained, some were absent, a few in North Africa, and the Communists were still in jail where Daladier had put them early in the war. Nevertheless, the majority was overwhelming and the Bill was assumed to have become law. In fact the Constitution of 1875 had laid down that any constitutional modification whatever must be voted by the two Chambers in session *at Versailles*, a wise provision since it implicitly required that the Government of France should be in free occupation of its own constitutional capital; the law could not be stretched to cover Vichy of all places. But Versailles was in enemy

[1] Gaston Bonheur.

hands and, said Laval, 'we will not allow our fellow-countryment to be subjected to the humiliation of voting under the control of the German Army;' legal or not, Vichy it must be. There were few objections, for not many politicians wanted to cross swords just then with Laval and all had confidence in the integrity of Marshal Pétain.

The Bill had been drafted by Raphael Alibert who, many years ago, had been a competent professor of constitutional law, who had thereafter proved his total incompetence in politics as in private business, and who was presently the subject of a diagnosis by Pétain's doctor, Ménétrel, in which it was stated that he 'suffers from megalomania with a certain tendency towards mental disequilibrium'. It was a condition that suited Pétain well enough; for, with Laval's help, the lunatic had given him a blank cheque. 'I liked Alibert very much,' he said afterwards, 'but he gave me very bad advice.' By then it was too late to undo the mischief.

The Bill, now Vichy's law, laid down: 'The National Assembly confers all powers on the Government of the Republic under the signature and authority of Marshal Pétain, President of the Council, to promulgate by one or more acts the new Constitution of the French State.

'This Constitution will guarantee the rights of Labour, Family and Country. It will be ratified by the nation and applied by the Assemblies it will have created.'

It was brief enough; and yet it was unnecessarily long, for only a portion of one sentence in the first paragraph had any real meaning. The Marshal, by his signature alone, would promulgate the new Constitution: 'by one or more acts.'

These 'acts', secretly drawn up by Laval and Alibert, were signed by Pétain on the 11th and published on the 12th. They had been drafted by Alibert a long time previously and their outline had been known to Pétain before the surrender at Bordeaux. That Laval should have favoured them was in keeping with his character and his views; he not only 'believed' in a German victory, he 'hoped' for it. But that Pétain should so readily have appended his signature to these extraordinary documents would seem to suggest that Alibert was not the only one suffering from megalomania and mental disequilibrium. By virtue of the first act, five lines only, the Presidency of the Republic was abolished and Pétain was named as 'Head of the French State'. By the second act he assumed for himself powers greater than those possessed before the Revolution by the kings of France, including the appointment of all government functionaries, civil or military, the making of laws, together with the right of reprieve and amnesty, the signing of treaties and sole control of the armed forces. A provision in this act denying him the right to make war 'without previous assent from the Legislative Assemblies'—a clause conceded by Laval before the voting on July 10—was neatly eluded in the next by putting the Assemblies in permanent cold storage, the third act bluntly laying down that the Senate and Chamber of Deputies were adjourned 'until further orders' and would not meet again unless 'convoked by the Head of State'—a convocation that was delayed *sine die* and in fact never took place.

The fourth act was even more fantastic. It revived the antique, pre-Revolutionary and royal rank of 'legitimate successor', the historic *delphinat*. By order of 'we, Philippe Pétain', the title *Dauphin*, echoing the chivalry, the honour and the glory of ancient France, was bestowed upon Pierre Laval. Had the consequences not been so tragic for France, it might well have been regarded as a joke, albeit in very poor taste.

Other more sinister acts followed. By a fifth, published before the end of July, Pétain announced the creation of a 'Supreme Court of Justice' whose 'organization, competence and procedure' were to be laid down by laws made subsequently. Since, by the second act, Pétain had already assumed all legislative power, he was now not only both judge and jury but also the sole dispenser of 'justice' according to laws he was empowered to manipulate. Not even Hitler could go farther than that.

Thereafter at reckless speed Pétain signed a vast number of laws and decrees that effectively abolished the Rights of Man, the one abiding achievement of 1789, and established a fascist dictatorship on the Nazi pattern, some of whose more hideous features—notably the appearance of statutes against Jews, in part even more stringent than German anti-Semitic laws—were presently reproduced on the advice of Alibert. But it is not enough to say that the Marshal was badly advised; he embarked upon the adventure deliberately, with his eyes firmly fixed upon the prize of kingly power, for the exercise of which he possessed not one of the requisite qualities. He had no real know-

ledge of practical politics or statecraft, save from the muddled views
served up by Alibert. He had no experience of governing, save that
gained, so long ago!, in the command of troops. He had, as yet, little
understanding of the implications of a totalitarian régime; he thought
of fallen France as comparable to Germany after 1918 or to Prussia
rising again in the darkness after Jena. Of how the resurgence of
France was to be achieved he had no clear idea, save that it would
involve 'moral regeneration' and 'more suffering' and a return to
agriculture. His broadcast utterances had a spurious profundity: 'A
field lying fallow is a portion of France dying. . . . Life is not neutral;
it consists in taking sides boldly. . . . May the springtime of our youth
soon expand into the springtime of renascent France.' Of his own
springtime nothing was left; he was old and going deaf, too old to
learn new tricks. He had married at sixty-five—and said afterwards
that he ought to have waited another ten years—had no children, yet
considered himself an expert on 'the family' and, after the manner of
elderly autocrats, the 'father' of all the people; in much the same way
he had once regarded as his 'children' the hardy and hirsute men of
the 33rd Regiment.

No doubt but that he had retained his cunning; during those first
ten days of July he had been, it was rightly said, 'very clever'—by
refraining from taking part in the Assembly's deliberations, by remaining silent and invisible within his suite in the Hotel du Parc, with
Alibert guarding the door and the telephone, by showing a paternal
affability to those few whom he received, by giving evasive replies to
awkward visitors whom he referred for more positive answers to
'Monsieur Laval', by allowing himself to be carried to power upon the
wave of adulation provoked by despair. But cunning was no substitute
for intelligence. He would have done better with a few grains of
common sense, the merest glimmer of foresight.

For after July, by his own acts, the barriers were down and the
road to perdition stretched out bleakly before him, the road upon which
he had first set foot at Bordeaux and from which, by virtue of his
assumption of autocratic power, he could no longer retreat. Along it
he marched with what an admirer described as 'that peculiar gait
which seemed to carry him so majestically', but which more nearly
resembled the heavy tread of a confident blindness; marched step by
step, after each minor and illusory concession taking a full stride

down the ever-steepening path at the foot of which, unmoved by good intentions, patient Nemesis waited with a judgment he was powerless to reverse.

But whilst a victorious Hitler beckoned, with false promises and genuine threats, it was Laval who led the way. Pétain might despise him for his coarse manners and vulgar speech, for the noisome cigarette that drooped perpetually from between the turgid lips, for the invariable white tie that, set beneath the cynical cruelty of the dark, toad-like face, seemed to him a constant mockery of honest virtues; yet Laval, in whom he found no 'spiritual worth', held him fascinated by the extraordinary success of his ruthless politics. By him he was guided; to him, although he struggled briefly to be free, he succumbed; through him he was lost. For Laval, too, Nemesis waited at the end of the road. He was the piper who called his own tune, and in the fullness of time, by the French people whose hatred had been aroused by his treachery, he would be paid his merited wage with the bullets of a firing squad.

In the summer and early autumn of 1940, however, he had things going his own way: the way of alignment with Germany at the expense of Britain. Paying scant attention to the many German breaches of the armistice agreement—notably the annexation to the *Reich* of Alsace-Lorraine and the detachment of northern Departments, grafted on to the German command in Belgium—and, negotiating first with Otto Abetz, German envoy and ex-spy, he progressed upward to Ribbentrop and eventually reached Hitler. On October 22, at the small railway station of Montoire[1] conveniently situated at the entrance to a tunnel, he made his first bow to the *Führer*.

Describing the encounter as a 'delightful surprise', at which he and Hitler had 'felt the same way', he reported back to Pétain at Vichy. He had received, he said, a very favourable impression of what might be expected from further meetings, and went on to explain that Hitler—'a great man'—had suggested a close understanding between France and Germany. He did not mention, however, what he later admitted, that he had replied: 'As a Frenchman, I can only say that I desire with all my heart a British defeat.' Pétain was led to believe that he might obtain some major concessions from the victor, together with an outline of peace terms, and very unwisely declared that he too

[1] North of the Loire, near Tours.

would be glad to meet the *Führer*. Laval hastened to gratify his wish.

Two days later, October 24, an event occurred that was to cast a long shadow. On the platform of Montoire station, Pétain, wearing the uniform of a Marshal of France, shook hands with Hitler. The warm handclasp was photographed, filmed, reproduced in the press; it was received by great numbers of French people with shocked amazement and a deep sense of shame. Worse followed. In Hitler's train Pétain sat down with the enemy and, foolishly trying to bargain with a man far more astute than himself—one, moreover, who held all the cards—was drawn into conceding the only point that, just then, Hitler intended him to concede. In return for a vague, verbal assurance that concessions might be expected, Pétain agreed to make an official announcement approving a policy of 'collaboration' with Germany. On October 30 the unhappy people of France heard their Marshal broadcast: 'It is in all honour and in order to maintain the unity of France . . . that I am today pursuing the path of collaboration. . . . This collaboration must be sincere. It must bring with it patient and confident effort.'

It was to be said that Pétain scarcely realized the gravity of the step he had taken, that he thought of the Montoire interview as an episode that committed him to nothing. But in fact he knew, from Laval as from Hitler, that the object of the policy was to co-operate, although as a non-belligerent, in the defeat of Great Britain and that, for a costly war, France would have to pay unless, Hitler had said, 'she decides to collaborate with Germany'. Towards the end of his broadcast he admitted full responsibility: 'This policy is mine. . . . It is I alone whom history will judge.'

For thousands of Frenchmen, dominated by fear of a hopeless future under the Nazis, secretly rejoicing at the news of Britain's continued resistance, there could be no waiting for the judgment of history. Even allowing for the evil influence of Laval, whom no one trusted, they were horrified by Pétain's words and action. The handclasp of Montoire changed everything. When it was followed by the announcement of 'collaboration' many, unable to understand and unwilling to follow, sensed betrayal. After the broadcast there was noted the first marked decline of unquestioning faith in the Marshal.

IV

De Gaulle's Manifesto from Brazzaville, coming less than three days after Montoire, was therefore timely. At this moment of renewed distress and uncertainty the people of France must be left in no doubt of the wholly unconstitutional nature of the Vichy government. Supporters inside the country, as well as the followers of Free France without, must be firmly assured that the Republic still existed and that all acts and decrees over Pétain's signature were null and void. At the edifice unlawfully erected by evil opportunists, with the assent of an elderly and complacent autocrat of singular ineptitude, the Manifesto struck the first shrewd counterblow.

In France, unfortunately, it was scarcely heard. Broadcast by the low-power Brazzaville wireless station, it was all but inaudible to those, now listening in secret, whose small sets were for the most part tuned in to London. Arrangements had been made, through the Carlton Gardens headquarters, for the entire Manifesto to be put out by the BBC; just then, however, the British Government, misled by reports that Pétain was about to conclude a damaging peace treaty with Hitler, was pursuing through its Ambassador in Madrid (Samuel Hoare) the negotiations initiated by the Vichy Ambassador on October 1; and the Cabinet was naturally anxious to avoid any action that might drive Pétain still farther into the enemy camp and provoke him to hand over the French fleet together with its Mediterranean bases. After keeping de Gaulle informed of the negotiations, as well as of the now rapidly dissolving rumours concerning a Vichy–German peace treaty, the Foreign Office cabled to him on October 31 that the Government had 'felt obliged to take action to prevent your organiza-tion from issuing in broadcasts and in the press denunciation of the Vichy Government which would certainly have been fully justified, had betrayal already been a matter of fact.'

The word 'betrayal' in this context referred to the reported peace terms, but the implication that without this renewed betrayal de Gaulle's 'denunciation' would *not* have been 'fully justified' was some-thing which the British Government knew to be absurd. Repeatedly since June, in the press, in broadcasts, in official declarations, the British Government had made plain its own condemnation of the government in France: by the broadcast statement of June 23 in which, after finding that the armistice terms were 'in contravention of agreements solemnly made between the Allied Governments', the British Government declared that it could 'no longer regard the Bordeaux Government as a Government of an independent country'; by the Prime Minister's statement of August 20 that, if France lay prostrate, it was the fault of 'this puppet Government'; by the violent action taken in the course of Operations *Catapult* and *Menace*, and again by action taken to protect Free French sea-communications off Libreville. 'Denunciation' could hardly have been sterner or more apparent.

For the British Government, however, the overriding consideration at this time was that the French fleet at Toulon should not fall into enemy hands, an eventuality which would seriously have affected the already precarious situation in the Mediterranean; and to attain this end was an imperative duty that fully justified any means, however arbitrary. De Gaulle himself was quick to appreciate (in a long telegram to Churchill dated November 2) the reasons for an attempted conciliation of Vichy and even for British hopes, in his view sure to be vain, of winning over certain prominent Vichy supporters, such as Noguès and Weygand. Nevertheless, it may seem regrettable that when, early in November, it became clear that 'collaboration' had been conceded by Pétain, the Manifesto should not have been given wider publicity and more profound attention on both sides of the Atlantic. It was an important document; closer study of its several clauses would have revealed a clearer picture of its author and his aims.

The first part of the Manifesto was in the form of an address in which, carrying a step further the appeals of June 18 and 19, de Gaulle clarified his intentions and declared his augmented responsibility. 'France,' he began, 'is going through the most terrible crisis in her history. Her frontiers, her empire, her independence and her very soul are threatened with destruction.

'Giving way to inexcusable panic some haphazard leaders have accepted and are submitting to the enemy's rule. . . . But there no longer exists a French government properly so called. For the body seated in Vichy and claiming to bear this name is unconstitutional and subject to the invader. In its condition of servitude this body can only be, and in fact is only, an instrument employed by the enemies of France against the country's honour and interest. A new authority must therefore take over the task of directing the exertions of France in the war. Events impose upon me this sacred duty. In it I shall not fail.

'My powers I shall exercise in the name of France and solely in her defence, and I solemnly undertake to account for all my actions to the representatives of the French people as soon as it shall have been possible to designate them freely.'

Announcing the formation of the advisory Empire Defence Council, which was to include such distinguished and irreproachable personalities as Catroux and de Larminat, Governors Eboué and Sautot, Professor René Cassin, d'Argenlieu and Leclerc, he made a further appeal.

'I call to war, that is to say to combat or to sacrifice, all the men and all the women of those French territories which have joined me. . . . The object is to defend, against the enemy or his auxiliaries, that part of our national patrimony which is in our hands, to attack the enemy wherever it shall be possible, to put to work all our resources, military, economic and moral, to maintain public order and to see that justice reigns.'

'This great task we shall accomplish for France, in the knowledge of serving her well and with the certainty of victory.'

To that high purpose he remained loyal throughout the years; to the principle of personal authority to which duty had called him he held with an unshakeable belief in its necessity to the cause he served; and at the end he kept faith and handed back to the people of France the power he had won by actions resolute, clearsighted and selfless. For some in Britain as in America, ignorant of the man, the verbal assurances of the Manifesto were not, at the time of its publication, a convincing guide to future intentions or even to practical politics; the road ahead was too long, too rough; Free France in the war was still infinitesimal, Vichy protected by German might seemed unassailable. No one man, it was said, could claim, without arrogant pretension, to rescue France from tyranny.

And yet little more than a cursory glance at the man's record, a brief personal acquaintance and an unprejudiced perusal of his writings and speeches should have been enough to reveal that, above and apart from mental ability, here was a character of rare integrity. Certainly his followers knew it, or at least the greater number of them; his past services, his peacetime predictions so fatally disregarded, the resolute stand and the simply worded statements of ineluctable fact, the ringing appeals and the commonsense views, the prompt decisions, even the austere dignity of manner, these things depicted for them stroke by stroke the portrait of the one leader exceptionally qualified to guide them through the darkness to their distant objective. Others, his opponents, seldom failed in their speeches to evoke the 'honour' of France; from his new post in North Africa, Weygand had recently gone so far as to declare, despite surrender and collaboration, that 'nothing contrary to the honour and interests of France . . . could be agreed to by a government headed by Marshal Pétain'. De Gaulle, too, spoke of 'honour', but to it he added 'victory'—a word no one under Vichy dared to utter.

From Brazzaville onwards the path he would follow, subject only to the outcome of the war and his own survival, was plainly discernible to those who were aware of his inflexible nature, his boldness and his vision. Twenty years after Brazzaville the *New York Times* wrote of him: 'His ideas are wise and statesmanlike; his courage is unbounded; his patience and tenacity are extraordinary.' What was to be said in 1960 could with equal truth have been said by any informed and fair-minded observer in 1940.

*   *   *

On November 17, having named de Larminat as High Commissioner for all the French colonies in central Africa and given instructions for the speedy utilization of French troops against the Italians, de Gaulle left by air for England. Nearly five months were to elapse before he passed through Brazzaville again on the way to Cairo and, eventually, to Syria.

16. Precept and Prejudice

Je ne suis pas de Gaule
Si vous donnez au mot un sens vilain et drôle!

*   *   *

Et si de tous les chants mon chant est le plus fier,
C'est que je chante clair afin qu'il fasse clair!

(*Chantecler:* Act III, Scene iv and Act II, Scene iii)

THE YEAR 1941, which saw the progressive widening of the War into global conflict, also witnessed a vast increase, inside France, in the numbers of those directly or indirectly supporting de Gaulle or sympathizing with his movement. Caused less by reports of decisive Allied successes—of which, on balance, there were few—than by German excesses, the increase became more notable as world-peace became more remote. External events provided the successive jolts necessary to open men's eyes; for the very prolongation and extension of the War made nonsense of the view, at the root of Pétain's actions at Bordeaux, Vichy and Montoire, that it had been both lost and ended. But it was the internal evidence, of humiliation, of loss of liberty, of worsening conditions affecting men personally, that supplied the continual nudge needed to dispel apathy and to awaken the dormant spirit of defiance. To this awakening the Vichy government's degradation, from open 'collaboration' to active military assistance, contributed greatly.

It would be a mistake, however, to attribute to Vichy's shameful compliance the sole, or even the chief, incentive to internal resistance. Vichy, after all, was only an effect—the effect of military defeat and national betrayal. The cause was the feral stupidity of German policy under the Nazis. For it is not too much to say that had Hitler been endowed with enough political wisdom to feign a magnanimity he did not possess he could, before the end of 1940, have produced a peace treaty that would have solaced the great majority of the people of France and have kept them in sulky but consenting neutrality until the end of the war.

It had been the 'proud' boast of the men of Bordeaux that the French fleet and air forces were still intact and would be trump cards wherewith to counter excessive enemy demands. Since then the value of the cards had been much reduced; the fleet, by *Catapult*, to no more than a powerful squadron, albeit with valuable bases; the air forces, by lack of supplies and production, to gradual obsolescence. But in any event Hitler's cards, had he chosen to negotiate peace, were far higher. He held two million prisoners, and he held Paris.

Had he released the prisoners and evacuated Paris he would have had, not only Vichy, but all France agreeing with Laval's opinion that he was 'a great man'. He might with advantage have gone further; he might without much risk have evacuated all occupied France, retaining only the Channel and Atlantic ports as submarine bases. The ports would have been bombed—as in fact they were—but the coasts about them and the hinterland would have been safe in the hands of defensively-equipped French forces, even more resolute than those at Dakar or, subsequently, in Syria, backed by a nation holding firmly to abstention for fear of instant reoccupation. A British refusal to recognize the neutral status would have been vain; against a determined and united French opposition a complete recasting of the plans, however distant, for re-entry to Europe would have become necessary, to the exclusion of France. With 'Vichy' translated to Paris—and doubtless legalized at Versailles—Pétain's triumph as 'peacemaker' would have been permanently sealed. Laval's anglophobia would have proved irresistible; and no one in France would have wanted to renew the fight for Danzig and the Polish Corridor against Germans who had shown themselves to be as generous as they were apparently 'invincible'. With the occupation army withdrawn France's own supplies, would have been ample for her needs; trade, with Germany, would have revived; and the great mass of the people could have resumed their peacetime avocations, comfortable spectators of a conflict that scarcely concerned them. De Gaulle's appeals would then have been laughed to scorn; for 'resistance' would have been meaningless when there was nothing against which to resist, and even 'liberation' would have had a hollow sound when there was so little from which to be freed and when the cost must be, from a new war, an even speedier defeat and a far deadlier occupation.

Such speculation is not altogether vain, for it was upon the negotiation of a peace treaty of somewhat similar scope that Vichy firmly counted and that all Frenchmen who believed in the Marshal hopefully relied. Thus, in the contrast between what might so easily have been and what in fact occurred, it can be seen how Hitler, through lack of vision and sheer meanness of mind, threw away an opportunity that might well, for him, have been decisive and, in so doing engendered the very conditions needed first to disillusion the French, then to provoke unrest, finally to stimulate hatred and active hostility. To Laval, at their first meeting, he had vowed that he had no desire for 'a peace of vengeance'; but from the outset the narrow vindictiveness of his measures, applied by his underlings with their customary callous indifference, was made plain in numerous breaches of the armistice terms. Already the spectacular vulgarity of Rethondes and the removal to Berlin of Foch's railway coach had evoked a shudder of dismay; it was not long before acts less obtrusive but of direr consequences were being imposed upon the vanquished.

Rather than release captives the tyrant demanded more, insisting upon the handing over by Vichy of German exiles who had thought themselves safe under French protection, later stretching out his hand to grasp at other foreign refugees, eventually, with Vichy's warm approval, reaching for the Jews. Rather than let bygones be bygones, he revived the ancient quarrel by re-annexing Alsace-Lorraine and, with a gesture as brutal as it was stupid, forthwith drove 200,000 of the population destitute into France. Rather than relax his Army's stranglehold he tightened its grip; the demarcation line, by the terms of the armistice no more than the limit of the German advance, became a frontier, a barrier to trade, commerce and communication.

He made no concessions. Instead of lightening the heavy burden of occupation costs, he vastly increased them by arbitrarily adjusting the exchange-rate in favour of the German mark. Instead of relieving the nation-wide difficulties of food distribution, dislocated by troop movements and war damage, he intensified them by sending endless freight trains stacked with plunder back to Germany where he retained the rolling-stock. And instead of sending back prisoners he sent, for re-burial beneath the dome of the Invalides, the body of Napoleon's son.

By this, his sole conciliatory gesture, Hitler set great store. All France, he appears to have thought, would be drawn to him by the touching generosity expressed, to a conquered nation, through the return from Vienna of the one-time King of Rome to lie beside the

Emperor whom the *Führer* considered as almost his equal. With so chivalrous an action he would win over the romantic French, not only to the collaboration announced by Pétain, but to the more positive military alliance he was negotiating with Laval. Just then, however, the French were less interested in the *Aiglon* than, the month being December, in the serious food and fuel shortages; they were neither moved nor hoodwinked by the *Führer*'s gift. Paris was contemptuous: 'We ask for coal, and we get ashes.' The population, expected to greet the event with cheers and tears, stayed at home; the ceremony fell flat. Hitler felt that he had been insulted.

Thereafter the restrictions were increased; Paris shivered and the poorer classes went hungry whilst the long freight trains rolled eastward, bearing away essential supplies. Daily the futility of attempting to conciliate an enemy whose rapacity remained insatiable became more evident as the policy of 'collaboration' became more one-sided, a matter of blackmail to which the only alternative was starvation. In the provincial towns and industrial areas the economic situation worsened steadily throughout the winter until men who, under a less rigorous domination, might have become reconciled to defeat were compelled to seek an outlet from despair. Increasingly they harkened to forbidden tidings spread by secret emissaries entering from Spain, landed on the coasts or dropped from the night skies, listened in cellars or attics to carefully tuned radio sets, striving through the maddening cacophony of enemy jamming to glean the news that should rekindle hope.

Of good news there was plenty that autumn and into the winter; good, that is, for those not enamoured of the German cause or spellbound by German might; and even Vichy might smile, remembering the stab in the back of June 11, at Mussolini's discomfiture. The Italians were being chased out of Libya and Cyrenaica; out of northern Epirus, too, and into Albania, towards Valona. For a while the Greeks seemed irresistible; on the French Mediterranean coast, facing the Italian border near occupied Mentone, jesting patriots painted a sign: *Armée grecque—Attention!—Frontière française!* Nor did the mighty Germans appear quite so invincible as during the previous summer; their much-advertised air assault on England had failed to bring the expected surrender; the seaborne invasion was still being postponed, as the Germans kept on repeating, 'because of the weather'; and now

British aircraft were retaliating over the French coast and into Germany. Clearly those French military experts who had declared that England's collapse was 'only a matter of weeks' had been mistaken. Perhaps then, many began to think, de Gaulle might be right in his estimate that 'France had lost a battle, but not the war'.

His voice was heard more frequently throughout the winter in the Free French broadcasting service from London, and his appeals, listened to by a small but growing audience, fell the more pleasingly upon French ears as the enemy press and radio increased the severity of their attacks upon him, his resistance movement and his colonial successes. Much free publicity had been accorded him since June 18, first through the announcement of the death sentence in August, then through the official jubilation at the 'miserable failure' of his attempt at Dakar. Opinion had then swung against him, since failure had seemed to mark the end of his 'rebellion'; but little more than a month later the howls of rage emitted by the enemy-controlled press and echoed by Vichy at the news of his successful operations in central Africa, coinciding and contrasting with the disastrous handshake of Montoire, had swung opinion back and gained him new adherents. Finally, before the winter's misery came to widen discontent, there had followed, hard upon the inexplicable announcement of 'collaboration', the incident near the Arc de Triomphe on November 11. To mark at the Unknown Soldier's Tomb the ever-memorable day of bygone victory, Paris students had marched bearing aloft in their midst two crossed staves—'*deux gaules*'—whose meaning escaped no one. Upon these young men the *Wehrmacht* foolishly opened fire, and 'gaullism' inside France gained its first essential martyrs.

The importance of this shift towards de Gaulle and the cause represented by the Cross of Lorraine must not, however, be exaggerated. There was nothing initially that could be classed as a national 'movement', nothing that gave the enemy so much as a moment's anxiety. Neither in the occupied territory nor in the so-called 'free' zone of German-dominated Vichy could there be open defiance of an authority overwhelmingly powerful. 'Resistance' was out of the question; there were no arms, no organization, no network of communications, no plan of action and no possibility of assembly save for a few in utmost secrecy. Such small bodies as began to form were little more than discussion groups, looking to a very remote, if rather more

De Gaulle meets the Allied Press—Conference Room at Carlton Gardens, 1941

Roosevelt's 'shotgun wedding'. Casablanca, January 1943
(Giraud, Roosevelt, de Gaulle, Churchill)

The Secretary of State confers with the 'marplot'.
Cordell Hull with de Gaulle, Washington, July 1944

The Day of Glory upon the Champs Elysées, August 26, 1944

hopeful future. A change of heart there was, brought about by exas-
peration as much by any firm belief in eventual British victory, a
turning of thoughts towards a dream of ultimate liberation by forces
outside of France, aided perhaps by those of de Gaulle; but there was
little physical action. The time was not ripe. Even such 'gaullist'
groups as were forming were suspicious of each other and deeply
divided in outlook and political complexion.

With the majority of Frenchmen, Pétain was still popular even after
the bitter blow of Montoire; it seemed incredible that he should have
accepted 'collaboration' unless it was a cunning move to gain important concessions, a matter of 'falling back the better to jump forward'.
When suddenly, in mid-December just before the *Aiglon* ceremony,
he dismissed Laval and had him put under arrest the action was
acclaimed as the first indication of a firmer attitude towards Hitler. It
was put about, and widely believed, that he was secretly in league with
de Gaulle, a supposition which, while it did no great harm to the
General, tended to renewed faith in the Marshal. His photograph was
everywhere, prominently displayed like that of a reigning sovereign
in all official places and public buildings, hung in hotels and restaurants,
flashed on cinema screens, distributed by the hundred thousand to all
parts of the country on either side of the demarcation line; in Paris
alone, it was officially if not very accurately stated, as many copies had
been sold as there were inhabitants. It is therefore reasonable to suppose that every man, woman and intelligent child in France was
familiar with the benign features of Marshal Pétain. De Gaulle, broadcasting from London, was still a man without a face.

*   *   *

Four years later, to the great majority of people inside France, his
features were still unknown. In June 1944 on the way to Bayeux—the
incident is related in his *Mémoires* and elsewhere—halting by the
roadside he saw, cycling peaceably towards him, two French policemen. Stopping them, he gave orders that they should return to Bayeux
to warn the people of his coming. The policemen hesitated, looked
puzzled. 'I am General de Gaulle,' he told them; and they obeyed with
alacrity. They knew the voice; they had not known his face.

The fact brings into clearer perspective both the nature and the
immensity of the task accomplished from the outer darkness of exile

and for the most part achieved from London during three war winters. It was not enough that he should call to a war outside of France his compatriots in the free world, so that some day they should march to the liberation behind the armies of more powerful Allies; he must appeal to those within, to the great mass of people helpless and immobile, so that in the end and at the right moment they should liberate themselves. He must speak to all men so that each would respond, however widely separated from his fellows by conditions physical or spiritual, practical or political, to the conjured vision of a France freed by her own sacrifice, united, independent and restored to greatness. He must stimulate the despairing, convince the undecided, calm the impatient; sympathize with suffering, but dispel apathy; temper boldness with prudence; condemn the defeatists, yet leave the way open for their future conversion; inspire faith where none existed, using arguments none could refute. Expressing admiration for Great Britain and gratitude for her support, he must at all times assert and prove that as French leader he was not subordinate to her policies. In words that could be understood by all and disapproved by few he must explain the purpose of Free France.

'The first article of our policy is to wage war. . . .

'We hold it as necessary that from the depths of the nation a wave, menacing yet salutary, should mount to sweep away the causes of disaster together with the scaffolding raised upon the capitulation. For that reason the second article of our policy is to give back to the people its voice, so that as soon as events permit free expression it shall make known what that people wants and what it does not want. . . .

'We speak of "Liberation" in the widest sense of the word, for whilst our labours must not cease before the defeat and punishment of the enemy it is also essential that they should have as their culmination conditions in which every Frenchman shall be able to live, to think, to work and to act, with dignity and in safety. There is the third article of our policy.'[1]

To the magnitude of his success the facts were to testify across the weary years of struggle. From the few sympathizers of early days, of necessity silent and inactive, the numbers swelled until at the moment

From a speech made at the Albert Hall, November 15, 1941.

of victory almost the whole of France recognized in him the only acceptable head of nation and state. The scattered supporters of 1940, rare, divided, unarmed, gained strength from his constant urging and tireless study of their problems. They were aided and organized, from London, by a brilliant Intelligence department for long under Colonel 'Passy'-Dewavrin and, from inside France, by men of such unforgettable heroism as Jean Moulin whose patron saint must surely be Saint Peter-Martyr, his finger for ever at his lips, silent under torture. It was Moulin who, on instructions from de Gaulle, brought together the groups which grew to be the French Forces of the Interior, 200,000 strong, united in acceptance of de Gaulle's authority, whose action so greatly contributed to the Allied triumph in 1944. Without those Allies there would, obviously, have been no triumph; but without de Gaulle there would have been no organized Resistance, no swift victory, and instead of 'liberation' there would have been civil war. Unchecked by de Gaulle the Communists, well organized and determined to dominate, would have fought the still powerful Pétainists, with their notoriously brutal Vichy 'militia' and the assistance of the Germans, would have fought them to the death; a third force, of independent groups armed and supported by the Anglo–Americans, would have intervened in the name of democracy; and the ensuing conflict would have prolonged the war against Hitler which it might well have outlasted. A million Frenchmen dead might have been the result, and at the end France devastated, self-destroyed, held down by Allied military force, must have been reduced to a despised and meaningless cipher among the nations.

De Gaulle spared her that. For an essential period of time he gave her unity; a unity of purpose in war that transcended the political divisions threatening her very existence and a unity of faith in the integrity of his leadership that compelled acceptance of his authority. The unity was dissolved with the liberation, but the authority he retained and asserted long enough to ensure France's active participation in the final victory and to regain her a voice in the councils of Europe and of the world. Then, with an abnegation unique among modern heads of state, he effaced himself. And in the finality of the gesture it seemed for a time that, to the golden thread of the pattern, the last knot had been tied.

Of the causes of his success it is evident that those having effect upon his followers outside France were markedly different from those at work within. They were in fact diametrically opposed. To all in the relatively few Free French forces enrolled under his command during the first year, in Britain, Africa and the Middle East, he was known by sight and, to a very large number, known personally. Exiles like himself, rebels in the name of France, many of the officers—Catroux, Larminat, Leclerc amongst others—like him condemned to death by Vichy, they were well aware that the only way home was the hard one to which he pointed. They saw him in their midst, proud, calm and resolute, '*le grand Charles*' striding confidently ahead: de Gaulle, the visible and acknowledged leader. To those inside France, whose hour was yet to strike, he was 'de Gaulle' the symbol.

Unknown, unseen, he held up to the increasing fraction the mirror of France through whose darkened surface they were exhorted to see the shadowy figures of Clemenceau, towering above the squalid Laval, of Marshal Foch obliterating Marshal Pétain—*Père-la-Victoire* eclipsing *Père-la-Défaite*—and, with memory stirred by the emblem of Lorraine, to glimpse the distant glory of Saint Joan. The reflected past, evoked in present humiliation, outlined heroically the perilous future. Then as now an arrogant foe had stamped across the land; then as now a solitary voice had called the people to rebellion against servitude, to unity in the name of France. Then, though the ancient enemy denouncing the heresy had destroyed the rebel, he had failed to destroy the rebellion; resistance had triumphed, and the sacrifice had been redeemed when the heretic was proved a saint. Might it not be the same now as then? Of the man who held up the mirror that banished apathy with the reproach of history, they could no more distinguish the features than they could those of the Maid of Orleans; yet since few could fail to perceive the similarity of spirit in a similar cause many came to regard the man as the successor to the saint and, in some sort, as her modern counterpart. Listening to his call to unity and to sacrifice, to the unemotional yet moving language of nocturnal broadcasts, his supporters, by the very fact of his physical remoteness and invisibility, came to endow his symbolic name with the spiritual qualities he invoked in the nation itself, so that in time the ideal of France and the ideals of 'de Gaulle' became almost synonymous.

This near-identification with his native land and her national saint, of which he was made aware by the growing number of young men escaping from France, increased de Gaulle's sense of mission; but it must be noted that he neither imposed nor suggested it. Though from the first he had felt impelled to speak 'in the name of France', he had at no time endeavoured to personify any leader other than 'de Gaulle'; such an impersonation would have been foreign to his nature. The declaration 'I am France' of the early days had been no more than a statement of fact, a matter of military necessity; the exclamation 'I am Joan of Arc', which Roosevelt was to attribute to him at a later date, was never made—not in that form, the expression most probably used being either 'they think of me as——' or 'for them I represent——' Certain it is that the idealized view of his symbolic leadership came from inside France, that the faith was spontaneous and that, for it, men were ready to suffer torture and death.

The effect upon de Gaulle, the awe such faith inspired in him, was to increase the severity of his own self-discipline and to accentuate the austerity both of his manner and of his mode of living. In London, at work all day and often late into the night at Carlton Gardens, he stayed at the Connaught Hotel where, in the privacy of his small suite, he sometimes dined with two or three of his close associates. Whenever time could be spared he spent a few days with his wife and the three children, living first at Richmond, later in Shropshire, eventually and more permanently in Berkhamsted where he took a house for them. In course of time and of many journeys he met most of the leading personalities in Government circles, was entertained by public bodies to whom he spoke in support of lasting Franco–British co-operation; spent the customary week-ends at Chequers where he endured the Prime Minister's erratic hours of work and play and survived, there as in Downing Street, his tireless energy and ebullient enthusiasm, his emotional moods, his hectoring and occasionally explosive wrath. Apart, however, from these necessary activities his life was devoid of what are usually called amusements; his visits to theatres or cinemas were rare; he was seldom to be seen in the great hotels, never in the expensive restaurants, elegant bars or well-known clubs. Had he shown himself more often he might well have become a more popular figure to the British, and later to the Americans; he would, in his own view, have been less worthy of France. Solace and relaxation he found only in the secluded family circle, in exile more restricted than ever. His son, Philippe, was growing up, presently to play his part in the

Free French Navy; his elder daughter was at Oxford, but the health of the younger was already causing grave anxiety. This one deep con-concern and personal pain aside, his absorption in the affairs of France was complete, his every action of everyday life determined by the need to justify the faith placed in him by her unhappy people.

At the end of the Syrian campaign a Vichy-French officer, depre-cating the armed opposition to the Allies, sought to explain the reasons: they had not known of the presence of German auxiliaries, Vichy had kept them in the dark, they had been ignorant of what was going on in the world, no one had told them anything. De Gaulle listened with patience, and at the end leaned forward confidentially: 'Between our-selves, let me tell you something. *The Germans are in Paris!*'

Much more than a bitter jest against those misguided men who, thinking to serve France under Marshal Pétain, were in fact aiding Germany under Adolf Hitler, it was the simplest possible expression of a truth that was never out of his thoughts. 'The Germans are in Paris!' No Frenchman could dismiss that lasting horror with a shrug. No Frenchman—outside of the military hierarchy, blind in its mis-taken estimate of the outcome of the struggle—could fail to see that in the long run the only way to get rid of the Germans must be to throw them out by force of arms and that to this end Free France and her British Ally were waging war. To rouse and prepare the people of France for the still distant goal, to organize step by step agents, groups, a network, eventually to equip and to arm for the fight, de Gaulle worked long hours in the darkness of wartime London, learning as he went and emerging unbowed from many a tussle with Government departments more interested in gathering positive Intelligence than in stimulating a Resistance whose ultimate worth was still uncertain.

London, as the centre of his activities, was the inevitable choice. Of the struggle against Germany, of the vital war at sea, of the war effort of the Commonwealth and Empire, of cable and wireless communica-tions with the entire world, London was the focal point. For the special purposes of Free France, whose central organization was now well established, it was the headquarters upon which depended the all-essential British support and supply, from which were directed the increasingly numerous air liaisons with France, towards which secret agents and new recruits converged, and in which was operated the supremely important Foreign Service of the BBC. As an independent 'capital' on French soil Brazzaville had its value; but it was too small, too remote, its wireless station was for long too low-powered to be effective. London it had to be.

Of his presence there the hostile press and radio naturally took advantage to describe him as a 'puppet of the English' living in comfort 'on the banks of the Thames', but since at the same time the enemy was gloating over the devastation caused by the *Luftwaffe* it did not appear to his French sympathizers that the 'puppet' had chosen a very safe refuge; indeed, as the much-tried Londoners bore up patiently to the German fury and as Churchill's voice continued to thunder its scornful defiance of Hitler and his 'tattered lackey', it seemed rather as though the British capital were the post of honour. By the ever-growing number of listeners in occupied France, as by the numerous 'gaullist' agents going to and fro on their perilous missions, the worth of de Gaulle's headquarters in London was not unappreciated, nor the reasons for his lengthy sojourns in England misunderstood.

All the more strange must seem the opinion of Cordell Hull. 'If he [de Gaulle], as an Army general,' the Secretary of State wrote, and later published in his Memoirs, 'had thrown himself wholeheartedly into the fight against the Axis in a military sense, if he had actually led French troops against the enemy wherever possible instead of spending most of his time in London, he could have rallied far more support to himself among the French. . . .' Given the many journeys made by de Gaulle to and from Equatorial Africa, Syria, Eritrea, Libya and, eventually, to Algeria and the front in Italy; given, too, the drab discomfort of London in wartime; the sneer emitted from the well-lit, and well-fed, warmth of Washington seems scarcely creditable to its author. And it must surely be a mathematical computation of some difficulty to estimate the support de Gaulle could have rallied to himself 'far more' than that of the entire French nation.

*   *   *

For Cordell Hull's annoyance there was, initially, some excuse. His policy, and that of Roosevelt, during the period of American neutrality and until the Allied landings in North Africa was to 'prop' Pétain's weakening resistance to German demands, to aid him in opposing enemy encroachments in Morocco and Algeria, and to warn him against the evil consequences of handing over the Toulon fleet. As events turned out, this policy achieved little of any consequence and was certainly pushed too far to be regarded with anything but distaste and suspicion by American public opinion; but, in the anxious days of 1940 and the first half of 1941, it had the warm approval of Churchill, prompted by the Prime Minister's very natural desire to be fully informed of Vichy's intentions concerning French land forces in Africa and Syria and French warships in the Mediterranean.

It was the apparent contradiction in the British attitude that made Hull so peevish: here was Churchill approving friendly relations with Pétain, and at the same time backing with supplies and propaganda that troublesome nonentity General de Gaulle. Some of the French colonies, he was forced to admit, had acclaimed the rebel General; in due course the United States would have to recognize the unwelcome fact and draw advantage from it; but inside France he had no real support whatever. Hull knew that, partly because he wished to believe it, since de Gaulle's movement ran counter to his policy of friendship with Pétain, partly because he was told so by the American Ambassador in Vichy.

There was nothing wrong with Admiral Leahy as a man and as a patriotic American. A loyal friend and assistant to Roosevelt, he discharged his mission of explaining the President's views to Pétain with firmness and ability. As a naval officer—retired, he was sixty-five in 1940—he was deeply conscious of the German menace to American security and thoroughly in agreement with the Lend-Lease policy towards Britain of 'all aid short of war'. He admired 'Britain's lonely, gallant stand' in 1940, and writing later of the Anglo-French tragedy of Oran-Mers el Kebir stated that had he been 'the British admiral on the spot' he too 'would have sunk the French ships'. Of France and the French, however, he knew little, being under the delusion, common to so many of his countrymen, that all Frenchmen entertained for America an ineradicable affection; whereas, as Admiral Darlan was to make quite clear (in an impertinent letter to Leahy, dated March 8, 1942), America was then all too frequently looked upon by Frenchmen knowing their history as 'a nation which owes its independence in a great part' to France and which therefore owed in return, and in perpetuity, material aid in times of peace and military aid in war. Since it was soon apparent that no substantial American aid of any sort would be available in 1941, any more than it had been forthcoming during the critical hours of 1940, enthusiasm for the United States remained at a very low ebb inside France, whilst the presence at Vichy of a fully accredited American Ambassador, tending to bolster Pétain's dwindling prestige, was regarded with strong disfavour by the Free French in exile.

Isolated in spy-ridden Vichy, debarred by his official position from establishing contacts of any real value outside governmental or diplomatic circles, it was next to impossible for Leahy to assess with any accuracy the true sentiments of the people of unoccupied France, and still less of those silent masses in the much larger occupied zone. His principal talks and negotiations were, naturally, with Pétain, Darlan and Weygand; so that, although far from gullible, it was almost inevitable that as time went on he should come to accept as facts some of their anti-Free French opinions. He heard Pétain express 'a special hatred' for de Gaulle: 'that viper'; listened to the aged Marshal's pathetic wail: 'He claims to be a patriot. Why doesn't he come back to France *and suffer with the rest of us?*'[1] And noted that 'a number of Frenchmen shared the Marshal's view'—which, in Vichy, was scarcely surprising.

Of the clandestine propagation of faith in the unseen leader he had scarcely any knowledge at all. Even when Vichy's increasing collaboration with the enemy during the first half of 1941 had led to a marked swing of popular opinion in de Gaulle's favour, the American Ambassador could still find it possible to assert that there was 'no indication in occupied France that the self-styled "leader of French resistance" had any important numerical following.' In his ignorance of conditions in the occupied territory—which, in his sixteen months as Ambassador, he was never able to visit—he does not appear to have realized that little indication was likely to be displayed upon the surface by those whose lives depended upon secrecy. On the other hand, if an underground movement existed, he was unwilling to admit that it had anything to do with the 'self-styled' leader. 'There was,' he wrote later, 'a group who called themselves "Gaullists". They were French, apparently attaching to themselves the ancient name of France, but they were not "de Gaullists".' Of this involved hair-splitting it may be observed that, had the members of the mysterious group wished to make use of the 'ancient name', they would have spelt it with

[1] Author's italics.

one 'l' and in all probability have called themselves '*gaulois*', and that no followers of the General were termed specifically '*de* Gaullists'.

As a corollary to his preconception that all Frenchmen loved all Americans he held the belief, fostered assiduously in Vichy, that all Frenchmen hated the British: a proposition which, by and large, was very far from the truth. Presently he was reporting to Roosevelt (August 26, 1941) that 'practically the entire population entertains a high regard for America, looks only to America for its salvation, and hopes for a British victory, although they expect little consideration from a victorious Britain without our assistance.' In other reports he was more explicit about anti-British sentiment, mistaking what he read in the enemy-controlled press for an expression of national feeling; with the result that, hearing Vichy Frenchmen say 'they looked upon de Gaulle as a paid British agent', he supposed that 'agent' to be included in an imagined anglophobia. Moreover, what he learned in Vichy seemed to be in keeping with Roosevelt's low opinion of the General; so that, although he had no facts to confirm his view, and no means whatever of discovering the thoughts of 'the entire population', he had already written to the President (July 28): 'The de Gaulle movement has not the following indicated in the British radio news or in the American press. Frenchmen with whom I can talk, even those completely desirous of a British victory, have little regard for General de Gaulle.'

Whilst the sources of information available to him in Vichy were limited to those 'Frenchmen with whom I can talk', it is impossible to acquit him of prejudice. From beginning to end of his mission—and subsequently in Washington—his scornful hostility to de Gaulle and his movement remained constant. However deeply he might distrust the majority of Vichy-Frenchmen, from frequent contact he too readily absorbed views that seemed to agree with his own preconceived notions; for de Gaulle he never had a good word, because in Vichy he never heard one. Later he was to write: 'From Vichy his movement appeared to cause nothing but trouble for the Allies.' From Vichy— and, unfortunately, from Washington.

Thus blinded, he failed altogether to observe, or even to guess at, the swing of popular opinion towards resistance that began in the summer of 1941 and, gaining momentum, continued throughout the months and the years until its importance could be denied only by men grossly misinformed or perversely refusing to perceive the truth. Admittedly, Admiral Leahy was beset by many worries of greater moment than the future of de Gaulle and his followers,[1] but it seems extraordinary that he should have contrived to overlook the many factors playing into the hands of the resistance movement: the effects of food shortage and worsening conditions upon the industrial masses, of open collaboration in the military field that resulted in the loss of Syria to Anglo–Free French forces, of political weakness that resulted in the loss of Indo-China to the Japanese, of repressive German measures denounced, not by Pétain, but by the pro-de Gaulle underground press, above all of Hitler's invasion of Russia.

The effect of the invasion was twofold. In the first place, despite the swift, and expected, initial successes of the German Army, the greater number of the people of France could not bring themselves to believe that in the end Hitler would win where Napoleon had lost; and, seeing that Britain had gained a new and powerful ally, took fresh hope in an eventual Allied victory. Secondly, it brought the French Communist party 'into the war' on the side of resistance against the Nazis with whom, hitherto, they had maintained harmonious relations by reason of the Russo–German agreement that had made the conquerors appear, in the distorted Marxist view, as 'the friends of peace among the peoples'. For their unnatural if well-disciplined aloofness in France's time of defeat and despair many party members had felt a deep sense of shame; with all the more zest they now threw themselves into the struggle. Thus for a while, as the wags put it, 'all Gaul was divided into three parties': Pétainist, Gaullist and Communist. But presently with Vichy once again crying out against the peril of a Bolshevik uprising—and giving assistance to the Germans in measures of increasing severity that included the slaughter of hostages selected because of their Marxist sympathies—the other two groups were drawn together in the common cause.

Their alliance, for the duration of the war, was not to be achieved without prolonged clandestine negotiation and much hard bargaining, and even then the Communists would endeavour to steal a march at the Liberation. But, for the practical purposes of resistance, their

[1] Towards the end of his mission he suffered, at Vichy, a great personal blow in the sudden illness and death of his wife.

union was brought nearer by three announcements of policy that reached the public within a week of Hitler's eastern attack. Churchill came first, with his prompt and forthright declaration of unqualified support for the Soviet Union in its fight against Hitler: his words broadcast to France, were heard with joy by the majority of listeners. Seven days later Vichy ranged itself squarely on Hitler's side by severing diplomatic relations with Russia in a manner so brusque and discourteous that the hand of its German master was clearly discernible: Bogomolov, the Ambassador, being curtly informed that he, his family and the entire Embassy staff were to be out of the country that same night and, in the meantime, were forbidden to communicate with Moscow. The significance of the gesture was not lost upon the 'gaullists', still less upon the Communists, and neither group was slow to perceive the obvious implication: Russia and Britain as allies, supported by Roosevelt's 'arsenal of democracy', were engaged in a fight to the death against Nazi Germany. In that fight the Pétain government would side with the *Reich*.

The community of interest now shared by the two principal resistance groups had been stressed, meanwhile, by the third announcement of policy. On June 24, General de Gaulle, cabling from Jerusalem whence he was anxiously watching the progress of the Syrian campaign, instructed the Free French authorities in London to announce at once, as Churchill had done, that 'we are very openly on the side of the Russians since they are fighting the Germans'. He further directed that Free French propaganda should immediately emphasize that: 'It is not the Russians who are crushing France, occupying Paris, Rheims, Bordeaux, Strasbourg. . . . Those German aircraft, tanks and soldiers which the Russians are now destroying, and will destroy in the future, will no longer be there to stop us from liberating France.'

To these words of practical common sense, swiftly made known inside France, he added instructions for an approach to be made to the Soviet Ambassador in London, Maisky. The ensuing negotiations, conducted by René Cassin, were friendly and fruitful; before long Maisky was able to announce the Soviet Government's official recognition of de Gaulle as Head of all Free Frenchmen wherever they might be, and to declare his Government's readiness to give aid and assistance to the Free French in their fight against Germany. Meanwhile, following upon Vichy's impolitic rupture of diplomatic relations,

Moscow radio had begun broadcasting approval of Free France and warm praise for its leader. The result was positive: the resistance groups, whatever their political colouring, were united under one authority.

Everything still remained to be done: organization, the chain of command, planning, method, equipment. Across the world the vast and terrible conflict had yet to be decided. But henceforth, as they struggled from the depths, the men of the Resistance could see upon a distant summit the pinpoint light of victory. Before the end of the year—with the Germans halted before Moscow, with hostages in occupied France being slain without protest from Pétain—if premature activity was restrained for fear of reprisals upon the innocent, hope had hardened into resolve. For many, whatever might be the cost to them in human suffering, the problem and its solution were seen to be simple: *'les Allemands sont à Paris.'* The Cross of Lorraine recalled Saint Joan's defiant answer: *'Nous les bouterons hors de France!'* Communists might not believe in the Saint, they could not disagree with her precept. Against it no prejudice could prevail.

17. Plots and Counterplots

Et toi, puissant moteur du destin qui m'outrage,
Termine ce combat sans aucun avantage,
Sans faire aucun des deux ni vaincu ni vainqueur.
(Corneille: *Le Cid.* Act V, Scene iv)

I

WHEN, IN December 1940, Laval was dismissed and arrested a ripple of hope had caressed the saddened hearts of the people of France. Now at last, they had thought, Pétain was standing up against 'collaboration', was resisting Hitler's demands and extortions, was insisting upon an honest observance of the armistice terms. Their disillusionment had been swift. The Marshal's momentary firmness evaporated; soon he was seen to be weaker than before.

In fact he had not even originated the plot leading to Laval's arrest. The conspiracy had been thrust upon him by a number of his ministers who, since they included Alibert and Darlan, cannot have been inspired as they claimed by hatred of the proposed military collaboration, but were certainly animated by deep hatred of Laval. Pétain's only independent contribution to the little *coup d'état* was to send for Pierre-Etienne Flandin, the able ex-Premier who had been one of the few statesmanlike figures in French politics during the last years before the War, and to put him in charge of Foreign Affairs in Laval's place. Since, however, Flandin, who had courageously opposed the abolition of the Republic in July, at once made it clear that he intended to resist German demands and oppose collaboration, he was wholly unacceptable to the enemy. Abetz, the German envoy, had come storming down from Paris to Vichy escorted by two armoured cars—in itself a breach of the armistice terms—and, refusing to recognize Flandin's appointment, had compelled the freeing of Laval whom he carried off to Paris. Thereafter, Pétain, tamely allowing himself to be drawn into discussions with the Germans relative to the composition of his government, had easily been persuaded to abandon Flandin. Then, forced to make his peace with Laval at a secret rendezvous, he had thought to display his strength and 'independence' by refusing to take him back, but had only been spared that humiliation—for a time[1]—by the fact that Hitler had lost interest in the man.

'The form of the French Government and the men who compose it,' declared the *Führer*, 'are profoundly indifferent to me. . . . The complaints made against him [Laval] today were, so it appears, largely known before I met him. Therefore, at the very least I must consider it a want of tact to have sent him. I might have been spared that meeting. . . .'

A new star was in the ascendant. Its baleful light had soon been recognized. On February 9 Flandin had resigned; on the 10th the *Journal Officiel* announced, over the Marshal's signature and with the gracious consent of the Germans, the accession to the princely title of *dauphin* and the appointment to the Vice-Presidency of the Council of François Darlan, Admiral.

*   *   *

Vichy apologists, even when critical of its more shameful personalities, have professed to see in men like Darlan, and even Laval, a motive force of elemental patriotism. For those, however, who suffered as the direct result of their actions the patriotic motive was not so easily discernible.

France, after all, was still at war with Germany. An armistice had brought military operations to a standstill, but France was not at peace, still less in alliance with the enemy whose forces held three-fifths of the country by armed occupation. For a Frenchman to give comfort or succour to that enemy, other than what was required by the laws of war or the terms of the armistice, must therefore be an act against France; and the universally accepted word for such an act is treason. Darlan, of his own accord and with Pétain's knowledge and agreement, gave economic aid and military support to Germany; the fact made him a traitor. The theory advanced that, because he believed in the enemy's victory, he was a 'patriotic traitor' can scarcely be admitted as a serious justification of misdeeds directly responsible for the death of many hundreds of his countrymen.

He was not possessed by evil in the same way or to the same extent as was Laval. The origins of his conduct lay in the fundamental weakness of a character that had all the earmarks of foolishness. He was

---

[1] Laval returned to power in April 1942 and remained in office until the Liberation when he fled to Germany.

vain and conceited. He boasted of his lack of erudition. A round of applause in an assembly would gain his unlimited favour. Awarded glittering decorations in the normal course of promotion, he stooped to beg for others to which he was not entitled. Headstrong, guided by prejudice, he was almost entirely unreliable, his actions rarely corresponding to any previously given undertaking. A feeble and childish sense of humour induced him to treat individuals and official bodies alike with an inane and scornful flippancy that alienated both trust and friendship. With too much power over his own service he regarded the French Navy as his personal property; immediately before the surrender he had ordered it to sea, upon his own responsibility, to continue the fight; it had scarcely sailed before, with none to gainsay him, he ordered it back to futile inactivity. The Navy band, an orchestra of eighty pieces, he took over as his own perquisite, causing it to follow him about wherever he went, from Vichy to his home at Nérac, beyond the Garonne, and even to Luchon in the Pyrenees where he went for an unnecessary cure. At a time when the people of France hungered and went on foot he lived in luxury and almost royal state, with a special train at the nearest railway station instantly ready to start at his sole order and regardless of time-tables.

Coming from a family that had long followed the sea, he had himself been keen and competent in his profession and as an officer of flag rank had done much to increase the strength and efficiency of the French Navy, most of whose members remained loyal to him to the end. The opinion of some of them, however, that he was a 'great' sailor is not borne out by the facts. During the first ten months of the War he showed none of the attributes of greatness and when, forsaking the sea, he embarked upon the muddy waters of politics his professional competence was obscured and his keenness diverted to self-aggrandizement. Anglophobia, born of ancient rivalry, he allowed to grow unchecked until it ruled his heart and dominated his military thinking. British determination and ruthlessness he did not question; it was British inefficiency and naval incompetence which, he convinced himself, would lose the War for Britain and therefore, inevitably, win it for Germany. Adding force to this opinion was the view, common to many a loyal but blinkered Frenchman, that none could conquer where France had been defeated: Germany was invincible.

Thence his nebulous thoughts led him to a conclusion well expressed in the brisk vernacular: 'If you can't beat 'em, join 'em.' Germany would win the War; to save herself France must be on the winning side. And at this point sanity left him. A wild dream of wishful thinking led him to the deadly belief that, were he to render 'some signal service', not to France as de Gaulle's phrase indicated, but *to the enemy*, then in the hour of victory Hitler would reward him with power and applause. More than that, under his, Darlan's, leadership a complaisant France would be restored by the *Führer* to independence and greatness. With Britain defeated and her ships all sunk, his navy reassembled would be second to none; with the colonial dependencies recaptured from the rebels, France would become one of the two most powerful nations in the world—in alliance with the enemy, with Nazi-Germany.

The vision of successful treachery held him in thrall, though he tried to explain it as political realism. Hitler was there to encourage him in his madness.

*   *   *

Darlan's first encounter with Hitler took place on Christmas Day, 1940—a fateful season for the Admiral. Two years later, in Algiers on Christmas Eve, 1942, he was to be assassinated by Bonnier de la Chapelle who, whatever his motives, certainly spared him the misery of a treason trial and the humiliation of a firing squad. By that time he was trying to climb back to power upon American shoulders. Of the band of unhappy lunatics and misguided traitors thrown up by Vichy, to him Nemesis was kind.

That first meeting took place in Hitler's train at a wayside station some twenty miles from Beauvais. It was not a pleasant interview, for when Hitler in his special coach came puffing out of the usual tunnel he was in one of his blackest moods. For one thing the Admiral, through no fault of his own, was three-quarters of an hour late for the appointment; and, for another, Hitler was already incensed with Pétain for rejecting military collaboration, for dismissing Laval, for snubbing him by not coming to the *Aiglon* ceremony and for showing ingratitude at imaginary 'concessions'. After treating the speechless Darlan to a long and violent harangue, he ended with the customary menace of blackmail.

'I declare solemnly that, for the last time, I offer a policy of collaboration to France. . . . Sooner or later France will realize, if she refuses collaboration, that she has taken one of the most regrettable decisions in her history.'

Though he resented the scolding, Darlan swallowed the insults and accepted the blackmail. Back in Vichy, after negotiating with Abetz in Paris, he worked to oust Flandin by adopting the very policy for advocating which Laval had been dismissed. Early in February, to a council of bewildered ministers, he declared his intentions. 'If we cease collaborating, we shall lose all the advantages we may expect from the armistice. For my part, I have made my choice. I am for collaboration.'

Pétain, who had caused Laval to be arrested for expressing similar intentions, now accepted the resignation of Flandin who refused to implement them. At the secret meeting he had held with Laval shortly after the arrest, the Marshal had been told to his face that he was nothing but a 'weathercock' and a 'marionette'. He had already proved himself to be the one, soon he was seen to be the other. Darlan, created *dauphin* in Laval's place and ordered to form an administration, took over no less than four key ministries: Vice-Presidency of the Council, Internal Affairs, Foreign Affairs, Information. In all but name, the Crown Prince was the Monarch.

For some two months, despite attempts at negotiation by both Pétain and Darlan, Vichy and occupied France were stretched upon the rack of Hitler's displeasure; diplomatic relations remained severed, with the demarcation frontier closed; serious breaches of the armistice convention increased, including the detachment of eastern departments of France to form the German dependency of *Ostland*. Then, when the rack had done its work, tension was suddenly relaxed and Darlan was permitted to see how he might win the *Führer's* favour. On May 3 Abetz called him to Paris, dangled the bait of possible concessions in return for military help, and put him in touch with an officer of the German General Staff who told him of Hitler's plan of campaign in the Middle East. Within three days an agreement was concluded (May 6) by whose terms Vichy undertook to wage war against Britain in Iraq.

On April 11 Pétain had stated in a broadcast speech: 'Honour demands that we should not undertake anything against our old allies'—meaning Britain. Within a month the 'weathercock' had swung about. The demands of Honour were importunate, Hitler was more vociferous. The Marshal agreed to support the *Führer* with military aid against the 'old ally'.

On May 11, summoned by Hitler, Darlan arrived at Berchtesgaden. He had cut the last hampering strings of sanity and was now obsessed by the lunatic vision of France, in alliance with Germany, taking the first place in Europe under Hitler's New Order. Hitler's threats may have made him shudder, the rewards of loyal collaboration were glittering: 'As compensation for the loss of Alsace-Lorraine, France might receive Wallonia and French Switzerland' and, in the way of colonies, 'certain spoils from the British Empire.' The usual harangue tending to prove that Germany was bound to win the War was hardly necessary. Darlan knew it already. What was far more exciting were the intended operations against Russia, revealed by Hitler on the following day (May 12): if Russia did not withdraw from the Baltic provinces 'she will be defeated in three weeks'.

Fascinated, the foolish Admiral let himself go. 'France,' he declared, 'is completely willing to help Germany win the War.' For 'France', had he been honest, he should have said 'Darlan'; and proved this a few moments later by angling for Hitler's continued support of his personal authority.

'I make a formal promise,' he announced, 'to direct French policy towards an integration with the New European Order . . . and to assure the continuity of this line of policy.'

To make certain that Hitler understood him he recalled the terms of the agreement made in Paris. 'France has already manifested her desire to collaborate with the *Reich* economically and militarily by lending effective support in Syria.'

On May 15 Pétain broadcast his approval of the policy of military collaboration; and war against Britain in the Middle East was begun, undeclared but open. Darlan, adding his confirmation, broadcast: 'It is a question of choosing between life and death. The Marshal and the Government have chosen life.'

In fact, for Vichy, there was no choice at all. Death was, and always had been, the wage of the unnecessary surrender. From the moment when Pétain and Weygand had conspired to ask for an armistice the outcome had been predictable, however the marionettes might dance, the weathercocks turn. Hitler was not, as some were to claim, 'obliged' to turn to Vichy for assistance in the Middle East. His attitude, from the day of Rethondes onwards, had been one of contempt for the conquered nation and indifference to its fate. France was a captured treasure chest from which he could snatch what spoils he wanted when he wanted them; when the chest was empty he would kick it to pieces without compunction. He had no intention whatever of restoring the chest, let alone the contents, to its rightful owners, no thought at all of allowing France to rise again to power and independence; if Darlan and the old Marshal believed they were striking a bargain, the more fools they. He was quite willing that they should 'collaborate'; thus they would give him freely what otherwise he would take by force. For the people of France it was slavery and death in any event, and the choice under Darlan was not whether they should live, but when they should die.

Darlan was to take pride in the fact that he did not hand over the French fleet. Hitler never asked him for it. He was determined that it should fulfil two conditions only: that it should not go over to the British or the Free French, which after Mers-el-Kebir was hardly probable, and that it should defend those North African dependencies which, with Pétain's France, had surrendered to him. Under Darlan's command the conditions were carried out to the letter. In nearly two and a half years, from the surrender of June 1940 to the act of suicide at Toulon in November 1942, the Vichy-French Navy, though it fired successively upon British, Free French and American allies, never once opened fire or took any action whatever against either German or Italian enemies. Thus, as a small 'fleet in being', a continual if minor source of anxiety to the Allies, it was of far greater value to Hitler than it could possibly have been had he insisted upon taking it over. For this contribution to the enemy's purpose Darlan was supremely responsible.

He was also responsible, under Pétain, for the tragic events in Syria and for the lasting damage they caused to France.

II

In Iraq, on May 2, Rashid Ali acting on the advice of Nazi *agents provocateurs* appealed to the *Führer* for assistance in attacking the small British garrisons maintained in the country under the terms of a long-ratified treaty of friendship. Hitler was ready to oblige. His forces had just overrun Greece; in Libya the *Afrika* Corps was rolling forward, rather unexpectedly, towards Egypt; a little additional trouble in the heart of the Middle East would keep the British quiet and deter both them and the Turks from attempting to aid Russia, the attack upon which was now less than five weeks distant. Abetz, in Paris, was given his orders: the usual carrot-like concessions were to be held before the donkey, and Darlan made to understand that now was the time to gain the *Führer's* favour and to strike a shrewd blow at the hated British.

Whatever confidence he may have felt in the reality of the concessions—time was to prove them almost entirely worthless—Darlan fully understood the importance of the enemy's military plan. He gave it all the assistance in his power. The agreement signed on May 6, which was implemented forthwith, included the following points:

> Three-quarters of the considerable French stocks of war material, arms and equipment in Syria (hitherto held under the Italian armistice commission) were to be transferred to the insurgents in Iraq. French officers and NCOs would be sent to instruct the Iraqis in the use of these arms.

> The French in Syria would permit the transit of German personnel, arms and equipment. They would give the *Luftwaffe* every assistance in transit or landing, whilst all British aircraft would be attacked on sighting.

> All German and Italian aircraft would be refuelled and maintained by the French. The airfield at Aleppo would be handed over for their use.

> The French would supply the German Command with all military information concerning the British in the Middle East. Operations would be undertaken subsequently against the Free French.

No time was wasted by the combined Vichy-German forces. Arms began to be moved across the border at once; German aircraft, crammed with Nazi agents, arrived at Baghdad. Between May 9 and the end of the month more than one hundred and fifty enemy aircraft[1] landed upon Syrian airfields, some flying on to Iraq, many remaining stationed in French territory.

These moves, by encouraging the insurgents, rendered the situation of the beleaguered British garrisons in Iraq precarious in the extreme

---

[1] Made up of approximately 110 German, 20 Italian, and 20 German aircraft with Iraqi markings.

and made inevitable an Anglo–Free French counter-move against Syria. As Churchill observed in a message to General Wavell at this time: 'If the Germans can pick up Syria and Iraq with petty air forces, tourists, and local revolts we must not shrink from running equal small-scale military risks.' Unfortunately, just then no risks could be regarded as 'small-scale' by the British Middle East command; indeed Wavell, with insufficient trained troops, short of arms, transport and aircraft, was in a considerable predicament. German pressure upon him was heavy; a part of his forces was still engaged in Abyssinia; from London the Chiefs of Staff ordered him to provide a force to attack Syria without detriment to operations in the Western Desert, while Churchill ordered him to provide this force without detriment to the defence of Crete and eventually of Cyprus. At the same time he was also ordered to take over responsibility for Iraq, normally outside his command.

This last demand upon Wavell's scant resources further complicated the situation, since to provide transport for the column ('Habforce') thrust across the desert to the relief of Habaniya, near Baghdad, the small British forces remaining in Palestine were all but immobilized. Initially, unless troops were withdrawn from the tottering Western Desert front, all that was available for the Syrian expedition were the Free French forces which, after greatly distinguishing themselves in Eritrea against the Italians, had just been moved up to Palestine by de Gaulle. But although, early in May, Wavell was informed—from London by the Chiefs of Staff, from Brazzaville by de Gaulle—that the road to Damascus was clear and that the Vichy forces would offer no resistance, he was reluctant to risk committing French against French, the more so since, as he reported to the Chiefs of Staff, the Free French 'were unable to move without transport he did not possess' and 'unwilling to move without British artillery support' which he could not provide. He therefore decided to delay the advance until he could assemble sufficient British troops to ensure a reasonable chance of success.

It was as well that he did so. As May wore on the reassuring information coming out of Syria and reaching de Gaulle was denied and reversed; the 'gaullist' sympathizers with whom General Catroux had been in touch were removed and replaced by Darlan's nominees; the unhappy General Huntziger was flown out to order the local Vichy commander, General Dentz, to resist to the utmost; German support was promised. Thus, when he laid his plans towards the end of the month for an advance early in June, Wavell was aware that he would be opposed by a total of 35,000 Vichy-French and native Syrian troops supported by 120 guns, 90 aircraft, and some 90 to 100 tanks.

The Allied forces, under the overall command of General Maitland Wilson, comprised: *British*—1 Australian Division minus 1 Brigade left to defend Tobruk, 1 Indian Brigade from Iraq, 1 regiment of Yeomanry mounted on horses, 1 Royal Marine Commando, no artillery, no tanks; the Navy supplied 2 cruisers and 10 destroyers to counter Vichy's 2 destroyers and 3 submarines at Beirut: *Free French* (General Legentilhomme)—1 battalion Foreign Legion, 4 battalions of Africans, 1 battalion *Fusiliers Marins*, a battery of artillery and a company of light tanks, no transport. At the start of operations the Royal Air Force could spare only 70 aircraft. Apart, therefore, from the grave disparity in artillery and tanks, the invading forces could muster but fifteen battalions to meet the Syrian–Vichy total of well over thirty.

Weygand had been quoted as saying that were the British to land in North Africa with ten divisions he would attack them, but that were they to bring one hundred divisions he would welcome them with open arms. Since, with some variation in the number of divisions, other Vichy authorities had at one time or another expressed similar views the policy could be taken as that of the military command in Syria. No high principles were at stake, no 'honour', no irreversible resolve to extirpate the Nazi tyranny such as compelled the Free French under de Gaulle. It was a matter of abject expediency, of siding with which-ever nation got in first with the greatest strength; to this miserable state had France been brought by the unnecessary surrender of Bordeaux.

Because of this policy, when the Anglo–Free French advance began on June 8 little resistance was encountered at first; but as soon as the Vichy forces perceived the weakness of their one-time allies, opposition became determined and, in some places, furious. Progress was thereby delayed and the operation, instead of a few days, lasted a month. It was not until July 9 that, with 'Habforce' returning via Palmyra and an Indian division from Iraq thrusting from Deir-es-Zor towards Aleppo, the Australians entered Beirut and Vichy begged for surrender terms. An armistice was negotiated at Acre and all fighting ceased at midnight July 11. By this time the Germans, seeing which way the wind was blowing, had withdrawn to Greece.

The cost in human suffering of Vichy's military collaboration with Germany was heavy. Total casualties—Vichy, Free French, Australian, English, and Indian—amounted to over 11,000 killed and wounded. It is safe to say that not one of these casualties would have been incurred but for Darlan.

*　　*　　*

Had Darlan, guiding the uncertain Pétain, refused Hitler's demands, had he retained his sanity and remained faithful to the basic principle 'France at war with Germany', he would have gained the sympathy of many of his compatriots and the respect of the Western democracies. Hitler would doubtless have exploded with rage, he could scarcely have augmented, though he might have accelerated, the severity of his oppressive measures; but without Vichy's complicity he could have done nothing in Syria and Iraq. Except by air he could not even reach Syria and, having lost the cream of his airborne troops in the Pyrrhic victory of Crete, he had no force with which to overwhelm the Levant had Vichy denied him the use of the airfields.

But the possibility of resisting Hitler's demands appears never to have entered Darlan's mind. The prospect of striking at British power in the Middle East so obscured his vision that, convinced Hitler would win because he wished him to win, he was unable to foresee the end of the adventure. When by his folly the lives of several thousand Frenchmen had been lost, he was surprised and pained to find that he had lost Syria too.

Vichy would not have lost it—not then at least, and not in that inglorious manner—but for Darlan's approval of German intervention. The British Government had not and, despite ineradicable French suspicions to the contrary, had never had the least intention of seizing for her own advantage French territory in the Levant. The position since the Bordeaux armistice had not been a comfortable one, yet hope of an amicable arrangement with the local Vichy authorities had not been abandoned; official consular relations between Cairo, Damascus and Beirut had continued and had led to the belief either that a state of not unfriendly neutrality would be maintained by the existing authorities or that, in course of time, the active agents of Free France would win these mandated territories over to the Allied cause. At all events a peaceful solution was both desired and expected; no compulsion by force of arms was contemplated, since it was believed that any German intrusion would be resisted by Vichy.

Rashid Ali's rebellion and appeal to Hitler set off the alarm bell; within a week the entire situation was changed. With the *Luftwaffe* upon Syrian airfields, not only was Iraq down to the Persian Gulf an easily reached objective, there were menaced at one and the same time Cyprus, Alexandria, Suez, and Britain's ally Turkey. Rommel pressed forward upon the left, Darlan–Hitler threatened the right. The occupation of Syria by Anglo–Free French forces became an imperative and immediate military necessity.

But the evil Darlan did was not to be effaced by the bloodshed of a brief campaign. The action to which his folly compelled the Allies created such a complex of problems political as well as military, such a host of embittered disputes dividing Britain and Free France, the Arabs intervening, as to outlast the War and to end, most regrettably, in the total elimination of France from the Levant.

III

De Gaulle, during his pre-war tour of duty, had noted: 'The only man who ever understood Syria was Catroux—that was why he left.' Now Catroux was back again, in charge of Free French affairs in Cairo and able to give the benefit of his wisdom and experience to the British Ambassador (Sir Miles Lampson) and to the Commander-in-Chief (Wavell), with both of whom he was on the best of good terms. Hoping until the last minute that Dentz in Syria would resist the Germans, the moment it became clear that Darlan's policy had prevailed he urged the necessity for British as well as Free French intervention and, perceiving that fighting might be severe and the issues confused, agreed to a suggestion that the Allied advance should be preceded by a declaration recognizing Arab national rights in Syria and the Lebanon where legitimate desires for independence, had, as he well knew, for too long been frustrated. With this suggested declaration, for which de Gaulle drafted the terms, the British authorities were in full agreement and, on the morning of June 8 when the advance began, Catroux, speaking in the name of Free France, broadcast from Egypt: 'I come to put an end to the mandatory régime and to proclaim you free and independent.' This was followed by a similar announcement from the British Ambassador who backed the declaration with the authority of the British Government.

From these two well-intentioned and equivalent statements grave divisions were to stem. Two days earlier Churchill had cabled de Gaulle that, concerning the Levant, 'our policies must run on parallel lines'. It was an unhappy simile, for like those lines the policies were never to meet, save head on.

There can be no question that from the outset de Gaulle intended to fulfil to the letter the terms of the declaration Catroux had made in his name. He reported the decisions it contained to the members of the Defence Council and to the Free France Delegation in London and, in a letter to Djemil Mardam Bey (former Premier of Syria) dated June 8, he wrote in warm support of 'this proclamation, whose spirit and terms I have approved'. His only mental reservation, a legitimate one, was in the matter of timing. So weighty a decision as the granting of independence to two new states could not be implemented, given the vicissitudes of war and the disturbed state of the country and of the Middle East generally, in a matter of weeks or even months; nor could France be rid in a day of the responsibilities of a League of Nations Mandate which she had held for twenty years. Indeed, as the Free France Delegation in London presently reminded him (July 3): '. . . the decision to put an end to the Mandate has been taken. The problem is to give it effect'—and further: 'It must be borne in mind that general peace alone will permit France to give definite form to the statute' [setting up the new states]. Plainly, this was no more than the truth: nothing could finally be settled, the Mandate could not be surrendered, the treaties of independence could not be ratified, until France herself was once more a free and independent power.

Made aware of these necessary, and quite unavoidable, delays de Gaulle might have done better to have risked the displeasure of both the British and the Arabs by making the reasons clear from the start. As it was he unwittingly allowed the impression to gain ground in the Levant that independence and the end of the Mandate were, not just round the corner, but immediately realizable certainties. In the letter to Djemil Mardam Bey he had written that Catroux's proclamation gave to 'the peoples of the Levant recognition of their status, guaranteed by treaty, as sovereign and independent peoples' without any qualification of time. Indeed by writing of the proclamation as 'this important event' he had seemed to imply that independence was an accomplished fact, an impression emphasized by his statement that the proclamation had been made in his name 'and in the name of Free France, that is to say of France'.

In this, if he went too far and too fast, the British Government unfortunately went much farther and faster. In his message to de Gaulle (June 6) Churchill had said: 'I welcome your decision to promise independence to Syria and the Lebanon, and, as you know, I think it essential that we should lend to this promise *the full weight of our guarantee*.'[1] De Gaulle had already protested to the British Ambassador in Cairo that no guarantee was necessary, that it was in fact slighting, since 'the word of France' was sufficient; and at this point the British Government would have been well advised to think again and to look carefully ahead. No one with any knowledge of the man could doubt the worth of de Gaulle's word of honour; but, in the context of his promise to the peoples of the Levant, the question arose: was he entitled to pledge 'the word of France'? The Free France organization under his leadership was not, and did not claim to be, the Government of France either 'provisional' or 'in exile'. By the terms of the Brazzaville Manifesto he had undertaken to administer such colonial territories as adhered to Free France and to render account to the French people at the Liberation; he had *not* undertaken —and by his very nature never could undertake—to give away French territory, even mandated, unless and until the liberated French people authorized him to do so. How then could the British Government 'guarantee' a promise to grant sovereign independence and to terminate a League of Nations Mandate, made by a leader, however honourable, who was not and *might never be* the acknowledged and fully authorized head of a free and legitimate government?

In 1941, with the Allies still an immeasurable distance from victory, it was evidently too early to grant to Free France the status of a Provisional Government whose authority would one day be accepted without question in the liberated homeland. Since, then, the British Government could not 'guarantee' the future of de Gaulle, it could not 'guarantee' the actions of post-war France. Nor had it any warrant for guaranteeing, without the specific authority of the Council of the League of Nations, the surrender of a Mandate granted to another

[1] Author's italics.

power. Whether the terms of de Gaulle's proclamation were fulfilled or not—and in time they were—the 'guarantee' did not give Britain the right to intervene by force, *against France*, in French mandated territory, well-justified though the intervention, *in alliance with Free France*, had been in time of war. Churchill and his Foreign Secretary, Eden, thought that it did.

France, it must be admitted, had not handled her affairs in the Levant with much adroitness between the Wars. But then Britain in neighbouring Palestine had been even less skilful and, wavering 'from policy to policy, irresolute, vacillating and bewildered,'[1] had been led by a succession of feckless politicians into an even more dismal *impasse*.

On France's behalf it can be said that in the Lebanon the position had not been unsatisfactory; French was the language most commonly spoken, the Christian population was about equal in numbers to that of the Moslems, few were resentful of French rule which brought them peace, prosperity and culture. In Syria, however, where the great majority of the mainly Arab inhabitants had rejoiced at the ending of Turkish rule and the birth of a new State under the Emir Feisal, the arrival of the French military administration under General Gouraud had, from the start in 1920, been anything but welcome and, as time went on and the new rulers made no move towards democratic government, clandestine opposition became open revolt. Yet, although the Druze rebellion of 1925 was extremely costly to the French, and the rising in Damascus of the same year was costly to the inhabitants, few attempts at conciliation were made by the French High Commissioner whose rule was absolute. The League of Nations Mandate had stipulated that a Constitution should be granted to Syria within three years (of 1923), but it was five years before an elected Assembly could meet; and then, having declared that Syria should be an independent republic, it was promptly suspended by the High Commissioner. The Constitution was nevertheless evolved, however slowly, and in 1934 a draft Franco–Syrian treaty was submitted to the recalled Assembly, which rejected it; whereupon the French suspended the Constitution. In 1936 a second treaty reached the stage of being initialled; but it was never ratified and, with negotiations dragging endlessly on, the Syrian president eventually resigned in protest (July 1939); the

[1] Sir John Glubb, *Britain and the Arabs*.

Constitution was again suspended and rule by the French High Commissioner was resumed. This position still obtained when the Anglo–Free French forces took over in July 1941.

Once Vichy had been ousted, and de Gaulle had wrested administrative control of the territory from the British military authorities, in itself a considerable achievement, General Catroux as Free French Delegate and Commander-in-Chief lost no time in honouring that part of the promise contained in his proclamation which could be fulfilled immediately. His loyalty to the promise and his skill as a patient negotiator were displayed against the dark background of violently divided opinions, where ex-Vichy officials hated the British and still regarded de Gaulle as something of a traitor, where the Free French, suspicious of 'collaborators', were even more suspicious of British intentions and were irritated by frequent reminders of the 'guarantee', and where the politically-minded people of Damascus, who had acclaimed de Gaulle as their liberator, were quick to complain that, despite the promises, all that had been done was to substitute for the rule of Vichy the rule of Free France. By autumn (1941) the first part of the task was accomplished and de Gaulle could write from London, in the name of the newly-formed French National Committee, to the Secretary-General of the League of Nations informing him that, in Damascus on September 26 and in Beirut on the 27th, the sovereign independence of Syria and the Lebanon had been proclaimed.

His letter, dated November 29, was circulated to fifteen nations which were members of the League and to two, Russia and the United States, which were not. After asserting that only the necessities of war would henceforth limit the sovereignty of the two States, a further paragraph wisely pointed out that complete independence was still conditioned by the terms of the Mandate. The proclamations of sovereignty did not, de Gaulle wrote, 'affect the juridical situation as it results from the Mandate Act. This situation could not, in fact, be modified except with the assent of the Council of the League of Nations ... and then only after the conclusion, between the French Government and the Syrian and Lebanese Governments, of treaties duly ratified in accordance with the legislation of the French Republic.' It was therefore clear to all concerned that, in de Gaulle's view, France was still the mandatory power, that the French National Committee was temporarily vested with authority, and that only the Council of the League could revoke this authority. Against this view not one of the eighteen nations notified (including Britain) appears to have registered any protest whatever.

Catroux remained as High Commissioner and, throughout the long months ahead, strove to hold a fair balance between the rival parties and to reach the next stage of political development: the holding of free elections. In the disturbed state of opinion in Syria and the Lebanon, still occupied by the Free French and British troops necessary both to back Turkey and to guard against possible German inroads from the Dodecanese, his task was not an easy one; and it was made no easier by the constant prodding of the British representatives and their perpetual fluttering of the 'guarantee', which served only to excite the truculence of place-seeking politicians in Beirut and Damascus. The elections, postponed during Rommel's advance to Alamein, were eventually held in the summer of 1943 and the results, as might have been foreseen, soon led to trouble. In November the new Lebanese Government passed a number of provocatively anti-French measures, including the abolition of French and the substitution of Arabic as the official language. The Free French representative, Helleu, then reacted by placing the members of the Government under arrest, to which the British authorities, waving aloft the 'guarantee', uttered loud cries of protest—unnecessary as it turned out, for de Gaulle, quietly disapproving Helleu's action, had ordered the immediate release of the Lebanese ministers. Tension was thereupon relaxed, hands were shaken, and discussions took place in December when it was agreed that the Free French authorities should relinquish their powers to the Syrian and Lebanese Governments on January 1, 1944. This left the ratification of the treaties and the ending of the Mandate as the only formalities to be concluded.

Here, however, delay was inevitable for the legal position was complicated. With the United Nations taking over from the moribund League, mandatory power would in future derive from the new organization to which France had not yet been invited to adhere, because de Gaulle's National Committee (by that time in Algiers) was still not recognized as the Provisional Government of France. With the liberation of France and the re-establishment of the French Government yet to be accomplished, it was therefore unlikely that the final settlement in the Levant could be effected before the end of the

War, and quite certain that no French troops would be withdrawn until then. Early in 1945 the treaties were ready for signature.

Hardly had the War in Europe drawn to its close, however, than Levantine political agitators—of whom there has never been any lack —saw how they might be rid of the French without the encumbrance of binding treaties. In the whole country there were only between 6,000 and 7,000 French troops; the Syrian levies outnumbered them, and the police—recently re-armed by the British—were hostile. Armed disturbances, small in scale but widely spread, would compel the French to take military action; the 'guarantee' could then be loudly invoked and the British 9th Army, some 50,000 strong—whose presence in Syria was now unwarranted by any military necessity—be asked to intervene.

Up to the last minute the French authorities, aware of the customary plotting, endeavoured to get the treaties signed; but by mid-May the planned risings at Homs, Hama and Aleppo had taken on so threatening an aspect that the French, fearing for their bases, their property and the lives of their nationals, were obliged to call in North African reinforcements which, landed at Beirut, were hurriedly marched inland.[1] Thereupon, the French were attacked at Damascus; there was fighting in the city where, in return, Syrian strongpoints were bombed and shelled by the French causing, the Syrians claimed, some four hundred deaths. With the situation on the point of being restored to normal, both the Levantine Governments, with an air of injured innocence, appealed to the Powers for help.

In all the circumstances it is almost impossible to imagine what other action the French could have taken. Their forces had an absolute right to be in the country, at the least until the treaties had been ratified and the Mandate formally terminated. Attacked, it was their duty to defend themselves and to ensure that sporadic outbreaks of violence did not degenerate into nation-wide anarchy. Too weak to safeguard life and property, it was incumbent upon them to call in sufficient reinforcements, and the obligation to reinforce was made the more urgent by the attitude of the British 9th Army, looking on impassively while the French were attacked by the police it had armed. Doubtless the neutrality of the British forces was technically correct, for they were in the country on sufferance only, but to the French it

---

[1] It should be noted that, whereas these reinforcements amounted to but 3,000 men, the British at about the same time moved in a division.

appeared callous, patronizing and, given all that had gone before, to some extent openly hostile. On the other hand, it had been recognized by the British Government that, even after the signing of the treaties, France's influence and interests in the area would be paramount; with the treaties still unsigned, France acted as any other nation, including Britain, would have acted in a situation of similar difficulty. She was entitled to sympathy, if not to support.

But, however justified, the French action stirred the British Government to a reaction as ill-judged and hasty as if this were the nineteenth century, with Palmerston in power and France the natural enemy; as if, moreover, its leaders were anxious, as Lord Alanbrooke noted, to 'put it across de Gaulle'. No time was allowed for tempers to cool, for less vehement counsels to prevail; the Arab case was listened to, the French case left unheard. Fighting had broken out in Damascus on May 29; on May 30, in the House of Commons, Eden replied affirmatively to the Syrian appeal, basing his reply not upon any carefully considered United Nations decision—which, incidentally, France could have vetoed—but upon the 1941 'guarantee' whose validity as an instrument of interference in a Franco–Syrian dispute was certainly open to question. That same evening Churchill telegraphed to de Gaulle, announcing that he had ordered the British forces to intervene and demanding that the French should cease fire immediately. By some culpable error which was never satisfactorily explained, the British Government's statement was made public in London more than an hour before it could reach de Gaulle in Paris; and this combination of bullying and blundering appeared to the French Government as tantamount to an ultimatum with the alternative of war— 'the language of Fashoda', Catroux rightly called it—and, since war with Britain was unthinkable, the French troops had perforce to withdraw (June 3) from Damascus which British troops then occupied.

Less heated, but prolonged and not very profitable discussions followed; and it was not until February, 1946, that at the request of the United Nations all French and British forces were finally removed. Syria was left to enjoy the delights of independence; but not for long. In 1941 de Gaulle, 'the Liberator', had been wildly acclaimed in the streets of Damascus; in 1945 the same people welcomed with the same fickle fervour the British forces coming to 'liberate' them from the Liberator; not a dozen years later they were madly to applaud the

loss of their independence to an Egyptian, 'smiling to deceive' and
bearing Russian arms.

At the height of the 1945 crisis (June 2) de Gaulle stated publicly
his belief that all France's recent troubles in Syria were due to British
encouragement of Arab aspirations. Although this was far from being
the whole of the story, it was a good deal nearer the truth than the
explanation put out by the British Government, in which Churchill,
denying de Gaulle's conjecture, invoked all the old familiar arguments
—the necessities of war, against Japan now, the security of communications with the East, the safety of the Suez Canal and, of course, the
'guarantee'—none of which was wholly devoid of substance. But
behind the smokescreen lay a jagged range of ugly fact.

Ever since 1941 the British Government had been reiterating that
in Syria it had no territorial interest, which was true, and no political
interest, which was not. The political interest, pro-Arab, constant and
thinly veiled, was to get rid of the French; and by their continual
pressure during the War and their all too frequent reminders of
Catroux's declaration, the British representatives in Syria and the
Lebanon had kept the Arabs upon the tiptoe of expectation: *the French
would go because Britain had promised*. The desired climax came in 1945.
With the ending of the War the Arabs, however disunited, were
everywhere restive; the winds of change, so often invoked, were
blowing from Libya to the Persian Gulf, from Aleppo to Khartoum,
and nowhere more strongly than in Syria's neighbour, the British
mandated territory of Palestine. There, with lofty insouciance and
almost unwittingly, Britain had given two promises, one to the Jews,
one to the Arabs; since each of these promises was flatly contradictory
of the other, neither could be kept; and the situation, long dangerous,
would soon become explosive. With the Arabs angrily, and not un-
justifiably, accusing Britain of bad faith, it had to be demonstrated that
in the matter of a simple promise, concerning a neighbour's territory,
an Englishman's 'guarantee' was still his bond. The demonstration was
made at the expense of France.

Whatever the rights and wrongs of France's action in the Levant
across the years—and of the unhappy dénouement Darlan's folly was the
root cause—it is scarcely surprising that many a Frenchman should have
been lastingly embittered by Britain's part in the closing events. It is a
measure of de Gaulle's magnanimity that he did not allow it to rankle.

IV

In 1941, however, other differences, more immediate if less enduring, bedevilled Anglo–Free French relations. Confusion over the
armistice terms to be granted to Vichy in Syria, military misunderstanding of French administrative rights, together with the ill-
concealed hostility of the British authorities, contributed to form a
sea of troubles such as few men in de Gaulle's position could have
navigated successfully. But if his uncompromising attitude on behalf
of France was so frequently misunderstood as to gain him the lasting
reputation of being 'terribly difficult to deal with', in the long run it
greatly served his cause in France and in the world.

No doubt there were valid excuses for the many blunders, *vis-à-vis*
the Free French, committed by the Foreign Office and by the local
British command. In the uncertain strategic situation in the Middle
East, it was evidently essential to terminate the Syrian sideshow as
rapidly as possible; almost any terms, even those favourable to Vichy,
were deemed acceptable by the Foreign Secretary provided that the
20,000 surrendered French troops were shipped out of the country
forthwith and the Levant, under British control, was made inaccessible
to the enemy. But these were not the terms formally agreed between
de Gaulle and Wavell; they not only permitted a considerable reinforcement of embittered pro-Vichy troops to French North Africa,
they made it impossible for Free French officers to talk to the men, to
win them over, and so perhaps gain an important increase of Allied
strength. The British, moreover, having entered Syria and the Lebanon
after a hard fight, tended to regard those countries as conquered
territory and all Vichy-French officials as personal friends of Hitler, a
view that was presently coloured by Vichy's vindictiveness in sinking
British merchantmen in Beirut harbour, in flying British prisoners
back to France as a gift for the Germans,[1] and in leaving behind the
nucleus of an Intelligence organization to spy on the British. De
Gaulle, on the other hand, strongly though he might condemn the
Vichy collaborators, saw in them Frenchmen, however misguided,
who would in time be converted to the cause of Free France and who

[1] Hearing of this the British promptly removed Dentz and other senior French officers
to Palestine as hostages. The British prisoners were thereupon returned.

must, meanwhile, remain in administrative control of French territory. To him the case was simple; this was an Allied campaign on French soil: 'when Field-Marshal Haig fought in France, civil power in those Departments in which his troops happened to find themselves remained wholly vested in the Government of the Republic.' Just then, to the British, the analogy seemed to have very little strength.

Despite Catroux's protests, instances of high-handed British action in the Levant territories continued to accumulate; French administrators were turned out, office buildings taken over, Free French officials prevented from functioning; in places the Tricolour was forcibly replaced by the Union Jack. In a week affairs came to such a pass that de Gaulle, who, in mid-July, had retired to Brazzaville to mark his disapprobation of the armistice terms, flew back to Cairo to announce a grave decision to the newly-appointed British Minister of State, Oliver Lyttelton (later Lord Chandos). Given the local military command's attitude, de Gaulle said, and the apparent insistence upon exercising British political control in the Levant, the Free French forces would be withdrawn by him from the British Command in three days' time and General Catroux instructed to assert his authority over the whole territory, whatever opposition was offered by anyone. Rather than allow the Anglo–Free French alliance to operate to the detriment of France, he added, he would terminate it and continue to fight the enemy alone.

The decision, and the detailed explanation of its causes, was announced with frigid anger; but there were no hot-tempered words, no violent gesticulations or thumpings of the table. At the end of the interview Lyttelton perceived two things: de Gaulle was not bluffing, and he had a strong case; in this sense the British Government was advised, the need for conciliation stressed. De Gaulle was then invited to renewed discussions, at which concessions were offered and agreed; and with tension relaxed he was able to go to Beirut (July 27), where he was received with wild enthusiasm by the entire population. Unfortunately, the new Lyttelton–de Gaulle agreement was either delayed in transmission or misunderstood by the local command; new and disturbing incidents occurred, culminating in a threat of martial law by the militarily capable but politically heavy-footed General 'Jumbo' Wilson. At once de Gaulle cabled to London requesting that Eden should be asked whether or not he wished to provoke a final

breach in Anglo–Free French relations. This brought Lyttelton up to
Beirut with explanations and apologies, and the situation was satisfactorily restored. By standing immovably upon France's undoubted
rights, de Gaulle had won his case.

Meanwhile, however, the Free French delegates in London, though
loyally supporting their leader's action, were becoming alarmed at
the possibility of an irreparable break with Britain, which, they
pointed out in several dispatches, would mean the end of Free France,
unable to exist without British supplies. Although they perfectly
understood his reasons and intentions, they begged him to modify his
intransigence.

To this de Gaulle made a memorable reply. By his forthright
methods he had succeeded; 'inadmissible' British claims had been set
aside. Modify his intransigence in matters relating to the legal rights
of France? Never. 'We shall have need of this intransigence up to the
Rhine inclusive.'

A phrase to inspire faint hearts. Distant by three years of ceaseless
effort, and two thousand miles by the shortest route—objective the
Rhine, and beyond. To the temporizing submissiveness of Marshal
Pétain, he opposed the brisk language of Marshal Foch.

Some at least of the outstanding points of difference had been
cleared up by the crisis; yet, of certain individuals, notably in Foreign
Office employ, de Gaulle remained suspicious. Previous experience
gave him cause for uneasiness. There had been the whispering campaign that had given him so much anxiety after Dakar. There had
been the unpleasant incident in London in the previous January, when
Muselier had been thrown into Pentonville Prison upon evidence so
obviously false it should have deceived nobody, let alone the Foreign
Secretary (Eden) who had ordered the arrest.[1] Lately there had been
the evasion by Eden of the armistice terms agreed by Wavell; and
now had come the dubious attempt to rob the French of their lawful
control in the Levant. And so it went on. Months later, Catroux was
reporting, from Beirut, (April 6, 1942) that an official British source
had been trying to impress him by claiming that 'divisions between
Free Frenchmen' had 'incensed the Cabinet', that the 'unity and
effectiveness of Free France' was 'no longer believed in', and by

[1] *Vide ante* page 124.

suggesting that de Gaulle was himself aware that he was losing his grip, that he was 'tired' and perhaps 'intending to liquidate the affair' of Free France. Since that same opinion was being quoted in London, it seemed clear that an enemy was attempting to play Iago to Churchill's Othello, with de Gaulle as a cantankerous Desdemona who disobligingly refused to be stifled.

Churchill was certainly influenced by these malicious whisperings. In a cable to de Gaulle before the start of the Levant expedition he had written (April 4, 1941): 'You, who have never faltered or failed in serving the common cause, possess the fullest confidence of His Majesty's Government and you embody the hopes of millions of Frenchmen and Frenchwomen who do not despair of the future of France or the French Empire.' After the occupation of Syria and the Lebanon such noble sentiments were replaced, more often than not, by expressions of the liveliest condemnation, inspired by reports from British sources in the Levant.

Admittedly, it was not easy for the Prime Minister, master in his own house, to accept that de Gaulle should be master in his, given that British troops had helped to put him there. Nor was it to be expected that one of Churchill's temperament should endure with equanimity the pointed retorts made by de Gaulle to the British Government's somewhat hasty accusations. When it was suggested that the Levantine peoples were discontented under French rule, de Gaulle asked in return whether the peoples of Palestine were contented under the British. When the demand was made for elections in Syria and the Lebanon to be held in the summer of 1942, de Gaulle replied that, with Rommel at the gates of Alexandria, the moment was scarcely well chosen: were the British permitting elections to be held in Egypt? And to the strong protests at Helleu's arrest of the rebellious Lebanese ministers in 1943—'kidnapping', Churchill called it—de Gaulle answered by recalling that, for very similar reasons, the British were holding under lock and key both Gandhi and Nehru.

Rather naturally such home thrusts, the more painful for being undeniable, left Churchill 'most indignant'. Nevertheless, through all the plots and counterplots, he contrived to remain loyal to the 1940 agreement with de Gaulle during the anxious months and years when the gravest threat to Free France came, not from Britain, not from Vichy and its German masters, but from Washington.

18. Three Blind Men—I

La Taupe: Je le hais parce que je ne l'ai jamais vu!
(*Chantecler:* Act I, Scene viii)

FROM PEARL HARBOUR, December 7, 1941, to the eve of the liberation of Paris in August 1944, the animosity of the American Administration towards the Free France movement generally and to de Gaulle personally was persistent, blatant and blind. The sentiment was far from being shared by all those in official positions in Washington and it was certainly at variance with the sympathies of a very great number of the American people. It did, however, dominate the thoughts and actions of three men at the head of American affairs: the President, the Secretary of State, Cordell Hull, and the Ambassador to Vichy, Admiral Leahy, who in July 1942 became the President's personal Chief of Staff. Greatly though these three may have contributed to Allied victory, in any portrayal of de Gaulle and his opponents it is their failings more than their qualities that must be delineated.

The causes of this animosity were rooted in anxiety. They were not originally due to the personality of de Gaulle, of whom the three men in Washington knew less than nothing in 1940. They were primarily evoked by the sudden shock of the collapse of France, and by the dire implications of that collapse for American security. Till then, comprehensibly if unwisely isolationist, safe from embroilment by virtue of the Neutrality laws, the United States Government had been able to take a calm and slightly supercilious view of a European conflict whose westward spread was contained by the two great barriers of the Royal Navy and the French Army. When with appalling swiftness the land barrier was swept away, leaving a weakened and gravely menaced Britain as the last outpost of democracy in Europe, the realization in Washington that with the Germans on the Atlantic seaboard a hole had been punched in the screen of isolationalism, through which either America would be drawn to the support of Britain or Nazi aggression would eventually reach to America, brought in its train a sense of deep resentment against the French Government and Army for having so easily surrendered. Unjust and illogical though that resentment undoubtedly was, it could not be denied; fear is notoriously a bad counsellor, and it was fear—of being compelled by events, of being involved in a war for which America, because of the isolationist policy, was morally and materially ill-prepared—that caused the resentment.

The French Army had for so long been regarded as the shield of western Europe, as a dominant factor in the preservation of peace on the Continent, had retained so much admiration over the score of years since its heroism had triumphed in 1918 and its leaders had won esteem as the foremost exponents of military art and science, that the violent disenchantment brought in rapid succession the sensations of incredulous amazement, of annoyance, of contempt. Some grief there was at the engulfment of Paris, some horror at the dismal mockery of Rethondes; for the French Army, and even to some extent for the French people, there was scorn. The Germans were strong, it was said, stronger than had been believed; but *the French had not fought.*

A full year later Admiral Leahy was to express the view held by many in Washington. At the time of Hitler's attack on Russia, he wrote, foreign diplomatic circles in Vichy were of the opinion that the German victory would be swift 'Nothing, they said, had stopped the *Wehrmacht*, not even the "magnificent French Army". To me, the "magnificent French Army" was only pretty fast on its feet. It almost got away—by running.'[1]

Grossly unfair though it must appear, it was to this damning verdict that the French Army had been laid open by Pétain's and Weygand's outdated military thinking before the War and by their treasonable surrender after a lost battle. Upon the President and Cordell Hull, sharing Leahy's ignorance, the effect produced was a distrust of all French soldiers as deep as that previously reserved for French politicians; and it was therefore with distrust as well as indifference that de Gaulle, just another French general of whose qualities they were unaware, was regarded from the start. When, however, events and his own leadership thrust him forward as a figure both political and military the distrust deepened to dislike and the indifference was supplanted by active opposition. To one of the two main objects of Washington's revised foreign policy he had become an obstacle.

---

[1] That this bitter sentiment was enduring is shown by its inclusion in Leahy's memoirs published ten years after the event.

Towards Britain the policy, wisely dictated by reasons of national interest far more than by any traditional sympathy, had been expressed in the phrase 'all aid short of war', and to this the policy towards Vichy became supplementary. As Hull first put it, the aim was 'to uphold that element in the French Government which opposes Hitlerism and Hitler'. More explicitly he told the Vichy Ambassador in Washington (Henry-Haye) in May 1941: 'the United States is thoroughly dedicated to the success of the British' and Vichy must therefore realize that 'any military aid rendered to Germany beyond the strict terms of the armistice is an attempt to slit the throat of the United States indirectly'. So forthright a declaration of policy and so clear a warning were invaluable in the dangerous period of uncertainty following the fall of France; had they been left at that, to be succeeded by firm action once Darlan's military collaboration had become known, no one on the Allied side could possibly have found fault with them. Unfortunately, the means chosen by Roosevelt and Hull to uphold such rare anti-Hitler elements as might be found at Vichy involved, by the appointment of Leahy as Ambassador, the recognition of Pétain's 'French State' as the legitimate Government of France, in direct opposition to de Gaulle's logically argued Brazzaville manifesto that declared the abolition of the Republic to be unlawful and Pétain to be a usurper. Upon this fundamental point, conflict between Washington and Free France was certain.

Moreover, the policy towards Vichy, at first directed almost exclusively—and with Churchill's warm approval—to keeping the Toulon fleet and the North African bases from a possible cession to Hitler, tended more and more to become a matter of keeping Pétain 'in the stirrups', as Hull phrased it, which in practice meant handling him so gently that the warning against giving military aid to Germany became idle in face of German threats of what would happen to France if military aid were refused. By persisting in his support of Pétain even after Darlan's open collaboration in the Levant, Hull alienated sympathy for his policy both in Britain and the United States; for the public in both countries were quick to see that, since Pétain was being compelled willy-nilly to serve the German cause, to support him was indirectly to support Hitler. Having outlived its utility, the policy was defeating its own aims.

To Hull, however, as well as to Roosevelt, it appeared for a time that American influence was in the ascendant at Vichy and that they had only to be patient to achieve a twofold success: the saving of Pétain from German domination and, even more important in their view, the bringing back of Weygand into the War on Britain's side. Strange cozenage! The strongest influence at Vichy remained, without question, that of the Nazi conquerors abetted by the collaborationist groups whose 'uppermost purpose', Hull admitted, 'seems to be to deliver France body and soul to Hitler'; from their toils nothing could now be done to extricate the Marshal. As for Weygand, upon whom Hull, advised by Leahy, pinned extravagant hopes, at no time did he evince any serious intention of re-entering the War on the side either of Britain or of Germany, with Free France or, later, with the Americans. He was ready, he said, to defend North Africa against anyone, but he had no desire to take any further part in the struggle. Admittedly, he had long since recovered from the panic of June 1940, but he could not now stand up and fight in Africa without conceding that he had been wrong in the first place to advocate surrender in France; to Pétain, his accomplice in the Bordeaux conspiracy, he was compelled to remain loyal.

When Darlan produced a second and more far-reaching agreement for military aid to the Germans—signed in Paris on May 27, 1941, and granting port and transport facilities in Tunisia—Weygand flew from Algiers to Vichy to protest, not, as Hull fondly supposed, because of 'fruitful contact' with American representatives, but because Pétain, horrified at the prospect of war with Britain, had requested his support against Darlan. Nor was the outcome of Weygand's intervention helpful to American interests, for although he contributed to restraining Darlan—thereby, however, only paving the way for Laval's return to power in April 1942—at Darlan's instigation he was dismissed from his North African post before the end of the year, and thereafter went into retirement.

Even then neither Hull nor Roosevelt abandoned their vain hope of drawing him back into the struggle. For their obstinacy there was a cogent reason: 'If Weygand stands up,' Hull had told the British Ambassador (Lord Halifax) in May, 'de Gaulle will have to become subordinate.' Since, according to Leahy, there was little support for de Gaulle in France and since, in Hull's view, the junior General was not only 'desperately temperamental' but 'showed few signs of political acumen', Weygand it must be. Early in 1942 a direct approach was made.

Churchill and Roosevelt having agreed in principle, at their first wartime meeting, to a North African expedition later in the year, Roosevelt sent a secret message to Weygand, delivered by one of Leahy's staff on January 20, asking him to return to North Africa and to lead the French in revolt by co-operating with the Allied forces when they landed. To this Weygand returned a flat refusal; he was, he replied through Leahy, 'a private citizen, completely loyal to Pétain' to whom he would at once communicate, although Leahy's representative begged him not to, the contents of the President's letter. When in addition Pétain refused, a few days later, to give any of the assurances requested in a special message from the President 'in regard to giving assistance to the Axis forces or in regard to the use of French ships', Leahy perceived that the policy of nursing Vichy was bankrupt. The alternative of his recall to Washington had already been threatened; he thought it should be given immediate effect. 'Too large a number of the members of the Vichy Government,' he wrote to the President, 'now share a belief with Admiral Darlan that the United States may always be depended upon to take no positive action whatever.'

But the less useful, and less popular, the policy towards Vichy became, the more Hull was determined to justify it. Although he and Roosevelt were now under 'heavy pressure' from 'various sources outside the State Department' to break with Vichy and to give at least a limited recognition to de Gaulle, Hull merely noted that 'fortunately, the President refused to let himself be swayed by advice so ill considered'. That Weygand was a broken reed, that Pétain was neither willing nor able to help the Allied cause did not constitute, in Hull's view, sufficient reason for breaking with Vichy, still less for recognizing de Gaulle who, since the St Pierre-Miquelon incident in December, had incurred his enduring enmity.

The incident itself had been trivial, but Hull's wrath was both violent and puerile. 'I pointedly accused de Gaulle of being a marplot,' he reported concerning a conversation with Churchill, adding that de Gaulle had acted 'directly contrary to the expressed wishes of Britain, Canada, and the United States, and I asked the Prime Minister to induce him to withdraw his troops from the St Pierre and Miquelon islands, with Canadians and Americans assuming supervision over the radio station at St Pierre.' This Churchill refused to do, and Hull had to listen to 'a violent diatribe against Vichy along with fulsome praise for de Gaulle', which almost reduced him to tears as he begged Churchill 'for just a few little words' in favour of Vichy.

But although neither Churchill nor Roosevelt was altogether happy about the incident, they had no desire to add to their troubles by quarrelling with the Free French at a time when their respective nations were facing the terrible consequences of disaster in the Pacific. Hull got no comfortable words and had to face almost alone the storm of criticism that arose throughout the United States at his official announcement concerning 'the action taken by the so-called Free French ships' in taking over, at the expressed wish of 98 per cent of the population of under 5,000 souls, two islets which had been French for several centuries—an action to which Hull objected on no better grounds than that 'it might seriously interfere with our relations with Marshal Pétain'. Since Pétain's government was now, as the American people were fully aware, irrevocably committed to collaboration, since it was also known that, under a Vichy administrator, the wireless station on St Pierre had been emitting a stream of meteorological information useful to the German submarines lurking off the North American seaboard, Hull's objection did not appear valid; and the suggestion contained in the State Department's bellicose announcement, that Canada should take steps 'to restore the *status quo* in these islands', was not allowed to take effect.

In fact de Gaulle had acted with perfect propriety and without undue haste. In October (1941) he had written to the Foreign Secretary, Eden, informing him of the desire of the islands' exclusively French population to join Free France, telling him that Free French vessels were in Newfoundland waters ready to carry out the operation, and asking for his opinion. To this Eden had replied that nothing could be decided without the agreement of the Canadian and United States Governments whom he promised to consult. The consultations were, however, delayed in Washington by the negotiations which Hull was then secretly carrying on with the Vichy Admiral Robert to secure control of the French West Indies, a command which included St Pierre and Miquelon; and de Gaulle, suspicious of American intentions, wrote to Churchill on December 10 to say that, unless there were objections to 'this little *coup de main*', he proposed to order Admiral Muselier—then at Halifax with three Free French corvettes —to proceed to the islands immediately.

With Churchill off to America, the Foreign Office then advised de Gaulle to wait until his and the British points of view had been put to Roosevelt; and to this postponement de Gaulle agreed on December 17. Hardly had he done so when, on the same day, the Foreign Office informed him that an agreement had been reached between Washington and Ottawa whereby, without prior consultation with either Britain or Free France, Canadian forces were to occupy the islands forthwith. This made it plain to de Gaulle that Hull, fully informed both of the Free French proposals and of the agreement to postpone action, was trying to steal a march before Churchill could put the case to Roosevelt. Feeling, justifiably, that this piece of chicanery released him from his agreement, de Gaulle ordered Muselier to sail at once from Halifax; and on December 24, amid rapturous enthusiasm, the island inhabitants were rallied to Free France.

*   *   *

Thwarted by the strength of American public opinion, unsupported by Roosevelt, rebuffed by Churchill, it was de Gaulle whom Hull never forgave. Thenceforward, to the Normandy landings and after, he missed no opportunity of decrying the importance of Free France and of attacking its leader by distorting his aims and traducing his character. In this, aided by Leahy's mistaken views, he was increasingly backed by the President whom he certainly misled.

He began by supplying Roosevelt, on the last day of 1941, with some spurious information based on guesswork arithmetic. 'Our British friends,' he wrote, 'seem to believe that the body of the entire people of France is strongly behind de Gaulle, whereas according to all my information and that of my associates, some 95 per cent of the entire French people are anti-Hitler whereas more than 95 per cent of this latter number are not de Gaullists and would not follow him. This fact (*sic*) leads straight to our plans about North Africa and our omission of de Gaulle's co-operation in that connection.'

Precisely what strength his double '95 per cent' left to de Gaulle's supporters was made clear in an embittered remark passed to the

British Minister in Washington, Ronald Campbell, on January 8, 1942:
'I wonder whether the British are more interested in a *dozen or so*[1]
Free Frenchmen . . . than they are in the World War situation itself.'
More than nine months earlier Churchill, with wider vision and greater
knowledge, had told de Gaulle: 'You embody the hope of millions of
Frenchmen and Frenchwomen.' Since then, by virtue of de Gaulle's
firm stand as much as by the march of events, some further millions
had raised their eyes to that same hope. When, however, Hull found it
impossible any longer to deny the figures he went on to deny the
worth of the individual members. 'One of the tragedies of the de
Gaulle situation,' he wrote later, 'was that de Gaulle had attracted to
himself not a single eminent Frenchman.' Not only was this an
inaccurate statement of fact—Mandel, Jeanneney, Herriot, Blum, and
Jouhaux all supported him—but considering the low opinion Hull and
Roosevelt held of almost all Frenchmen, eminent or otherwise, it is
not easy to discern the element of tragedy.

But although by mid-1942 Hull was asserting 'to the world that the
Vichy Government did not represent the French people', while at the
same time admitting reluctantly 'that larger segments of the French
population were rallying to de Gaulle than before', upon one point of
policy he was not to be moved; in the forthcoming North African
operation de Gaulle must have no place. After the St Pierre incident:
'The President and myself . . . regarded him as more ambitious for
himself and less reliable than we had thought him before'; and,
according to Hull, it was the President who first decided that he and
the Free French should be kept out. In June, Churchill endeavoured to
get the decision reversed on the grounds that Free French help might
be invaluable and that, in any case, it would be extremely difficult to
keep the secret from them; but 'the President', Hull noted, 'was still
resolved that General de Gaulle should not be included in this expedition or even informed of it'. The decision was upheld. French North
Africa—Algeria and Morocco—was to be an American preserve, in
the occupation of which the British might be allowed to help, but not
the Free French.

[1] Author's italics.

19. Three Blind Men—II

Put on him what forgeries you please; marry, none so rank
As may dishonour him . . .

(Shakespeare: *Hamlet*)

HULL WAS seventy in 1942 and had served almost ten years as Secretary of State under Roosevelt. A hard-working lawyer, he was devoted to his office and to the interests of the United States; but with little humour and considerable pomposity there went a lawyer's worst failing, the uncontrollable urge to prove himself right even when he knew he was wrong. Concerning the affairs of France he appears to have convinced himself that he knew more than the French themselves and certainly a great deal more than the Free French and de Gaulle; so that arguing endlessly against the evidence, contradicting the facts when they dared to contradict him, under his guidance the State Department developed in high degree the ability to back the wrong horse.

To send Leahy to 'help keep Pétain in the stirrups' in the uncertain autumn of 1940 had seemed a reasonable bet even to Churchill, though it is difficult to agree with Hull's view that 'a contrary policy might well have been disastrous'; but by the spring of 1942 it was plain to all that, in the Allied victory stakes, the Marshal was a non-starter. By that time, moreover, Weygand had scratched, Darlan had fallen and Laval was running hard in the wrong direction. Yet, when it came to North Africa, rather than back de Gaulle the blind punters in Washington put their money on General Giraud, an outsider who was in honour debarred from starting at all by reason of a letter he had written to the Marshal, in which he expressed his 'complete loyalty', his 'utter devotion', and gave his 'word as an officer to do nothing in any way to hinder our relations with the German Government or to impede the labours with which, under your high authority, Admiral Darlan and President Pierre Laval are charged with accomplishing.' A dark horse indeed for the American selection, but even running with a broken word he was thought to be safer than the unmanageable de Gaulle.

Negotiations with Giraud were left to the military commanders, Eisenhower and Mark Clark, but the authority to employ him in

North Africa came from Washington; and, despite Churchill's approval, a worse choice could scarcely have been made. In France he had enjoyed a modest reputation in peacetime and, to his credit, as Governor of Metz he had praised Colonel de Gaulle's handling of the famous Tank Regiment, but his battlefield experience in May 1940 had been curtailed by capture before he had had time to assume a vital command; so that it would appear that his only recommendation for service with the Americans was derived from his recent spectacular, and slightly mysterious, escape from the fortress of Königstein. A quiet, obstinate man, more ambitious than talented and inclined to stand upon his dignity, he entirely misunderstood the purpose for which his co-operation had been requested, vainly imagining that it was to lead a vast Allied army back into France within a matter of days. From the start he proved to be a greater nuisance than he was worth.

Breaking his word of honour by leaving France to join the Allies, he haggled over a point of honour regarding the manner of his departure; some deep resentment, either at the Syrian campaign or at the more recent occupation of Madagascar by British troops against Vichy opposition, forbade him to travel in a British submarine; and HMS *Seraph*, the only vessel available, had to be provided with an American naval officer in nominal command so as to conceal her nationality. On landing at Gibraltar Eisenhower took him into his office under the Rock and briefly explained the part he was expected to play in bringing Vichy troops over to the Allied side; to which Giraud replied blandly that, as he understood it, he was forthwith to become Supreme Allied Commander-in-Chief. When the tactful Eisenhower disillusioned him, he demanded a passage back to France, and when this was refused he remained sulking on the Rock while the landings took place against considerable resistance. Agreeing to move to North Africa only when the landings had been successfully accomplished despite the heavy losses he had been expected to prevent, he then found that the majority of Vichy officials both civil and military, aware of his letter to Pétain, regarded him as a forsworn traitor with whom they would have nothing to do. The fighting continued.

It was then that the American Command turned to Darlan. He had come to Algiers a few days previously to see his son who was stricken with poliomyelitis; but, although he is said to have been in ignorance

of the forthcoming Anglo–American landings, the fact that, according
to Mark Clark, he had already tried through the American Consular
representative, Robert Murphy, 'to feel out the American attitude
towards accepting his assistance' would seem to indicate that rank
opportunism had something to do with his timely arrival. Clark at
once seized upon him and extracted an order for the Vichy forces to
cease fire, to which no one would have listened had it been given by
Giraud. Darlan was obeyed because, whilst it was known that he had
no real political power, he was still the *dauphin*, heir to the Marshal's
throne, and still the nominal Commander-in-Chief of Vichy's armed
forces; he was therefore thought to be executing Pétain's orders. Had
Clark left it at that, used Darlan as a convenient tool and then removed
him as a suspected traitor, the initial agreement would have been
entirely justified; unfortunately, once the cease-fire had been complied
with, he went on to negotiate with the Admiral and, after four days of
argument, left him in power as High Commissioner for North Africa.
But although Clark afterwards accepted all the blame for this unwise
action he was not by any means solely responsible. An energetic and
skilful military commander, he was quite inexperienced in politics and
had felt bound to take the advice of the man on the spot, Robert
Murphy; moreover, though in command at Algiers, he was under the
overall command of Eisenhower, and Eisenhower was under the
supreme command of Roosevelt who informed Hull of the Darlan
agreement, and Hull implemented the policy.

According to Hull the estimated saving of British and American
lives caused by accepting Darlan's cease-fire was probably 16,000. But
Darlan's presence in Algiers was, to Washington's knowledge, wholly
fortuitous; and therefore, but for his presence, and on the basis of the
actual casualties incurred, 20,000 British and American lives would
have been lost in the invasion of a region about which Hull had
claimed that he knew everything and over which he had pretended to
exercise some measure of control. His claims had provided the excuse
for prolonging the pro-Vichy policy and for sending relief supplies to
the North African population: 'We had,' he noted early in 1941, 'an
efficient staff of control officials in North Africa, watching events like
a thousand hawks. They were indispensable in preparing the ground
for our invasion.' To this he added in the summer of 1942: 'by continuing our close contact with French North Africa we could count on

a large portion of the civil and military administration when the time came.' And the result, when the time came, was confusion, heavy loss of life, the futility of Giraud and the chance advent of Darlan who, according to Hull, 'had been of great assistance to our landing', but by whose acceptance as an ally, according to Churchill, 'a brilliant military episode had been tarnished and tainted'. Much of this, and most of the subsequent bitter political struggle, might have been avoided had the agents and adherents of Free France been set to work ahead of time; but of their existence Hull was unaware, the eyes of his 'thousand hawks' had not been sharp enough to discern them.

So far no one in Washington had been able to blame de Gaulle for anything that had happened in North Africa; deliberately held at arm's length he had at no time been consulted. But from the moment when the storm of execration at Darlan's appointment as High Commissioner blew up simultaneously in Britain and America, when in the British press and parliament it was angrily asked how it had come about that this notorious anglophobe and pro-Nazi collaborator, who had hitherto done his utmost to ensure the German victory for which he hoped, had been welcomed with open arms and selected to rule in French North Africa whilst the leader of 'Fighting France',[1] who for more than two years had striven for Allied victory and the liberation of his country, was treated as an outcast, almost as an enemy agent—as soon as the name 'de Gaulle' was advanced as that of the man best qualified to unite the people of French North Africa in the common cause, so soon did the blind men of Washington turn upon him a stream of vilification whose purpose was clearly to paint him so black that a half-demented traitor must seem white by comparison.

Leahy was in the van of the attack. Capable naval officer though he may have been, his sixteen months as Ambassador to Pétain had gained him a reputation for expert knowledge of France that was almost entirely unmerited. As an old friend of the President and now his personal Chief of Staff, his advice was listened to by Roosevelt, by his entourage, and by members of the State Department who sought his opinion. Of de Gaulle he knew next to nothing; he had never set eyes upon him and his only information had come from the embittered

---

[1] The new designation—*France Combattante*—for the Free French movement had been officially recognized by the British Government in July, 1942.

Pétain or from prejudiced Vichy administrators. For Darlan, deeply though he distrusted him, he entertained a curious feeling of friendship, based apparently upon the 'brotherhood of the sea' and the fellowship of Admirals. Thus, biased and ignorant, when the storm of protest broke in America against the whole pro-Vichy policy of which he had been the instrument he counter-attacked with calumny based on gossip. Referring to 'the so-called "leader of the French resistance", who at that time was a highly advertised hero in England and in this country', he reported that 'when de Gaulle read news of the invasion in the newspapers he almost had an apoplectic fit. His Gallic pride had been insulted. He was in a terrible frame of mind.' To this he added inconsequently and with total disregard for the truth: 'Of course, we knew that his organization was impregnated with German spies, and if we had given him advance information the Germans might have known it. We just could not accept the risk of telling him.'

Of this discreditable nonsense which Leahy should have been ashamed to publish in his memoirs the facts are that de Gaulle—from whom, according to Leahy, 'plans for the landing had been kept a complete secret'—was informed by Churchill, on November 8, of what was being done in North Africa and that, concealing his anxiety, he received the news with his customary equanimity,[1] not only because of his exemplary self-restraint, but also because, through his representatives in Washington and his agents in French North Africa, he had been aware of all the main points of the Allied plans *since August*. As for 'German spies', there is no evidence whatever to suggest that even a single enemy agent was at work in de Gaulle's entourage.

For the six weeks of Darlan's reign at Algiers, Leahy continued to exert his considerable influence against any *rapprochement* with de Gaulle. On November 14 he told Lord Halifax that the British Government's suggestion to send Free French representatives to North Africa would be 'disadvantageous to our military effort'. Two days later he drafted a cable from the President to Churchill, informing him that Eisenhower had been ordered to abstain from making any political agreements with the British or Free French—a cable that, in his view, 'stopped de Gaulle and Churchill from trying to take

---

[1] It was only subsequently, on hearing news of the American agreement with Darlan, that he displayed a momentary flare of anger and was with difficulty restrained from sending Roosevelt a cable of stern rebuke.

Eisenhower into their camp' against Darlan. A State Department official[1] then asked his advice concerning a practical suggestion of getting de Gaulle to send a representative to North Africa to discuss matters with Giraud; to which Leahy replied that he 'could see no advantage to us in the suggestion, but would offer no objection providing that care was taken to avoid offending Admiral Darlan' because the Admiral 'was sensitive to criticism'. By December, 'after many discussions with the President' who was himself sensitive to the 'public furore' against Darlan, Leahy 'accepted' the view that de Gaulle was in 'competition for future political power', whereas Darlan was the 'representative of Marshal Pétain, the regularly constituted legitimate Government'.

Too blind to perceive that Pétain's Government never had been legitimate, Leahy ought at least to have seen that with the whole of France now occupied by the Germans, with the remains of the French fleet scuttled in Toulon harbour, and with Pétain virtually a prisoner, there was properly speaking no French Government at all. Moreover, since Darlan himself admitted that he had been 'disavowed by Vichy', Leahy's view that he had a 'claim to legitimacy' was no longer valid.

*   *   *

The sorry episode of the Darlan–Washington collaboration was brought to a close on Christmas Eve by Darlan's assassination; but the stubborn fight against de Gaulle was taken up and prolonged by Cordell Hull. The Secretary of State, remembering his painful experience in the matter of St Pierre and Miquelon, started off with the idea that for the 'violent attacks against the French set-up in North Africa' —by which he meant the American set-up of Giraud and Darlan— de Gaulle's 'propaganda machine in England' was responsible. Ignoring the 'polecats' in his own country whose criticism of the 'set-up' had been deafening, he incautiously tried to get Churchill to muzzle the British press which, he claimed, 'was supporting in the loudest and most extravagant ways de Gaulle's desire for supreme political control of France'. Repulsed by both Churchill and Eden, and finding that the criticism was continuing unabated, he expressed himself in terms certainly unwise and, towards an Ally, not far from impertinent.

'I insist,' he told the Foreign Secretary shortly before Darlan's

[1] Ray Atherton.

assassination, 'I insist that where there is a plain and palpable interference with the prosecution of the North African campaign by pure
brazen politics it is high time, in my opinion, that this should receive
the serious attention of the British Government.'

Such language was not calculated to achieve his purpose any more
than was the rather less intemperate tone of his message to Eden of
February 3, 1943, in which he stated that 'the President has shown
some annoyance at the continued propaganda emanating from the
de Gaulle headquarters in London. The President labels their attitude
as a continuing irritant . . . and hopes you can further steps to allay the
irritation.' Not only did those 'professional agitators', as Hull called
them, continue to irritate, but the press in Britain also offended by
persisting in its advocacy of de Gaulle even after the Casablanca conference had, at the President's demand, temporarily united him with
Giraud. To hear Hull it might almost be thought that de Gaulle had
joined the ranks of the British press-lords: he had 'the support of
large British newspapers . . . which at times he turned loose on us with
bitter criticism of certain attitudes and policies of this Government that
did not please him'. This, he claimed, 'had the effect of confusing
public opinion'.

American public opinion was certainly confused by the Administration's continued support of Giraud to the exclusion of de Gaulle,
and once the North African campaign had come to a victorious end,
Hull was compelled to shift his ground. 'The issue at stake,' he
announced, was 'not only the success of our future military operations,
but also the very future of France itself.' And in that future there must
be no room at the top for de Gaulle, because, as Hull had told the
President a year ago: 'It is clearly evident that the French people who
have rallied to General de Gaulle as the head of a military movement
are not prepared to regard him as the future leader of France.' When,
by midsummer of 1943, this was not quite so 'clearly evident', Hull
came round on the other tack and declared that those who did regard
de Gaulle as their future leader were the wrong sort of people: he had
'permitted to come under his umbrella all the most radical elements in
France'. On the other hand, he had 'fascist tendencies'. Worst of all:
'The Communists in France . . . have announced their insistence that
de Gaulle be their leader.'

Fascists, Communists, Radicals, the greater part of the French

Empire—it began to look as if de Gaulle had accomplished the miracle of uniting France. Hull refused to admit it; still less that such popular support, as the General might find in France and her Colonies entitled him to any political power in North Africa, because the duumvirate at Algiers, with the newly-formed French Committee of National Liberation under de Gaulle–Giraud, presented an 'increasingly troublesome and serious, not to say dangerous problem'. The campaign of disparagement was therefore continued, with Hull bringing every possible pressure and argument to bear upon the British Government to abandon de Gaulle: the General 'had quarrelled with the British in Syria', had made use of 'false propaganda', his 'adventures in the political field' had 'excited suspicion', his own countrymen 'distrusted him or could not work with him'. But, although Churchill was forced to walk carefully and to admit that 'he and Eden found de Gaulle terrible to get on with', nothing was gained by calumny: 'the British just could not throw him overboard, notwithstanding his many very objectionable and difficult ways'.

And so it went on, month after month. At Quebec, in August (1943), Hull had to listen to Churchill saying that 'all the liberal elements in the world, including the Governments-in-exile and the Soviet Government, were demanding an immediate decision granting full recognition to the Committee [of National Liberation]'. To which Roosevelt replied with Hull's now well-established slogan: 'we had to think of the future of France herself'. Of what that future was to be immediately after the liberation the draft plans submitted in October gave an unpleasant foretaste; for whereas it was stated that the 'ultimate' aim was to give the French people a free choice of 'the form of government under which they wished to live', it was made plain that meanwhile France was to be treated in the same way as any conquered enemy country, with the entire civil administration in the sole charge of the Supreme Allied Military Commander, an American, who whilst permitting freedom of speech and of the press would endeavour to 'hold the scales even between all French political groups'. Unfortunately, the draft appealed not only to Hull, but also to the President; from Cairo, in November, Hull quoted him as saying: 'The thought that the occupation [*sic*] when it occurs should be wholly military is one to which I am increasingly inclined.' Despite the British Government's view that it was 'contrary to their conception of government to

permit important political decisions to be taken by a military commander' and their reiterated belief that 'all Frenchmen would rally in
support of de Gaulle', neither the President nor Hull would submit to
the obvious.

'Mr Roosevelt and I,' Hull wrote later, 'continued throughout 1943
to resent de Gaulle's ambitions', and presently, 'carried into 1944 the
deep-seated suspicions he and I entertained regarding de Gaulle'. To
maintain these resentments and suspicions, even up to the Normandy
landings, Hull went to extreme lengths of evasive argument. That the
French Committee had 'shown us numerous reports that they said
came from the French underground, showing a great majority support
for de Gaulle', could not be allowed to pass without the denial: 'but
we had had other reports from inside France to the opposite effect.'
To what possible 'other reports' could he be referring? For the success
of the operations in France the Allied Military Commander, Eisenhower, was relying upon the support of nearly a quarter of a million
men of the French Resistance, every one of whom acknowledged
de Gaulle as leader. No evidence 'to the opposite effect' could be
anything but false.

Quite suddenly and without comment Hull admitted defeat. 'The
great majority of the French people,' he wrote of events in the summer
of 1944, 'freely accepted the leadership of General de Gaulle and the
administration he had set up on French soil. . . . Once this last point
appeared assured, our political backing became cordial and wholehearted'—which was not strictly true. For it was not until October
23 that the Government of the United States, under British and
Russian pressure, gave full recognition to de Gaulle's authority in
Paris as that of the Provisional Government of the French Republic.

Thus, after all the calumnies and recriminations, after the determined
opposition, and the equally determined support of Pétain, Darlan and
Giraud, Hull's unbending policy was bent back to de Gaulle's starting-
point four years earlier at Brazzaville. There is nothing to suggest that
Hull ever read the Manifesto; had he done so he might have spared
himself and everyone else a great deal of time and unnecessary trouble.

20. Three Blind Men—III

Il faut rire pour ne pas pleurer.
(Beaumarchais)

ROOSEVELT'S PLACE in history is not to be determined by the single facet of his dealings with France. It is necessary to stress this very obvious truth, because were he to be judged solely by his attitude to Fighting France and his treatment of de Gaulle scarcely any of the attributes of greatness would be discernible in his character. For his ignorance in the early stages of Free French resistance there was some excuse, guided as he was by the faulty intelligence concerning de Gaulle supplied by Hull, Leahy and Robert Murphy. Moreover, his initial careless prejudice against de Gaulle had been stimulated first by British reports alleging Free French responsibility for the non-existent Dakar leakage, later by the vehemence with which Hull had denounced the 'marplot' of St Pierre and Miquelon; and the prejudice thus enhanced led to the almost casual, but stubbornly maintained, decision to exclude de Gaulle from the North African operations. But by November, 1942, there was no excuse whatever for the President's pretended ignorance of the aims and objects of Fighting France, of its moral strength in the world, of the intentions of its leader.

He had before him all the evidence, from the Brazzaville Manifesto to the many speeches and broadcasts made by de Gaulle, the substance of which had always been unswerving devotion to the cause of Allied victory, of the liberation of France and the restoration of democratic liberty to her people. He had before him, if he chose to read them, the reports of the American Ambassador in London, John Winant, who after long and profitable interviews with de Gaulle had undertaken to 'make every effort to see that the General's true character was understood in the United States'.

He knew, or he ought to have known for the facts had been published all over the world, that de Gaulle's armed forces, small though they might be, had fought with great gallantry on many fields, notably in Eritrea against the Italians and more recently in Cyrenaica against Germans and Italians in the memorable rearguard engagement of Bir Hakeim. He knew—he can hardly have ignored the fact altogether since it involved his signature—that Lend-Lease aid had been extended in November 1941 to territories under Free French control, whose defence by Free France was recognized as 'vital to the defence of the United States'. He must also have known that as recently as July (1942) his Government had handed to de Gaulle a Memorandum setting forth the terms of an agreement reached between the United States and the French National Committee; and he cannot possibly have been unaware that paragraph 2 of this Memorandum stated unequivocally that his Government recognized 'General de Gaulle's contribution, and the efforts of the French National Committee, in keeping alive the traditional spirit of France and of her institutions' and that consequently 'all military assistance and every possible support' would be given to the Committee as 'the symbol of French resistance' to the enemy everywhere. He was fully informed of the British Government's agreement of August 1940, recognizing de Gaulle's leadership, as of its declaration of July 13 (1942) reaffirming that 'Fighting France' represented 'all French nationals, wherever they may be, and all French territories, who unite to co-operate with the United Nations in the war against the common enemies', and stating that the National Committee was 'the directing organization' of these nationals and these territories who 'refused to accept the surrender and . . . contributed to the liberation of France'.

And yet, notwithstanding the accumulated evidence of de Gaulle's integrity and of his high standing as the leader of a movement supported by 'millions of Frenchmen and Frenchwomen', Roosevelt regarded him as no more than an 'irritant', a member of one of the '*émigré* factions', to be classed with the turncoat Darlan who had striven for German victory and with Giraud the forsworn ambitious nonentity. In a letter to Churchill, dated November 12, 1942, he lumped together indifferently 'all three of these prima donnas'; and followed this up a few days later with the remark to Hull that the best solution of the French North African problem was to 'place Admiral Darlan, General Giraud, and a de Gaulle representative in one room alone and then give the government of the occupied territory to the man who came out'.

In this scornful jest the words 'occupied territory' provide the key to his attitude then and later. With a lack of sympathy for the affairs of France, based less upon blind ignorance than upon a patronizing and often sneering indifference, he regarded himself as the master on French soil and, heedless of the obvious claims of Fighting France and the growing strength of the gaullist Resistance, was determined that his will should prevail. Whether a Darlan, a Giraud or some other submissive instrument was chosen to serve that will, it would not be de Gaulle. He was 'difficult' and he claimed to know more about France and the feelings of Frenchmen than either Roosevelt or Churchill, and that was 'preposterous'.

At the time of the Casablanca conference (January 1943) de Gaulle, forced under a threat of excommunication to accept the Churchill–Roosevelt 'invitation', was not alone in expressing dismay and measured indignation at the President's attitude. General Eisenhower, whose observations were confirmed by minutes taken at a staff meeting in Washington, noted some very disturbing indications.

'I found,' he wrote, 'that the President ... did not always distinguish clearly between the military occupation of enemy territory and the situation in which we found ourselves in North Africa. He constantly referred to plans and proposals affecting the local population, the French Army, and governmental officials in terms of orders, instructions, and compulsion. It was necessary to remind him that from the outset we had operated under policies requiring us to gain and use an ally . . . but he nevertheless continued, perhaps subconsciously, to discuss local problems from the viewpoint of a conqueror.'

At that same time Eisenhower also observed something which de Gaulle had long suspected. The President, he wrote, 'speculated at length on the possibility of France's regaining her ancient position of prestige and power in Europe and on this point was very pessimistic. As a consequence, his mind was wrestling with the questions of methods for controlling certain strategic points in the French Empire which he felt that the country might no longer be able to hold.' There could be no doubt of it: de Gaulle would have need of his intransigence 'up to the Rhine inclusive' and beyond—to the Caribbean, to the Pacific, perhaps even to West Africa.

Of the meeting between de Gaulle and Giraud, which was a principal object of the Casablanca conference, the President spoke with a flippancy that revealed the contempt of the 'conqueror' for the conquered. The meeting he dismissed as a 'shotgun wedding' in which 'the temperamental bride showed no intention of getting into bed with the bridegroom'—an analogy that seems to have pleased both Hull and Churchill, each of whom quoted it in his memoirs. It was given fuller treatment in the journal kept by W. D. Hassett,[1] for more than three years Roosevelt's press secretary, friend and confidant, where it was described as 'the really funny incident of the Casablanca pilgrimage', although the only element of humour lay in the President's manner of relating it.

According to Hassett's version, the President said: 'My job was to produce the bride in the person of General Giraud while Churchill was to bring in General de Gaulle to play the role of bridegroom in a shotgun wedding. . . . I was on hand with the bride—waiting at the church—but there was no bridegroom. At last Churchill showed up with de Gaulle. . . . I had several conferences with both Giraud and de Gaulle and tried, with difficulty at first, to bring them to a realization and recognition that the first job in hand was to get the Germans out of France. But it was an uphill task.'

Hassett went on: 'At one conference, the President said, de Gaulle said again and again that he represented the spirit of France—the spirit of Jeanne d'Arc. . . . "That spirit, de Gaulle said, must be reincarnated," the President continued. "He thought he represented it. He was suspicious and distrustful of Giraud." At another conference, FDR said, de Gaulle told him that in the present emergency he felt he must play the role of Clemenceau, with Giraud acting as Marshal Foch. "I almost laughed in his face," remarked the Boss. "On Friday you are the reincarnation of Jeanne d'Arc, and today you are Clemenceau." '

In these and other tales, assuming that Hassett reported Roosevelt accurately, and there is every reason to think that he did, there is audible the authentic cracked ring of untruth, of facts distorted to make a good yarn in which the point of the joke is invariably directed against de Gaulle. After Casablanca there could be no excuse either for ignorance or for failure to appreciate, however dimly, de Gaulle's honesty of purpose and strength of character, not to mention the strength of the cause he represented; any informed observer not beset by prejudice or corrupted by power could have perceived that here was a man not to be dismissed with mockery.

Before the President there were now all the facts relating to the two-and-a-half-years' struggle to bring France back into the War, in

[1] *Off the Record with F.D.R.*

which de Gaulle and only de Gaulle had played the leading part; the facts of willing co-operation, in central Africa by the supply of airfields and port facilities, in the Pacific by the provision of island bases; of gallant fighting most recently displayed by Leclerc's astonishing campaign through the Fezzan; of able representation in Washington by men of such high quality as Adrien Tixier and René Pléven, assisted at one time or another by Maurice Dejean, André Philip, Thierry d'Argenlieu and Colonel de Chevigné, who had long since stressed that Free France was not a beggar with outstretched hand cupped to catch the charitable penny, but an Ally requesting arms wherewith to fight. In addition there was the fact that, at the time of the Africa landings, the President had received from de Gaulle a letter (dated October 26, 1942) in which, at considerable length and with unexceptionable arguments, the case for France in the War and for Fighting France as sole champion of her rights and liberties was clearly and convincingly stated. Whether he bothered to read it or not is unknown; the letter was certainly handed to him by André Philip, the Resistance leader who had just made his escape from occupied France; but, perhaps because the facts it contained were unanswerable, he made no reply. Nevertheless, the letter was there to be studied; and to it had been added the final fact necessary to dissipate the last lingering mist of ignorance: the meeting face to face, the chance to understand and to know. He missed the opportunity. Instead of making an objective assessment of the man's character, he made a 'funny' story.

After Casablanca, Roosevelt's hostility increased noticeably and became more personal. Since ignorance of de Gaulle's achievements and intentions could no longer be pleaded, it became more and more apparent to impartial observers that the President's blindness was deliberate. In the mounting enmity, in the flat and persistent refusal to recognize in de Gaulle any quality or virtue, he seemed bent upon the elimination of the one man capable of thwarting his arbitrary handling of a France not so much liberated as, in his view, reconquered. It was to be a fight to the finish, from which the President could not turn back without loss of face and in which the opponent must surely succumb since, by his own admission, he was 'no politician' and only a two-star General. It may be that Roosevelt suspected, though perhaps no more than subconsciously, that the man he disparaged and mocked was made of truer steel than himself. The façade of charm and easygoing bonhomie, the patrician manner, and the undeniable fortitude with which he endured a crippling physical disability, concealed a shallow intellect given to careless habits of thought and an egotism, ruthless, domineering and vindictive, akin to the moody temper of a spoiled child and the very antithesis of the character and qualities of de Gaulle. It may thus have been jealousy, arising from an intuitive sense of inferiority, that urged him to destroy the man who, daring to challenge his will, walked with the dignity of a king and championed France with the panache of a medieval knight. He began by undermining, with the glad assistance of Hull and Leahy, the sympathy and support of Great Britain.

Churchill, on a visit to the United States in May (1943), noted 'a very stern mood', but being 'at this time most indignant with de Gaulle' he did nothing to counter it. 'Not a day passed that the President did not mention the subject to me. Although this was done in a most friendly and often jocular manner, I saw he felt very strongly indeed upon it. Almost every day he handed me one or more accusing documents against de Gaulle from the State Department or the American Secret Service.'

The State Department must have been saving up for Churchill's visit; the production of fresh documentary evidence of this sort 'almost every day' for a fortnight was a circumstance so remarkable that, but for the quality of Pickwickian gullibility displayed by the Prime Minister when in the company of his 'very dear friend' the President, it could hardly have failed to arouse suspicions of a put-up job. That it was done 'in a most friendly and often jocular manner' can well be believed; it was Roosevelt's way of sugar-coating the poisoned pill of denigration. In Hassett's journal the 'manner' is frequently illustrated; the President is reported as 'kidding' and 'wisecracking', but the words and incidents quoted show him as facetious rather than funny, a spiteful and superficial scoffer; never once in three years is any remark cited showing the least generosity towards de Gaulle or any acknowledgment whatever of his merits. At the time of the Casablanca meeting the President conceded that 'he liked the spiritual look in his eyes'. The rest was venom.

Coming from 'the Boss' the poison spread downwards and outwards. In London, General Marshall could hardly be brought to speak to de Gaulle who came to seek his advice on the use to be made of French Resistance forces; neither he nor Admiral King 'told him', according to Mark Clark who was present, 'as much as he could have learned by reading the morning newspaper'. Of this, his first meeting with de Gaulle, Clark's report is so ill-natured as to make it plain that, in one usually fair, it was inspired from above. De Gaulle was described as 'obviously displeased' on entering: 'after a curt handshake he shrugged his shoulders'; a bottle of champagne was produced, but he 'refrained from drinking'; getting no response from Marshall he 'became impatient' and 'rose stiffly', gave a handshake labelled this time as 'cool' and 'marched out', accompanied by 'a stiff-necked aide'.

Meanwhile, in Washington, Leahy equated him with Laval; and Hull, although obliged to admit that 'troubles did not stem entirely from de Gaulle', noted without regret that Roosevelt's 'resentment against de Gaulle was still lively'. From North Africa, Murphy reported that 'not 10 per cent of the people' supported the General—a foolish estimate for which de Gaulle exacted a mild revenge. When, upon his first public appearance in Algiers, a throng of some 100,000 people massed to greet him, Murphy came forward to exclaim admiringly: 'What an enormous crowd!'

'They represent,' replied de Gaulle with his little smile, 'some of your ten per cent.'

Even Eisenhower was swayed at first by the prevailing prejudice. Only after personal and amicable negotiations at Algiers did he confess, with admirable candour, that he had allowed himself to be misled—thereby evoking de Gaulle's exclamation in seldom-used English: *'You are a man!'*

*   *   *

With a broad section of American public opinion Roosevelt was far from finding approval of his opposition to de Gaulle and on more than one occasion, thought fit to twist the truth to hide the inconvenient facts. 'At his press and radio conference today,' Hassett wrote in his journal on July 16, 1943, 'the President spent a long time in clearing up the French situation, muddled by continuous and persistent stories in the press . . . most of them greatly distorted, emphasizing the antagonism of the Roosevelt administration towards General Charles de Gaulle.' As if to reassure himself, Hassett added: 'This is untrue'—meaning the antagonism which, in fact, continued unchecked.

Because of it there developed, through the latter part of 1943 and the first half of 1944, a situation of high absurdity in which, with de Gaulle at Algiers moving irresistibly towards the goal of sole authority now patently desired for him by the great majority of French people at home and abroad, London and Washington trailed far behind each disconcerting move, protesting, threatening, powerless. After Casablanca, Washington had backed Giraud to the hilt as Civil and Military Commander-in-Chief under American control and in accordance with the Clark–Darlan agreement, thus thinking to exclude de Gaulle. But at Algiers, on June 3, de Gaulle—who had foreseen this very situation at Lagos in October 1940 and had wisely laid plans to counter it—compelled the formation of the National Committee of Liberation in which he and Giraud were co-equals. Roosevelt, mixing his own metaphor, threatened force against 'the bride'; on June 5 he cabled Churchill that 'North Africa is in the last analysis under British–American military rule, and for this reason Eisenhower can be used on what you and I want', meaning de Gaulle's suppression. To which Churchill replied that he thought they could 'safely work' with the new Committee, because in it de Gaulle would be 'in a minority of five to two, and possibly completely isolated'—only to learn within a matter of days from an indignant Roosevelt that it was Giraud who was in the minority, liable to be outvoted and forced to retire from the Committee. And the Churchill–Roosevelt correspondence then degenerated into an academic argument concerning the degree of recognition to be granted to a Committee already recognized by informed opinion everywhere in the Allied world.

Churchill to Roosevelt, July 21: 'I am under considerable pressure . . . to "recognize" the Committee. . . . What does recognition mean? One can recognize a man as an Emperor or a grocer.'

Roosevelt to Churchill, July 22: 'I do not think we should at any time use the word "recognition". . . . Perhaps the word "acceptance" . . . comes nearer to expressing my thought.'

Churchill to Roosevelt, August 3: '. . . your proposed formula'—Roosevelt had suggested *co-operation with* instead of *recognition of*—'was rather chilling and would not end the agitation there is for recognition in both our countries.'

Roosevelt to Churchill, August 4: 'I earnestly hope that nothing will be done in the matter of recognition . . . until we have an opportunity to talk it over together.'

Roosevelt at Quebec, August 22, quoted by Hull: 'said he did not want to give de Gaulle a white horse on which he could ride into France and make himself master of a government there.'

Out of Quebec, after laborious discussion, there did at length come an American declaration of very limited recognition, which Churchill vainly hoped would be welcomed by the French 'in most cordial terms' so as not 'to rouse new flames of resentment in the State Department'. But de Gaulle was already several moves ahead. Churchill, agreeing with Roosevelt, had said that he would be 'strongly opposed to Boisson being dismissed from his post' in West Africa; de Gaulle, remembering his subservience to Vichy, dismissed him. Roosevelt had imposed Peyrouton, one time member of Pétain's government and ex-Vichy Ambassador at Buenos Aires, as Governor-General of Algeria; Peyrouton resigned and offered his services to de Gaulle. The ageing General Georges—'whom I got out of France', Churchill wrote, 'and who is a personal friend of mine'—was voted off the Committee and went into retirement. More wounding still to Roosevelt's pride, Giraud's position on the Committee was steadily weakened by his own obstinacy and lack of vision; his small influence dwindled to nothing, his appeals for American support were unavailing and in the Committee he had no support at all; early in November he retired from it. For a while he retained the post of Commander-in-Chief of the French Forces, but his stubborn persistence in regarding himself and the Army as independent of the Committee's authority—notably in the liberation of Corsica where his forces treated the local, and victorious, gaullist Resistance leaders almost as enemies—so diminished confidence in his reliability that eventually it was found necessary to remove him. Treating him with the utmost kindness and patience de Gaulle then appointed him (April 1944) to the lesser but still useful post of Inspector-General of the Army; whereupon Giraud reverted to the selfsame attitude he had adopted on first meeting Eisenhower at Gibraltar. He would be 'Commander-in-Chief or nothing'. Presently he was nothing.

Meanwhile, in October, another important step forward had been taken at Algiers with the gathering together from France of Resistance representatives and political leaders of all parties, including the Communists and excluding only the most compromised of the 'collaborators'. Upon this broad basis there was formed a provisional Consultative Assembly which, meeting for the first time on November 3, clearly outlined the political future. By common consent, indeed by common insistence, de Gaulle was appointed sole President of the National Committee. And with Churchill 'disturbed' and Roosevelt 'angry' the whole argument concerning recognition of the new organization began all over again, to be kept up spasmodically throughout the winter and into the spring with much the same fatuity as when, in doomed Constantinople, points of Christian dogma were argued while the Turkish artillery was battering down the walls.

In April (1944) the National Committee declared that it was now to be regarded as the Provisional Government of the French Republic. Roosevelt turned his back on it. 'If anyone,' Hull quoted him as saying, 'could give him a certificate proving that de Gaulle was a representative of the French people he would deal with him, but that otherwise he had no idea of changing his mind.' Nor was he willing to change his mind even when, after June 15, the 'certificate' could plainly be read in the news from France: in the vitally important contribution to Allied success being made by the French Forces of the Interior commanded, in de Gaulle's name, by General Koenig attached to Eisenhower's staff; in the wild acclaim accorded to de Gaulle on his first visit to Bayeux; in the swiftly vanishing portraits of the Marshal; in the ready acceptance of gaullist administrators. The signs were obvious to all; Roosevelt refused to see them.

Hassett's journal for June 23: 'At his press and radio conference the President indicated his disapproval of the action of General Charles de Gaulle, head of the French Committee of National Liberation [sic], in appointing prefects and sub-prefects in the liberated areas of Normandy. He said more French territory must be liberated before the problem of civil administration, which involves the question of recognition of de Gaulle's committee as a provisional government, would be considered in Washington.'

In fact, Roosevelt was still clinging tenaciously to his own solution of the problem of civil administration. Suggestions made by de Gaulle had been entirely ignored and, in September 1943, the document

(Associated Press)

ᴀʙᴏᴠᴇ. The Road to Victory. Generals
de Lattre, de Gaulle, Devers, Patch.
At Saverne, Alsace, February 1945

ʀɪɢʜᴛ. The Rhine Crossing, Kehl,
April 1945. A French Division going
forward, German prisoners streaming
back

(Etienne Krafft)

RIGHT. The End of the Road. French trumpeters sound the 'cease-fire' below Hitler's chalet, Berchtesgaden, May 1945

BELOW. Presentation to General Eisenhower of a Sword of Honour made for Napoleon I, Paris, 1945

containing the decisions of the United States Government concerning
France had been communicated to the British Government. By the
terms of this document—withheld from the National Committee
which, however, had managed to obtain a copy—French liberated
territory was to be treated in precisely the same manner as enemy-
occupied territory; the Allied Commander-in-Chief would nominate
all civil administrators; he would, if the situation required it, suppress
all troublesome political organizations and intern their leaders;
although he would not negotiate with the ex-Vichy Government, he
would transfer its authority into his own hands; and he would only
deal with liaison officers from the National Committee if he thought it
advisable to do so. Such terms were naturally wholly unacceptable to
the French; and de Gaulle, having informed Churchill and Eisenhower
of his refusal to agree to their application, instructed the Provisional
Government at Algiers to proceed with its long-prepared plans.
Thereupon, throughout the summer of 1944, carefully selected civilian
administrators were moved into France by air, to take over from
ex-Vichy officials in the liberated areas and even, with the help of local
Resistance units, in districts not yet liberated by Allied forces. They,
and with them de Gaulle's authority, though presently challenged by
the Communists, were accepted without demur by the inhabitants.

Recognition of authority in civil affairs could no longer be reasonably withheld. But Eisenhower had already foreseen the principal
obstacle: 'President Roosevelt was flatly opposed to giving General
de Gaulle this specific and particular type of recognition.' And
Churchill, aware of the dangerous deadlock, saw the need to arrange
a meeting in Washington, to which de Gaulle assented on condition
that he was invited by the President. About issuing the invitation,
however, Hull found the President 'extremely difficult', because he
'could not invite him as Head of the United States Government and
State—de Gaulle being neither'. When, at long last, he did invite him
he pretended that it was de Gaulle who had asked to come.

Hassett, June 9: (The President) 'told his press and radio conference
he had assented to a request by General Charles de Gaulle for a visit
to the White House, apparently on a personal basis.' June 27: 'The
President told his news conference that the much-discussed visit of
General de Gaulle may take place between July 5 and 9. He said he
was informing the General those dates would be satisfactory.' July 1:

(The President) 'impatient because nothing has been heard from General de Gaulle concerning the time of his arrival. . . . The President is greatly inconvenienced by de Gaulle's continued failure to reveal his plans.' Shedding further light on the President's state of mind, Hassett added: 'When I told the Boss what de Gaulle was quoted as saying in an interview in Rome yesterday'—(*If I go to the United States to present our greetings to Mr Roosevelt and the American people, I will be very happy and honoured*)—'he cut in: "He's a nut." '

Despite wartime transport difficulties, the 'nut' arrived punctually. Hassett, July 6: 'President put final touches on plans for reception of de Gaulle this afternoon, insisting that his honours be limited to his status as a brigadier-general, although the Frenchman claims to be major-general. . . .' Here Hassett might well have inserted his earlier comment: 'This is untrue.' But from close contact over the years he had been infected with the President's venom; when de Gaulle arrived at the White House, 'he stepped from the automobile with an air of arrogance bordering on downright insolence, his Cyrano de Bergerac nose high in the air'.

There followed four days of conferences about which Roosevelt was very reticent, but from which de Gaulle emerged calmly victorious. Hassett, July 11: '. . . the President told his news conference that this Government has granted to the French Committee of National Liberation the status of a working "de facto" authority in civil affairs in French liberated territory.' Remembering the President's 'funny incident', however, Hassett could not resist a last bitter comment: 'Now let's hope the temperamental Gaul keeps his feet on the ground with no delusions about his reincarnation as Joan of Arc or Clemenceau.'

Even then, in making the President's recognition of de Gaulle's authority effective, there was a singular lack of haste. Between London and Washington agreement on the details of French civil administration, already efficiently worked out by the Provisional Government, were slowly completed. So slowly that they were only released by the Allied Supreme Headquarters on August 24.

By that time, however, Paris, in flaming rebellion, had thrown off its chains. Leclerc and his 2nd Armoured Division had fought their way into the heart of the city. And de Gaulle, from Rambouillet, had ordered the Government at Algiers to join him in the capital. He had no need for the President's 'white horse'.

21. Arrival

O vous, noirs ennemis qui vous glissez dans l'ombre,
Disparaissez à l'approche du jour.
(Racine: Hymns from the Roman Breviary)

IN THE evening of August 25, at the *Hôtel de Ville*, de Gaulle spoke to a packed assembly of Resistance leaders. The liberation of Paris was accomplished. Five days of sporadic fighting, of fierce rebellion fiercely contested and costing some four thousand dead on either side, had been brought to an end on the sixth day by the swift action of Leclerc's Division compelling the surrender of General von Choltitz and the surviving German garrison of fifteen thousand men. A crackle of distant fire still came from the north where, at Le Bourget and Montmorency, the enemy rearguards held momentarily against the advancing French detachments; within the city limits the struggle was over. Vast Allied operations had opened the way, but the capital of France had been freed by Frenchmen.

'Why should we hide the emotion that grips us all?' said de Gaulle. 'These minutes will outlast each of our little lives.'

That night, while he rested at the War Ministry in the rue St Dominique—where in four years nothing had been changed, no single detail altered, where even the little tickets against the bell-buttons on the Minister's desk showed the same names as in June 1940, so that it seemed as if Time had been holding its breath since that dark morning when Weygand had tripped jauntily in to postulate surrender—throughout the night the hastily repaired wireless stations broadcast the announcement of the coming day's event: the simple yet grandiose ceremony marking the climax of liberation in the recognition of the liberator. From dawn onwards, in a Paris deprived of cars, buses and subway, the streets echoed to the unaccustomed clamour of an advancing multitude coming from every quarter of the city and from all its sprawling suburbs, shuffling on worn-out shoeleather or clattering upon wooden soles, single-minded in its determination to gain some point of vantage along the processional route, to see—at last!—the man whom few had ever seen, yet to whose voice all had at some time listened. By noon the greatest crowd ever assembled in the long and turbulent history of Paris had thrust itself into jammed immobility from the Étoile to Notre Dame.

The route was lined—it needed to be, to leave the way clear—by men of the F.F.I. (French Forces of the Interior), by the Paris police who had led the insurrection, by Leclerc's Armoured Division one quarter of whose force was still engaged in clearing the enemy from the north-eastern outskirts. Leclerc had that day received a curious order from the American general commanding the Army Corps to which his Division was attached, an order that seemed to reflect the ill-will still smouldering in Washington. By it Leclerc was told to disregard any instructions given him by de Gaulle, and was further told that none of the troops under his command were to take any part in the ceremony whatever. The occasion, however, was too great to be marred by foreign interference and the order was rightly ignored.

Punctually at three o'clock de Gaulle arrived at the Arc de Triomphe. A crowd of officials was waiting to receive him by the Unknown Soldier's grave: members of the Government, of the National Council of Resistance, of the Liberation Committee of Paris, the Prefects, the Generals—some of them his companions from the earliest days of the struggle, risen to high rank by skill and gallantry: Leclerc de Hautecloque, one time 'Mr Clark' passenger for Lagos and Duala, Koenig, hero of Bir Hakeim, Thierry d'Argenlieu, priest and Admiral. When he had rekindled the flame over the tomb, de Gaulle turned to inspect the officers and men of an armoured unit standing by their vehicles, men of the 'Chad Regiment' for whom in the uncertain days after Dakar he had woven the pattern of a dream so distant, so fantastic it still seemed a dream even now that it had come to pass, even to him who had invoked it—until suddenly, at the end of the line, with the crowd of officials opening before him, the dream was surpassed by unimagined reality.

The wonder of it was to linger in his *Memoires*: 'Before me, the Champs Elysées. Ah!— but it's the sea! An immense throng piled up on either side of the avenue. Perhaps two million souls. The very rooftops black with people. At every window a compact mass entwined with flags. Bunches of men like grapes hanging from ladders, from flagpoles, from lamp-posts. As far as my eyes can reach—a living swell of ocean, beneath the sun and beneath the tricolour. I go forward on foot.'

The walk itself was of the stuff of dreams. No pomp of planned pageantry, no clatter of cavalry; no sheen of breastplates or measured tramp of marching men; no reverberating words of command or crash of arms presented. Just one man striding down the centre of the great roadway, his long legs carrying him so fast the ragged wave of followers had to run to keep up with him. Just one brigadier-general (temporary) with a high-crowned *képi*; wearing no glittering stars or serried rows of medal ribbons, only an emblem that was not an award but a symbol of dedication: a miniature plaque bearing the Cross of Lorraine. One man; and only one sound, but that deafening. It came at him from both sides at once; tumultuous, resonant, drowning all other cries; the deep double percussion of his name. *'De Gaulle!— De Gaulle!'*—an echo of Duala, of the encouragement, so warm but so thin, accorded in the days of darkness, grown now to the full diapason of the day of glory; thunderous, triumphant, unceasing.

He strode on at speed and, ahead of the growing column of those who now seemed more like pursuers than followers, almost alone. Glancing continually from side to side, up to the windows, higher to the rooftops, his smile was broader than usual, certainly happier, yet still restrained, modest, almost shy. Seen from afar by those craning their heads to catch a first glimpse, the tall angular figure springing forward with long, elastic stride appeared to be floating clear of the ground, the impression heightened by the ceaseless rise and fall of winglike arms that seemed to raise him up and the whole vast crowd with him and to extend, to each and every one of the people of Paris, not a military salute, but a greeting, a handclasp, friendly and familiar.

It was, just then, all that he had to give: 'For the attitudes and gestures that please the crowd I have neither the physique nor the inclination.' Yet in that hour, for those who called his name and waved and wept for joy, it was enough. They did not welcome him as a mighty conqueror; rather did they express their gratitude for hope given in the hour of defeat, for pride restored after the years of humiliation, and by their immense acclaim give thanks for all he had so nobly preached and so steadfastly practised in the name of France. 'To give back to the nation the voice of the people'—this he had promised. And the people, with voice regained, declared their will with one accord. Even by those who, putting party before patriotism, planned to seize power, even by those in whose hearts there lingered regret for the fallen Marshal, carried away by the receding tide of invasion, the unity of the millions was proclaimed: '*De Gaulle!*— *Vive de Gaulle!*'—and, to his ears, the sweeter sound of '*Vive la France!*'

Outwardly calm, smiling, repeating incessantly the almost mechanical two-sided greeting, he was uneasy under the overwhelming burden of frantic applause; at the same time deeply moved and coolly unaffected in his far-seeing judgment. This would not last; this was but the moment of explosive joy, of mutual understanding, of recognition, the moment in which he had been confirmed by popular acclaim as sole leader and head of the Republic. Beneath the surface the bitter enmities were too deep and too violent for unity to endure unless he struck while the iron of enthusiasm was still white hot. The liberation of Paris, even of all France, was not an end, but a beginning—of fresh trials for the French people, of a renewed testing of his own integrity. There could be no relaxation, no resting upon laurels however selflessly earned. 'Independence' he had promised, but it was now less a matter of liberation from a defeated enemy than of security from the ruthless opportunism of Communist ambition. 'Restoration of the greatness of France'—from the outset he had announced the national aim to the nation which now applauded him; but greatness was not to be had for the asking. 'France,' he had written long ago, 'would not be France without her Army.' So it had proved to be for four long years. To be recognized once again as a great nation, all France must be brought back into the struggle whatever the cost.

He had been careful to stress the necessity in his improvised speech at the *Hôtel de Ville* on the previous evening. 'France has come back to Paris,' he had said, 'more certain than ever of her duties and her rights. I speak of her duties first, and I can sum them up by saying that, for the time being, they are the duties of war. The enemy is tottering, but he is not yet beaten . . . we shall therefore continue to fight to the last day, to the day of total and complete victory. All those here present, and all those in France who hear us, know that this duty of waging war demands national unity. The nation would not tolerate that, in the present situation, this unity should be broken. The nation knows well that in order to win, to rebuild, to become great, it must have with it all its sons and all its daughters . . . and that all the sons and all the daughters of France must march together, hand in hand, towards the achievement of the aims of France.'

But, however high his personal reputation, however warm the present popular approval, moving speeches and fraternal greetings were not enough. Action, swift and decisive, was needed. The Government must govern; and in that Government his was the sole voice of authority. 'For the time being,' he might well have repeated without vainglory, 'I am France.' At this very moment his personal authority was unchallenged, respected, desired by the great majority; were it to be relaxed catastrophe would surely follow. For the danger was real and immediate; the danger that the well-knit Communist party, long and secretly preparing for this very occasion, would take advantage of the blended enthusiasm and confusion of the liberation to seize power by force of arms. That the peril was pressing had been made clear by information reaching him from all sides within the past few days; it was to be further emphasized by the events of that evening.

With a solid phalanx now at his back and the crowds ahead closing in upon him, he paused momentarily at the Rond Point to greet a section of Leclerc's armour, standing ready to move off to the north should the enemy attempt a last despairing dirve into the city; turned aside to salute the rugged statue of Clemenceau, thrusting forward through the trees by the Petit Palais; and marched on between the chestnuts that recalled the vision of Rostand's *L'Aiglon* which had so deeply moved him in boyhood. On the Place de la Concorde a rapturous mob hemmed him in, so that he had difficulty in reaching the entrance to the rue de Rivoli. There a car waited with an armed escort to convey him at greater speed, first to the Hôtel de Ville, then to Notre Dame.

The *place* before the Cathedral was densely packed; de Gaulle's car drew up amid cheers. But even as he mounted the steps where the clergy waited to receive him, a wild fusillade broke out from the garret floors of houses upon the north side. Promptly answered by the small arms of the escort, it was returned from the rooftops; in the hastily scattering crowd many were hit or else injured in the crush. At the same hour, at widely separated points in the capital, similar incidents occurred; the plan to spread alarm was concerted. Blamed by the Communists upon non-existent German elements conspiring with collaborators, it was intended to demonstrate the need for the fighting groups to retain their arms so as to preserve order. Upon a people just rid of Nazi tyranny it had the opposite effect; Paris refused to be cowed by its own Resistance.

Within the Cathedral, meanwhile, a volley of shots rang out from the galleries high above the nave down which, in slow procession, de Gaulle paced impassive and erect. No shot was aimed at him; but more than once in history the stray bullet has changed the course of events; had he been killed then no one in France could have taken his place. In his Government as in his Army there were men of proven quality, of integrity and high intelligence; none of them was known as he was known, none commanded the respect of the nation, none echoed in a name the magic of 'de Gaulle'. France already half destroyed, becoming a prey to bitter strife Communist-inspired, might never have risen again within the lifespan of any of those present that day. Seldom in the history of nations has so much depended upon one man's survival.

It may be that such an eventuality as chance assassination occurred to him later; just then his thoughts were elsewhere. The firing in the upper galleries continued fitfully, the shots reverberating beneath the high vault to punctuate incongruously the full-voiced *Magnificat* intoned by the choir. Stone splinters and ricochets flew down, wounding members of the packed congregation. To avoid further casualties, de Gaulle cut the ceremony short.

Thus the day of glory ended, upon a discordant note. Clearly, not all the F.F.I. were to be trusted with weapons now that the Germans had been driven out, least of all the Communists. That night, moreover, the people of Paris were reminded that Liberation did not mean the end of the War; *Luftwaffe* bombers raided the eastern quarters of the city, causing a thousand dead and wounded.

22. Assertion

'On veut de l'autorité.'
(General Leclerc to de Gaulle, August 27, 1944)

IN THE course of the following day reports began to come in from all over the country, clarifying a rapidly developing situation civilian as well as military. With the Allies upon the Loire and across the Seine above and below Paris, with General de Lattre's army driving up the Rhône valley after freeing Toulon and Marseilles, the German forces were flowing away from the centre as from a watershed, one part hurrying eastward before the gap should close, the other withdrawing westward to crowd into Atlantic strongpoints in the vain hope of halting the Allied advance by closing the ports. By this hasty withdrawal considerable areas of central and southern France were being automatically liberated almost overnight; and, in the absence of the civilian administrators appointed by de Gaulle's Provisional Government who had not yet had time to arrive, effective authority was increasingly—and, in the absence of French regular troops, inevitably—being imposed by local Resistance Committees and groups of the F.F.I.

Taken as a whole the lightly armed Forces of the Interior had played a valiant part ever since the Normandy landings, harassing the enemy, cutting his communications, greatly delaying and even immobilizing some eight urgently needed German divisions. In many regions they had suffered heavy losses in hand to hand fighting, and those captured had more often than not been tortured to death. 'Throughout France,' wrote Eisenhower, 'they had been of inestimable value in the campaign. . . . Without their great assistance the liberation of France and the defeat of the enemy in western Europe would have consumed a much longer time and meant greater losses to ourselves.' In such forces, however, secretly recruited and armed for a deadly purpose, there were serious weaknesses which, once the purpose was accomplished, declared themselves openly. Leclerc, reporting to de Gaulle on August 27, estimated that '10 per cent' were 'very good, very honest, genuine fighters; 25 to 30 per cent follow the example of the first; the remainder worthless or negative'. By these, the worthless 60 per cent, the new-found unity of France was threatened.

'The immense majority of the population,' Leclerc further reported, 'particularly in Paris, magnificently French and national, ask only to be commanded so as to remake France.' To de Gaulle the necessity of granting the desire and of asserting his authority seemed paramount if law and order were to be restored behind the retreating enemy. The lessons of an earlier tragedy were there to instruct: in 1871, at the end of the siege of Paris, failure to collect the arms distributed to the civilian defenders had led to the horrors of the Commune. On the following day (August 28), summoning before him the members of the National Resistance Council, he first congratulated them upon their undoubted achievements and then—to the obvious dismay of some who had hoped to control the Government by maintaining under arms a 'patriotic' (i.e. Communist) militia to enforce the will of 'the people'—announced his firm decisions.

Published over his signature that same day, they included a number of essential measures. The command and staff organizations of the F.F.I. were abolished in all liberated territory; their functions would be exercised, in Paris, by the military governor, General Koenig, in the liberated departments by the generals commanding military regions. Such of the F.F.I. units as could at once be used in further operations would be incorporated in the Army forthwith. All other F.F.I. officers, NCOs and men in liberated territories would be regularly enrolled, stock would be taken of their arms and equipment which would be handed over under conditions to be fixed by the generals commanding military regions and, for Paris, by General Koenig.

Of de Gaulle's Government in metropolitan France these were the first important measures; and in Paris and the areas held by the Allied armies they were effective. But in the south, over much of the vast area enclosed between the Atlantic and the Mediterranean, the Loire and the Rhône, they were not easily enforced against the will of local resistance leaders who deliberately ignored them. Groups often no more than a hundred strong, under 'officers' flaunting badges of high rank to which they had no title, roamed the countryside and, following upon the heels of the retiring enemy, seized power in towns and villages before the Government authorities could take over. Largely, but not exclusively, of Communist affiliation, from harassing the Germans they turned with alacrity to hunting those of the French

whom they suspected, with or without evidence, of having supported
Vichy, collaborated with the enemy, or merely of having taken no
part in the Resistance. Thousands were thrown into prison or herded
into the camps of a new captivity; thousands more were summarily
executed, frequently without so much as the mockery of an illegal
trial. Big towns, such as Toulouse, Limoges, Lyons, Nice, were
subjected in the course of liberation to reigns of terror rivalling those
of the Revolution, in which, often for motives of personal vengeance
or personal gain, houses were broken into and pillaged, the occu-
pants slaughtered. The total of those slain in these outbreaks of criminal violence and anarchy—intended, in so far as they were planned,
to further Communist domination—can never be known with any
certainty; enemy action and Allied air attacks were held responsible
for much and helped to conceal murders which the authorities were
ashamed to admit. It has been put as high as 100,000, as low as one
tenth of that number; de Gaulle, in his *Mémoires*, gave the figures of
10,842 executed without legal trial and 779 put to death by verdict of
properly constituted tribunals; but the hidden total of assassination
was certainly very much higher and probably between thirty and forty
thousand.

The effect of these provincial disturbances, which it took all
de Gaulle's personal authority to limit and eventually to terminate,
was enhanced by the widespread miseries of war. Gone in a matter of
days was the near-unanimity of insurrection against the invader, gone
the unmixed joy at seeing the enemy depart as suddenly as he had come.
Anxiety bred dissension, expressed in the regained freedom of speech.
The 'worthless or negative' majority of the F.F.I., their heroic
minority absolved but soon forgotten, were scorned and detested.
The Communists, foiled in their plot to seize power by armed force,
but highly successful in numerous bank robberies, fell back upon the
more subtle, and more dangerous, methods of corruption and blackmail. The country people and peasantry who, for all their sorrow and
humiliation, had for the most part known four years of compulsory
peace and even, in certain districts, of considerable prosperity, were
dismayed to find that in many a zone of operations the new liberty
brought in its train the most terrible consequences. Fierce passions
aroused by appalling Nazi reprisals—that of Oradour-sur-Glane being
only the most notorious among many—were vented against traitors

who had either informed or blatantly befriended the enemy, were then turned against those who protested at a vengeance too brutal and too blind; at length were allayed by the spectre of approaching famine.

Without transport, with all means of communication cut—and restored only along the line of the Allied advance—with ports sealed against relief from outside, scanty stocks were quickly depleted until, in the towns as in communities in unproductive districts, no more than the barest necessities of life remained. Flames of pure patriotism seldom burn steadily in empty stomachs, soon only the embers were left; and the great mass of the people could hardly be blamed, once the enemy had gone, for finding in the struggle for existence something of greater moment than that for the resurgence of France among the nations. In a land half ruined by battle, hardship and undernourishment brought swift disenchantment, until national pride was no longer sufficient to stifle a yawn of lassitude.

To counter this moral and physical exhaustion, to infuse a new spirit of duty and sacrifice in the people at a time when it was impossible to increase their material comfort or even their meagre rations, was a formidable task, the more so since the situation was one of which de Gaulle had not been sufficiently informed ahead of time. In planning the immediate future of the nation he had been led to suppose that once the people had cast off their chains they would throw themselves with Revolutionary fervour into the two-fold labour of fighting the war whilst rebuilding the country. It was a belief that had been fostered in the days of Fighting France in exile both by the immense courage and devotion of the Resistance leaders, risking torture and death, and by the eager patriotism of the young men who in increasing numbers had made their way out to join the French Forces. Kept in ignorance of the Allied invasion plans until the last moment, he had not been able to appreciate fully the extent of the material damage it would be necessary to inflict upon the territory of metropolitan France in order to loosen the German grip. Churchill might well, on the eve of D-day, have warned him of the intended destruction; instead he appears to have told him rather testily that, rather than find fault with Roosevelt's plan for civil administration, he should be grateful that the Allies were 'willing to risk the lives of scores of thousands of their men to liberate France'[1]—which was almost the exact opposite of the truth. The Allies were not condescendingly 'willing' to liberate anything; they had chosen France as the battlefield upon which to defeat the German Army, thereafter as the broad highway over which their forces would march into the heart of Germany. To achieve this end it was evident that, in the initial stages, a vast injury would have to be inflicted upon the soil and people of France whose liberation would be incidental to the forward sweep of the victorious Allies.[2]

In the First World War the grim desolation of the battlefields had been confined to the north-eastern corner of France; behind the Western Front the life of the country had continued almost undisturbed. In 1944, within the space of five months, destruction and demolition dotted over the length and breadth of the land brought national activity to a standstill. Already impoverished by four years of Nazi spoliation and ruinous occupation costs, lacking the physical strength, to work or to fight, of nearly three millions of her men detained in Germany—as prisoners of war, as compulsory labour in German factories, as political deportees in those death-camps in which 150,000 French citizens died—France became the anvil upon which, largely by the hammer-blows of Allied air power, the enemy's cohesion was smashed. By these blows, added to the widespread and brilliantly efficient work of the Resistance forces, the enemy was defeated and rolled back. But France was paralysed.

With the coming of autumn the ineluctable consequences became apparent. Aside from the armies hurrying eastward or closing in about the enemy-held ports, scarcely any movement was discernible in the country. More than three thousand road bridges had been blown; over the principal rivers, the Rhône, the Loire, the Lower Seine, there were no railway bridges at all. Ten thousand locomotives, out of twelve thousand, had either been destroyed or removed by the enemy; only one tenth of all mechanized vehicles remained and for that tenth there was scarcely any fuel. Communication centres, road and rail junctions, marshalling yards, factories used by the enemy had been bombed intensively, sometimes with pinpoint accuracy, too frequently

---

[1] Churchill: *Second World War*, Vol. V, page 556.

[2] The damage caused by Allied action and enemy counter-action in France was several times greater than that inflicted upon Britain by German bombing. Alone the figure of 2,000,000 dwelling-houses destroyed or seriously damaged gives some measure of the tragedy.

with an unfortunate spilling over into non-military areas; occasionally targets had been missed altogether with disastrous and tragic results. Numerous towns had been partially devastated: Rouen, Orleans, Tours, Cherbourg, Toulon and Marseilles; others in the battle-zones had been half obliterated: Caen, St Lô, Vire, eventually Le Havre, Calais, Brest. Telegraph and telephone lines were everywhere down, power cables had been cut; many places had neither light nor heat and very little food; heavy industry and mining had ceased, and in the north-east the remaining coal stocks had been requisitioned by the Allies who, unable to deliver promised relief through the blocked ports, could offer only the receding hope of speedy victory. Small wonder that, facing winter, the people of France should feel discouragement in the present, anxiety at the future. It is the measure of de Gaulle's strength of purpose, and also of his clear-sighted ability as an administrator, that he rescued the country from paralysis and anarchy and the people from their torpor.

He began, despite the extreme difficulty of communication, by enforcing the central Government's authority against the local Resistance committees usurping power, by strengthening the police, moving in detachments of regular troops, re-establishing the magistrature, insisting upon obedience to the orders restricting the activities of the F.F.I. Late in September he followed up with a rapid tour of the country: to the south, to Toulon and Marseilles; to the south-west, to Toulouse and Bordeaux; northward to Britanny, the Loire valley, the towns of Normandy; north-east to his old garrison-town of Arras, to his native Lille; south again through his home-village of Colombey, south-east to meet the advancing army of de Lattre thrusting up towards the Belfort Gap; back via Dijon to Paris.

The effect of these first visits was more decisive than any Government edict. His popularity was enormous. In every town and village dense crowds assembled at his coming, surrounded him crying their gratitude, grasping his hand, cheering, weeping. Of the man himself, of his personality and appearance, they had scarcely known what to expect and yet what they saw seemed, mysteriously, to exceed their expectations. His presence was commanding yet unassuming, his manner friendly, courteous, sympathetic. To the common people he was easily approachable, devoid of pomposity or arrogance, yet maintaining a measure of restraint beyond his own natural reserve, enough to remind those about him that he who had shared their sufferings and inspired their hopes was now, by their own acclaim, supreme head of France.

He spoke frequently, with the simple eloquence to which they had become accustomed during the years when they had listened secretly to his broadcasts. He gave them the slogan 'order and ardour', two factors 'without which nothing great can be done': the 'Republican order under the only valid authority, that of the State', and the 'concentrated ardour' necessary for the rebuilding and renewal of that State. Rehearsed or impromptu, his speeches were outspoken and direct, avoiding those hollow phrases of oratory of which the French people over the years had swallowed a surfeit. Scoffers who came to stare at the 'symbol' stayed to listen to the man who, warning them that the way ahead must be hard and recovery slow, outlined the practical measures that would make that recovery sure. Under the impact of his presence Communist 'generals' fell strangely silent. Those in local Resistance committees who questioned his decisions he treated in much the same manner as the recalcitrant 'deputation' that, four years earlier, had come aboard the *Duboc* off Duala: listened patiently to their objections, silent, unsmiling, with that occasional little jerk of the head which his associates had come to know so well—an upward thrust of the chin as though his collar were too tight or as if he were squaring his shoulders to ease a burden—listened to the end, and then strode forward imperturbably to reply with arguments of unanswerable logic and plain common sense, announcing his clear-cut conclusions quietly, almost gently, yet in a tone of authority that few thought to defy.

By the end of October pacification was assured; 'Republican order' had to a large extent been reestablished throughout the liberated territory. Of the F.F.I., 50,000 of the best trained and disciplined were added to de Lattre's Army; 50,000 more were held in reserve pending the supply of uniforms and equipment; of the remainder an important fraction was joined to the regular troops investing the German-held ports, notably at the mouth of the Garonne; and the rest were dissolved, not without protest, and their arms slowly recovered. The first freight trains began to grind over hastily repaired lines, nosing an uncertain way over makeshift bridges; rare lorries burning a variety of strange substitute fuels clattered down the broken roads; with the peasantry stubbornly working their fields and herding their cattle, the desperate shortage of the towns was gradually alleviated.

With the provisional Government broadened and the Consultative Assembly enlarged, in anticipation of the day when the war situation would permit the holding of municipal and departmental elections, the social reforms announced by de Gaulle put new heart into the people long before the measures could be effective. The *Banque de France* and various key-industries were to be nationalized. The wage-level throughout the country was to be raised by 50 per cent forthwith, with family allowances, grants and pensions to follow; there might 'always be the poor, there would be no more pauperism'. To halt, temporarily at least, the consequent inflation a 3 per cent Government loan was launched, and met with overwhelming response. In agriculture tenant-farmers were given greater security of tenure, with option to purchase. The many who, in industry or commerce, had made fortunes by working for the Germans were to be made to disgorge their illicit gains. Collaborators, informers and traitors, responsible for the torture, deportation and death of their compatriots, were to be tried by a specially convened High Court of Justice.

Although, internally, the continuing difficulties of distribution through lack of communications and transport remained disheartening obstacles to recovery, in external affairs successive events did much to steady the morale of the nation. Persistent reminders by de Gaulle's Ambassadors in London and Moscow had persuaded the Governments of both those countries to bring pressure to bear upon Washington in the still vexed matter of 'recognition'. Despite Churchill's reluctance to do anything that might hinder his 'friend's' re-election to the Presidency, and Roosevelt's reluctance to do anything that might conceivably help his 'friend' de Gaulle,[1] Washington was at length compelled to admit the obvious and, on October 23, six months after its inception at Algiers and more than eight weeks after its arrival in Paris, to recognize as legally valid the Provisional Government of France. The Allied Governments-in-exile, which had long urged the advisability of the move, promptly announced a similar recognition and were followed by most of the friendly Governments of the world;

[1] In Washington, in July, Roosevelt had given him a photograph with the curious inscription: 'To General de Gaulle who is my friend'.

(*Associated Press*)

The Road from Colombey, May 1958

Mme de Gaulle greets Mr. Macmillan at Rambouillet, March 1960

(*Keystone*)

Twenty Years After: '*J'ai conscience de parler au nom de la France.*' President de Gaulle in Westminster Hall, April 6, 1960. (*right*: M. Geoffroy de Courcel)

Algeria, December 1960

diplomatic representatives were exchanged, France resumed a part in international politics. Modest to start with, under de Gaulle's impulsion it was soon more worthy of her ancient traditions.

The first notable event was the official visit, at de Gaulle's invitation, of Churchill and Eden. They came in November, in time for the victory parade on the 11th, an occasion which gave the Prime Minister an opportunity to display his customary emotionalism and, in a subsequent speech, to praise de Gaulle for having restored France to greatness as 'the champion of liberty and independence'. It was, he said, a fundamental principle of British policy that the alliance with France should be unshakeable, continuous and effective. De Gaulle, remembering the recent past, his eyes wide open to the uncertain future, took this assurance with a wary pinch of salt, knowing as he did that Churchill's policy just then was to keep in step with Roosevelt, in whose nebulous ideology France traced no more than an unwelcome shadow. Offered a draft treaty that appeared to be little more than a reaffirmation of the old *Entente Cordiale*, he suggested a more comprehensive pact that, by linking the two nations in a common policy for all Europe, should provide a powerful buffer between the slapdash intentions of Washington and the darker ambitions of Moscow. With this farsighted plan, however, Churchill—who in 1940 had backed the fantastic scheme for total and indissoluble union between France and Britain, their peoples, governments and empires —would have nothing to do. Too trustfully 'leaning upon the bosom of the urgent West', he missed what may have been the one great chance of rescuing eastern Europe from Roosevelt's high-handed folly and Stalin's crafty realism. By January it was too late, and presently the War was ended with a betrayal similar to that by which it had been preceded. De Gaulle's integrity, and Roosevelt's spite, saw to it that France played no part in that betrayal.

Free French endeavours, steadily pursued since 1941, to establish firm and friendly relations with Soviet Russia were now rewarded. On November 24, at Stalin's invitation, de Gaulle, with a party that included his Foreign Minister, Georges Bidault, left for Moscow where, after a slow roundabout journey, he arrived on December 2. Negotiations for a Franco–Russian treaty of alliance in the war against Germany, and for mutual assistance thereafter, were commenced at once and lasted, day in day out, for the whole of the week's visit of which no less than fifteen hours were spent in personal discussions between the two heads of State. From these prolonged encounters de Gaulle was quick to discern Stalin's character and intentions, perceiving beneath the blunt speech and easy-going manner 'the cunning and implacable champion of Russia', whose passion for personal power and national expansion burned so fiercely as to emanate, through all his dissimulation and insincerity, 'a kind of sombre charm'.

About the treaty itself, the details thrashed out by Bidault and Molotov, there was relatively little difficulty; but it was soon made plain that the price attached to the document would be an annexe whereby France recognized the Communist 'Lublin Committee' as the Government of Poland to the exclusion of the lawful Government in exile; and this price de Gaulle calmly but resolutely refused to pay. He well understood, he told Stalin, Russia's fear of a recurrent German aggression and her consequent need of a friendly neighbour; but Poland, France's traditional ally for whom she had declared war in 1939, must be restored to complete freedom and independence: 'the future Government of Poland is the concern of the Polish people, and this people must, in our view, be able to express itself by universal suffrage.' He was ready to conclude a mutual security pact with Russia; he would neither recognize nor treat with the Lublin Committee; and, as previously arranged, he would leave Moscow by train on the morning of December 10.

Upon this ground he stood firm throughout his visit, outwardly unmoved by displays of pomp and power, by grandiose receptions at the Spiridonovka, by ballets at the Bolshoi, by inspections and reviews—including that of his own *Normandie-Niemen* air squadron, the only Allied unit to have fought upon the Russian front—by a culminating banquet of barbaric splendour in the Kremlin. Subjected to Stalin's bluff and cajoling eloquence, to Molotov's unsmiling persuasiveness, de Gaulle never wavered. Well aware of his inability to prevent the subjection to Russian domination either of Poland or of other eastern European countries, foreseeing that Britain and the United States might presently give in to Soviet pressure, he remained unshakeably determined: France would not condone the crime of Polish enslavement. It was a matter of principle, a point of honour that might in the long run redound to France's credit. 'The future lasts a long time,' he was to write. 'Some day anything may happen, even this: that a deed consonant with honour and honesty should eventually appear as a sound political investment.'

To the last day, almost to the last hour, Molotov and his grim-faced subordinates persevered; at Stalin's command arguing tirelessly, manoeuvring, bargaining in favour of the Treaty-plus-Lublin, while de Gaulle, informed of events by Bidault, remained aloof and reserved. At the conclusion of the impressive banquet on the last evening of his visit (9th), and after the countless toasts had been drunk, light entertainment was provided with the showing of Russian films. At midnight, with the films only half shown, de Gaulle rose from his chair and, giving Stalin his hand, thanked him for his hospitality, remarked that the train would soon be leaving and bade him *au revoir*. Bowing to the amazed and suddenly silent assembly he strode slowly out of the room, made his way down the great stairway and, getting into his car, was driven back to the French Embassy where Bidault presently joined him. It was the perfect exit, marking in a manner courteous but firm the end both of the visit and of the negotiations, and it had a remarkable effect.

At two o'clock in the morning (10th) an emissary arrived from the Kremlin, bringing a modified draft of the agreement in which, it was now suggested, France would not officially recognize the Lublin Committee, but would announce an exchange of representatives. De Gaulle turned it down. At Molotov's invitation Bidault then returned to the Kremlin, and at about half-past three yet another draft reached the Embassy. This time there was no mention at all of the Lublin Committee.

Approved by de Gaulle, the draft was then rushed back to the Kremlin where the guests left over from the banquet were still anxiously hanging about under Stalin's watchful eye and where, in the next room, final touches were hastily put to the text. At four o'clock, notified that all was ready, de Gaulle himself returned and, a few minutes later, the treaty of alliance valid for twenty years was signed in his presence by Bidault and Molotov. 'Let's celebrate!' cried Stalin. And immediately tables laden with food and drink were rushed in by a host of lackeys; and presently Stalin was once again proposing a long series of grandiloquent toasts: 'To the Slavs—free and independent everywhere! . . . To the friendship of France, Poland and Russia! . . . To Poland, strong, independent and democratic!' And de Gaulle, responding politely but abstemiously, silently meditated 'the great gulf that, in the Soviet world, divides words from deeds'.

*   *   *

Paris was well pleased with the Treaty which, while it took much of the wind out of Communist sails at home, re-asserted France's influence abroad. Status in international affairs appeared to have been restored together with military prestige; for already, just after Churchill's visit, France, at the invitation of Russia, Britain and the United States, had joined the London European Commission upon a footing of equality with the great Powers; and on the eve of de Gaulle's departure for Moscow had come the announcement of the brilliant operation carried out by the 2nd Armoured Division resulting in the capture of Strasbourg and the arrival—first of the Allied forces— of French troops upon the Rhine. It seemed almost as if the war were drawing to its close and, although 100,000 German troops still held their ground in the encircled western ports, a large proportion of the French people facing the acute problems of daily life, lost interest in a campaign whose outcome was a foregone conclusion.

Complacency was shortlived. Hardly had de Gaulle returned when, on December 16, in an early winter of exceptional severity, the enemy made his last desperate thrust through the Ardennes; and the depth and swiftness of penetration filled with dismay the wearied people of the north-east, so recently delivered and never wholly recovered from the heartbreaking shock of 1940. Ominous names of unhappy memory began to be heard again: Marche, Libramont, Bastogne, the line of the Meuse, Dinant. Scanty reports in the insufficient press increased the general anxiety, rumour ran riot: paratroops in American uniforms were being dropped far in rear of the Allied armies, the murderous Vichy 'militia' was returning, Paris was menaced. By de Lattre's army it was learned that, to shorten the line, the Allied Command had ordered the Americans to withdraw from Metz and Lorraine, thus compelling the French on their right to evacuate Strasbourg and abandon Alsace.

On January 1, with a German diversionary attack developing, the retirement began. But de Gaulle would have none of it. The liberated territory of Alsace could not under any circumstances be handed back to the enemy who, under the local command of Himmler, would wreak a vengeance the more terrible for the recent wild welcome accorded to the liberators by the inhabitants. Asserting his authority as head of the French Government, he gave orders that, whatever the American forces did, the French army would stand fast and if necessary alone. Strasbourg must be defended to the end. Consideration for the people of Alsace apart, France would not accept the news of a retreat without a fight; not on this front and by French troops. A display of weakness at this stage of the War would lead to loss of faith in the Government, to demoralization in the chilly and ill-fed towns, to riots and anarchy. 'De Gaulle' would no longer be the symbol of resistance and victory.

On January 3, at the Allied Headquarters in Versailles, de Gaulle informed Eisenhower of his decision not to withdraw and of his reasons for the decision. By this time the German drive to the Meuse had been halted and, with sufficient Anglo–American strength to counter-attack in the north, there was no need to bring back divisions from the south; nevertheless the argument was protracted and warm. Eisenhower began by telling de Gaulle that 'the French Army would get no ammunition, supplies or food unless it obeyed' his orders. To which de Gaulle retorted with justifiable frigidity that, were the French Army left, in isolation and without supplies, to be destroyed by the Germans, the then uncontrollable wrath of the French people would be turned against American communications by rail, road and wire with the same skill and fury as earlier against those of the enemy; the Allied campaign would end in disaster.

After this the discussion was continued upon a more sensible level. To get a military order revoked, said Eisenhower, 'de Gaulle's argument seemed to be based upon political considerations'. But, de Gaulle answered, 'it is to serve the political aims of states that armies exist'. Eventually, admitting that 'the crisis in the Ardennes was well past', Eisenhower gave way with his customary good grace; the order to withdraw in Alsace-Lorraine was rescinded. Strasbourg was spared from destruction and massacre; and presently, with the enemy everywhere thrown back, France breathed again. 'Intransigence' based, as usual, upon sound reasoning had scored another point.

23. Exclusion

The only real tragedy in life is the being used by personally minded men for purposes which you recognize to be base.

(Shaw: Preface to *Man and Superman*)

MEANWHILE, HOWEVER, as if to admonish the French Government and people for a too rapidly returning confidence and self-respect, the Allied Powers went out of their way to make it clear that France, in the settlement of international affairs, counted for nothing. Early in January, without any official communication to Paris, the information was 'leaked' through the press that Stalin, Roosevelt and Churchill were shortly to meet, not only to concert plans for the ending of the War, but also to decide the subsequent fate of Europe. From this meeting de Gaulle was to be excluded.

However wounding to national pride, the exclusion, adding but one more injury to the many suffered over the years, in no way surprised de Gaulle. 'Whatever progress had been achieved along the road leading France back to her rightful place, I knew too well whence we had started to believe that we had yet arrived.' What alarmed him were the reasons for the exclusion. Because, although Moscow surreptitiously placed the blame upon Washington, it was plain that Stalin had no desire to see at the conference table one who had so steadfastly refused to recognize the Lublin Committee. London, too, allowed it to be known that but for Washington's opposition France would have been invited, yet made no move to insist upon the invitation. Admittedly, de Gaulle was wrong in thinking that Churchill intended, at the conference, to gain political advantage for Great Britain in the Middle East at the expense of France; for, by mid-January, with victorious Russian forces overrunning Poland in pursuit of the irretrievably broken German armies, the Prime Minister was far more deeply concerned at the prospect of Soviet domination of all eastern Europe, a danger greatly increased by the naïve trust placed in the Russian Government's honesty by Roosevelt and his entourage. But although, when the conference met, Churchill was warmly to support France's right to a zone of occupation in conquered Germany and to a seat on the Allied Control Commission, he would certainly have done better to have insisted beforehand, at whatever cost in diplomatic wrangling, upon the presence of France at Yalta. With de Gaulle to make an uncompromising fourth at the table, there would have been no agreed signing of the loosely-worded formula, adopted at the plenary session on February 10, whereby the Lublin Committee was recognized as 'the present Provisional Government of Poland'. Doubtless Stalin, already in possession of Poland, would have acted subsequently exactly as he did and would not have been deflected by the wrath of Allies who, still needing his help to end the War, were in no position to resist him by force, but he would not have had their sanction. As one distinguished historian of the period[1] was to put it: 'The real issue for the world and for the future was not what Stalin would or could have taken but what he was given the right to take.' In the case of Poland this right had been refused him by de Gaulle at Moscow. Since the refusal was a matter of 'honour and honesty' it would have been rigidly maintained by de Gaulle at Yalta.

So deluded were Roosevelt and his advisers, and even Churchill, by Russian professions of good faith and by artful 'concessions' as illusory as those Hitler had dangled in front of Chamberlain before the War, that they failed to see that, together with Poland, they had betrayed almost the whole of eastern Europe—and, in the Far East, much else besides—into the hands of a cunning and ruthless despot. Beside Yalta, 'Munich' must appear reasonable and almost virtuous. And yet, perhaps captivated by Stalin's 'sombre charm', the Western leaders thought they had acted wisely and even honourably. Roosevelt, addressing a joint session of Congress, declared: 'I am sure that— under the agreement reached at Yalta—there will be a more stable political Europe than ever before.' Churchill, reporting to the House of Commons, told of his impression 'that Marshal Stalin and the Soviet leaders wish to live in honourable friendship and equality with the Western democracies. I feel also that their word is their bond.'

De Gaulle did not share this simple faith, nor had he much confidence in the outcome of negotiations from which France was excluded. Broadcasting to the French people on February 5, while the Yalta conference was in session, he told of the warning he had issued to the Governments of the three Powers: 'As regards the future peace settlement, we have made it clear to our Allies that France would, of

[1] Chester Wilmot, *The Struggle for Europe*, page 654.

course, not be bound by anything whatsoever that she had not been able to discuss and approve on the same level as the others.' That the warning had been effective was evident when the three-Power declaration at the conclusion of the conference, after announcing that France was to be invited to become the fourth Power in the occupation government of Germany, expressed the hope that the French Government 'would be willing to associate itself' with the various measures to be taken in 'liberated Europe'. Upon one point, however, to which was linked a second, that hope was not expressed.

To the handing over of Poland to the Lublin Committee, without any guarantee of free elections under universal suffrage and the secret ballot, France's agreement was not sought; she was not even consulted. Similarly, Yugoslavia, France's ally in peace and war, was permitted to fall under Russian influence and Tito's dictatorship without so much as a passing reference to French opinion. Stalin, already aware of de Gaulle's uncompromising attitude, doubtless thought that to seek his agreement would be a waste of time; but a deeper and far less excusable motive underlay the failure of the two Western leaders to invite the comments of the French Government. The omission was not an oversight, it was deliberate; because to submit the Polish agreement to de Gaulle who had refused to recognize the Lublin Committee would be to invite him to expose it for what it was, neither 'honourable and honest' nor even 'a sound political investment'. To avoid hearing what de Gaulle had to say, they prevented him from saying it.

Of the other matters in the Yalta Protocol, those with which it was hoped that France would associate herself, there were some concerning the post-war settlement with Germany that required prolonged consideration by the French Government. It could evidently not be said immediately and with certainty that everything accepted at Yalta by the 'Big Three' would be acceptable to France as one of the 'Big Four'; and it was partly to avoid giving the impression of a precipitate French approval that de Gaulle refused Roosevelt's invitation to meet him at Algiers on his return from the Crimea.

There were of course other cogent reasons for the refusal. For one thing, although the slight may well have been unintentional, it was adding a careless insult to previous injuries for the American President to invite the recognized ruler of France to a meeting—for which, he said, *he* would announce the time and the date—at a place on French soil selected by him, when, in the previous November, he had rejected an invitation to visit Paris and, only a month ago, had excluded de Gaulle from Yalta on grounds far from flattering to France. Had the positions been reversed, had de Gaulle—returning, say, from some Allied conference from which he had excluded the United States—invited Roosevelt to meet him in Hawaii after refusing an invitation to the White House, the American people would no doubt have approved their President's rejection of the summons as loudly as they now denounced de Gaulle's refusal to come to Algiers. Roosevelt's personal resentment was displayed upon his return to Washington when, reviving an elderly and—concerning the head of an Allied State—thoroughly tactless jest, he referred before Congress to the opportunity for a useful meeting that had been missed by 'a certain temperamental prima donna'. It never seems to have crossed his mind that scores of French patriots had faced the firing squad triumphantly shouting the name of the 'prima donna' who had inspired their heroism.

It was his last recorded jibe at de Gaulle. The year before, during the visit to Washington, he had taunted him with another and far from original 'wisecrack' to the effect that, before the War, so frequent had been the changes of government in France, he had scarcely been able to remember the name of the current French Premier. His own position, from being exactly opposite, was no less obnoxious. For there was growing up a generation that could hardly remember a time when Roosevelt had not been President; his tenure of office seemed to be permanent, almost unchallengeable. Suddenly, in April, death ended his reign. It was too late to save Poland.

Of the danger inherent in the Polish formula adopted at the conference, Leahy had warned him. 'Mr President, this is so elastic that the Russians can stretch it all the way from Yalta to Washington without ever technically breaking it.' And stretch it they did, even whilst Churchill and Roosevelt were loudly reaffirming the high principles of the Atlantic Charter. But, as de Gaulle was to write, 'even the highest principles are made valid only by their actions'; the principles having been abandoned, no action was possible. Roosevelt gave way to Stalin; Churchill found it expedient to give way to Roosevelt. De Gaulle, unheeded, alone stood firm.

*   *   *

The underlying reasons for which France had been excluded from Yalta by Roosevelt had become known to de Gaulle at the end of January through the President's confidential man-of-all-work Harry Hopkins. France was not to be forgiven for 1940, that was the long and short of it. Now was to be heard again the old story of resentment at France's failure told by those who had not fought. Now could be seen the full extent of the damage done to France's reputation by the Pétain–Weygand surrender, by the Darlan–Laval collaboration with Hitler. Now, because of the stupefaction once felt at France's defeat, of the scornful anger aroused by the swift collapse of that barrier which had been expected to shield both western Europe and American neutrality, it was said that a great nation having fallen so low could not again be allowed to play a great part. De Gaulle?—the grudging admission of his achievement was coupled to the reflection that in all probability he would last no longer than a pre-war French Premier.

That in the minds of ordinary citizens, far from the scene and insufficiently informed, such careless contempt should subsist was, however regrettable, perhaps comprehensible. That it should be expressed by Roosevelt and his close associates must appear inexcusable, and understandable only as part of a deliberate intention to prevent France from interfering in a predominantly Russo–American settlement of affairs and, by keeping her weak, to deprive her on the grounds of incapacity of some at least of her overseas bases and colonial dependencies.

By January 1945 neither Roosevelt nor Hopkins, nor any other Presidential adviser, could be unaware of the recent resurgence of France in the War. However arrogant their disdain they could not, save by the exercise of resolute ill-will, be wholly unappreciative of, for instance, Eisenhower's report of the 'services of inestimable value' rendered by the Resistance forces throughout France; of General Devers' reports of de Lattre's rapid advance (with the French 1st Army) up the Rhône valley through the Belfort Gap and into Alsace to the capture of Mulhouse; of General Patch's opinion of Leclerc's 2nd Armoured Division (then attached to the U.S. 7th Army) in its brilliant penetration of the Vosges and subsequent capture of Strasbourg; least of all of General Mark Clark's strong views on the 'decisive' contribution to the battle for Rome made nearly a year earlier by General Juin's 'magnificent French Expeditionary Corps'.

Of this Corps Clark was to write that it made 'one of the most brilliant and daring advances of the war in Italy', that only 'the utmost determination made this attack possible', and that 'the French displayed that ability during their sensational advance which Lieut.-General Siegfried Westphal, the Chief of Staff to Kesselring, later described as a major surprise both in timing and in aggressiveness'. Praise could hardly have been higher; of it Roosevelt, who knew and admired Clark, cannot have been entirely ignorant.

Of the growing French contribution in all fields of warfare the facts were widely known. At sea, with the Royal Navy's virtual annihilation of the German Navy and the total surrender to Britain of the Italian fleet, with the Japanese fleets decisively defeated and progressively destroyed by those of the United States, the French Navy, though small in relation to the vast Anglo–American armadas, had regained third place in the world. The mighty *Richelieu*, with a flotilla of auxiliary vessels, had joined the Allied forces in the Far East (whither a small expeditionary corps had also been sent); in the Mediterranean half a dozen fine cruisers and as many destroyers operated against the German flank in Italy; in the Bay of Biscay cruisers, destroyers, the battleship *Lorraine* helped to block the German-held ports and to assist General de Larminat, commanding on land, in their gradual reduction; in the Channel not a convoy sailed for France that had not French warships among its escort vessels. In the air close upon a thousand aircraft manned by Frenchmen—shades of Odiham and the solitary Free French squadron!—operated in France, in Italy, in Russia, over Germany from bases in England. On land eight divisions faced the Rhine, two the Alps; the equivalent of three (including F.F.I.) were under Larminat; two more were provisionally held in reserve. Pending the arrival of new equipment from America, no further large units could be provided with modern weapons; even so the total of fifteen French divisions represented, together with their ancillary services, almost a quarter of all the forces under Eisenhower's command in France.

With these facts before him, with the additional knowledge that, Vichy having been swept away and the Communists rendered innocuous, de Gaulle's position both as military leader and political head of the French Republic was one of unassailable strength, Roosevelt had not, in honour or in reason, the least shadow of an excuse for denying

France's right to a place at the conference table. But though he had no excuse he had a purpose. By belittling France, by holding up the cracked mirror of Vichy to distort her present appearance and cast doubt upon her future worth, he sought to stifle de Gaulle and his unaccommodating principles until his own arbitrary plans should have been made irrevocable; and the speed with which he changed his attitude to France once he had succeeded proves the purpose. At Yalta, no sooner had he denied the Atlantic Charter by signing the discreditable agreement on eastern Asia and by conceding the fatally 'elastic' Polish formula than he blandly nominated the hitherto despised Republic of France to a position of equality with the Great Powers, a seat on the Control Commission and a zone of occupation in Germany. To this, secure in the knowledge that the Polish agreement was not to be subject to French disapproval, Stalin promptly assented.

24. Victory

Therefore, my lords, omit no happy hour
That may give furtherance to our expedition;
For we have now no thought in us but France.

(Henry the Fifth: Act I, Scene ii)

DE GAULLE, after the Hopkins interview, had wasted no time in recrimination. In a brief note to Bidault (who had not been present at the interview) he wrote, on January 27, that he did not think it was in France's interest to appear annoyed at her exclusion from Yalta; for one thing it was too late to obtain any real benefit from insistence, for another 'we shall be much more free to deal subsequently with the European imbroglio if we have taken no part in the forthcoming confused babbling, which may well end in rivalry between those present'. The forecast was no less accurate for being an understatement.

But although, after the conference, his wise restraint had seemed to be rewarded by the invitation to join the three Powers, the advantage reaped, if it enhanced France's prestige, was in reality almost negligible. The Powers had decided what was to be done with Germany; if France was reasonable and agreed with the decision she would be allotted a zone of occupation of unstipulated size and location; if she objected no one would pay much attention, the War would be won without her. It was all very well for the Powers to declare concerning the future of liberated Europe that they intended to build 'a world order under law, dedicated to peace, security and freedom and the general well-being of all mankind'; de Gaulle had heard such fine phrases before, and both his reading of history and his four years of hard schooling in statecraft had taught him that for all the talk of high principles what established a nation's rank among the Powers were not its learning or its ancient traditions, its noble ideals or its civilizing influence, but, now as ever, its armed strength. 'The Pope? How many divisions has he?'— Stalin's cynical question stressed an enduring verity. For the nation that had fallen in battle, however unjust its fate, there was no compassion; unless it could rise again by its own fighting strength it was subject to the law of the liberator, however just its cause. To that law Poland had succumbed.

Unless France proved her armed strength, unless she fought her way to victory, not merely in the field of diplomacy but upon the field of battle, she would be remembered only, as Hopkins had shown, by the débâcle of 1940. Alone amid her 'ruins and her principles', her voice would not be heeded. At the end of the Yalta banquet, when the powerful guests had departed, she had been asked in like a poor relation to partake of a dish of left-overs; meek acceptance would gain neither credit with her friends nor respect from her enemies; only by the sword could she regain her necessary place in Europe. In the conquest of Germany she must march with, and not behind, the Allied Powers. She must share their losses and be seen to win. To this end, long foreseen, de Gaulle now worked with speed and skill.

It was no easy task. For one thing, in the matter of supply and equipment the French Army was almost entirely dependent upon America, and with the available tonnage taken up by the requirements of their own forces the American authorities saw no advantage in burdening transports with equipment for new French divisions that would probably not be trained in time to be of use in Germany. Differences concerning the scale of French rearmament had existed since 1943 in North Africa and, despite de Gaulle's urgent pleading to Churchill and to General Marshall, no upward revision of the schedule could be obtained now. On the Army level and in the combat zone, where American co-operation was as warm and willing as in Washington it was frigid and reluctant, some artful juggling was connived at whereby the French, entitled to replacements in tanks, guns and transport, were allowed to retain the weapons and vehicles, classed as worn out, for which the replacements had been requested. Thus de Lattre's divisions were brought up to something more than full strength and at the same time it was found possible to equip a number of new regiments formed from the many thousands of young volunteers and ex-members of the F.F.I. But no new divisions could be armed and, despite American assurances, the supply uncertainties remained to the end of the War.

An even greater obstacle to French participation in the final campaign lay in the absence of any top-level French representation in the Allied Supreme Command. In the initial operations in Normandy, General Koenig, commanding the F.F.I., had been attached to the staff of Supreme Headquarters and informed of Allied plans; but after

the liberation of the major part of French soil and the absorption of
the F.F.I. into the regular forces he had been withdrawn and appointed,
by de Gaulle, military governor of Paris. Thereafter, whilst the British,
with their Deputy Supreme Commander (Tedder) alongside Eisenhower and with Montgomery in command of an Army Group,
concerted future operations with the Americans, the French 1st Army
(de Lattre) remained in the dark and received only orders from the
Army Group commander, General Devers.

In the planning and execution of the campaigns of invasion from
Normandy and Provence a unified and exclusively Anglo–American
command had appeared essential to success; but now that the forces of
three great nations were about to set forth, from the common base of
France, to the final conquest of Germany it might have seemed both
reasonable and wise to invite de Gaulle to send a deputy to Eisenhower's headquarters, if only for information. De Gaulle's suggestions
to this effect appear to have passed unnoticed; at all events nothing
was done; so that with no personal representative in the Supreme
Command organization it was impossible for him to discuss or
comment on future plans since he was in ignorance of them until
they were fixed beyond recall.

Thus it was not until early in March, when Montgomery and
Bradley had reached the Rhine and Devers was preparing to break
through the Siegfried Line to overrun the Palatinate, that de Lattre
learned of the part his army was to play in the forthcoming 'Operation
Eclipse', designed to take the Americans on his left across the Rhine
and into the heart of southern Germany. For the French it was an
'eclipse' indeed: from north of Strasbourg to the Swiss frontier they
were to stand motionless upon the defensive; only in the event of a
German collapse would they be allowed to follow in the wake of
General Patch and the American 7th Army to the peaceful occupation
of some small fraction of the old Grand-Duchy of Baden. France was
not to be allowed to fight her way into Germany; after all she had
suffered under the Nazi tyranny she was to be led forward by the
hand, like a lost child retrieved by a kindly policeman.

It should have been obvious, if not to Eisenhower who was concerned only with military objectives, at least to the British and American statesmen who were concerned with the political aims of strategy
that this apparent humiliation of France in the face of the enemy was

certainly unwise and even more certainly bound to be rejected out of hand by de Gaulle. By this time, after all, they should have known something of the character of the man whose patriotic pride had never fallen with his country's fortunes and who had for so long stood uncompromisingly for that country's interests and honour. Even before Eisenhower had formulated plans for the final battle, the Allied statesmen would have done well to have remembered that, in order to reassume the role of great nation, it was essential for France to defeat on German soil the army which had defeated her in 1940 and that she must achieve this victory not for the sake of military glory but as a matter of practical European politics.

In fact de Gaulle took the affair out of Allied hands. Sending for de Lattre the moment he learned of the 'Eclipse' operation, he studied the military situation in detail and made his own decisions. Now could be seen in action the strength of purpose and clarity of vision which in the French nation's darkest hour—with all Europe in the Nazi grip, with Darlan backed by Pétain giving military aid to Germany in Syria, with Leclerc's minute force a forlorn hope in the Sahara—had bidden him declare to his wavering followers 'we shall have need of our intransigence up to the Rhine inclusive'. Informing Eisenhower of his rejection of the purely passive role allotted to the French Army, he virtually took over personal command of all French forces in the field and instructed de Lattre to cross the Rhine whatever Allied orders he received to the contrary.

De Lattre was only too willing, but here again the task was far from easy. To begin with, however keen, efficient and well-armed the troops, his Army was not overabundantly supplied with ammunition, its air component was relatively small, and the essential bridging material had been withdrawn from its Armoured Divisions for Allied use farther north. Across the broad river he was faced by the superior strength of the German 19th Army standing in well-sited positions prepared in 1939 and backed by the steep slopes and wooded heights leading to the great massif of the Black Forest. Certain to be costly, the crossing and frontal attack would be hazardous, success no more than conjectural.

The way out of the difficulty, de Lattre had explained to de Gaulle, was for the French to extend their front downstream so as to find, beyond the Siegfried defences, an easier crossing zone and open country to the east. To do this, however, it was necessary for the French Army to insinuate itself between the Rhine and the right of the American 7th Army (Patch), and de Lattre had to approach the Army Group commander, Devers, before any move could be made. Here again co-operation on the lower level was wholehearted; Devers sanctioned the first part of the French plan (i.e. for the northward advance) and, when the attack was made in mid-March, Patch was glad enough to have upon his right flank the French 2nd Corps under General Monsabert, the Siegfried Line being at its deepest in this area. But even then, on the level of Supreme Headquarters, there was some reluctance to open the road to the French; for when, after several days hard fighting, the German defences were pierced and, with Patch driving hard for his intended crossing-place of Worms, Monsabert thrust downstream past Leimersheim (March 24th) to reach for Speyer, access to this latter town was refused the French on the grounds that it was needed by the Americans. De Gaulle at once took the matter up with Eisenhower, but it was not until March 28 that Speyer was included in the French Army zone. By that time Patch was over the Rhine, in Mannheim, and heading south into Baden.

Devers' directing of Patch's 7th Army to the south with Stuttgart as the first objective was in accordance with a plan that discounted any notable French contribution east of the Rhine. Ill-will did not enter into it; rather was it due to the somewhat careless assumption that the French Army, lacking massive air support, amphibious craft and bridging material, would be unable to cross the river in sufficient strength and at sufficient speed to affect the battle in South Germany. But, however reasonable the assumption and honest the intention, the effect of the 7th Army's move south was plain to de Gaulle: the French forces, squeezed into the narrow strip of Baden territory bordering the Rhine, would be deprived of their just vindication in battle. Protests in writing to Eisenhower took time; and with Montgomery and Bradley driving across the northern plains, with Patton striking at the centre and Patch across the Neckar, time was short. On March 29 de Gaulle telegraphed to de Lattre: 'My dear General—You must cross the Rhine, even should the Americans not agree and even should you have to cross in boats. This is a matter of the highest national interest. Karlsruhe and Stuttgart await though they may not desire you. . . .'

After dark on the 30th the crossing was begun by advanced parties of several divisions, using a variety of craft from rowing-boats to barges and taking the weak enemy defences by surprise. The movement was continued on successive days while General Dromard, commanding Engineers, built up two bridges—constructed with remarkable ingenuity from makeshift material recently collected—which were open to traffic by the evening of April 2, allowing the greater part of Monsabert's Corps to assemble on the eastern back by the 3rd. At de Lattre's command splitting his force (130,000 strong, with armour and transport) into three columns, Monsabert, his north-eastern flank protected by Patch upon the Neckar, marched south on the 4th. The outer column, from Speyer, struck at Pforzheim (taken on the 7th); the centre aimed at Freudenstadt; and the third, moving on Karlsruhe which it captured the same day (4th), proceeded to roll up the German Rhine defences from north to south in an operation skilful, audacious and swift. Seizing in rapid succession Rastatt, Baden-Baden and Kehl —where it opened the crossing from Strasbourg to General Bethouart whose divisions struck due east at Freudenstadt—the column hastened on to the south, took Freiburg-im-Breisgau, opened yet another crossing at Breisach, and reached down to Lörrach opposite Basle. Thence, turning east along the Rhine frontier of Switzerland, it marched to the Schaffhausen salient where it encountered Bethouart's divisions hurrying south from Freudenstadt through Donaueschingen. In little more than two weeks the German 19th Army, which de Lattre had driven ahead of him from the coasts of Provence, had been firmly encircled. For another week it fought on, desperately striving to break out to the east; then it surrendered, and the great natural redoubt of the Black Forest fell into French hands with a hundred thousand prisoners.

De Gaulle, however, was still bent on expanding to the east the area of French conquest and, on the 15th, gave de Lattre a direct order to capture Stuttgart ahead of Patch. Four of Monsabert's divisions moved up at once from the Freudenstadt–Pforzheim area and, against considerable enemy opposition, entered the capital of Württemberg on the 20th. The protests of the Allied Command were immediate and violent, rising from Devers to Eisenhower, eventually to the recently installed President Truman; but to these de Gaulle wrote reasoned and conciliatory replies that turned away wrath, while at the same time maintaining his hold upon Stuttgart. Eisenhower's renewed threats to cut off the French Army's supplies if it did not comply with his orders were unavailing; Patch was allowed unobstructed right of way through the town, but a French garrison remained in control.

Crossing the Neckar at Tübingen, Monsabert then marched south-east to the Danube and, capturing Ulm, asserted his hold upon an eighty-mile stretch of the river. Thereafter, against diminishing resistance, both he and Bethouart thrust at Austria, one column ascending the valley of the Iller, the other following the shores of Lake Constance, to meet upon the Arlberg, having captured on the way the newly-formed German 24th Army. Had the enemy forces to the south not already surrendered, doubtless the French columns would have entered Italy from the north.

But this had in fact been done from the west. In the Alps, where four German and Italian-fascist divisions held positions of great natural strength, de Gaulle had increased his forces, with such troops as he could spare from the 1st Army, to a total of three divisions with additional artillery and engineers. These forces, under General Doyen, opened a general attack in mid-April towards the passes of the Little St Bernard, Mont Cenis, Mont Genèvre and Tenda, and after two weeks of bitter fighting broke the enemy's resistance. By the 28th French troops were moving down the Val d'Aosta, the Po and the Stura. By May 2, when fighting ceased, they had reached Turin.

On the Atlantic, meanwhile, Larminat's forces, temporarily rein-forced by Leclerc's Armoured Division and a brigade of American artillery, had moved to the assault (April 14) of the powerful German positions held by 15,000 men on either side of the Gironde mouth. Very heavy fighting ensued and lasted until the 20th when all resist-ance ended, save on the island of Oléron which had to be carried by assault on the 30th. That same day Larminat opened a violent attack upon the 20,000 Germans strongly entrenched about La Rochelle where, after storming the defences in a three-day battle, he received the garrison's surrender on May 2. In Brittany the enemy pockets at St Nazaire and Lorient then gave up without further ado. After nearly five years the Atlantic coast was clear; it had been freed at the last by French forces.

Rushed back from the Gironde, Leclerc's Division was hurried into Germany to rejoin Patch and the 7th Army. In company with the

American 3rd Division, it drove hard to the south-east to forestall the Nazi intention of holding out in the Bavarian Alps, plans for which were already far advanced. Thus, before the fighting ended, it came to Berchtesgaden; and the odyssey that had begun upon an August night in 1940, with twenty defiant men at Duala, came to its destined end in the *Berghof* where Hitler had once gloated unctuously over fallen France, where Laval had plotted and Darlan schemed and each in turn had hoped for the triumph of tyranny.

In Berlin, together with the British, the Russian and the American delegates, de Lattre, at de Gaulle's command, witnessed the signing by the Germans of the instrument of total surrender. Well might de Gaulle broadcast to the French people from Paris on May 8: 'This is the victory of the United Nations, *and it is the victory of France!*'

It was, concerning France, no more than the truth. But none save de Gaulle had the right to say it, since but for de Gaulle it would not have been true. The tragedy was that, with six Armoured Divisions, it could have been true in 1940.

25. Departure

'. . . if you fail to take into account the lessons of our political
history over the past fifty years and, in particular, of what happened in 1940 . . . you will move towards a situation such that,
some day or another, I predict, you will bitterly regret having
taken the road which you will have taken.'

(de Gaulle to the Constituent Assembly, December 31, 1945)

IN PARIS on the bleak Sunday morning of January 20, 1946, de Gaulle
gave effect to a decision as momentous as any he had made since
June 1940. Summoning the members of the Government to the War
Ministry in the rue St Dominique, where once as Under-Secretary he
had battled with Weygand for the honour of France, where since the
liberation as President of the Provisional Government he had laboured
to restore his country's fortunes, in a room vast and frigid, hung with
tapestry and stocked with medieval armour, he renounced his powers.
He was, he declared without preamble, withdrawing forthwith, handing in the resignation of the Government to the president of the National
Assembly; the decision was irrevocable and not open to discussion.

It was said firmly, without emotion, and in less than a minute the
ceremony was over. At the end, after the quick, customary handshake
with each of the seventeen Ministers present, he strode out of the
silent room, collected personal papers from his office; left the building,
left Paris. Behind him, of the bewildered men suddenly chattering—
anxiously, despondently or with relief, according to the political
complexion of each—only one seems to have glimpsed the true
significance of the occasion. Maurice Thorez, whose innate patriotism
conflicted so violently with an obtuse party loyalty, noted that the
departure was 'not lacking in greatness'. Indeed it was not, for the
departure had not been compelled by any force of circumstances that
de Gaulle could not have controlled by the forces of order. The
alternative was clearly visible: pleading the nation's need of authority
he could have remained in power, almost unchallenged save by a
whisper of conscience. Between an easy highway and a narrow path,
he had chosen the path.

It was no snap decision, no impatient gesture of irritation at political obstruction as his critics in France and abroad were to aver. The moment of departure had been fixed as far back as the autumn of 1940 when, in the Brazzaville manifesto, he had undertaken to hand back political power to the elected representatives of the people once they could again act freely, a promise redeemed in full by the elections held on October 21, 1945. Then, together with the general election for a new National Assembly, a referendum had put two questions to the people: first, was the Assembly to elaborate a new Constitution; secondly, was it to confine itself to this work, with a time-limit of seven months? Since to each question the answer had been an overwhelming Yes, and since the Assembly had begun its labours (November 23) by unanimously electing de Gaulle to be the head of the new provisional Government, his leadership was assured until the new Constitution had been promulgated and thereafter for as long as the Assembly wished and he agreed.

Immediately after this promising beginning, however, it had become apparent that the three main political parties, in approximately equal strength—Communist 152, Socialist 142, MRP (*Mouvement Républicain Populaire*) 141—together with the smaller groups (totalling 120 seats), were up to the old party tricks again, with some even of the same old political birds befouling the same old nests—such as the verbose and vacillating Herriot who had changed his coat at least three times since 1940 and was now pecking ponderously at de Gaulle. Indulging in time-wasting disputes and confused arguments increasingly critical of the Government, the parties were soon craftily intriguing for future power while neglecting the vital needs of the country whose post-war situation was still almost desperate. Moreover, as the year drew to its close, it had become known to de Gaulle that the members of the commission appointed by the Assembly to draft the Constitution were devising a system of government the exact opposite of what he believed to be essential if the errors and weaknesses of the past were to be avoided in the future. France, they laid down, was to be ruled by a single Chamber with virtually absolute powers. A Premier would be elected by the Chamber, but only to obey orders; hedged about with restrictions he would have no real authority and would be lucky to survive the vote required by the Chamber before he could even take office. As for the President of the Republic—that there would have to be one was only reluctantly conceded—deprived of all political power he would be no more than a cypher, a lay figure for display purposes. Thus the tail would effectively wag a headless dog and, with the parties endlessly bickering and manoeuvring, the pre-war merry-go-round of recurring crises and successive Premiers would be re-established and merely speeded up. De Gaulle, who had recently warned the Assembly of the urgent need to ensure 'the responsibility, the stability and the authority of the executive power', at once made it clear that the draft Constitution was a document to which he could not possibly subscribe.

Once, long ago, at a staff meeting in London in June 1940, he had felt a similar frustration: had slapped his hands down upon the conference table, thrust back his chair and got to his feet. 'I cannot go on,' he exclaimed bitterly. 'Not one of you is giving me any help.' But upon the instant second thoughts and the muttered protests of his staff had brought him back. Since then, the long years of self-discipline had intervened; there would be no impulsive gesture now.

Early in January, for the first time in seven years he had taken a week's holiday and gone south to Antibes; not, however, for the sake of 'dance, and Provençal song, and sunburnt mirth', but to meditate at peace and make his grave decision. Away from the din and dissension of Paris the issues had seemed clearer than any faced since the year of disaster. Before the end of the month the Assembly would debate the draft Constitution; given its recent attitude, it appeared certain that it would reject his advice; and the Constitution, at best slightly modified, would be enacted as that of the Fourth Republic. To stay on, a voiceless symbol impotently presiding over a régime doomed from its inception, was unthinkable. To go, to mark by his own abdication the gravity of the errors about to be committed and thus to convince the nation before it was too late—there lay the solution most compatible with reason and with honour. Only the date of his departure had remained to be decided. When he returned to Paris on the 14th, his mind was made up.

There was, of course, an alternative. From the events of ninety-five years ago, almost to the month, the *coup d'état* offered a notorious precedent; and for all the dissimilarities in the men there were obvious similarities in their situations. Then, with an elected assembly split by the two main, monarchical parties unable to agree upon the person of the monarch and dominated by the fear of a 'social revolution' menaced by those who were beginning to be known as 'Communists', there had appeared to the Prince-President the opportunity, almost the necessity, to bring back that 'order and stability' for which the country yearned. True, by his arbitrary assumption of personal power he had violated the Constitution of the Second Republic, but success had condoned the violation; there had been remarkably little bloodshed and an even more remarkable expression of popular support in the ensuing plebiscite. Louis-Napoleon had invoked the name of the great Napoleon; de Gaulle could have invoked 'de Gaulle'. The indignant politicians would have indulged in furious polemics, the Communists would have screamed that 'democracy' was being murdered, there might have been disorders; but the people would have sided with him. After the testing years of Resistance, vindicated by Liberation and Victory, the record would have told in his favour, and the nation following him into the era of Reconstruction might gladly have welcomed, ahead of time, the Constitution that was to be evolved in the end for the Fifth Republic.

If the idea did not tempt, it certainly occurred to him. On January 20 he told the assembled Ministers that, strongly though he disapproved of the reappearance of rule by the political parties, he had no means of preventing it 'short of setting up by force a dictatorship which I do not want and which would probably end badly'. Thus, apart from considerations of narrow legalism, the issue was decided on grounds of commonsense realism. Dictatorship did not agree with his concept of the new Republic; moreover, the experiment would be dangerous for France. Rather than assert his power, he gave it up.

Henceforth, whatever the outcome, it would be for the political parties in the Assembly to choose between constitutional strength and weakness. That they would make the wrong choice appeared certain; but, although from outside the Government he might continue to advise and to warn, for the time being his stated task of 'guiding the country to its liberation, its victory and its sovereignty' had been accomplished.

He left the political stage no richer than on the day in June 1940 when he had first stepped upon it. No pension or grant of money was awarded, no honours showered upon him; and he refused the offer, made by the Government, to 'regularize' his rank and to raise it to the highest in the land. He took with him the affection of the people, the respect of his enemies, and a name that had rung through the world to the honour of France.

26. Return and Fulfilment

One equal temper of heroic hearts,
Made weak by time and fate, but strong in will
To strive, to seek, to find, and not to yield.

(Tennyson: *Ulysses*)

DE GAULLE'S departure, if it surprised the world, was variously interpreted. In France, whilst the political parties were for the most part glad to be rid of his strict tutorage, the majority of the people, distrustful of the politicians, regretted the withdrawal of his wise counsels and careful control. Communist party members, though admitting the quality of 'greatness' perceived by Thorez, regarded the voluntary renunciation of power as an act of folly from which they might hope to profit. Less openly, the numerous one-time supporters of Vichy, the retired officials and senior Army officers, the many in the Navy who still secretly sympathized with Pétain, were not wholly displeased at the going of one who, if in the end he had led them to victory, had never gained their unqualified approval; the image of the bold swimmer striking out to cross an ocean alone and unaided had never appealed to them, rather had they seen him as a sort of insubordinate Lord Jim who had jumped from the derelict ship in which they had remained mournful passengers tortured by divided loyalties. To these, his presence being a constant reproach, his departure seemed gratifying.

Abroad the critics were sharper. Few of those who had been wont to disparage the 'temperamental Gaul' and his 'lust for power' were able to discern any element of greatness in his resignation, since it was widely stated and generally believed that he had gone 'in a huff' and without any previous consideration of the step. The fact that, already in December (1945), he had given clear warning of his views and intentions was ignored. Yet the warning had been repeated in a speech to the Constituent Assembly on January 1.

'The régime of government by an Assembly,' he had said, 'is conceivable, but it is not the conception of the Government. . . . What is needed, in my opinion, is a Government that bears, and bears alone—I repeat, alone—the whole responsibility of executive power. If the

Assembly, or the Assemblies, refuse all or part of the means considered necessary for the executive to carry responsibility—well, this Government will resign. Another Government will appear. And that, it seems to me, is exactly what will happen.'

After that his departure three weeks later had seemed logical enough. As he wrote in his letter of resignation to the President of the Assembly (Félix Gouin), if he had agreed to remain at the head of the Government since November it was both in answer to the Assembly's unanimous request that he should do so and in order to bridge a period of transition. With the Assembly in session and debating the Constitution: 'That transition is now achieved.'

There, as events were to prove, he was too optimistic. Drawn out by the unending dissensions of the rival political parties and splinter groups, the period of executive weakness and uncertainty was to last for twelve years. That the draft Constitution initially proposed was rejected by the nation in May did nothing to improve the situation, for the one accepted in October was little better and could scarcely be expected to endure without revision. But to revise wisely, to place power in the hands of the executive as de Gaulle had counselled, implied a surrender of power by the Assembly, something the parties refused to consider seriously until it was too late to avert the fall of the whole system whose lamentable instability had by then been proven by the fall of fifteen Premiers.

The enfeebling succession of Governments, for which the parties responsible for the system were clearly to blame, did not fail to discredit the régime in the eyes of the people. With individual successes marred by lack of continuity, with failures frequent and cumulative, with continuing inflation and political scandals destructive of public confidence, with unalleviated tragedy in Indo-China, the ultimate dissolution soon appeared almost as desirable as it was inevitable. Thus, when in Algiers, in 1958, the Army found its pretext for revolt, all France was ready to accept the change and, looking back, to see in the Fourth Republic little more than an uneasy transition from the Third to Fifth.

But if from the beginning the impermanence of the Constitution enacted in October 1946 had been evident to many, rare were those who, advocating a return of more authoritative government, had envisaged the return of de Gaulle to supreme authority. However great his personal prestige, since the only permissible road to national leadership lay through the dark and polluted labyrinth of party intrigue, place-seeking rivalry and not infrequent corruption, it had seemed highly improbable that one of de Gaulle's non-partisan integrity could ever come back to the tribune when once he had stepped down into the arena. For a time the political movement (*Rassemblement du Peuple Francais*: R.P.F.) to which he gave his patronage had gained, together with a large measure of popular support, sufficient parliamentary strength to influence the party game in the Assembly and even, joining in the merry-go-round in uneasy alliance with other groups, to put Bidault in office for a few months in 1950. But political 'gaullism' in time of peace, concealing many who were not 'gaullist' at all, had little of the unifying altruism of 'de Gaulle' in time of war. Weakened by inner antagonisms and disputes on policy, the movement eventually split and lost all meaning. In 1953 de Gaulle withdrew his support, thereby withdrawing from most of his supporters their last lingering hope of his return to power.

Until then he had seldom been out of mind or out of sight of the people, to whom with notable speeches he had continued to plead the cause of national unity under a stronger system of government. His frequent personal appearances in France had culminated in a world-tour of French dependencies during which, a private citizen, he had been received everywhere with military honours and popular rejoicing. But although his words were listened to with respect, his political influence declined with the fortunes of the R.P.F. and at length, falling silent, he went home to a more permanent retirement.

As the years passed, and the War receded and new wars threatened and the attention of France was increasingly distracted from worldwide uncertainties to colonial unrest and decline, it began to look as if, for de Gaulle, Destiny had run out of thread. Renunciation had tied the last knot in an uncompleted tapestry and already, in the acceleration of history, the pattern was blurred; he was being forgotten. Not as the great national figure, heroic, unique; that glory was undimmed; but the once broad and urgent stream of inspiring leadership, carrying all before it with the practical ideals of enlightened patriotism, had been reduced to a trickle that seemed bound to end in quiet Lethe amid the trees and the lengthening shadows of the oasis at Colombey.

Autumn was upon him and, as evening drew in, he found solace in the ancient classics and in the Latin texts: '*Soon with silent step comes bent old age.*' He was not unaware of it. Visitors were becoming less frequent; there were blank pages in the appointments book. To one who came to discuss the chances of future action, he shook his head resignedly: '*Je suis une page tournée*'—a back number.

Mission accomplished? Not yet. A major task remained to be achieved so that the pattern might be completed and the 'signal service' rounded off by a permanent service to the nation's history. The facts must be placed on record: 'Since all things always begin again, sooner or later what I have done will inspire new ardour when I have gone.' More than that, France in her future must be warned by her past, the story of disaster told in full, the military reasons explained and the political lessons brought home, to the end that, together with the tale of sacrifice and heroism, the half million French dead of the Second World War should not have died in vain.

The burden assumed was no light one: three volumes, a thousand pages, a thousand selected documents. No great team of clerks and scholars eased the labour; he worked in solitude, in a first-floor study whose long windows faced the sunset across a vast and empty plain. Despite much practice, with his early works, with wartime speeches, broadcasts and despatches every one of which he had drafted himself, writing never came easily to him. Perhaps no great writing ever does, and this writing was great. As with some noble symphony the theme is simply stated in the first phrase to be developed later through successive variations, so with the first dozen words the subject was set: '*Toute ma vie je me suis fait une certaine idée de la France.*' Upon that idea, 'inspired by sentiment as much as by reason', the work was founded; from it the development followed logically, and presently the story was unfolded with deceptive ease and notable magnanimity. The first volume was published at the end of 1954. It was twenty years and six months since the publication of *Vers l'Armée de Métier*.

Without a break the work was continued. At the steady rate of regular hours the second volume would appear in the summer of 1956, the third two years later. The time-table was not set by chance, for now infirmity faced him with an unenviable choice. He was losing his eyesight; if he worked too hard he would not see to write; if too slow he might not see the end. Beyond the dilemma the other enemy was beginning to beckon; old friends were going—Leclerc, de Lattre; even poor foolish old Pétain in his island prison. Two of his brothers were dead. Anne, the beloved invalid, had died at Colombey in February 1948. His other daughter and his son were married and if now, in holiday-time in summer, the house woke to the cries of his grandchildren, to the writer's necessary silence melancholy was no stranger. 'How many the hours that pass, when, reading, writing, dreaming, no illusion sweetens my bitter serenity.' At the end he saw himself as an 'old man, sated with trials, remote from action, sensing the approach of everlasting cold, yet never weary of watching in the shadows for a gleam of hope.' For France the hope, for himself nothing; the shadows were lengthening, the light fading. He was in his sixty-eighth year and persistent cataract was closing his eyes.

Suddenly, like some outdated contrivance of drama, the off-stage thunder of revolt in Algiers brought the dénouement to the tangled scene of political weakness and mounting incompetence; and Destiny, waiting in the wings, led forward de Gaulle as though in answer to a long-expected cue. Events beyond his control had their fated effect; the disasters of war had brought him up, the menace of civil war brought him back. In a matter of weeks, even of days, the ageing writer-philosopher became again the man of action and swift decision.

The third volume of *Mémoires de Guerre* was ended with the end of winter 1958, to be revised with the coming of spring. 'The traveller climbing the hillside,' he had said long ago in London, 'sometimes makes a brief stop to measure the distance covered and to take his bearings upon the goal.' The pause had been exactly sufficient; the backward glance had supplied the just perspective by which he could face forward with confidence.

One Sunday in May—it was the 11th—he strolled through the village of Colombey, with every one of whose three hundred and fifty inhabitants he was acquainted, to the annual meeting of its fifty-eight old soldiers. In friendly conversation one of them said: 'Things are looking bad. You don't suppose they'll recall you, General?' The answer, with its gentle irony and faint smile, was prompt as ever: 'I do not believe things are bad enough yet for that.' Doubtless he re-called that other May, eighteen years earlier almost to the day, when belatedly acknowledging the justice of his predictions a despairing

Chief of Staff had asked him to save France with a paper division of tanks. From that bitter memory some slight encouragement might be drawn for the future: de Gaulle was the man they sent for when all others had failed, a sort of Foul-weather Jack only summoned to the bridge when it was quite certain that the ship was sinking.

Things 'not yet bad enough' on the 11th were soon much worse. Within three days the first approaches, tentative, secret, were being made simultaneously from Algiers and Paris; wild rumours, true for once, began to spread concerning a military *coup*; and presently a winged annunciation swept the skies of Colombey. Once from a field at Odiham a flag had flown bearing the Cross of Lorraine; now, above a remote village of the Upper Marne—one hundred and twenty-five miles from Paris, only forty from Domrémy—a squadron of jet aircraft rushed past in Lorraine Cross formation. Soon all France was calling; not for the Army, for the man who would save her from the Army. De Gaulle declared his readiness to serve, and left for Paris; returned to Colombey while the Government hesitated to accept his terms, returned to Paris when it trembled and fell.

By the end of the month, at President Coty's invitation and just in time to save the nation from the Army's planned seizure of power, he was forming the last administration of the tottering Fourth Republic. On June 1 the discomforted party politicians, who, had he appeared before the Assembly a month earlier, would have cried treason and ordered his arrest, accorded him a comfortable majority.

He had never made any secret of his intention—he had stated it publicly often enough since 1946—to strengthen the executive power of the Government, at the expense of the parties, in order to ensure that essential 'authority, dignity and responsibility', lack of which had led to disaster, and to do so lawfully and with the full approval of the electorate. There was now no other way to save France from the alternative of anarchy or military dictatorship; no other man in France could lead the way to salvation. With the return to political power there had returned to him the earlier sense of mission and the selfless ambition to serve. It was no happy adventure. To achieve national unity, without which nothing, he must once again 'shoulder the burden though it should break his back'. There was no one else to do it.

With parliamentary sanction the new Constitution was drafted during the summer. In the autumn it was put to the people. In an exceptionally heavy poll, amounting to 85 per cent of the electorate, no less than 80 per cent voted Yes to de Gaulle and the Fifth Republic; and there can be little doubt that of the 20 per cent who, out of party loyalty, voted No, many had Yes in their hearts. The record had spoken for him with a louder voice than any propaganda; with more than half a million copies of the *Mémoires* in circulation, the nation voted for the man who, in the thirties, had foretold the catastrophe of 1940, who had predicted in 1946 the disastrous confusion of 1958, and who to each foreshadowed peril had foreseen the simple remedy.

In December de Gaulle was elected President; and when, upon the day of his inauguration, he drove through the streets of Paris the unforgetting massses welcomed his accession with a joy, less delirious for being more reflective, such as they had not expressed since the Day of Glory upon the Champs Elysées. The political parties had got the Constitution they deserved, the people the ruler they wanted.

Observers at the time compared de Gaulle to Cincinnatus, a comparison chiefly remarkable for the distance from which it had to be fetched. For to be unable to discover a valid analogy save by turning back the pages of history a matter of two thousand five hundred years is to mark the exceptional nature both of the man and of the circumstances in which he was recalled to power. Even more remarkable, however, was the discovery by the same observers that, in the twelve-year interval of retirement, he had grown older, as though they had expected to find in the possessor of so many qualities the ultimate quality of eternal youth. Some went further and professed to perceive, in the normal changes of appearance and manner, if not a fundamental alteration of character, at least a notably mellowed temperament. He seemed gentler, less intransigent, warmer.

In fact it was not the man who had changed so much as the conditions under which he had to face the problems of leadership. In the past those conditions had imposed upon his conduct a vigilance that could never be relaxed in public. De Gaulle the unknown had been compelled at all times to submit to 'de Gaulle' the symbol, a figure whose every word and action in the name of France must be controlled by a rigorous self-discipline, the leader acknowledged by a popular acclaim largely emotional and unstable, the head of a Government that by his own undertaking could be no more than provisional. The stress of war, moreover, the bitter enmity of Roosevelt, the uncertain temper of Churchill, the strain of his lonely eminence as champion of fallen France and inspirer of her resurgence, had forced upon him the characteristics of unaccommodating severity which, thirty years earlier in the lectures to the War School so portentously inaugurated by Pétain, he had described as habitual to the man of action; so that to many his naturally reserved manner, accentuated by an austere dignity, had appeared frigid, repellent and constantly wary.

The change upon his return to power was thus largely psychological. To some extent the positions were now reversed: France called to him before he called to France. However fierce the opposition of the political parties, on his side there was the great mass of the people; and even before the overwhelming verdict of the Referendum he had learned that which he had always wished to know: 'what this people wants, and what it does not want.' Sure of his authority he no longer needed continually to assert it. Always magnanimous, he could afford to be conciliatory to old enemies; among old friends he could relax, smile, converse, unbend. However great the perils ahead, temporarily at least the man of action could be cloaked by the gentle philosopher.

Disarmed by these apparent signs of a more affable de Gaulle, foreign observers were shaken to discover, as 1959 wore on, that—particularly in his desire to reform the NATO command—the characteristic intransigence had been no more than dormant. But although his abrupt removal of the French fleet from NATO's Mediterranean command evoked a considerable outcry in the capitals of the Western world, the conditions in that command appear to have amply justified the decision; in the pungent phrase of Field-Marshal Montgomery, who from long experience certainly knew what he was saying, the organization was no better than a 'dog's breakfast'. When further examples of the old uncompromising attitude followed—notably in the matters of French determination to develop nuclear weapons and French refusal to allow American nuclear weapons to be stockpiled in France save under French control—the critics abroad reflected sadly that de Gaulle had not changed very much after all.

It could scarcely be denied, however, that France under his leadership was rapidly regaining her ancient prestige among the nations. For years, largely because of the shifting policies of frequently changing

Governments, French influence in international affairs had been so largely discounted that the very name of France had rarely appeared in the news unless linked with some misfortune or to a further devaluation of the franc. Now, in a remarkably short space of time, the effects of political stability and continuity were to be seen in an improving economy due in part to the wise implementation under the Fifth Republic of policies devised under the Fourth—the reconciliation with Western Germany, for instance, and the development of the European Common Market—and were reflected abroad in the suddenly enhanced respect accorded to France and to de Gaulle himself.

But respect was not immediately accompanied by affection; indeed as time went on it seemed more generally to be accompanied by mounting impatience. Towards the end of the year his supposed obstinacy in insisting upon a postponement of the 'Summit' conference, into which Western statesmen were being stampeded, aroused so much popular indignation outside France that when, only a little later, the Army-sponsored conspiracy in Algiers flared up in open rebellion the rumour that the Generals who had put him in were about to put him out was received without dismay. Foreign commentators, listening to the mocking voices of political opponents relegated to obscurity, reported that he was losing his grip, that his persistent cataract was symbolic of his diminished foresight, and that his dreams of French greatness were no more than an old man's *folie de grandeur*.

All the more surprising was the sudden flowering of popular regard, in America as in Britain, in the spring of 1960. At one and the same time, within a matter of three months, it came to be appreciated that, if Algeria still smouldered, he had damped down the worst of the flames, that his cautious approach to the 'Summit' had been both skilful and wise, and that in France, whatever partisan critics might argue against the virtual suspension (under Article 38 of the Constitution) of parliamentary government, he had the support of the people on all essential matters and to an even greater extent than before. In January, at the height of the Algerian crisis, a television broadcast to the French nation had been seen and heard by millions in Britain, upon whom the firmness and obvious sincerity of his speech had not been lost. '*Eh bien! mon cher et vieux pays, nous voilà encore ensemble devant une situation tragique. . . . Une fois de plus, j'appelle tous les français.*' To his own countrymen a poignant appeal, it had not left

British listeners altogether unmoved. Reminding them of their share in his heroic past, it added to the exceptional warmth of London's greeting in April.

Ensuring the success of the State Visit the national newspapers, which by and large had never been wholly unsympathetic to his cause, enumerated his qualities and sought to explain his 'enigmatic' personality, discovering in the process at least one characteristic he had never possessed. 'His admirable arrogance' was the typical comment—a phrase taken straight from Churchill: 'I understood and admired, while I resented, his arrogant demeanour.'[1] But to those who understood de Gaulle and his predicament, he had never appeared arrogant in the accepted sense of the word. Proud certainly, to his opponents perhaps excessively so, but not proud of himself or of his talents, of which he thought so little he sometimes doubted whether they could be equal to the heavy burden of leadership. His pride, deliberately grafted upon an inner humility, was impersonal and dedicated to France. In her blackest hour, when the world despised her and even Frenchmen could be heard to say that they were 'ashamed of being French', it had raised him up above a crowd despondent, uncaring or contemptuous. It was rooted in an unconquerable faith in the resurgence of the great nation that only through faulty leadership had 'lost a battle, but not the War'; and for a while, expressed by a cold and haughty manner whenever France's honour and interest were at stake, it had been his only weapon. More than admirable, pride had been essential.

With another Churchillian judgment the people of London, for all their enduring affection for their wartime leader, were very far from agreeing. 'I knew he was no friend of England,' Churchill had written after the War[2]; surely a strange statement to come from one who was in possession of all the relevant facts. True, first and foremost de Gaulle was the friend and protagonist of France. But in 1940 he had come to England because Britain was France's friend and ally; and with Churchill he had approved the great scheme for the union and integration of the two countries, in itself a proof of deep and trusting friendship. Subsequently, and throughout the War, Free French troops

[1] Churchill: *Second World War*, Vol. IV, p. 611.
[2] *Ibid.*

under his command had fought valiantly alongside British forces upon many a front, from Eritrea to Italy. In public speeches he had denounced the common enemies and stressed the need for enduring friendship between France and Britain; and at the end of the War he had proposed, to Churchill, an agreement involving a common policy in Europe under Britain's leadership that, had it been followed up, might well have averted the evils arising from Yalta. As a Frenchman fighting for France, it would seem that he could scarcely have done more for Britain.

It may therefore be in his often quoted reply to Eden—who, at the time of the Free French departure for Algiers in 1943, asked him what he thought 'of us'—that the underlying cause of Churchill's animosity can best be found. 'I think your people are admirable,' de Gaulle had answered. 'But I cannot say the same of your politics.' To the Prime Minister who believed he 'understood the soul of France', and who could speak of British military commanders as 'my generals' in the manner of an emperor, it must have been singularly galling to have a junior French general standing up to him and rejecting his policies with an authority and a logic as disconcerting as they were unanswerable.

But disapproval of Churchill's politics was not necessarily a crime against friendship; if it had been, then by the War's end half Britain would have been guilty. Indeed the very fact that an exile without resources had had the courage and the wit to speak up in the name of his stricken country in opposition to the mighty rulers of Britain and America had appealed to the romantic tendency of the English to back the underdog. They had never been happy in Britain at the idea of negotiating with Pétain or Darlan, even when wartime emergencies had seemed to dictate the necessity. De Gaulle was the only man for their money. At a time of extreme anxiety his defiance of the enemy had matched their own stubborn resolve, and his imperturbable courage in an adversity greater than theirs had set so gallant an example that they had come to regard him as a fighter after their own hearts. Now, returning, to the people of London he appeared as an old and trusted friend. They recalled how he had come to them, with little else than his faith in victory, to share the perils of the *blitz*, the menace of invasion and the long tedium of the blackout; and remembering his staunch few, the 'little dust' of Free Frenchmen, and their sobriquet *le grand Charles*, they bestowed upon him the endearment of a Cockney shout: 'good old Charlie!'

In passing it may be noted that whilst, in the boisterous *milieu* of Roosevelt's court, it had always been 'Winston' and 'Ike', and Bill (Leahy) and Harry (Hopkins), and in Africa Bob (Murphy) and Harold (Macmillan), no one had ever thought of calling de Gaulle by his first name. It might be the 'temperamental Gaul', the 'prima donna', or the 'marplot'; it was never 'Charles'. Well-disciplined reserve had its advantages. A necessary armour to the champion of France, the dignity expected of 'de Gaulle' was also that required of the President of the French Republic.

But if dignity, traditional and ceremonial, ordered the measured pageantry of his reception in Westminster, it was even more the astonishing consistency of the qualities that had brought him there which struck the imagination. For although, in the great hall that eight centuries earlier had echoed to the French of Norman kings, it was now the ruler of France who addressed the Lords and Commons, those who recalled his wartime arrival could see standing upon the dais, the ever-faithful Courcel at his side, that same de Gaulle who twenty years before, unknown and alone in a broadcasting studio, had been impelled to pronounce words he might well have repeated now. '*J'ai conscience de parler au nom de la France.*' Destiny may have opened the road, his own constancy had brought him to the fulfilment.

* * *

Since de Gaulle himself now seemed politically unassailable for as long as he remained in office as President, the emaciated body of criticism, comprising discredited party leaders at home and pinhead demagogues abroad, turned to a vinegary disparagement of the régime. In Britain, where few had ever been able to conceive 'democracy' in any other form than that practised in their own country, highly-paid professional entertainers posing as informed political broadcasters referred to 'de Gaulle's France' in terms that equated it with Hitler's Germany, and jauntily forecast the wrath to come. Upon one point they harped with mournful monotony. De Gaulle might be, they were willing to concede, a man of unimpeachable moral rectitude, of irreproachable private life and selfless ambition, the possessor of great talents and a wide knowledge of affairs; he had one great failing. He was mortal. Things too terrible to contemplate—or, it seemed, accurately to predict—must ensue for France upon his death.

It does not seem to have occurred to the critics that the eventuality of his death in office might already have been contemplated by de Gaulle. And yet the possibility had clearly been taken into account in the Constitution: in the event of the President's demise or incapacity the President of the Senate assumed full powers until elections could be held for the appointment of a new President of the Republic. It was a matter of common sense. To shrink from the inevitable, to fear the ultimate shipwreck and fail to make ready for it, these things were not in de Gaulle's character. Death was not an unfamiliar thought; for long hours he had pondered it in the 'bitter serenity' of Colombey, and since then more than one old comrade had tiptoed into the shadows, most recently Pierre de Gaulle, his close associate and last of his brothers. The 'everlasting cold' could not be so far away; it did not dismay him, he prepared for it as thoughtfully as for an unwelcome military campaign that could not be avoided though it might be postponed.

From his long record in peace and war, from the evidence of his writings as from the more recent testimony of an intellect unimpaired, his intentions were not beyond all conjecture. Political realism and keen vision, the ability to see the wood despite the trees, were not obscured by illusions of perfection and permanence. He had no magic wand to wield, though many had thought on his return to power that, in the matter of Algeria, 'de Gaulle' would solve the insoluble in a twinkling. He had not invented a new system of government to endure for a thousand years or be overthrown in the next; indeed he had it in mind that since the days of ancient Greece it had been unlikely that any man could say anything new, though he might conceivably be able to say it differently. Long ago (at Bayeux, in June 1946), he had quoted Solon's reply to those who asked him to name the ideal constitution: 'First tell me for which people and in which age.' The people he knew; across the centuries they had changed little: 'All our history,' he had told them, 'has alternated between the immense sufferings of a people divided and the fruitful greatness of a free nation gathered beneath the shield of a strong State.' It was the age that was uncertain, and against that uncertainty he sought to insure the nation's future.

Dictatorship was not the answer, nor had it ever been his aim. On that point his views had seldom been more clearly expressed than in the long letter to Roosevelt in October, 1942. 'Were we'—the Free French movement—'to nourish sentiments so low as to wish to defraud the French nation of its future liberty, we should give proof of a singular ignorance of our own people. To personal power the French people, by their very nature, are most opposed of all. At no time has it been easy to impose that power upon them. But . . . after Pétain's odious experiment . . . who would be foolish enough to imagine the establishing and maintaining of personal power in France? The dreamer who should attempt it would bring against him a unanimous opposition, whatever services he might have rendered in the past.'

Although this was no more than the truth, it was true only by reason of the key-verb 'to impose'. For if throughout the centuries the French people have shown a certain readiness to revolt against oppression, real or imagined, and more especially against oppressive taxation, their willing acceptance of enlightened personal power has frequently been in evidence and has largely contributed to the happiness, prosperity and greatness of France. Examples are numerous and notorious. Louis XII, for all his absolutism, and his costly defeats in Italy and Flanders, was regarded affectionately as 'the father of his people'; the personal rule of Henry IV was esteemed for its benevolent care of the people's welfare; under the autocracy of Louis XIV a contented nation flourished for a while as never before; and the period of Bonaparte's Consulate earned not only the enthusiastic approval of the French nation, but also the admiration of the civilized world. Under the First Empire, France as a whole had been happy enough until too many of her sons had been swallowed up in too many victories: '*être vainqueur, c'est beau, mais vivre a bien son prix!*' Under the Second Empire, the last plebiscite, taken within a few weeks of the military disasters of 1870, had given overwhelming support to Napoleon III. Nor could it now be contested that de Gaulle's power was personal and that, notwithstanding some noisy grumbling both at the length of the Algerian war and at the austerity essential to maintain the stability of the currency, it continued to enjoy the warm support of the very great majority of the people.

From all this it was not altogether unreasonable to deduce that, in France, personal power over the people, provided the people agreed to the person, might be the most suitable form of democracy. But if safeguards there must be to ensure the free expression of the people's will to choose the person, even stronger safeguards were necessary to control the unruly minority's will to change him. For without such safeguards, valid in law and backed by force, it would be too much to expect that, after de Gaulle, the successors of the political helmsmen who since 1789 had sailed France through no less than thirteen Constitutions would refrain from embarking upon a fourteenth, if only to satisfy the insatiable Gallic propensity for political argument often brilliant, generally violent and always inconclusive. A further Constitution could only mean, since everything else had been tried at least once, a permutation of things that had already failed, by which its own failure would be assured. But hard upon one more Constitutional breakdown it could be predicted that totalitarian tyranny, Left or Right, would almost certainly follow; and with even greater certainty it could be said that this was not what the French people wanted. To power imposed by political extremists they infinitely preferred the personal power freely accorded to de Gaulle.

By his critics it was then said that, in assuming the special powers conferred upon him by the Constitution, de Gaulle had debased parliamentary institutions; but in the popular view the institutions had long ago debased themselves by their own ineptitude. The nation was now so tired of the domination of the score of wrangling political groups, whose cumbersome machinery and power-seeking manoeuvres under the Fourth Republic had both strangled efficient government and stifled the voice of the people, that few disadvantages could be perceived in the temporary limitation of the powers of parliament when all could see the immediate advantages of the powers wielded by de Gaulle and his expert assistants. The improvement over the years since May 1958 had in many ways been startling. Impressive plans developed since the War, but held up hitherto by the frequent changes of Government, had been completed by unchanging authority. Sound economic policy backed by a stabilized currency had advanced the country's general prosperity, despite the drain of Algerian warfare. Re-equipped railways, plentiful electricity, and oil supplies more than matching its needs, had added to the nation's wealth. Close ties with the 'Six' of the Common Market, and close friendship with the Federal German Republic, had restored to France a large measure of leadership in Western Europe, whilst a shrewd and forceful foreign policy had enhanced her influence upon the affairs of the Western World. It would not have been so without de Gaulle. True, the Algerian problem remained; personal prestige and the patience available to a lasting Government could yet solve it.[1] Token strikes and customary demonstrations were no more than symptoms of a democratic freedom said by the critics to be dead; and the protests against 'censorship' in the French press could carry little weight when under the law, in matters concerning libel and comment upon cases *sub judice*, it could still take greater liberties than could the press in Britain. Despite the mounting perils inherent in the acceleration of history, France in a new age was reaching towards new greatness. To consolidate her achievements the essential requirement was continuity.

*   *   *

To this, the problem of continuity after his departure, de Gaulle himself had supplied the solution. 'It is simple,' he told a questioner. 'You have only to find another de Gaulle.' It was no mere quip illustrative of the height of impossibility; touching France his wit was pointed, never flippant. Nor was it a light-hearted shrug of indifference to the future, a careless equivalent of '*après moi le déluge*'. Others might imagine solutions complicated or sinister, his own was a matter of practical common sense, of not looking farther than the obvious. Here, after all, was the edifice of a State not unsoundly built, founded upon principles not untested and having the approval of the people; here were the safeguards required by democracy; here the powers necessary to stability, to avoid those 'ephemeral governments' which had strained the loyalty of better men than Weygand. To crown the edifice what was needed first was a period of success; he must take the risk of a fatal time-limit. Thereafter, the people would choose—not, it was to be hoped, the first political adventurer who offered himself, nor some ambitious General inexperienced in statecraft and none too competent in his profession; but a man honest, impartial, dedicated to the service of the people—a man of character. Such a man, in France,

---

[1] In the referendum held on January 8, 1961, approximately 75% of the electorate of metropolitan France recorded a 75% approval of de Gaulle's outline of policy for Algeria. In Algeria itself, despite the terrorist demand for abstention, nearly 60% of the electorate gave a 70% approval.

was not unimaginable. Yet, in the end, what de Gaulle would leave far greater than a Constitution would be an example, a pattern of integrity.

But to accustom the people to the idea of a continuity, and a probity, they had not enjoyed for generations, to prove in practice the advantages of the new régime and to show that, if unity was the 'secret' of strength, the converse could also be true that the strength of a stable government might foster national unity, the period of political *détente*, of freedom from party divisions and parliamentary obstruction, must be prolonged under the personal rule of the President. In forcing this lull he was accused of holding the nation down under an anaesthetic; yet, in an age much given to the taking of sedative drugs, the administering of a political tranquilizer, lawfully prescribed, seemed reasonable enough. If the patient was somnolent during the operation of economic austerity and tax-extraction he would be unlikely to complain when he awoke to new health and vigour. No one, meanwhile, could question de Gaulle's purpose, whether or not the critics agreed with his methods.

Guided by his selfless ambition, he seemed to stride forward into the seventies of his age with undiminished energy, unsparing of physical strength. If he had outlived most of his contemporaries, he had not outlived his talents and the years that had broadened his outlook had not dimmed the clarity of his thoughts. Within the limited period of his term of office a great labour remained to be accomplished and from it there could be no respite; until the major problems had been solved and the future assured he must continue 'to strive, to seek, to find' for the sake of France and the good of all men. Then, at length, 'made weak by time and fate', he might leave the sunlit peaks and seek enduring peace beneath the trees at Colombey.

At the time of his return to power a former Resistance leader, observing his altered appearance and failing eyesight, and noting the bitter opposition of the political parties, had remarked with an irony doubtless intentional: 'On his side, he has only the people.' They were still on his side as the years sped by; and the great majority of those who, with feelings of anxiety and personal sorrow, had seen him drive away from the rue St Dominique, who twelve years later had rejoiced at his unexpected return, found a comforting reassurance, not unmixed with national pride, in the thought of his imperturbable presence at the Elysée. In their hearts even his enemies were glad.

* * *

There was one person, however, who while not altogether regretting the departure of 1946 had not been overjoyed at the return of 1958 and to whom residence in the Elysée Palace, at best no more than temporary, was not a source of unalloyed pleasure. Madame de Gaulle, perhaps more than most women, had a deeply rooted aversion to moving house. At the outset of her married life she had, of course, been aware that with a keen and talented young army officer for husband occasional moves were only to be expected; but the early years in Paris, his appointments and initial successes had encouraged the belief that advancement would lead to a more permanent settling down. With the first unexpected posting—to the Rhine instead of to the General Staff—a period of uncertainty had set in, and it had been with the determination to find a fixed home while her husband was shuttled between Mainz and Paris and Metz that in 1934, largely for the sake of the children, she had chosen the house at Colombey: *La Boisserie*, midway between the capital and the eastern frontier. Alas for hopes of domestic tranquillity! In a dozen years she had spent little more, on average, than eighteen months in any one place.

After the restless wartime wanderings—the years of exile, Algiers, the return to Paris—retirement to Colombey, sadly though it had started with the death of Anne, had come as a relief, providing the longest period of contentment and self-expression she had ever known. Thus the recall to Paris, alive though she was to its necessity in the cause of France, came as a not very welcome interruption. Even less welcome was the move to the Elysée, where the imposed formality of the President's Palace, and public curiosity concerning the President's wife, emphasized another marked trait in her character.

Her dislike of personal display, and of personal adulation, of fuss, of any attempt to thrust her into the limelight, was lifelong and ineradicable. More than a matter of shyness, an innate modesty bade her shun publicity. It was not in her nature to give herself airs; and the heights to which her husband's mission had carried her she found uncomfortably breathtaking. For him it was different; all his life he had been 'on parade', trained to overcome his reserve and to face the staring crowd. For such a part she felt unsuited, and as much as possible she avoided ceremony and continued at the Elysée the quiet routine of family life in the provinces, giving her orders personally to the household staff and keeping a watchful eye upon the accounts. An official car might take her shopping, she would permit no escort, police or other; and the store selected, usually on the more familiar 'left bank', was warned against lining up an obsequious reception committee; only one assistant was allowed to attend to her, one she knew of old.

Nevertheless, when circumstances of state demanded her presence, she could play the role of leading lady with a poise the more appealing for an unassuming simplicity, a gentleness of manner and, perhaps the most striking feature after forty years of married life, something of the ingenuous freshness of youth. But modesty was always tugging at her sleeve. The dignity and protocol expected of the President's wife were complied with willingly because they were necessary to the successful performance of her husband's duty to France; but she never enjoyed the compliance.

Between them understanding ran deep; no more than his wife had de Gaulle any great liking for ostentation, for splendid functions or rigid ceremonial posturings, though as a soldier, a Catholic and a convinced traditionalist he was deeply conscious of the value of such outward forms to a nation's spiritual greatness. 'We lead a very simple life,' he had said long ago. 'It is a matter of personal taste, and also of what is fitting.' This similarity of taste had drawn them together in the first place, and upon what was 'fitting' their agreement in all essential matters was profound and tacit. He could count upon her following his lead, not tamely, but with a strength of purpose that matched his own; so that at moments of crisis he had no need to consult her, he could be certain of her approval. In 1940, waiting at Colombey, she had answered his summons unhesitatingly: packed, gathered the children and their faithful companion Marguerite Potel—piled up the suitcases, and hastened to Brittany and the hazardous chance of the last boat out. That he learned of her arrival in England without surprise, gives the measure of the reliance he placed upon her courage and ability.

In England no doubt she would have been lost without him; but without her, without the constant support of her sympathy, it seems unlikely that he would have been able to carry the burden to the end;

the 'navigator peering through the gloom' could hardly have made his landfall without her light. Throughout the years of wartime exile, as through the longer years of retirement at Colombey that, to him, so much resembled exile, on into the years of supreme authority, she was the sharer of his secret hopes, the ever-dependable confidant and companion, as necessary in the days of darkness as later upon the glittering occasions of state, and never more so than during the restless solitude in which was woven the noble pattern of the *Mémoires de Guerre*.

Doubtless it was then, in the quiet house at Colombey, that she found her happiest moments. Sometimes in the evening of a busy day they would sit alone, or with some old and trusted friend, and the General would lay out the cards for a game of Patience. Once, while he was playing, staring hesitantly at the cards through horn-rimmed spectacles, *la Générale* leaned forward to exclaim that he had missed a move. '*Je le sais, Yvonne. Je le sais,*' he answered tolerantly, making a belated adjustment. And she sat back and said nothing, content that this time, without her, he would not have known it at all.

But as a rule, of course, he did know. There was nothing of consequence that escaped his attention in the long run. And assuredly, in that vaster game of Patience he had played for so long with such courage and skill, there were few moves he had ever missed for the good of the people and the greater glory of France.

Postscript

HARDLY HAD the last chapter been written when the thunder pealed again in North Africa and rumbled over France. It was not unexpected. But added to the other and far more alarming storm-signals discernible not only in Europe but across the world it confirmed my impression that, rather than extend the portrait as I had been thinking of doing, it was high time to bring the canvas in out of the rain without waiting for the skies to fall.

To continue painting, to fill in with greater detail the post-war political history of France and the personal history of de Gaulle and to bring them both to a date nearer the present than the point at which I had left them, was certainly tempting. But considerations of space apart I had to remember those conditions I had myself imposed in the preface: that once a 'recognizable likeness' has been drawn and the traits of a 'comprehensible character' brushed in the painter must come to a stop even if his painting is not full face, full length and life size. With these limitations in mind, the question was whether the Portrait had in reasonable measure fulfilled its purpose.

Given the known facts of the Subject's life, has enough been depicted of his origins and growth, of his deeds even more than of his words, of the lonely road he travelled and of the obstacles he encountered upon the way, to establish the character of integrity attributed to him? It may be thought that the effect is one of uncritical adulation; the truth is that, judged by the few simple principles which are common to humanity and as old as the hills, this man is great; to praise him is not to say that he is never wrong, but to stress what his critics find to be his most objectionable quality, that of being almost invariably right. And the test of the portrait's accuracy is whether, in the light of events subsequent to its painting, he continued to act in a manner predictable from the character to be discerned in the drawing. The first event in point of time was the revolt of the Generals at Algiers in the spring of 1961.

To understand the situation which then arose two factors must be taken into consideration. In the first place, it is essential to remember that the French settlers had been in Algeria for some one hundred and thirty years—equal to the period between the *May-flower* landing and 1750—during which they had developed the region as their homeland, giving it law and order and creating all its wealth, with scant assistance from a thinly-spread indigenous population largely unenlightened, unprogressive and indolent. By the mid-twentieth century the situation of these French-Algerian settlers was not dissimilar to that of the New England colonists in the mid-eighteenth. So it was that when the settlers, under pressure on the one hand from a rebellion, fomented, fostered and financed by 'nationalists' for the most part living outside the country, and on the other from ill-informed 'anti-colonialists' living outside Europe, perceived that the probable outcome of French policy under the Fourth Republic would be to abandon them to those who were attempting to destroy them, to seize all they had built and to drive them from the land of their birth, they reacted in much the same way as would have, one is entitled to suppose, the New England colonists had they been informed by the government of George II that, in the high-sounding but specious names of 'democratic freedom' and 'self-determination', they and their country were to be turned over to an assortment of Redskins, massacring and torturing at the behest of an enemy beyond their frontiers. With the initial revolt of the settlers against their government's policy all in France were in sympathy, including de Gaulle.

But—and this is the second factor—in the three years from 1958 to 1961 conditions not only in Algeria but in all Africa had altered radically and, with few exceptions, for the worse. For one thing, although the hard-fighting French army had largely succeeded in holding down the Algerian terrorists and in holding off the 'nationalist' forces invading the country, it was clear to most Frenchmen that not even the half-million troops engaged could hope to stifle a rebellion nourished and continually reinforced from neighbouring and supposedly neutral states; unless a solution could be found the war might continue for years to drain France of men and treasure. Moreover, whilst the more truculent Arab states were cheering on the rebels from the side-lines, the delighted Communist bosses were busily urging an intensification of the conflict, happy in the knowledge that, by the slaughter of thousands of Arabs as well as Frenchmen in Algeria, France was distracted and the West embarrassed.

For as all could now see the pinning down of the greater part of the French army in North Africa gravely weakened the defences of the West at a time when tension was steadily mounting in Europe. Thus de Gaulle's gradually evolved and tentatively outlined policy of conciliation came slowly to be recognized in France, resentfully by some, regretfully by all, as both logical and inevitable. It was based upon negotiation with the 'nationalists', followed by a period of transition, leading eventually to carefully supervised elections that were to decide Algeria's future as an autonomous state more or less closely linked to France. By many of the more extreme settlers, however, the policy was denounced as a betrayal of their hard-won rights, a view expressed by their violent action at the 'barricades' in Algiers early in 1960. Nevertheless, when a year later the question whether or not de Gaulle should proceed with his policy was put to the test of a referendum, over two-thirds of the electorate in France and more than half of that in Algeria authorized its initiation.

Against this background of broad national support for the policy of cautious negotiation which offered at least an issue from the ruinous impasse of an endless war, the revolt of the Generals in the spring of 1961 stands out as an act of reckless folly. In no circumstances could they hope for lasting success since they had no constructive long-term policy other than to continue the war against the will of the French people who supplied the men, the money and all the warlike supplies; and since even a short-term success must lead inevitably to civil strife, it was certain that their act of treason could only destroy that which they sought to preserve: the prestige of France and the honour of its army. However deep their anxiety for the settlers, and it was far less a matter of altruism than of military pride, the conduct of the four ringleaders—Challe, Zeller, Jouhaud and Salan—thus appears not only unprincipled but silly; and the plea of one of them, Challe, when, the revolt having failed, he was brought back to Paris to stand his trial upon the gravest charge known to the law, that he had acted 'for the good of the country', sounds so illogical as to raise serious doubts of his sanity.

Admittedly, the rebel plan of action had been a bold one. With the greater part of the effective army in Algeria, with the bulk of the remainder across the Rhine and staffed with supposedly disgruntled officers sent back from North Africa after the abortive *putsch* of 1960, the plotters believed that the defenceless home government, under pressure from a handful of political malcontents and a few armed emissaries airborne from Algiers, could swiftly be compelled to come to terms. The Generals would then take over with a semblance of parliamentary support and de Gaulle, shorn of all power, would either be reduced to an innocuous figurehead or sent back under escort to Colombey—and all this to the end that the war in Algeria might continue without any prospect of settlement.

In any event shortsighted, the scheme was doomed from the start by an extraordinary miscalculation. For incredible as it seemed, even at the time, the Generals and their reluctant associates failed to take into account both the climate of popular opinion and the character of the man at the head of the Republic. They forgot that when, in 1958, the army leaders in Algiers had started to move against the tottering Fourth Republic, seizing power in Corsica as the first step towards seizing it in France, it had been de Gaulle, coming out of retirement to accept office from President Coty, who had stopped them with the full force of popular approval. They forgot, further, that this was no longer the Third Republic under President Lebrun lacking constitutional power to deal with a national emergency, but the Fifth Republic under a man who had applied the lessons of 1940 and who could, by invoking Article 16 of the Constitution, counter a threat to the State with the weapon of supreme personal power. They even forgot to take into their calculations the fact that de Gaulle, at the Elysée, was not Louis-Philippe, at the Tuileries, with a cab waiting in a sidestreet ready to trot him away into tearful exile at the first mutter of mutiny.

Upon the instant when the gravity of the revolt became known in Paris, de Gaulle reacted in precisely the manner which his enemies should have been able to predict from his past record. He had never failed, in peace or war, as soldier or statesman, to face the unexpected with prompt decision, to 'accept risks' and to 'raise the stakes', to 'shoulder the burden' of leadership though it should 'break his back.' Article 16 of the Constitution he invoked at once

in agreement with the Council of State. In Paris and the provinces
armed police forces assumed authority; tanks were moved into the
capital, roads were blocked, airfields closed. Strict orders went out
to all in outlying commands in Algeria to refuse obedience to the
rebellious Generals who were summarily stripped of all rank; the
Mediterranean fleet was alerted and presently despatched to the
blockade of Algerian ports. Unable immediately to call upon the
distant army for support, he called upon the people. At no time had
he been ignorant of 'what that people wanted and what they did
not want', and in this hour of crisis he knew well that what, above
all, they did not want was to be dictated to by a clique of unreliable
military adventurers without a policy, without experience, without
popular support. Of the response to his television appeal—'*Fran-
çaises, Français, aidez-moi!*'—there was never any doubt. Im-
pressed as much by his firmness as by the speed of the measures,
and angry with the plotters for the alarm they had caused, almost
the whole nation rose up to bar the way to rebellion. Of those few
who, at first blush, had been inclined to side with the mutineers
some were arrested, others went prudently underground. The army
beyond the Rhine declared, and showed, its loyalty to the government; in the outlying districts of Algeria the great majority of local
commanders refused to support the revolt with which, save for a
relatively small hard-core of Paratroops and Foreign Legionaries,
the conscript rank and file were clearly out of sympathy. Thus,
isolated, condemned by the government and people of France, the
rebel Generals and their fellow-conspirators faced within a matter
of hours that certain defeat which they should have had the sense
to foresee when they first set foot upon the path of treason.

The ground-swell raised by the storm, the waves of unrest rolling
over France and North Africa, did not wholly subside with the
ending of the revolt at Algiers. 'Fifty million Frenchmen,' the old
song has it, 'can't be wrong.' But coming from perhaps the most
intensely individualistic people in the world fifty million different
opinions cannot all be right at one and the same time; and those
who had nothing to say and no voice to say it with contrived to
make themselves heard by sporadic bomb explosions, senseless and
frequently murderous. They did not deter de Gaulle from pursuing

the policy of peace and self-determination in Algeria. Praised for his firmness not only by a majority in France but, for once, by the nations of the West, he was now as much master of the situation as he had always been of himself. Outwardly calm, he had only once during the early stages of the revolt displayed to the nation his innermost feelings when, in the course of the broadcast, the one word '*hélas!*' repeated three times upon a falling inflexion had expressed the grief felt at this latest betrayal of France. For the rest he remained imperturbable as when, more than twenty years earlier, Churchill had first seen him in the hour of defeat—or as when, upon the quarter-deck of the *Duboc,* he had replied to that 'deputation' of would-be mutineers with forthright arguments of uncompromising logic.

Negotiations to bring the Algerian 'nationalists' to a conference table were opened at once, with the kind assistance of the Tunisian leader Bourguiba who at this time was sitting astride a shaky fence, maintaining friendly personal relations with de Gaulle while continuing to harbour some thousands of 'nationalist' troops harassing France in Algeria from across the Tunisian border. Meeting at Evian, the conference was opened upon de Gaulle's instructions with a notable gesture of magnanimity : the order to the army in Algeria to cease fire and the simultaneous release of a large number of Algerian prisoners in France. To this gesture the 'nationalists' failed to respond; the French truce—observed by the army for three months to its considerable disadvantage—was angrily brushed aside and, even as the talks proceeded, the 'nationalist' forces continued their tip-and-run campaign of terrorism and murder from the 'neutral' soil of Morocco and Tunisia. From this and from their attitude at the conference, where all French attempts to negotiate were persistently blocked by preliminary demands for impossible concessions, it soon became apparent that the 'nationalists' had no intention of allowing an agreement to be reached for the good of the people in an autonomous and democratic Algeria ; but rather that they were playing a political poker-game from which, by a combination of bluff and blackmail, they were determined to rise the sole winners and, in Algeria, the sole masters.

Adjourned, then resumed, the Evian conference reached deadlock over the Sahara problem. It had been foreseen by the French that the great desert region lying to the south of Algeria proper, and now known to be the lid of a vast reservoir of oil, gas and water, would be a subject of dispute with the 'nationalists', who naturally coveted its wealth since they had done less than nothing to develop it. To avoid endless discussion and future strife the French government therefore proposed an equitable settlement of great vision and generosity, whereby France would continue to supply technicians, equipment and marketing facilities for Saharan oil and gas, whilst the profits of the undertaking would be shared by the states bordering the region including (as well as Algeria) Morocco and Tunisia. Since it was immediately apparent that the two last-named states were ready to welcome a scheme of such openhanded liberality, the dismayed 'nationalists', deprived of the jackpot, were quick to perceive that by their own greed and obstructiveness, as much as by French concessions and honest dealing, they were about to lose the game. Their bluff called, unable to count for the future upon the blackmail threat of armed intervention by the North African states, they threw down their cards, kicked the table over and drew a gun.

In fact it was Bourguiba who obligingly drew the gun for them. Jumping off the fence from which he had for some time been smiling at the West, he first stirred up the Tunis mob with a rabble-rousing speech against France and then, without further delay and regardless of his amicable understanding with de Gaulle, whom he had openly lauded in Washington and London, launched a strong force of troops against the naval base at Bizerta. Here the small French garrison, reduced to little more than 120 effective fighting men during the period of friendly relations, fought back as vigorously against the violent and unexpected attack of Bourguiba's Tunisians as, under similar conditions, United States forces at Guantanamo would have fought back against an attack of Castro's Cubans. Very properly de Gaulle reinforced the garrison with troops from Algeria, and the assailants were driven back with some loss of life on both sides. Two things then happened: the 'nationalists' broke off the Evian talks—for no sufficient reason, since Bizerta had nothing to do with Algerian self-determination—and Bourguiba uttered piercing screams which, echoed in the United

Nations, were heard by the Secretary-General who came running Presently, through the babel-clamour rising from a section of the Afro-Asian choir ably conducted from Moscow, there could be distinguished the no longer very astonishing theme: a French garrison had been fired upon, hard-pressed it had fired back, *ergo* France was the aggressor. *'Cet animal est très méchant—Quand on l'attaque il se défend.'* A nineteenth century lyric was becoming in the twentieth a tenet of international politics.

Getting little satisfaction from the West, Bourguiba turned to the East, calling upon Khrushchev to rescue him from the defenders of Bizerta much as, twenty years earlier, Mussolini had called upon Hitler to rescue him from the defenders of Greece, and with even less reason since the French, at the request of the United Nations, had already ceased fire. Happy to be offered yet another spot in which to stir up trouble for the West, Khrushchev brandished bombs and rockets and announced his forthcoming descent upon Tunis in much the same tone of gloating menace as that used, in September 1940, by Hitler to warn the people of Britain impatient of in-vasion delays: *'Warte nur—er kommt!'* De Gaulle was not im-pressed by such wild threats any more than by the intemperate language of the Afro-Asians demanding immediate evacuation: Bizerta's value as a naval base might have diminished for the West. but without guarantees he was not going to hand it over to the East to become a substitute for Albania or an outpost for Alexandria. Turning away from what he termed, not without justification, the 'incoherences' of the United Nations he reduced the giant-like ap-pearance of the Tunisian imbroglio to its true scale of minor episode concerning France alone and strove patiently to divert the stream of Bourguiba's bellicose speeches into the deeper channels of a quiet diplomacy from which the quarrel, if there was one, should never have overflowed.

Far less excusable than the outcry in the United Nations, directed at France by men largely ignorant of the Bizerta problem, were the bitter comments directed at de Gaulle by sections of the English-speaking press, apparently wholly ignorant of the man. Incapable, it seemed, of an impartial let alone a friendly understanding of France's difficulties, gripped once again by the folly of 'appease-ment' some correspondents of London newspapers filed reports encouraging the Tunisian hot-heads by placing the blame for the Bizerta episode squarely upon de Gaulle and by reviving, against the President, the twenty-year-old phrases of disparagement used against the General. How well the mud of ancient 'denigration' had stuck—*'Calomniez, calomniez, il en restera toujours quelque chose!'*—could be read in the summary of de Gaulle's character sent from Tunis by an English correspondent: 'arrogant, chauvinistic and stubborn,' a judgment made more foolish by its bracketing with a similar assessment of Bourguiba—as well equate rock with water. Later, the same correspondent quoted Bourguiba's far from original view that de Gaulle was 'living in another century'—which was true enough; in his vision of world affairs, of European affairs in particular, he was living not in the mid-twentieth, but already in the twenty-first. Yet a London paper, said to be 'conservative,' forgetting that it was the 'nationalists' who had broken off the Evian negotiations and sparked off Bourguiba's attack if indeed they had not requested it, implied that de Gaulle's action at Bizerta had cost the West a 'valuable ally'; whereas in fact Bourguiba had never been an ally and his small, backward and largely arid country was of no great value to anybody unless strongly supported with military, economic and financial aid. 'Our policy [is one] of non-alignment,' he had declared. 'We will accept aid from East and West and from anyone else.' Since he had already accepted many millions from both France and the United States, it could perhaps be deduced that by firing upon French troops and then accusing de Gaulle of 'blind stubbornness' in allowing them to fire back he was intending to display his impartiality by turning for further aid to the East.

Less prejudiced critics of de Gaulle, rather than impute blindness or chauvinism, preferred the more temperate label 'old-fashioned' whenever, as frequently happened, they failed to understand the long-term implications of his policies at home or abroad. But to be old-fashioned is not necessarily to be wrong; in fact, since the pendulum always swings, the more old-fashioned a man's ethics the more likely he is to be ahead of his times. And certainly to some of his more farsighted contemporaries de Gaulle was beginning to appear not as a man outdated and quixotic, but as one prescient and from a nobler epoch, amenable to reason but never pliant, a figure towering, tireless, indomitable and essential. The burden he had taken up at the call of the people was by his own choice made heavier; in his seventy-first year the hours worked and the tasks accomplished would have seemed prodigious for a man half his age. An absolute dedication stayed the corruption of absolute power; every waking hour was pressed into the service of France for whose government he was now solely responsible, whose every major action he alone must decide. Throughout the prolonged periods of crisis and anxiety he continued the series of exhausting provincial tours: whirlwind visits to major towns, with a new speech and formal reception at each, less formal calls upon smaller communities, brief halts at remote villages Acclaimed officially, cheered by the people—to the consternation of foreign critics who had supposed he would at least be booed—he strode forward into the familiar crowds, the same de Gaulle who had called to them in the nightmare of defeat, who had kindled hope in the years of darkness, who had led them and led them again, and who now stood forth as their one sure defender against confusion and anarchy—strode, ageing but erect, into the press of smiling people, to an endless clasping of outstretched hands, heedless of the chance that some demented Ravaillac might be lurking among them.

It may be true that to some extent they clung to him for fear of what might follow if he went; but in the warmth of their constant greeting there was affection as much as respect, a realization that about his qualities, as distinct from his talents, what was so extraordinary was that they were so ordinary, the simple virtues that at heart all sensible men admired: courage, steadfastness, understanding, a selfless devotion and an unswerving fidelity to 'honour and honesty'. In an age when it could be said with at least as much truth as in Thoreau's day that the mass of men led lives of quiet desperation, de Gaulle had repeatedly shown the people of France that common sense forbade despair, provided they remained united in adversity and faithful to their own 'old-fashioned' principles. '*Tout est toujours à recommencer,*' he had told them in his *Mémoires;* and all could see that from every setback, however deeply disappointing, he faced forward again; not unmoved, for Churchill's curiously-worded yet penetrating judgment—'a remarkable capacity for feeling pain'—was still valid, but undaunted and outwardly unruffled, a fighter absorbing punishment and refusing to give in.

He had raised the stakes to the maximum now: the numbered days of his life wagered against the remaining obstacles—to a settlement in Algeria, to tranquillity in prosperous France, to the splendid vision of renascent Europe. The Algerian problem would remain unsolved only so long as men ill-willed or illogical, whether French settler or Arab 'nationalist', fought against a fair and logical solution; and the army, relieved of the hampering truce, would continue to fight only for so long as the rebels of either side continued to outrage humanity with the gross brutality of murder and counter-murder. For France herself, if the present was bright, the future could be brilliant. The economy was sound, the currency stable; inflation had been halted, minimum wage-rates kept pace with costs; productivity was rising, unemployment non-existent. Industrialists co-operated with Ministers to evolve a practical plan of development; the Trades Unions upheld the régime and stood firm against those who plotted its downfall. The only challenge came, not from the customary grumbling of an honest minority, not from the few brief strikes, not even from the protracted and much-advertised 'peasants' revolt' but from small irreconcilable groups of extremists, of outlawed politicians and ex-generals, of men embittered by their own incompetence, hysterical, paranoiac and desperate, who by continuing their insensate guerrilla war of explosions and gun-fighting sought to extend to metropolitan France the murderous climate of Algiers. Against this threat to stability and national confidence the maintenance of Article 16, with its powers of arbitrary arrest and imprisonment, was certainly justified; and if foreign critics uttered cries of horror at the strong-arm methods of the French police, by the great majority of the French people disgusted with the methods of the terrorists the forceful actions of the police were generally approved. No one in his senses could feel sympathy for bomb-happy extremists so foolish as to think that de Gaulle could be frightened with off-stage noises, however loud the bangs.

Of faltering in the affairs of France in Europe he gave no sign as the days of uneasy summer led on once more to the crisis of a stormy autumn. Even as from the dark recesses of the Kremlin the raucous voice of Khrushchev rose to threaten the obliteration of the several nations of the West, using almost the same words with which Hitler had once threatened the obliteration of Britain: '*wir werden ihre Städte ausradieren*' echoed by 'we shall wipe out Britain in a day,' and extended to include France and Western Germany and 'the orange groves of Italy' and 'the Acropolis'—even whilst the Russian dictator was mouthing his monstrous policy of destruction from Moscow, the leaders of the Common Market nations were elaborating their life-giving policy of construction in Western Europe. Whatever shape it might eventually assume, the development was epoch-making, the realization of a dream that since the days of Henri Quatre had appeared to men of vision only to vanish in the flames of recurrent warfare. By de Gaulle the dream had long ago been brought into the realms of practical politics, not in the unwelcome form of a federated 'united states' on the American model—something which France, for one, would scarcely have found acceptable—but as an association of autonomous nations, politically co-ordinated yet retaining their identity: '*l'Europe des patries*' linked, under the Treaty of Rome, by a common interest in trade that became, under the Soviet menace, a common interest in survival. In any event a noble vision, to the three hundred millions of Western Europe it offered a fresh impulse, a chance to evolve from a new conception a new Renaissance greater than the old. But since without a permanent Franco-German conciliation there could be no rebirth at all, and since for the cementing of that friendship French influence and French leadership were essential, together with some divesting of sovereignty, it was clearly from motives far removed from 'chauvinism' that de Gaulle gave to the grand design a support that for being prudent and farsighted was not the less wholehearted.

But the old defamatory labels were not easily effaced. Against all the long-accumulated evidence of character and purpose his detractors, misunderstanding the man, continued to misrepresent his actions. His commonsense policy of direct discussions between France and Tunisia, localizing the Bizerta flare-up, was attacked as nothing more than a spiteful 'policy of snubbing' the United

Nations. Because he failed to display any marked enthusiasm over Britain's request for admission to the Common Market—after successive British governments had for years refused to have anything to do with it—he was said to be 'stubbornly opposed' to the admission when all he wanted to know was whether Britain was quite sure of what it was she wanted to join. At length, as the Soviet-contrived Berlin crisis rose to its expected climax, he was accused of 'dragging his feet' in the face of world-war when, by a cautious approach to negotiation, he was trying to prevent the dispute from dragging the West into another 'Summit,' another Munich or another Yalta.

Misrepresentation was nothing new to de Gaulle; he had endured it for a matter of thirty years and, disdaining slander, made no effort to restrain it. Misquotation was another matter; he could guard against it by an even stricter rule of silence, by a further reduction of official pronouncements that, misinterpreted, would appear to commit him to some course of action which 'contingencies', political or military, might prevent him from taking. Of this wise reserve, however, the unintended effect was that the less he said the more his listeners extracted from what he did say, until into every phrase he uttered a cryptic meaning was read. Even his parting words to President Kennedy, at the end of the formal visit to Paris in the early summer of 1961, were found to be enigmatic. What had he intended, the critical voices asked: to give unwanted advice, to talk down 'arrogantly' to a junior, to hint incautiously at the advantages of one-man rule? Mystery!

And yet it seems simple enough. '*N'écoutez que vous-même,*' he had told the President. *Hamlet* he knew of old and sometimes quoted; it was to *Polonius* he turned for the ancient watchword of integrity: '*To thine own self be true.*' It had guided him ever since he had first set forth, boldly determined to render 'some signal service'. It could well have formed the opening line of this work; it provides perhaps the most fitting last stroke to the Portrait.

INDEX

Abetz, Otto, 182, 206
Air forces, compared, 70
Alanbrooke, Lord, see Brooke, Gen. Sir
Alan
Algiers revolt, 301, 305
Alibert, Raphael, influences Pétain, 35,
176, 181; drafts Constitution, 179; and
Laval's arrest, 206
Alsace-Lorraine, annexed, 182; renewed
threat to, 277
Anti-Semitism, 180
Arab policy, 217–19, 225
Ardennes, 'impassable', 77–8; 1945 thrust,
276–7
Argenlieu, Thierry d', on Cross of Lor-
raine, 121–2; at Dakar, 141; Libreville,
171; Washington, 251; Paris, 260
Armoured Divisions, concept of, 62;
standing army of, 63–9; use of, 78–85,
89

Baudouin, 19, 102–3, 105
Bécourt-Foch, 141
B.E.F., 99–103
Belgium, unco-operative, 71; surrender,
89–90; and see Plan D
Berthier, Lt, 117
Besson, Gen., 97
Bethouart, Gen., 290–1
Bidault, Georges, 273, 299
Billotte, Gen., 69
Blum, Léon, 65, 69
Bogomolov, 204
Boislambert, Capt. de, 43; to Cameroons,
116; reports on Dakar, 137; arrest, 138
Boisson, Gov.-Gen. Dakar, 127, 142; dis-
missed, 255
Bonhomme, Capt., 87
Bonvin, Louis, 158
Bordeaux Government, 101, 105–6
Bourdillon, Sir B., 156–7
Brazzaville, 116
Breton redoubt, 100

Briand-Kellog Pact, 59
British Press, on Oran, 113–14; on Dakar,
152–3
Brooke, Gen. Sir Alan, 100–3

Casablanca Conference, 249
Cassin, René, 186, 204
Catroux, Gen., refuses surrender, 33–5;
to replace de Gaulle? 154; joins de
Gaulle, 170; advice on Syria, 217; in
Syria, 221–2
Chad, 115, 169
Chevigné, Col. de, 251
Churchill, Winston, helps de Gaulle, 26;
on de Gaulle, 39; sees Weygand, 97;
warned of surrender, 100; proposes
union, 107; perpetuates Dakar 'leakage'
story, 125; supports Russia, 205; Syria
policy, 224, 229; opposes Roosevelt on
Free French, 237, 252, 254–5; invited to
Paris, 273; de Gaulle on, 307
Clark, Gen. Mark, 238–40
Communism, 'the real peril', 73; effect of
invasion of Russia, 203; after Libera-
tion, 262–4, 266–7
Consultative Assembly, 256
Corsica, 255
Courcel, Geoffroy de, 38, 43
Cross of Lorraine, 67, 120–2
Cunningham, Adm., 131

Dakar expedition, see Chapters 10–12
Dakar 'leakage', 123–5
Daladier, 65, 72
Darlan, Adm., 35; anglophobe, 112; and
Oran, 112–13; and Laval, 206; dauphin,
207; character, 207–9; meets Hitler,
209–10; forms government, 210; at
Berchtesgaden, 211; assists German
attack on Iraq, 213; U.S. choice for
North Africa, 239–40; assassination,
209, 243
Dejean, Maurice, 251

331

DATE DUE